Complexity Thinking and China's Demography Within and Beyond Mainland China

"This book is an essential read for anyone interested in demographic changes in China. Adopting a multidisciplinary perspective, this edited book provides a much-needed update on the legal, social, political, and economic context shaping demographic trends and thereby offers an insightful analysis into state-society relations in China. It will help both students and practitioners better understand contexts, perspectives, and policy changes in China's demography."

—Genia Kostka, *Freie Universitaet Berlin, Institute for Chinese Studies, Germany*

"This book makes significant and valuable contributions to our understanding of the local and global political implications of China's changing demography. The text highlights the two-way connection between politics and population dynamics, including population size, low fertility, aging, and migration. The originality of this work lies not only in shedding light on an under-studied topic, but also its multidisciplinary approach."

—Melanie S. Brasher, *University of Rhode Island, Department of Sociology and Anthropology, USA*

"This is a bold book that does not shy away from the difficult task of explaining the many, often contradictory, facets of contemporary China. In a world and time where simplistic and populist worldviews are ubiquitous, the contributors to this book apply anthropological, multidisciplinary, and complexity approaches to in-depth analyses of China's demographic transition within and beyond its borders. This book is recommended for those who wish to explore China's approaches to one of the key challenges of our time."

—Katja Levy, *Norwegian University of Science and Technology – NTNU, Department of Sociology and Political Science, Norway*

"This book reflects a socio-cultural anthropology approach to demography with a political perspective in a context of complexity thinking. It shows value of interdisciplinary aspects which combines IR, legal insight, socio transformation and public policy. This book is a useful work which provides us to have a better understanding of changing of state-society relations in China."

—Chin-Peng Chu, *National Dong Hwa University – NDHU, Department of Public Administration, Taiwan*

"This book offers an essential deep dive into the demographic shifts that are poised to redefine China's future and, by extension, the global landscape. The authors illuminate the complexities of policy-making in the face of these changes. It's a good read for anyone eager to understand the nuances of the demographic challenges facing the world's most populous nation."

—Bingqin Li, *University of New South Wales – UNSW, Social Policy Research Centre, Sydney, Australia*

Armando Aliu
Editor

Complexity Thinking and China's Demography Within and Beyond Mainland China

A Geopolitical Overview

palgrave
macmillan

Editor
Armando Aliu
Faculty of the International
and Political Studies
Jagiellonian University
Kraków, Poland

ISBN 978-981-97-0171-1 ISBN 978-981-97-0172-8 (eBook)
https://doi.org/10.1007/978-981-97-0172-8

This Palgrave Macmillan imprint is published by the registered company Springer Nature Singapore Pte Ltd.
The registered company address is: 152 Beach Road, #21-01/04 Gateway East, Singapore 189721, Singapore

Paper in this product is recyclable.

For
My Precious Mom 'Zize'

Preface

This book is about complexity thinking, China's demography, and population-driven geopolitics within ***mainland China*** and beyond the territory governed by the People's Republic of China (PRC). It contributes to concepts inextricably intertwined in complexity thinking (CT) and China's demographic antecedents and tenets, which involve perceived risks of China's demographic characteristics, the shrink in China's population, and China's demographic power and influence on geopolitical relations. From a multidisciplinary perspective, it combines international relations (IR) approaches, demography research, and law as a social discipline to conceive the recent demographic trends and social transformations in China and across the world.

This book draws attention to how China's population changes and demographic engineering interplay with politics, law, and transnational relations. Leading scientists from a wide range of disciplines argue many political and policy aspects of demographic shifts and demographic transition periods in China.

I met with prominent scientists in China studies, IR theorists, political sociologists, anthropologists, and demographers in the 'Horizon Europe' workshops that were organized by the Jagiellonian University Center for International Studies and Development and held between October 17 and 19, 2022 (1st Roundtable Meeting), and December 5 and 7, 2022 (2nd Roundtable Meeting), and Complexity Winter and Summer Schools held between February 13 and 17, 2023, and July 3 and 14, 2023, in Kraków (Poland). The debates revolved around connectivity projects of China and EU, complexity and China–EU–US relations, population-driven geopolitics, Dragon's footprint and engagement in the EU, population-driven area studies, China's pragmatic and rational foreign policy, principle of indivisibility, Chinese cultural integration and diplomacy, China's grand strategy motivated by the Belt and Road Initiative (BRI), elite recruitment and state-building, China's integration with Western civilizations, China's relations with local communities, China's soft power in Southeastern Europe, research in a complex world (methods and cases), understanding the complex world, complex IR, methods and tools of complexity, dynamic tools for understanding the complex world, network analysis in a complex environment, foresight in the complex and turbulent world, and so on. These discussions, invaluable and timely exchanges, and conversations helped me sketch out the first thoughts for this edited book project and outline the first draft of the book.

For this volume, we wanted to offer a wide scope across five dimensions. First, we attempted to prioritize the anthropological viewpoint to demographic research to provide a better understanding of demographic phenomena from a multidisciplinary viewpoint and combine an anthropological demography perspective with CT and geopolitics. Second, we sought to find concrete solutions to the root causes and drivers of population change, demographic shifts, demographic transitions, demographic dividend, inbound and outbound migration, the causes, and consequences of control mechanisms on politics of demography and population change. Third, we particularly argued the demographic shifts and population changes in mainland China and the significant effects of China's population control, policies, and plans on global challenges, sustainable development, and geopolitical relations. Fourth, we expanded China's population change and many facets of demographic shifts by discussing China's policymaking, China's commitments to the UNSDGs 2030, legitimacy and political power, public policy, eldercare system, Chinese exceptionalism, new foreign relations law, and supervision system reform. Fifth, we focused on the future of China's demography in terms of legal, social, political, and economic reforms and analyzed anticipations and speculations for the future.

Kraków, Poland
Hamburg, Germany
December 2023

Armando Aliu

Acknowledgments

I would like to thank all of the contributors to this edited volume for their perseverance and dedication in producing their chapters, the quality of their work, and their patience. The strength of this book is a testament to their commitment and contributions that comprise a blend of various theoretically innovative and methodologically diverse intellectual approaches. The idea for this particular book started in the autumn of 2022 when I joined the 'Promoting Order at the Edge of Turbulence (POET)' project group. The POET project is conducted at the Faculty of International and Political Studies, CISAD, Jagiellonian University in Kraków (Poland). The book is accompanied by a project website on the official website of Jagiellonian University CISAD, and the current URL is https://isad.uj.edu.pl/en_GB/poet. This book was developed within the framework of the POET Project, and 'the Project is co-financed by the Polish National Agency for Academic Exchange under the NAWA Guest Professorship program' and the 'Polish National Agency for Academic Exchange within the NAWA Chair program'. The editor and POET project team members wish to acknowledge the financial assistance of the NAWA grant (PPN/PRO/2020/1/00003/DEC/1) from the Polish Academic Exchange Council and the NCN grant (ZARZADZENIE NCN 94/2020) from the Polish National Science Council. I am grateful to NAWA and NCN for the funding that made the research collaboration possible. I am indebted to the CISAD and the Faculty of International and Political Studies at the Jagiellonian University in Kraków for having such an excellent and vibrant research ecosystem in which I could explore and develop the ideas that are central to the edited book. I also thank the international visitors at the CISAD during the Winter Semester 2022/2023. I am grateful to the international visitors and audiences for their insightful debates, constructive remarks, and feedback. In particular, I wish to express my sincere thanks to the conversations I have had with the following prominent fellows and administrative staff, at these events or elsewhere, on topics related to this work: Paweł Laidler (Jagiellonian University, Poland), Monika Pająk (Jagiellonian University, Poland), Carol Wise (University of Southern California, USA), Wolfgang Muno (University of Rostock, Germany), Jeremy Garlick (Prague University of Economics, Czechia), Csaba Moldicz (Mathias Corvinus College, Hungary), Monique Taylor (University of Helsinki, Finland), Karolina Pomorska (Leiden University, Netherlands), Antje Jantsch (Leibniz Institute of Agricultural Development in Transition Economies, Germany), Katrin Bohm (Univeristy of Rostock, Germany), and Jungmin Seo (Yonsei University, South Korea). I am especially thankful to Senior and Junior Fellows in Leuven Institute for Advanced Study (LIAS) at KU Leuven for their thoughts, scientific contributions, and constructive remarks during roundtable discussions in Holland College: Hilde Debois (KU Leuven), Bart Pattyn (KU Leuven), Joost Van Meerbeeck (KU Leuven), Rose Gilroy (Newcastle University), Outi Hannele Jolanki (Tampere University), Masi Mohammadi (Eindhoven University of Technology), Atiyah Mahmood (Simon Fraser University), Habib Chaudhury (Simon Fraser University), Thibauld Moulaert (University of Sherbrooke), Cillian Ó Fathaigh (Universidad Complutense de Madrid), Jelle Zeedijk (KU Leuven), and Elisa Cardamone (University of Edinburgh). I am especially grateful to Palgrave Macmillan Commissioning Editor Jacob Dreyer, Project Coordinator Ashwini Elango, and Aurelia Heumader for their help, recommendations, and support. Thanks also to Alfredo Tuzi (Vatican Apostolic Archives) and Bishop Sergio Pagano (Prefect of the Vatican Apostolic Archives).

I am grateful to the speakers and participants who debated at the '7th Max Planck Symposium for Alumni and Early Career Researchers' that was held between September 27 and 28, 2022, at Harnack House in Berlin. I would like to thank the Leuven Institute for Advanced Study (LIAS) at KU Leuven, LIAS Foundation and Metaforum at KU Leuven, the German Institute for Global Area Studies (GIGA) in Hamburg, Vatican Apostolic Archives, the US-Asia Law Institute at NYU School of Law, the China Studies Centre at the University of Sydney, the Australian Centre on China in the World at the Australian National University, China and Global Development Network at the Hong Kong Polytechnic University, the Cambridge Group for the History of Population and Social Structure at the University of Cambridge, the Max Planck Institute for Social Anthropology, the Max Planck Institute for Demographic Research (MPIDR), the School of International and Public Affairs at Columbia University, and the Office of Population Research at Princeton University. As a member of the European Association for Chinese Studies—EACS and the Academic Council on the United Nations System—ACUNS, I am likewise grateful to the EACS and the ACUNS team members who have nurtured and grown these organizations.

I am indebted to the Secretariat and panel participants of the 17th Annual Conference of the European China Law Studies Association that was held between September 20 and 22, 2023, at the Faculty of Law, University of Helsinki (in cooperation with the Finnish China Law Center) in Helsinki (Finland). The European China Law Studies Association (ECLS) is a major international venue to gather scholars, practitioners, and policymakers to debate on the development of law in China from both comparative and interdisciplinary perspectives. The annual conference of the ECLS is a leading international academic forum for the exchange of information and ideas on Chinese law and China studies. I also thank the secretariat and participants of the Conference of the Association of Southeast Asian Nations (ASEAN)–Social Work Education and Social Development 2023 which was organized between August 1 and 2, 2023, in Hanoi (Vietnam).

Contents

1 **Introduction: Anthropological Perspectives of Demographic Phenomena and Political Demography** 1
Armando Aliu, David O'Brien, and Dorian Aliu

2 **Eldercare Services in Urban China** 27
Björn Alpermann and Christina Maags

3 **China's Population Change and Its Geopolitical Impact** 65
Xu Zhu, Shuzhuo Li, and Zhongshan Yue

4 **The PRC Belt and Road Initiative: An Accelerator to Achieve the United Nations Sustainable Development Goals?** 99
Yin Liu and Jonathan Harrington

5 **Creating Legitimacy and Exercising Political Power: An Analysis of the Functions of the Chinese Constitutional Preamble Based on a Linguistic Study** 129
Kathrin Tremml

6 **Revisit Chinese Exceptionalism Through the Lens of New Foreign Relations Law** 155
Zixuan Yang

7 **Coordination and Interaction Between Intra-Party Regulations and National Laws in the Context of Supervision System Reform** 165
Ma Sijie

8 **What Influences Fertility Plans of China's Migrant Populations? Mechanism Analysis Based on House Prices Perspective** 193
Jingwen Tan, Shixi Kang, He Shi, and Qi Zhang

9 **The BRICS are 'Getting Old Before Getting Rich': Trends and Prospects** 215
Lauren A. Johnston

10 **Conclusion: Future of China's Demography—Legal, Social, Political, and Economic Reforms** 249
Armando Aliu, Karolina Kaczmarczyk, and Jakub Stefanowski

Index 283

List of Contributors

Armando Aliu Centre for International Studies and Development (CISAD), Faculty of International and Political Studies, Jagiellonian University in Kraków, Kraków, Poland

Dorian Aliu Department of Business Administration, University of New York Tirana (UNYT), Tirana, Albania

Björn Alpermann Julius-Maximilians-Universität of Würzburg, Würzburg, Germany

Jonathan Harrington Troy University, Troy, AL, USA

Lauren A. Johnston University of Sydney, Sydney, Australia

Karolina Kaczmarczyk Centre for International Studies and Development (CISAD), Faculty of International and Political Studies, Jagiellonian University in Kraków, Kraków, Poland

Shixi Kang University of Wisconsin-Madison, Madison, WI, USA

Shuzhuo Li Xi'an Jiaotong University, Xi'an, China

Yin Liu Huaqiao University, Xiamen, China

Christina Maags University of Sheffield, Sheffield, UK

David O'Brien East Asian Politics Section, Ruhr-University Bochum, Bochum, Germany

He Shi University of Copenhagen, Copenhagen, Denmark

Ma Sijie College of Administrative Law, Northwest University of Political Science and Law, Xi'an, China

Jakub Stefanowski Centre for International Studies and Development (CISAD), Faculty of International and Political Studies, Jagiellonian University in Kraków, Kraków, Poland

Jingwen Tan University of Copenhagen, Copenhagen, Denmark

Kathrin Tremml Ludwig Maximilian University of Munich, Munich, Germany

Zixuan Yang Hamburg University, Hamburg, Germany

Zhongshan Yue Xi'an Jiaotong University, Xi'an, China

Qi Zhang University of Copenhagen, Copenhagen, Denmark

Xu Zhu Xi'an Jiaotong University, Xi'an, China

Abbreviations

AAAA	Addis Ababa Action Agenda
ACUNS	Academic Council on the United Nations System
ADL	Activities of Daily Living
AIIB	Asian Infrastructure Investment Bank
APEC	Asia–Pacific Economic Co-operation
ARF	ASEAN Regional Forum
ASEAN	Association of Southeast Asian Nations
BBB	Build Back Better Plan of the United States of America
BFA	Boao Forum for Asia
BRI	Belt and Road Initiative
BRICS	Brazil, Russia, India, China, and South Africa
CCP	Chinese Communist Party
CDB	China Development Bank
CGD	Center for Global Development
CIDCA	China International Development Cooperation Agency
CISAD	Centre for International Studies and Development
CMFA	China Ministry of Foreign Affairs
COVID19	Coronavirus Pandemic
CRC	Convention on the Rights of the Child
CSGs	Coordinating Small Groups
CT	Complexity Thinking
EACS	European Association for Chinese Studies
ECLS	European China Law Studies Association
EDT	Economic Demography Transition
EPFIs	Equator Principles Financial Institutions
EUGG	EU Global Gateway

EximBank	Export-Import Bank of China
FDI	Foreign Direct Investments
FYPs	Five-Year Plans
GDP	Gross Domestic Product
GIGA	German Institute for Global and Area Studies
GMD	Guomindang
GZAR	Guangxi Zhuang Autonomous Region
ILO	International Labor Organization
IMAR	Inner Mongolia Autonomous Region
IMF	International Monetary Fund
LIAS	Leuven Institute for Advanced Study at KU Leuven
LSGs	Leading Small Groups
LTC	Long-term Care
MERICS	Mercator Institute for China Studies
MGI	McKinsey Global Institute
MPIDR	Max Planck Institute for Demographic Research
NAWA	Polish National Agency for Academic Exchange
NBS	China's National Bureau of Statistics
NCN	Polish National Science Council
NDB	New Development Bank
NEPAD	New Partnership for Africa's Development
NHAR	Ningxia Hui Autonomous Region
NPFPC	China's National Population and Family Planning Commission
PLA	People's Liberation Army
PPPs	Private-Public-Partnerships
PRC	People's Republic of China
RCEP	Regional Comprehensive Economic Partnership
RMB	The Renminbi (Official Currency of the PRC)
SAMOA	SIDS Accelerated Modalities of Action
SASS	Shanghai Academy of Social Sciences
SC	Several Commissions
SCO	Shanghai Cooperation Organization
SDRM	Sovereign Debt Restructuring Mechanism
SOEs	State-owned enterprises
TAR	Tibet Autonomous Region
TTIP	Transatlantic Trade and Investment Partnership
UN	United Nations
UNDESA	United Nations Department of Economic and Social Affairs
UNIOM	United Nations International Organization for Migration
UNPD	United Nations Population Division
UNPDF	United Nations Peace and Development Trust Fund
UNSDCF	UN Sustainable Development Cooperation Framework, 2021–25
UNSDGs	United Nations Sustainable Development Goals 2030

USD	United States Dollar
USSR	Union of Soviet Socialist Republics
WHO	World Health Organization
WTO	World Trade Organization
XPCC	Xinjiang Production and Construction Corps—Bingtuan
XUAR	Xinjiang Uyghur Autonomous Region

List of Figures

Chapter 2

Fig. 1 Population aging in Shanghai 40
Fig. 2 Population aging in Beijing (*Source* Beijing Municipal Government Reports, 2006–2018) 47
Fig. 3 Comparing eldercare service development in Shanghai and Beijing (*Source* Shanghai Municipal Government Reports 2006–2018, Beijing Municipal Government Reports 2006–2018) 53

Chapter 3

Fig. 1 Trends in total fertility rates of China, the USA, India, Japan, and South Korea, 1950–2050 (*Data source* United Nations Department of Social and Economic Affairs, United Nations World Population Prospects 2022, https://population.un.org/wpp/ [2024–2050 are projected]) 71
Fig. 2 Percentages of population above 65 in China, the USA, India, and Japan in 1950–2050 (*Data source* United Nations Department of Social and Economic Affairs, United Nations World Population Prospects 2022, https://population.un.org/wpp/ [Data for 2024–2050 are projected]) 74

Fig. 3 Sex ratios at birth of China, India, Myanmar, and Vietnam in 1950–2050 (*Data source* United Nations Department of Social and Economic Affairs, United Nations World Population Prospects 2022, https://population.un.org/wpp/ [Data for 2024–2050 are projected]) 75
Fig. 4 Mechanisms of the effect of demographic change on geopolitics 81

Chapter 5

Fig. 1 Lengths of paragraphs 135
Fig. 2 (Change in) lengths of paragraphs (1982–2018) 138
Fig. 3 Number of characters per sentence 139

Chapter 7

Fig. 1 The construction of the internal party regulatory system with the "1 + 4" basic framework 172

Chapter 8

Fig. 1 Before-matching kernel density 206
Fig. 2 After-matching kernel density 207

Chapter 9

Fig. 1 Population estimates, China and India (1950–2021) (*Source* DESA [2022]) 216
Fig. 2 Population forecast (medium estimates), China and India (2022–2100) (*Source* DESA [2022]) 216
Fig. 3 Senior population share average by income group (*Source* The World Bank [2023]) 218
Fig. 4 Aggregate GDP, selected years, BRICS countries (*Source* The World Bank [2023]) 220
Fig. 5 Under-Five Mortality Rate, BRICS (1960–2021) (*Source* The World Bank [2023]) 221
Fig. 6 Total Fertility Rate, BRICS countries (1961–2021) (*Source* The World Bank [2023]) 222
Fig. 7 Life Expectancy (years), BRICS countries (*Source* The World Bank [2023]) 223
Fig. 8 Median population age, BRICS countries (years of age) (*Source* The World Bank [2023]) 224

Fig. 9 Share of Population Aged 65 and over (%) (*Source* The World Bank [2023]) 225
Fig. 10 Projected Population Structure, Brazil (millions of people, estimates) (*Source* The World Bank [2023]) 226
Fig. 11 Projected Population Structure, Russia (millions of people, estimates) (*Source* DESA [2022]) 227
Fig. 12 Projected Population Structure, China (billions of people, estimates) (*Source* DESA [2022]) 229
Fig. 13 Projected Population Structure, India (billions of people, estimates) (*Source* DESA [2022]) 230
Fig. 14 Projected Population Structure, South Africa (millions of people, estimates) (*Source* DESA [2022]) 231

List of Tables

Chapter 4

Table 1	The seventeen sustainable development goals	123

Chapter 8

Table 1	Variable description	198
Table 2	Descriptive statistics results	199
Table 3	Baseline results	204
Table 4	Instrumental variable regression results	206
Table 5	Propensity score matching results	208
Table 6	Moderating effect of culture infrastructure	209
Table 7	The effect of housing stress	210
Table 8	Heterogeneity analysis	211

Chapter 9

Table 1	Year of BRICS Country Reaching 'Ageing' Thresholds	225
Table 2	Overview of China's economic demography transition strategy	233

CHAPTER 1

Introduction: Anthropological Perspectives of Demographic Phenomena and Political Demography

Armando Aliu, David O'Brien, and Dorian Aliu

1 Why Have Anthropological Perspectives Become Essential for Political Demography?

Discussions about the population and demographic structure of China have intensified even more, especially during the Coronavirus (*COVID19*) pandemic era. Demography discipline is statistically dominated; however, our approach adopted here is to consider demography not as a numerical exercise but instead as an essential factor for arguing the attributes of anthropological demography, such as sociocultural components, gender aspects, comparative political economy of aging, demographic conjunctures, legal perspectives, and gerontocracy

A. Aliu (✉)
Centre for International Studies and Development (CISAD), Faculty of International and Political Studies, Jagiellonian University, Kraków, Poland
e-mail: armando.aliu@uj.edu.pl

A. Aliu (ed.), *Complexity Thinking and China's Demography Within and Beyond Mainland China*,
https://doi.org/10.1007/978-981-97-0172-8_1

(Bernardi 2007; Bernardi and Hutter 2007; Coast et al. 2007; Johnson-Hanks 2007; Tepe and Vanhuysse 2009). A socio-cultural anthropology approach to demography is useful for interpreting demographic indicators, including human population change rates, life expectancy, migration, fertility/natality, mortality, marriage, family reunification, women's status, and household (DeWitte 2017; Johnson-Hanks 2007; Kertzer 2005).

In this chapter, we will sketch out broad issues to stimulate the current state of the art in anthropological demography and political demography. It is crucial to stress that anthropological demography goes beyond the boundaries of demography that investigate quantitative changes in population size and structure. In an anthropological demography approach, the demography and anthropology disciplines are intertwined in a more comprehensive approach where the cultural components, cognitive science, aging, migration, fertility, and gerontology are very much involved and interact in the complexity of agents and institutions.

Coast et al. (2007) highlighted that there is a shift from seeing anthropological demography as primarily concerned with the geographically distant "other" to being able to address issues much closer to "home." From this point of view, a significant change in the demography of China will have a great impact not only on mainland China but also elsewhere. There is a dual process, in turn, moving from regional to local and from local to regional levels. Therefore, the participation of China's demography studies increasingly at "local levels" (including autonomous regions) can help to better design the dynamics of the entire region.

Combining a socio-cultural anthropology approach to demography with political demography creates a complex structure where demographic indicators are considered as inputs of politics, public policies,

D. O'Brien
East Asian Politics Section, Ruhr-University Bochum, Bochum, Germany
e-mail: david.obrien@ruhr-uni-bochum.de

D. Aliu
Department of Business Administration, University of New York Tirana (UNYT), Tirana, Albania
e-mail: dorianaliu@unyt.edu.al

and polities (Goerres and Vanhuysse 2021). Political demography is also associated with state control and intervention in population change and demographic engineering (Bookman 2002; McNamee and Zhang 2019). Population control as a matter of means is interwoven and logically separate from disagreements about goals. Population control is a policy regime designed to modify fertility trends through deliberate interference in reproductive behavior, with the aim of influencing demographic outcomes (Coole 2018).

According to Freedom House, China's demographic engineering programs accelerated demographic change and restructured population dynamics by providing more advantages to Han Chinese ethnic groups in the Xinjiang Uyghur Autonomous Region (XUAR), the Tibet Autonomous Region (TAR), the Inner Mongolian Autonomous Region (IMAR), the Guangxi Zhuang Autonomous Region (GZAR), and the Ningxia Hui Autonomous Region (NHAR)[1] (Freedom House 2023a, b).

In China, "Ethnicity"—*"minzu"*—is "an official classification positioning every citizen as one of 56 recognized ethnic groups. One's ethnic category appears on ID cards and many other official documents and therefore is continually flagged as a key constituent of one's identity." All of the 56 ethnic groups together are conceived of as making up the national "Chinese family": *Zhonghua minzu* (O'Brien and Brown 2022). In contrast to the Soviet Union, which established a "system based on federal republics with a theoretical right to secession for its national minorities, the PRC instituted a system of limited territorial autonomy to manage ethno-national differences" (Clarke 2011). On October 1, 1955, Xinjiang was formally integrated into the People's Republic as an autonomous region, comprising of autonomous counties, districts, and prefectures.

The Uyghurs are "the largest and titular ethnic group living in the Xinjiang Uyghur Autonomous Prefecture, a vast area in northwest China of over 1.6 million sq. km. They make up 45.21 per cent of the population of Xinjiang, numbering 8,345,622 people. The Han, the largest ethnic group in China, make up 40.58 per cent in the region with

[1] According to Freedom House, the Chinese government has been continued to pursue policies that alter the demographics of ethnic minority regions, such as XUAR, TAR, and IMAR. Recent analysis has provided strong evidence that the governmental actors were involved in the design and implementation of the demographic engineering for ethnic minority regions (Freedom House 2023a, b).

7,489,919." A Turkic-speaking largely Muslim ethnic group, the Uyghurs traditionally inhabited a series of oases around the Taklamakan desert in the south of the region, which is known as "East Turkestan",[2] to Uyghurs outside of China. Their complex origin is evidenced by "a rich cultural history that can be traced back to various groups that emerged across the steppes of Mongolia and Central Asia. Uyghur communities are also found in Uzbekistan, Kyrgyzstan, and Kazakhstan, with significant diaspora groups in Australia, the US, Germany, and Turkey" (O'Brien 2021).

In the early part of the twentieth century, "Uyghurs briefly declared two short-lived East Turkestan Republics in 1933 and again in 1944, but the region was brought under the complete control of the Chinese state after the Chinese Communist Party (CCP) came to power in 1949" (ibid). Like its predecessor the Qing, the Communist Party of China saw Han settlement in Xinjiang as key to gaining control over the region and its people. Unlike the Qing, however, they proved much more successful in actually getting Han settlers to stay in Xinjiang.

From a low of 7 percent in 1953; by 1964 they comprised 33 percent of the population (54 percent Uyghur). Among those were tens of thousands of former Kuomintang soldiers who had also been sent to the region after their defeat in the Chinese Civil War (Joniak-Lüthi 2013). A decade later, at the beginning of the Chinese economic reform in 1978, the demographic balance was 46 percent Uyghur and 40 percent Han (Toops 2004; Xinjiang Statistical Yearbook 2011).

[2] Interior brackish seas and lakes, fed by the more constant flow of larger rivers, have played an important role in the history of the two great desert basins of Eastern and Western Turkestan. The lacustrian is united with the alluvial zone, and this is more often the case in Eastern Turkestan, where flying sands are divided into several wide nuclei by long rivers that traverse the basin. The grazing areas of Turkestan, taken in the aggregate, are so large that even at the present time stock-raising forms a very important part of the industry of the land. The animal industry seems to approach more closely to the character of that of modern Turkestan, especially when one considers that in the course of centuries, under the influence of the changed religious observances, the breeding of swine and cattle has been still more suppressed. Therefore, the Turkestan-Iranian sphere of culture remained free from foreign influences, and the domestic animals were autochthonous products. Certainly, the physiographic changes were one of the primeval causes of the frequent emigrations to Europe or Southern Asia undertaken by the cattle-breeding nomads of ancient Turkestan. In Chinese Turkestan many cities have been reexposed by the shifting dunes that swallowed them over a thousand years ago (Pumpelly 1908).

"Of particular importance to increasing the Han population was the creation of the Xinjiang Production and Construction Corps (XPCC) (*Xinjiang Shengchan Jianshe Bingtuan* 新疆生产建设兵)." The *bingtuan* (兵团) as it is commonly known in Xinjiang, was initially made up of demobilized People's Liberation Army (PLA), Guomindang (GMD) and Ili army troops and was a direct descendent of the Qing-era military farms. Much like the earlier Han settlers during the Qing, the Xinjiang Production and Construction Corps—Bingtuan (XPCC) was "originally mandated to reclaim land, garrison the frontier region, and populate strategic border regions and transportation corridors within Xinjiang" (Gaubatz 1996). "The XPCC was initially focused on settling, cultivating, and developing sparsely-populated areas such as the fringes of the Taklamakan Desert under the principle of not competing for benefits with the local people." It also provided a reserve military defense for the region which was particularly important in light of the worsening relations with the Union of Soviet Socialist Republics (USSR) (O'Neil 2008; Rossabi 2004). "Much of Xinjiang's population growth in the 1950s up to the 1970s involved migrants resettled and employed by the *bingtuan* and it remains a hugely significant economic factor, if less so militarily, in Xinjiang today. From 1954 to 1957, the *bingtuan* population grew from 200,000 to 300,000 and by 1966 it numbered 500,000–600,000. During the Great Leap Forward famine years (1959–1961), the *bingtuan* handled more than 2 million Han refugees from outside Xinjiang and processed another 1.6 million Chinese rusticated youth. Although many of these returned to the East when they could, a 1975 report claimed that some 450,000 had settled in Xinjiang" (Millward and Tursun 2004). The *bingtuan* was and remains overwhelmingly Han.

Of its 2.5 million members today, roughly 88 percent are Han (O'Neil 2008). "The corps has over 16 million *mu*[3] of farmland, nearly a third of Xinjiang's arable land and its members comprise nearly 12.9 per cent of Xinjiang's population, or nearly a third of Han registered within the province" (Becquelin 2004). "While the XPCC is administered by both the central government in Beijing and the government of XUAR, it has sub-provincial powers on par with sub-provincial cities and its economic and social development are administered separately from that of Xinjiang" (Becquelin 2004; Bovingdon 2010; Zhu 2000).

[3] 1 *mu* equals 1.65 acres.

This system avoids the appearance of colonialism and keeps non-Han officials in positions of visible authority in the region, while ensuring that the real power is held by Han officials. It also had the distinct advantage of putting Uyghurs into competition with other *minzu* groups and divided any sense of a shared Turkic identity (Millward and Tursun 2004). The CCP has long tried to inculcate both patriotism and the notion that "elder brother" had arrived to assist his "younger brothers" to develop their own language, customs, religious beliefs, and traditions. They were also adamant that any act leading to a split 'of the unity of the various nationalities' would be prohibited at all costs. As Matthew Moneyhon has written 'the CCP essentially offered its left hand to sustain minority culture, while its right erased any hope for true autonomy or self-determination' (Moneyhon 2003: 133). Gardner Bovingdon gives a succinct interpretation of "autonomy" in Xinjiang:

> The division of Xinjiang into a number of smaller autonomies was a stroke of administrative genius. In parceling "sub-autonomies", the Chinese Communist Party simultaneously satisfied the goals of embodying the idea that Xinjiang belonged to thirteen different *minzu* and of counterbalancing the Uyghurs' overwhelming political and demographic weight. To a certain extent, the political and material interests of each of the other groups were therefore aligned with the central government and against the Uyghurs. By the end of 1954, more than 50 percent of the area of the province had been allotted to autonomous townships, districts, counties, and prefectures. (Bovingdon 2010: 45–46)

The dramatic demographic changes in Xinjiang have seen the Uyghurs who once numbered 80 percent of the population now make up just above 50 percent. This has come about through both official and unofficial waves of Han migration. From the ideologically driven mass settlements of the 1960s and 70s to the economics migration of the 80s and 90s the story of the XUAR is written by the waves of new arrivals and those who have felt displaced.

Chih-yu Shih (2002) argues that the study of ethnic consciousness in China is, "a study of the relationship between the small numbers of ethnic minority people and the vast majority of Han Chinese." In Xinjiang, however, the Han are (just about) a minority, but a minority who occupy the position of elite. In order to understand how each group sees itself, it is vital, therefore, to understand how each group sees the "other."

"In 2009, a major outbreak of violence in the capital Urumchi saw hundreds die and many more imprisoned. The years 2013 and 2014 were also crucial turning points with deadly attacks on passengers in train stations in Kunming and Yunnan, bombings in Ürümchi, and a suicide attack in Tiananmen Square in Beijing, all blamed on Uyghur terrorists" (O'Brien 2021). "The 2016 appointment of Chen Quanguo, the former Party chief of the TAR, to replace Zhang Chunxian as XUAR Party secretary saw a significant escalation of repression of the Uyghur and other non-Han ethnic groups" (O'Brien and Brown 2022). "The roll out of electronic surveillance into almost every aspect of life and the establishment of a system of internment camps that would see in excess of million people being held without trial for what the government terms vocational training" (Byler 2018), have brought widespread international condemnation and unprecedented focus on the region.

"Known for his hardline tactics in Tibet, Chen quickly adopted a similar approach in Xinjiang. According to Adrian Zenz and James Leibold (2017), a total of 31,687 security-related positions were advertised in 2016, a more than threefold increase over the previous year."

Edward Schwarck (2019) writes that "regardless of whether Beijing faces a genuine threat of terrorism in its western regions, the Party evidently sees the problem as serious enough to implement a costly and utterly inhumane policy of mass internment and brainwashing." "Numerous reports by academics, journalists, and human rights groups claiming that more than one million members of the Uyghur and other Muslim ethnic minority peoples have been imprisoned without trial" (Chestnut Greitens et al. 2020; Human Rights Watch 2018; Zenz and Leibold 2017; Anderson and Byler 2019; Sudworth 2021). Harrowing testimonies from Uyghurs who have been through the camps paint a picture of serious systematic repression (Hill et al. 2021). The government's official position on ethnic tension in Xinjiang is that it exists only due to outside instigation.

"That ethnic minorities' poverty, and its attendant ignorance and lack of opportunities, has been taken advantage of by external forces spreading religious extremism, and it is religious extremism which has caused ethnic minorities to become prejudiced and perceive themselves as Muslims over and above being Chinese." So-called "Re-education" camps thus provide vocational training to "address their poverty, and education to address their wrong-thinking. Besides the cruelty to individuals and destruction of communities forced incarceration and fear of it is causing, one thing which is tragic about this situation is that it cannot but fail to address much of the ethnic tension in the region, because profound prejudice, distrust, and resentment are not limited to marginalized Uyghurs" (O'Brien and Brown 2022).

Alongside the mass interment of a significant proportion of the Uyghur population, a campaign of "Sinicization" attempts to create an idea of a "shared past", between the Uyghur and the Han. The "shared past" being articulated in Xinjiang is one that symbolically emphasizes Xinjiang as part of the Chinese imagined community (Brown and O'Brien 2022). In practice, this campaign involves a variety of things, taking place across varied regions: examples include propaganda emphasizing the "Chinese Socialist Characteristics" being placed outside of mosques (Brown and O'Brien 2020), media emphasis on Uyghurs engaging in Han cultural practices as a demonstration of their loyalty to the state (Anderson and Byler 2019), as well as the removal of visible signs of Islamic history and culture. The latter includes the removal of architectural features including minarets, domes, and crescents from mosques, as well as removing Arabic script which used to be placed alongside Mandarin script on storefronts, restaurants, etc. (Stroup 2019; Ruser et al. 2020). "Ruser et al. (2020) have used satellite imagery of Xinjiang and other data to identify a variety of religious sites, including mosques, shrines, and graveyards, which have been demolished or damaged since 2017, including many which were ostensibly protected under Chinese law." They characterize this as "cultural erasure", "stripping away any Islamic, transnational, or autonomous elements" (Ruser et al. 2020: 3), and also as a means of symbolically severing Xinjiang's traditional culture from visually resembling the varied cultures of the region.

Sean Roberts (2018, 2020) offers a biopolitical reading of the use of internment to deal with ethnic tension in the XUAR. Roberts is not alone in offering a biopolitical reading of the PRC (e.g., Anagnost 2004), or specifically, the CCP's approach in Xinjiang (e.g., Zhang et al. 2018; O'Brien and Brown 2022).

Roberts focuses upon the ways official discourses use the [potential] "terrorist" label to justify inhumane treatment toward those so nominated (an expansion of earlier similar arguments made by scholars focusing upon the US "War on Terror" (Butler 2009; Tagma 2009). Furthermore, both "extremism and separatism are likened to a disease from which the "normal, healthy" population needs to be "quarantined." Rather than framing such threats as ideological attacks upon a political order, the danger is presented as a threat to the general population"—this allows for the state to claim a pastoral role as the protector of the population, while situating part of that population as culpable for posing this threat. As David Tobin writes "for *Zhonghua Minzu* to be a benevolent, attractive civilisation *and* a modern state of 56 equal *minzu,* it needs Xinjiang to be Chinese *and* to be marginal. However, it is this perceived need that lies at the heart of China's security problems in Xinjiang" (Tobin 2020: 31).

Complexity thinking can make it clear to understand the geopolitics of China's demography by explicating China's strategy to expand its population (i.e., the Han Chinese) within and beyond mainland China and the changing trend in demographic composition in the XUAR, the TAR, and other local indigenous ethnic groups. Apparently, Beijing has encouraged the Han people to migrate, especially to the XUAR and the TAR. Contemporary ethnic relations concerning rival ethnic and religious groups and hybridization of the Han, Uighur, and Tibetan cultures are very delicate issues, and scientists are reluctant to further foreground and dig deeper through research projects and fieldwork.[4]

China's demography is a geopolitical novelty that advances asymmetric strategies and hybrid warfare. China's perspective of "ethnonationalism" fills in the Sino-cultural mission, Sinicization, and "rejuvenation narrative" that is a powerful contemporary strategy. According to *Xi Jinping*, China needs a great revival and/or rejuvenation of the Chinese nation (Economy 2018). Since the 20th CCP National Congress on October 16, 2022, China has been stressing a centralized unified leadership, national identity, and the revival/rejuvenation of the Chinese nation based on traditional cultures and national values/interests.

However, there is a "decoupling" of societal structures in China—i.e., the juxtaposition of cosmopolitan Chinese and traditional Chinese. This is a contradictory point as occurred in China's history (e.g., Chinese living during the Tang Dynasty "618–907 A.D." were more cosmopolitan (Lewis 2009), while Chinese living during the Ming Dynasty "1368–1644 A.D." were more traditional). Now, it is the time for Chinese

[4] Scientists can be sentenced to life imprisonment by the Chinese state authorities just because they express their free will and freedom of expression (e.g., *Ilham Tohti*, a Uyghur economist, was sentenced to life imprisonment by the Urumchi People's Intermediate Court for his separatism-related thoughts and interpretations related to the Uyghur issues) (Tohti 2022).

people to decide in which culture and society they will choose to live, a cosmopolitan or traditional culture and society. On the other hand, Communist China has always been totalitarian and imposed on those who valued traditional Chinese culture and forging national consciousness. For this mission and the ultimate objective, the CCP adopted ethnonationalism as a political ideology in the party documents (Minzner 2018). The political strategies of the Chinese authorities are becoming extremely coercive ideologies that limit the cosmopolitan nature, the embeddedness of "ethnopluralism/ethno-differentialism", the creation of "common/democratic collective identity", and the openness of the Chinese society. As a result of these political strategies, there is always a risk of "demographic de-cosmopolitanization." It is basically the main problem that these authorities still insist on designing the Chinese population through demographic engineering, incentive programs, and putting great pressure on the freedom and independence of Chinese women and girls. Is Chinese authoritarianism/totalitarianism a driving force for the decline of the Chinese population? Do the demographic engineering policies of the Chinese government really cause a "backlash", a very powerful and unexpected adverse reaction to the demographic development of Chinese people who are in favor of cosmopolitanism, ethnopluralism, and openness? Is it possible for Chinese people (both traditional and cosmopolitan Chinese) to see the same "Chinese dream of great rejuvenation of the Chinese nation?"

All these questions enable us to speculate that China is currently located in between its past and future and there is a dichotomy of tradition and modern age, an ambivalence of ancient and contemporary (Arendt 2006). Undoubtedly, the dichotomy of ethnonationalism and ethnopluralism will cause social conflicts, class struggles, self-determination, and ambivalence in socio-cultural and demographic trends, and it is vital to distinguish "political action" and "political philosophy" in this respect. Is the decline in demography and a rapidly slowing down trend in population a natural evolutionary process or a responsibility of an authority? Is it a multifaceted process in which both nature and humans are in action? For example, migration flows due to climate change consider both natural reasons and climate/green politics. On the contrary, forced migration as a consequence of war and internal rebellion can be understood as a human responsibility where natural conditions do not significantly affect the influxes and the decline in the population of the conflict zones (Goldstone 2002). Returning to the traditional-cosmopolitan debate, Arendt stressed the philosophical aspects of the notion of "tradition." Arendt raised criticism of Marx and his interpretation of the 'tradition.' Arendt rejected the idea of Marx that tradition evolved with human action forming a kind of philosophy. Instead, Arendt argued that the tradition began with philosophy's changing the action into a kind of philosophy. In this context, we may allege that the ethnonationalist perspective adopted by the authorities in China is contradictory to Chinese philosophy and its universality principle and cosmopolitan nature.

The very basic nature of the ethnonationalist perspective is to create a strong bridge with China's "traditional past" and "transformations of today" by denying China's "cosmopolitan future." But is China considering cosmopolitanism, ethnopluralism, and multiculturalism as a threat to its traditional culture and society? Can cosmopolitanism, ethnopluralism, and multiculturalism form a pluralist "political philosophy" that can later turn into an undeniable "political action?"

Central and local authorities in China are still hold onto the idea that if a state improves living infrastructure, urbanization, and tangible aspects of economic demography and development, they can abruptly increase the population and migration to these developed areas. However, it is really a secondary issue. Of course, urbanization has an impact on people's lives, globalization, and connectivity with other areas. However, it cannot be a major driving force for changing fertility rates, population planning, and migration. Instead, we offer to consider intangible driving forces of demography and population change that have synthesized demography studies with other disciplines, such as anthropology, political science, philosophy, etc. Therefore, we stressed that the Shanghai Academy of Social Sciences (SASS) team predictions based on scientific arguments and methodology do not only have a meaningful input for China but also for the entire world, where all states are in a very high level of interdependency and cannot resist on global economic and commercial relations without a stable China.

The *COVID-19* case is the best example for testing and measuring to what extent an unstable China can have a negative consequence for the entire world. Thus, the disappearance of almost half a billion (UNDESA 2021) or one billion of Chinese population (SASS 2022a, 2022b) from the world in less than 75 years of timeframe will have a devastating effect on all aspects of both production and consumption, distribution channels, transport lines, etc. In this context, the key question can be raised as such: "Is the world ready to confront this huge demographic change?"

According to data from China's National Bureau of Statistics (NBS), the China's population increased by 480,000 in 2021. However, the SASS team extrapolated an annual average decline of 1.1 percent after 2021, pushing China's population down to 587 million (or even less than half a billion[5]) by 2100 (Aliu 2023; Sydney Business Insides 2022; The World Bank 2022; World Economic Forum 2022). China's population reached its peak size and experienced a decline during 2022. In 2022, at 1.2 births per woman, China had one of the world's lowest fertility rates. In China, the most notable policies were the "later, longer, fewer" campaign of the 1970s, as well as the stricter "one-child" policy (1980–2015). Among people younger than 25 years in 2023, there are 116 men for every 100 women in China (in 2023, India has overtaken China as the world's most populous country). Between 2023 and 2050, the number of people aged 65 or older is expected to nearly double in China. By 2040, people aged 65 or older in China will outnumber those under age 25; and by 2050 they could comprise 30 percent of the total population (UNDESA 2022, 2023).

The total number of "Overseas Chinese" has reached approximately 10.7 million (approximately 60 million, if their descendants are included). According to the United Nations International Organization for Migration (UNIOM), there are currently about 281–284 million migrants (around 37 million of them refugees) in the world and Chinese migrants amount to more than 40 million (estimated total number of Chinese migrants is much higher than the total number of refugees in the world) and are scattered across 130 countries. (Academy for Cultural Diplomacy 2023; Guotu 2021; McAuliffe and Triandafyllidou 2021; The World Bank 2023). Overall, the ambiguity and vagueness of the statistical data on the demography of China create a misconception about how to capture the real image of the country.[6]

[5] Can the shrinking population in China ensure reverse power relations? The disappearance of almost 1 billion Chinese from the earth by 2100 may sustain reverse power transition processes, encourage radical revisionist movements, and prevent war, bilateral tensions, and system-wide global conflicts between global hegemons (Chan 2008). According to power transition theory, an interesting argument is that the population decline in China can also be conceived as a basis for peace, stability, and symmetric relationships at the global governance level.

[6] The announced statistical data from China's National Population and Family Planning Commission (NPFPC) do not overlap and even lack consistency with the NBS and the UN Population Division (UNPD). China's demography statistics have contradictions and

2 China's Demography and Population Studies: A Matter of Concern for Global Challenges?

We are aware that the demography and population studies within and beyond mainland China are indeed a matter of concern for global challenges. One of the main driving forces of China's grand strategy is to expand its population beyond mainland China and increase its influence on the global governance arena. The BRI prepared a ground for investments from Chinese banks and multinational enterprises and the migration of Chinese youth and workers to the Silk route countries; however, these Chinese people will get older before becoming richer. It creates a barrier to the holistic development of the Chinese population beyond mainland China.

Johnston emphasized China's consequential discourse "getting old before rich" on economic demography transition (EDT) and the analysis of the EDT matrix of 182 economies from 1996 to 2016 identified China as one of many old poor economies (Johnson 2019a). Therefore, China is becoming a key international investor in the Maritime Silk Road in countries of the Indian Ocean under the umbrella of the BRI (Johnson 2019b). The social and economic consequences of China's discourse of "getting old before rich" will ensure demographic competition and population-linked resource scarcity, where the effects of youth bulges on social stability, population aging, immigration policies, resettlement programs, and issues of the diaspora will become a part of China's strategic national interests (Weiner and Teitelbaum 2001). Thus, China's political approach to the demography transition is "interventionist" through "demographic engineering and securitization of the demographic transition."

Weiner and Russell implied that demographic transition processes can create security concerns and violent conflicts within and between states and regions (Weiner and Russell 2002). Weaponization of demography and population power can be instrumentalized by using migration as a demographic transition process and the state intervention method. Extreme right-wing, nationalist-populist movements, and political actors

scientists are skeptical about the reliability and validity of the data. Complex anticipations cause indispensable scientific quarrels, and scientists are very much aware of the fact that gathering reliable and valid data from China both at national level and local level is a grueling work.

capitalizing on fear politics use ethnocentric self-determination based on pure ethnic population of a territory and pro-natalist population policies (Bookman 2002; Ricci 2020). Overpopulation and underpopulation can be considered as a dilemma for a particular region, and it is quite difficult to set up criteria and principles to offer an optimum population at the macro level. This dilemma pushes us to enforce the understanding of a population size entering the common utility function as a separate argument (Dasgupta 2019). This point will enable us to distinguish optimistic plausible assumptions from pessimistic interpretations or critical remarks on whether a population decline in a particular area can be considered as an opportunity or threat to development or not. However, this is not an issue relevant to "equilibrium or balance of population" but an issue of population ethics. It has become harder to extrapolate the future based on the scrutiny of demographic data due to the lack of data or insufficient data (Dorling and Gietel-Basten 2018). But it is also an uneasy task to underpin effective implementation of population policy and shape the future of demography and population size. In essence, demography shapes political actions and vice versa. There is a symbiotic relationship between politics, migration, and demography. So far, many government officials have abandoned "keeping the door open for migrants and refugees", and a sense of political alienation has become dominant in political rhetoric and diplomatic communication.

Political concerns about the future of demography and population size can increase due to migration policies, a rise in fear, hatred, and racist attacks. Should governments increase their control mechanisms over migration? Why? Undoubtedly, any control measure of governments over migration will be the main factor in shaping the demographic structure and population size of a particular region. Public institutions have the capacity to build any system, procedure, process, and other means of eliminating, preventing, reducing, and mitigating the risks of demographic change and population shrink that may be caused by sudden adverse events, such as outbursts of infectious disease, famine, war, sub-replacement fertility, persistently low birth rates, high mortality rates, and continued emigration.

The consequences of climate change, famine, war, and epidemics have been neglected in the demographic transition literature. For instance, China experienced a demographic decline during 1958–1961 due to the great famines that occurred in China. In the great famine case, Zhao and Reimondos explored that fertility and marriage rates declined everywhere in China, child mortality increased sharply, and rural areas were more severely affected than urban areas (Zhao and Reimondos 2012). Similarly, China faced almost the same catastrophic consequences of the *COVID-19* pandemic, and the demographic effects were a kind of *déjà vu* for Chinese society. In any kind of socio-demographic inventory and social transition, it is very difficult for women and children to prevail, and there is always a gender bias, diversity, and paradoxical effect of male chauvinism (Attané and Guill 2012). The gender perspective in China has an ambivalence as women mainly remain dependent on men, and the repercussions of demographic gender-based discrimination (Greenhalgh and Li 1995) can be witnessed in the marriage, labor market, and socio-political representation of women. Regulation of fertility in China is part of social engineering and a state-building endeavor (Sommer 2018). As a result, there is an imbalance of gender perspectives and there is a significant impact of male aspects of demography on population and family structure in China. There is a lack of awareness of woman-related demographics, such as the fertility rate, political status of women, women's economic empowerment, etc.

In light of these considerations, the area of political demography constitutes an interconnection between demography and political science, and alleged demographically determined shifts occur in the international balance of power relations (Teitelbaum 2015). Although the Chinese government formally announced the end of the one-child policy in October 2015, China had a birth control policy in place, especially with restrictions on births at parity three and above (Wang et al. 2018). However, the COVID-19 pandemic has forced the Chinese government to abolish all forms of mandatory birth control and ensure demographic determinism and multidimensional demographic complexity in Chinese society.

Incontrovertibly, the unprecedented nationwide zero-COVID protests were China's boiling point or tipping point (O'Riordan and Lenton 2014), and have encouraged more human rights activism and the demand for more freedom and justice to achieve the United Nations Sustainable Development Goals 2030 (UNSDGs) in China. Therefore, China's approach and roadmap to achieve the UNSDGs 2030, and its solutions developed to solve complex global problems have been considered strategically important for global governance, sustainable development, and the global demography outlook.

3 Complexity and China's Demography: UNSDGs 2030, Sustainable Development, and Transcending the Boundaries of Demography Phenomenon

Complexity thinking (CT) structures "interconnectedness" (and/or disconnections at the same time) between systems, knowledge, forms of life, and technology, and as a result, forms a spillover effect on everything else in our world that contains an inexplicable behavioral phenomenon (Jervis 1997). A structurally complex system can behave in a simplistic manner. Demographic change and population growth are easy for us to understand; however, it is almost impossible to extrapolate and create forecasting models due to the unpredictable nature of actors and systems in a complex structure. Casti coined the term "complexification" which is not based on a set of rules as occurred in the philosophy of science, but at the level of observations themselves and how these "uncoded" observations are transformed into measurements and models (Casti 1995, 2022).

From an ontological viewpoint, CT has compositional, structural, and functional aspects. Thus, a system in CT is a matter of the quantity and variety of its constituent elements and the elaborateness of their interrelational structure, be it organizational or operational (Rescher 1998). As a marginal and emergent phenomenon, CT is never fixed or secure, and it is always momentary, and the marginal moment of emergence is inevitably complex. In CT, finite systems are not closed, but are open and thus incomplete, and some systems involve recursive relations, and cannot be understood in terms of linear models of causality. In other words, in a non-linear system, a recursive way can by no stretch of the imagination be described in terms of first-order predicate logic (Cilliers 1998). "In recursive systems, it is not possible to measure initial conditions with enough precision to determine causal relations, and therefore unpredictability is unavoidable. Unlike linear systems, in recursive systems, complex feedback and feed-forward loops generate causes that can have disproportionate effects" (Taylor 2003). Non-linearity, self-assembly, and dynamical systems analysis in CT bring an array of transformations on the edge of chaotic and turbulent order (Urry 2005).

CT offers a powerful lens for viewing and modeling the complex, and highly dynamic terrain in which public policy is situated. This lens over-emphasizes the role of agent-based actions and the behavioral economics of interacting with people and groups (Room 2016). As a result, CT has insufficiently developed a corresponding framework for making sense of the larger co-present and co-determining organizational patterns in which multi-agent behavior is situated, as in the case of political and institutional power or economic conflict and group privilege. Thus, while CT can play a central and essential role in the analysis of policy dynamics, it must be combined with an appreciation of institutions and political economy. From a multidisciplinary complexity-informed social science viewpoint, there is a good deal in common with classical economic thought, public policy tradition, and real politics, as these were framed in the tradition of political economy and heterodox economists are more and more engaged with CT literature (Byrne and Callaghan 2014).

From a CT's point of view, the 17 SDGs of the United Nations (UN) transform the future of global demography and population outlook by considering the principle of utilitarianism and benefit for all. There is a distinction between the "effectiveness of China's demography and population policies" and the "efficiency of the adoption of the UNSDGs 2030" in China.

In this framework, it should be noted that all UNSDGs 2030 are to some extent relevant to demography and population studies (Sachs et al. 2021a, 2021b, 2022). In this context, it is vital to make an inquiry at this point: Has China been facing a complex turn to meet the UNSDGs 2030? Efforts to track commitments and objectives in SDG transformations are limited by the complexity of policies and the absence of nationally and internationally agreed targets.

China's overall SDG rank score is 56/163, SDG index score is 72.38/100, spillover score is 94.85/100, and spillover rank is 76/163.[7] Taking into account the commitments and efforts of the governments for the SDGs scores, China was classified as one of "low SDG commitment countries" (Sachs et al. 2022). China promoted synergy between BRI and the 2030 Agenda, deepened South-South cooperation, and provided financial assistance through the China-UN Peace and Development Fund and

[7] The overall score measures the total progress toward achieving all 17 SDGs. The score can be interpreted as a percentage of SDG achievement. A score of 100 indicates that all SDGs have been achieved. Each country's actions can have positive or negative effects on other countries' abilities to achieve the SDGs. The spillover index assesses such spillovers along three dimensions: environmental & social impacts embodied in trade, economy & finance, and security (Sachs et al. 2022). A higher score means that a country causes more positive and fewer negative spillover effects.

the South-South Cooperation Assistance Fund in collaboration with the China International Development Cooperation Agency (CIDCA). High-quality Belt and Road cooperation and deeper international collaboration on connectivity will provide strong support not only for China's economic development, but also for global post-COVID recovery (Ministry of Foreign Affairs of the People's Republic of China 2021). Three strategic priorities have been identified for the 2021–2025 UN Sustainable Development Cooperation Framework (UNSDCF) for China to support the development priorities of China. The three strategic priorities are as follows: "(1) *People and prosperity* (Priority 1): Creating innovation-driven, coordinated, and shared development. Equitable and high-quality economic, social, and human development for all throughout the life course; (2) *Planet* (Priority 2): Achieving green development toward a more sustainable and resilient environment; and (3) *Partnerships* (Priority 3): Realizing the full potential of China's international engagement to promote its open development and partnerships to accelerate achievement of the SDGs across the world" (UN 2020).

Analytical input and technical assistance from the UN have helped to strengthen China's capacity to design and implement evidence-based and gender-responsive policies and programs to sustainably address China's demographic transition. "With UN analytical inputs and technical assistance, China is better able to provide equitable, high-quality and gender-responsive health and care services accessible to everyone throughout the life-course, designed to respond to the country's changing demographics and disease burden. However, China also faces a complex and difficult macroeconomic environment. The demographic dividend has gradually vanished, and the ageing of the population accelerates" (Sachs et al. 2022; UN 2020; UNDP 2022).

In summary, it is critical that major international infrastructure investment programs, including the Build Back Better (BBB) plan of the United States, the European Union Global Gateway (EUGG) strategy, and the BRI of China, align with the SDGs and modernize production systems and connectivity in developing countries (Sachs et al. 2022). However, to date, there has been relatively little action to address the complex multi-sectoral agenda in a systematic way while increasingly recognized by policy makers in countries, international organizations, and businesses (Sachs et al. 2021a). "Policymakers currently lack the capacity, actionable information, and integrated analytical tools to address complex challenges and uphold a common vision through effective policy design in their respective local contexts. The challenge of tracking action and its possible effects is further amplified by varying and highly fragmented policy approaches, in the context of substantial technical complexity and diffuse boundaries. Similarly, measuring government efforts in support of the SDGs is challenging, due to the broad and complex nature of the goals" (Sachs et al. 2021b). Individual and collective behaviors rely on what the actors do; and the dynamics and inputs of the system are rooted in their incentives, goals, and calculations. However, "local predictability" produces a high degree of complexity and "unpredictability" as outcomes and patterns are formed interactively (Jervis 1998).

This book posits that it is timely to raise the issue of anthropological demography lens as a philosophical aspect and sociological insight that will capture the rarely visible points of demography and population studies. Our contributors attempted to draw our attention to CT, the nexus of demography and population studies with geopolitics, and the realistic viewpoint of demography and population change. These were related to ongoing debates on elderly people, gender aspects, population planning, migration, and public policy. Our endeavors are, first and foremost, to contribute to eldercare services in China, geopolitical impact, the nexus of the BRI-UNSDGs 2030, legitimacy and political power, Chinese exceptionalism, and foreign affairs, reform of the supervision system, fertility plans of China's migrant populations in a glimpse of complex macro level analyses.

References

Academy for Cultural Diplomacy. (2023). Chinese diaspora across the world: A general overview. https://www.culturaldiplomacy.org/academy/index.php?chinese-diaspora. Accessed November 10, 2023.

Aliu, A. (2023). Demographic indicators and future predictions of China, Hong Kong, Macao, and Taiwan: A comparative perspective. *Harvard Dataverse*. https://doi.org/10.7910/DVN/CBU8Y2. Accessed November 10, 2023.

Anagnost, A. (2004). The corporeal politics of quality (Suzhi). *Public Culture*, 16(2): 189–208.

Anderson, A. and Byler, D. (2019). Eating Hanness: Uyghur musical tradition in a time of re-education. *China Perspectives*, (3): 17–26. https://www.cefc.com.hk/issue/china-perspectives-20193. Accessed March 9, 2023.

Arendt, H. (2006). *Between the past and future: Eight exercises in political thought*. London: Penguin Books.

Attané, I. and Guill, E. (2012). Being a woman in China today: A demography of gender. *China Perspectives*, 4(92): 5–15.

Becquelin, N. (2004). Staged development in Xinjiang. *The China Quarterly*, 178: 358–378.

Bernardi, L. (2007). An introduction to anthropological demography. *Max Planck Institute for Demographic Research (MPIDR) Working Paper WP 2007-031*. Rostock: MPIDR.

Bernardi, L. and Hutter, I. (2007). The anthropological demography of Europe. *Demographic Research*, 17(18): 541–566. https://doi.org/10.4054/DemRes.2007.17.18

Bookman, M. Z. (2002). Demographic engineering and the struggle for power. *Journal of International Affairs*, 56(1): 25–51.

Bovingdon, G. (2010). *The Uyghurs: Strangers in their own land*. New York: Columbia University Press.

Brown, M. S. and O'Brien, D. (2020). Defining the right path: Aligning Islam with Chinese socialist core values at Ningbo's Moon Lake Mosque. *Asian Ethnicity*, 21(2): 269–292. https://doi.org/10.1080/14631369.2019.1636637

Brown, M. S. and O'Brien, D. (2022). Making the past serve the present: The testimonial tourist gaze and infrastructures of memory in Xinjiang (XUAR) China. *Journal of Current Chinese Affairs*. https://doi.org/10.1177/18681026221121828

Butler, J. (2009). *Frames of war: When is life grievable*. London: Verso.

Byler, D. (2018). China's government has ordered a million citizens to occupy Uighur homes. Here's what they think they're doing. *ChinaFile*. October 24, 2018. https://www.chinafile.com/reporting-opinion/postcard/million-citizens-occupy-uighur-homes-xinjiang. Accessed March 9, 2023.

Byler, D. (2019). The 'patriotism' of not speaking Uyghur. *SupChina*. January 2, 2019. https://supchina.com/2019/01/02/the-patriotism-of-not-speaking-uyghur/. Accessed March 9, 2023.

Byrne, D. and Callaghan, G. (2014). *Complexity theory and the social sciences: The state of the art*. Abingdon: Routledge.

Casti, J. L. (1995). *Complexification: Explaining a paradoxical world through the science of surprise*. New York: HarperCollins Publishers.

Casti, J. L. (2022). Complexity. Encyclopedia Britannica. https://www.britannica.com/science/complexity-scientific-theory. Accessed January 10, 2023.

Chan, S. (2008). *China, the US and the power-transition theory: A critique*. New York: Routledge.

Chestnut Greitens, S., Lee, M. and Yaziki, E. (2020). Counterterrorism and preventive repression: China's changing strategy in Xinjiang. *International Security*, 44(3): 9–47. https://doi.org/10.1162/ISEC_a_00368

Cilliers, P. (1998). *Complexity and postmodernism: Understanding complex systems*. London: Routledge.

Clarke, M. (2011). *Xinjiang and China's rise in Central Asia 1949:2009: A history*. London: Routledge.

Coole, D. (2018). *Should we control world population?* Polity Press.

Dasgupta, P. (2019). *Time and the generations: Population ethics for a diminishing planet.* Columbia University Press.

DeWitte, S. N. (2017). Demographic anthropology. *American Journal of Physical Anthropology*, 165(4): 893–903.

Dorling, D. and Gietel-Basten, S. (2018). *Why demography matters.* Polity Press.

Economy, E. C. (2018). *The third revolution: Xi Jinping and the new Chinese states*. Oxford: Oxford University Press.

Coast, E. E., Hampshire, K. R. and Randall, S. C. (2007). Disciplining anthropological demography. *Demographic Research*, 16(16): 493–518. https://doi.org/10.4054/DemRes.2007.16.16

Freedom House. (2023a). *Countries freedom in the world 2022: China.* https://freedomhouse.org/country/china/freedom-world/2022. Accessed November 10, 2023.

Freedom House. (2023b). *Countries freedom in the world 2023: China.* https://freedomhouse.org/country/china/freedom-world/2023. Accessed November 10, 2023.

Gaubatz, P. R. (1996). *Beyond the great wall: Urban form and transformation on the Chinese frontiers*. Stanford: Stanford University Press.

Goerres, A. and Vanhuysse, P. (Eds.) (2021). *Global political demography: The politics of population change*. Cham: Palgrave Macmillan.

Goldstone, J. A. (2002). Population and security: How demographic change can lead to violent conflict. *Journal of International Affairs*, 56(1): 3–22.

Greenhalgh, S. and Li, J. (1995). Engendering reproductive policy and practice in peasant China: For a feminist demography of reproduction. *Signs: Journal of Women in Culture*, 20(3): 601–641.

Guotu, Z. (2021). The overseas Chinese: A long history. The UNESCO Courier. https://en.unesco.org/courier/2021-4/overseas-chinese-long-history. Accessed November 10, 2023.

Hill, M., Campanale, D., & Gunter, J. (2021). Their goal is to destroy everyone": Uighur camp detainees allege systematic rape. BBC News, https://www.bbc.com/news/world-asia-china-55794071 Accessed November 10, 2023.

Human Rights Watch. (2018). Eradicating ideological viruses: China's campaign of repression against Xinjiang's muslims. September 9, 2018. https://www.hrw.org/report/2018/09/09/eradicating-ideological-viruses/chinas-campaign-repression-against-xinjiangs. Accessed March 8, 2023.

Jervis, R. (1997). *Systems effects: Complexity in political and social life*. Princeton University Press.

Jervis, R. (1998). Complexity and the analysis of political and social life. *Political Science Quarterly*, 112(4): 569–593.

Johnson, L. A. (2019a). The economic demography transition: Is China's 'not rich, first old' circumstance a barrier to growth? *The Australian Economic Review*, 52(4): 406–426. https://doi.org/10.1111/1467-8462.12325

Johnson, L. A. (2019b). An economic demography explanation for China's 'Maritime Silk Road' interest in Indian Ocean countries. *Journal of the Indian Ocean Region*, 15(1): 97–112.

Johnson-Hanks, J. (2007). What kind of theory for anthropological demography? *Demographic Research*, 16(1): 1–26. https://doi.org/10.4054/DemRes.2007.16.1

Joniak-Lüthi, A. (2013). Han migration to Xinjiang Uyghur autonomous region: Between state schemes and migrants' strategies. *Zeitschrift Für Ethnologie*, 138(2): 155–174.

Kertzer, D. I. (2005). Anthropological demography (pp. 525–547). In: Poston, D. L. and Micklin, M. (Eds.). *Handbook of population*. New York: Kluwer Academic/Plenum Publisher.

Lewis, M. E. (2009). *China's cosmopolitan empire: The Tang dynasty*. Cambridge, MA: Harvard University Press.

McAuliffe, M. and Triandafyllidou, A. (Eds.) (2021). *World migration report 2022*. Geneva: UNIOM.

McNamee, L. and Zhang, A. (2019). Demographic engineering and international conflict. *International Organization*, 73(2): 291–327.

Millward, J. and Tursun, N. (2004). Political histories and strategies of control: 1884–1978 (pp. 63–100). In: Frederick Starr, S. (Ed.). *Xinjiang China's muslim borderland*. Armonk: ME Sharpe.

Ministry of Foreign Affairs of the People's Republic of China. (2021). *China's VNR report on implementation of the 2030 agenda for sustainable development*. Beijing: Ministry of Foreign Affairs of the PRC.

Minzner, C. (2018). *End of an era: How China's authoritarian revival is undermining its rise*. Oxford: Oxford University Press.

Moneyhon, M. (2003). China's great western development project in Xinjiang: Economic palliative, or political Trojan horse? *Denver Journal of International Law and Policy*, 31(3): 491–523.

O'Brien, D. (2021). Uyghurs. In: Wright, T. (Ed.). *Oxford bibliographies in Chinese studies*. New York: Oxford University Press. https://doi.org/10.1093/OBO/9780199920082-0187

O'Brien, D. and Brown, M. S. (2022). *People, place, race, and nation in Xinjiang, China: Territories of identity*. Singapore: Palgrave Macmillan.

O'Riordan, T. and Lenton, T. (2014). *Addressing tipping points for a precarious future*. Oxford: Oxford University Press.

O'Neil, M. (2008). The conqueror of China's wild west. *Asia Sentinel*, April 13, 2008. http://www.asiasentinel.com/index.php?option=com_content&task=view&id=1148&Itemid=31. Accessed March 9, 2023.

Pumpelly, R. (Ed.) (1908). *Exploration in Turkestan: Expedition of 1904 prehistoric civilizations of Anau—Origins, growth, and influence of environment*. Washington D.C.: Carnegie Institution of Washington.

Rescher, N. (1998). *Complexity: A philosophical overview*. New Jersey: Transaction Publishers.

Ricci, D. M. (2020). *A political science manifesto for the age of populism: Challenging growth, markets, inequality, and resentment*. Cambridge: Cambridge University Press.

Roberts, S. (2018). The biopolitics of China's 'war on terror' and the exclusion of the Uyghurs. *Critical Asian Studies*, 50(2): 232–258. https://doi.org/10.1080/14672715.2018.1454111

Roberts, S. R. (2020). The war on the Uyghurs: China's campaign against Xinjiang's muslims. Manchester: Manchester University Press.

Room, G. (2016). *Agile actors on complex terrains: Transformative realism and public policy*. Abingdon: Routledge

Rossabi, M. (Ed.) (2004). *Governing China's multi-ethnic frontier*. Seattle: Washington University Press.

Ruser, N., Leibold, J., Munro, K. and Hoja, T. (2020). Cultural erasure: Tracing the destruction of Uyghur and Islamic spaces in Xinjiang. *Policy Brief Report No. 38/2020*. Australian Strategic Policy Institute. https://www.aspi.org.au/report/cultural-erasure. Accessed March 9, 2023.

Sachs, J. D., Kroll, C., Lafortune, G., Fuller, G. and Woelm, F. (2021a). *The decade of action for the sustainable development goals: Sustainable development report 2021*. Cambridge: Cambridge University Press.

Sachs, J. D., Schmidt-Traub, G., Kroll, C., Lafortune, G. and Fuller, G. (2021b). *The sustainable development goals and COVID-19: Sustainable development report 2020*. Cambridge: Cambridge University Press.

Sachs, J. D., Lafortune, G., Kroll, C., Fuller, G. and Woelm, F. (2022). *From crisis to sustainable development: The SDGs as roadmap to 2030 and beyond—Sustainable development report 2022*. Cambridge: Cambridge University Press.

Schwarck, E. (2019). The failure of China's security policy in Xinjiang. *RUSI Newsbrief*, January 11, 2019. https://rusi.org/publication/newsbrief/failure-chinas-security-policy-xinjiang. Accessed March 8, 2023.

Shanghai Academy of Social Sciences—SASS. (2022a). China's population and projections. https://english.sass.org.cn/. Accessed December 2, 2022.

Shanghai Academy of Social Sciences. (2022b). China working-age population, 65+ population. https://english.sass.org.cn/. Accessed December 2, 2022.

Shih, C. (2002). *Negotiating ethnicity in China: Citizenship as a response to the state*. London: Routledge.
Sommer, U. (2018). Women, demography, and politics: How lower fertility rates lead to democracy. *Demography*, 55(2): 559–586.
Stroup, D. (2019). The de-Islamification of public space and Sinicization of ethnic politics in Xi's China. *All About China. Middle East Institute*. September 24, 2019. https://www.mei.edu/publications/de-islamification-public-space-and-sinicization-ethnic-politics-xis-china. Accessed March 9, 2023.
Sudworth, J. (2021). China defends detention of Uighur model in Xinjiang. *BBC*, August 18, 2020. https://www.bbc.com/news/world-asia-china-53809345. Accessed March 9, 2023.
Sydney Business Insides. (2022). China's baby bust will change the world. https://sbi.sydney.edu.au/chinas-baby-bust-will-change-the-world/. Accessed December 2, 2022.
Tagma, H. M. (2009). Homo sacer vs. homo soccer mom: Reading Agamben and Foucault in the war on terror. *Alternatives: Global, Local, Political*, 34(4): 407–435. https://doi.org/10.1177/030437540903400403
Taylor, M. C. (2003). *The moment of complexity: Emerging network culture*. Chicago: University of Chicago Press.
Teitelbaum, M. S. (2015). Political demography: Powerful trends under-attended by demographic science. *Population Studies*, 69(1): 87–95.
Tepe, M. and Vanhuysse, P. (2009). Are aging OECD welfare states on the path to gerontocracy? *Journal of Public Policy*, 29(1), 1–28.
The World Bank. (2022). World development indicators: Population dynamics. http://wdi.worldbank.org/table/2.1. Accessed January 10, 2023.
The World Bank. (2023). *World development report 2023: Migrants, refugees, and societies*. Washington, DC: World Bank.
Tobin, D. (2020). *Securing China's northwest frontier: Identity and insecurity in Xinjiang*. Cambridge: Cambridge University Press.
Tohti, I. (2022). *We Uyghurs have no say: An imprisoned writer speaks*. London: Verso.
Toops, S. (2004). The demographics of Xinjiang (pp. 264–275). In: Frederick Starr, S. (Ed.). *Xinjiang China's muslim borderland*. Armonk: ME Sharpe.
United Nations. (2020). *UN sustainable development cooperation framework for the People's Republic of China 2021–2025*. Geneva: UN.
United Nations, DESA, Population Division. (2021). *Global population growth and sustainable development. UN DESA/POP/2021/TR/NO. 2*. New York: United Nations.
United Nations, DESA, Population Division. (2022). World population prospects 2022. http://population.un.org/wpp/. Accessed 10 June 2023.

United Nations, DESA, Population Division. (2023). India overtakes China as the world's most populous country. *Policy Brief No. 153*. New York: United Nations.

United Nations Development Program—UNDP (2022). *Reducing inequality in the decade of action to achieve the SDGs and accelerate post-pandemic recovery*. Bangkok: UNDP.

Urry, J. (2005). The complexity turn. *Theory, Culture & Society*, 22(5): 1–14.

Wang, F., Cai, Y., Shen, K. and Gietel-Basten, S. (2018). Is demography just a numerical exercise? Numbers, politics, and legacies of China's one-child policy. *Demography*, 55(2): 693–719.

Weiner, M. and Russell, S. S. (2002). *Demography and national security*. New York: Berghahn Books.

Weiner, M. and Teitelbaum, M. S. (2001). *Political demography and demographic engineering*. New York: Berghahn Books.

World Economic Forum. (2022). China's population is about to shrink for the first time since the great famine struck 60 years ago: Here's what that means for the world. https://www.weforum.org/agenda/2022/07/china-population-shrink-60-years-world/. Accessed 10 January 2023.

Xinjiang Statistical Yearbook. (2011). *Xinjiang Weiwu'er Zizhi Tongjiju. Xinjiang Tongji Nianjian 2011*. Beijing: Zhonguo Tongji Chubanshe.

Zenz, A. and Leibold, J. (2017). Xinjiang's rapidly evolving security state. *China Brief*, 17(4): 21–27.

Zhang, X., Brown, M. S. and O'Brien, D. (2018). No CCP, no new China: Discourses of pastoral power in the Xinjiang region of China. *China Quarterly*, 235: 784–803. https://doi.org/10.1017/S0305741018000954

Zhao, Z. and Reimondos, A. (2012). The demography of China's 1958–61 famine: A closer examination. *Population (English Edition)*, 67(2): 281–308.

Zhu, P. (2000). *20 Shiji Xinjiang Shi Yanjiu (Research on the History of Xinjiang in the 20th Century)*. Urumchi: Xinjiang Renmin Chubanshe.

CHAPTER 2

Eldercare Services in Urban China

Björn Alpermann and Christina Maags

1 Introduction

Since the beginning of the Reform and Opening up period commenced in 1978, the central government has sought to redefine and restructure its relationship with subordinate tiers of government (such as on the provincial, municipal, and county levels).

While the early days of the reform period were characterized by widescale decentralization,[1] later reforms have sought to take back

[1] Following Mok (2004), decentralization refers to a number of processes which involve the transfer of responsibilities/tasks and decision-making authority from the central to local government levels. It therefore includes deconcentration, delegation and devolution processes. In contrast, centralization refer to processes which reconcentrate tasks and authority at higher government levels.

B. Alpermann (✉)
Julius-Maximilians-Universität of Würzburg, Würzburg, Germany
e-mail: bjoern.alpermann@uni-wuerzburg.de

C. Maags
University of Sheffield, Sheffield, UK
e-mail: c.maags@sheffield.ac.uk

A. Aliu (ed.), *Complexity Thinking and China's Demography Within and Beyond Mainland China*,
https://doi.org/10.1007/978-981-97-0172-8_2

control through recentralization (Naughton 2018: 62, 101; Zheng 2007). Since then, the Chinese government has initiated several rounds of “loosening” and “tightening” of central control over local power (Cho 2020). Most recently, under the leadership of president Xi Jinping, the People’s Republic is said to be undergoing a renewed phase of recentralization (Lee 2017), seeking to concentrate political power within himself, marginalize factional voices, and reign in local government autonomy (Sarkar 2020).

Although mostly studied in relation to economic and fiscal policies (Tsui and Wang 2004; Cai and Treisman 2006), decentralization has had a tremendous impact on social welfare. Central government devolution of key social welfare areas, such as health care (Ramesh et al. 2014), education (Ngok 2007), or social assistance (Solinger and Hu 2012), has left local governments, particularly municipalities, with the responsibility to finance and provide a variety of social welfare programs. This devolution process resulted in a fragmented system of social welfare provision, which differs greatly not only between urban and rural areas but also between localities across China, leaving many with insufficient social protection (Leung and Xu 2015: 172–173).

However, following broader recentralization efforts under Xi Jinping, recent scholarship suggests that this decentralization of social welfare is changing. Comparing health care, pensions and basic education, Zhu (2016), for instance, has argued that “China has moved from decentralization to recentralization in enacting its social welfare system, to address increasingly more serious social unrest stemming from loosened control over public welfare provision on the part of the central government during the decentralizing market reform era” (2016: 251). Other scholars have echoed this shift toward recentralization in social welfare (Hong et al. 2018) as well as other policy areas (Kostka and Nahm 2017; Chen and Lees 2018). Yet, in contrast to these claims around recentralization of social welfare, recent studies continue to regard decentralization as the root cause for insufficient welfare provision and regional inequality (Hipgrave et al. 2012; Qian and Mok 2016; Mok and Han 2017; Shi 2017).

This study seeks to shed light on this empirical puzzle. As we argue, the on-going use of the binary of “decentralization versus recentralization” blurs the complexity and at times antithetical processes underlying central-local relations. After all, scholars have suggested that central-local relations do not necessarily follow either one of these logics exclusively.

As Chien (2007), for instance, notes the central state has frequently engaged in "asymmetric decentralization" which includes centralization of political power under the party, while leaving key economic and fiscal responsibilities decentralized. Mok (2004) instead speaks of a "centralized decentralization", in which "operational decentralization is combined with the centralization of strategic command" (2004: 7). He therefore attests to the coexistence of trends which are centralizing, decentralizing, and recentralizing all at the same time. Moreover, focusing on this binary does not shed light on, for instance, how local governments respond to recentralization efforts (Schubert and Alpermann 2019). A focus on the relations between central and local governments also deemphasized the role of non-state actors which, as Teets (2013) notes, have gained substantial influences despite the state's various forms of indirect control. In other words, while Zhu (2016) might be correct in arguing that certain policy instruments are leading to greater recentralization of social welfare, the focus on the binary "recentralization versus decentralization" obscures key factors and processes, such as remaining sources of local government power, local responses to centralization and the role of non-state actors needed to obtain a full picture of the developments under scrutiny.

To contribute to our understanding of central-local relations and their impact on social welfare in China, this study employs "political steering theory" (Mayntz and Scharpf 2005; Mayntz 2009) to analyze eldercare service development in local China. As demonstrated by Schubert and Alpermann (2019), "political steering theory" offers a more comprehensive tool than the centralization/decentralization binary to examine Chinese political processes as it enables us to analyze various modes of coordination under the central government's "shadow of hierarchy". This allows us to, on the one hand, retrace the relationship between central and local governments; and on the other hand, examine modes of interaction between various levels of local governments (including township, villages), corporate actors, collective actors (e.g., social organizations) and individual actors. We employ "political steering theory" to examine how decentralization and recentralization impact local government development of eldercare services and by extension influence the local "welfare mix" of public, private, and third sector eldercare service provision on the ground. Ultimately, by combining the use of "political steering" and the "welfare mix" theories, we link the discussion of recentralization/decentralization to related developments of privatization and marketization in social welfare provision (Mok 2004).

In comparatively studying eldercare service development in Shanghai and Beijing, we contend that:

In comparatively studying eldercare service development in Shanghai and Beijing, we contend that while decentralisation has resulted in greater leeway for local governments to determine the time and way in which central regulation and plans are implemented, local governments must demonstrate compliance with central initiatives, particularly when the centre uses centralising tools, such as FYPs which signal central-level priorities. Consequently, waves of decentralisation/recentralisation occur due to central-level steering efforts. If they are strong, it is mandatory for local governments to act, but if they are weak or absent, local governments are more able to counter-steer, shirk or negotiate, resulting in the "loosening" and "tightening" mentioned in the literature.

We argue that local variations in policy implementation are determined by 1) the interplay of central steering efforts and local-level responses and, borrowing from historical institutionalism, 2) the timing and sequence of these efforts and responses. This is evident from our case studies below: Since Shanghai acted upon the centre's first steering approach in the late 1990s (1996 Law), it commenced the development of its eldercare service sector much earlier than Beijing. It was moreover influenced by trends and priorities in eldercare services (community-based care) much earlier than Beijing (where home-based care only became a trend later) and has historically been more open to a larger role of SOs than Beijing. This demonstrates that service development in each case took a different "route" to achieving the 3-tier system envisioned by the central government, by emphasising different types of care service and governance structures. However, recurring central steering efforts make sure that local variation is streamlined to a certain extent. Despite commencing on different paths, after 12 FYP both Shanghai and Beijing started to focus more on the tier they had neglected before to fulfil the 3-tier objective of the centre.

These findings demonstrate how the timing and sequence of local-level responses impacts the resulting welfare mix. Examining ownership structure, in the case of Shanghai, social organizations were able to proliferate and take over market segments early on, while in Beijing they were only supported rather late and mostly in relation to community-based care. Therefore, Beijing's eldercare services are dominated by for-profit providers. In addition, the two municipalities vary in their development of different service types. This has consequences for older persons, who may receive greater access to a specific type of service at different times, leading to unequal access to care across space.

In what follows, we first provide a more detailed description of our conceptual and methodological framework, before examining central government's reforms in eldercare services. The main section of this study comparatively examines the development of the welfare mix in Beijing and Shanghai's eldercare service sector under the "shadow of hierarchy" of the central government. A discussion and brief conclusion round up the paper.

2 Conceptual and Methodological Framework

In political steering theory, central-local government relations are conceptualized through multi-level steering processes. The center aims to "resolve identified social, economic, and political problems within a given society by either 'hard' or 'soft' modes of state intervention or guidance of policy implementation at all administrative levels of a political system" (Schubert and Alpermann 2019: 206). In studying political steering, one needs to differentiate between (a) steering objects (social systems whose autonomy is to be steered in a certain direction, such as city governments or the Communist Party) and (b) steering subjects (such as local governments, corporate, collective, and individual actors) who are the ultimate addressees of the steering effort (Mayntz 2009: 42). However, as local governments are steered by the center, while steering subordinate governments themselves (e.g., township or villages), they are simultaneously steering subjects and objects (Schubert and Alpermann 2019: 208). Political steering theory thus allows us to examine the relation between the central and local governments, as well as between local governments and local non-state actors at the same time. This enables an analysis of central-local relations and their influence on networks between state, business, and third sector actors.

In addition, political steering theory can analytically differentiate between steering modes and steering outcomes (Mayntz 2009: 9, 43). In its steering efforts, the center and local governments (as steering objects) have multiple steering modes, instruments, and tactics at their disposal. Whereas superordinate government levels can engage in hard steering, such as direct governmental intervention, they can also allow negotiation, competition or make use of soft steering modes (e.g., discursive modes of steering). Commonly, a mix of steering modes is used in any given policy field. Local governments in turn can respond by steering (in line with top-down command), coping with, negotiating, shirking, or counter-steering against top-down steering (Schubert and Alpermann 2019: 211). In differentiating between these modes, instruments, and tactics, political steering theory can differentiate between top-down policy making and implementation, on the one hand, and bottom-up processes of selective compliance on the other (Mayntz 2003: 29). Steering outcomes depend on the steering capacity (extent to which steering objects can be molded) and steering governability (extent to which steering subjects can be molded) by the center. The success or failure of steering efforts can be measured by examining implementation effectiveness (outcome is in accordance with predefined objectives) and outcome efficiency (the policy formulation reflects an understanding of the common good) (Schubert and Alpermann 2019: 211).

As Mayntz and Scharpf (2005) argue political steering lies on a continuum ranging from vertical, top-down steering to horizontal, bottom-up steering processes which resemble horizontal modes of cooperative governance outside of government control as described in governance theory. However, as Schubert and Alpermann (2019) emphasize, while non-state actors play a role in Chinese political processes, due to its authoritarian nature, the Chinese party-state does not operate like democratic systems in which the state mainly acts through a regulatory structure. Instead, interaction between the Chinese party-state and society is hampered by the CCP hegemony. Any form of coordination therefore takes place under its "shadow of hierarchy". Depending on the central government's attitude, this shadow can expand or contract. In other words, it is the center that—at any given time—can enforce compliance by local governments (as they do not enjoy any constitutional autonomy) and replace more cooperative with hard steering modes (Schubert and Alpermann 2019).

This article applies political steering theory as outlined in relation to the Chinese policy process (Schubert and Alpermann 2019) to examine the impact of central-local relations on local public service development. To examine the interaction between local governments, businesses, and third sector actors on the ground we moreover employ the concept of "welfare mix". The welfare mix refers to the "configuration of relationships between the state, private and non-profit suppliers" (Ascoli and Ranci 2002: 17) and other actors such as families, employers, charities, and communities as a whole (Powell and Barrientos 2011). By assessing the role of regulation, finance, and provision it is possible to examine the emerging welfare mix by identifying whether responsibilities are delegated to the private or public realm (Powell 2014: 523). In so doing, scholars commonly differentiate between public, commercial (for-profit), and non-profit welfare provision (Longo et al. 2015: 2). However, due to hybridization, these categories can be difficult to discern in China (Maags 2021). In the Chinese context both for-profit and non-profit providers are subsumed under the label "civilian-run" (民办) in contrast to publicly run (公办) (Li et al. 2018).

In many countries, the welfare mix has recently shifted from state-led welfare provision to more complex arrangements where welfare is increasingly provided by other actors. This development is commonly associated with austerity measures resulting from increasing welfare expenditure, particularly due to aging populations (Taylor-Gooby et al. 2019: 2). Consequently, many central governments—in democratic and authoritarian states alike—have attempted to devolve welfare planning, financing, and provision to local-level governments (Andreotti et al. 2012). Basing our analysis on "political steering theory" (Schubert and Alpermann 2019) and the notion of "welfare mix", we examine the ways in which the center is steering local governments in their efforts to ensure eldercare service provision. In so doing, we seek to understand how and to what extent multi-level steering efforts influence the emerging welfare mix within the eldercare service sector.[2]

To do so, we have conducted a comparative case study of two first-tier cities, Shanghai and Beijing. We have selected these two cases, firstly, as population aging and by extension eldercare services are more advanced in these municipalities. Secondly, we chose "centrally administered" municipalities which are more directly influenced by the steering efforts by the central government. Thirdly, developments pioneered in these municipalities often serve as precursors for national-level regulations. To assess the

[2] In the following, eldercare is understood as "assistance mostly from family members, friends or professional caregivers in so-called activities of daily living (ADL)" (Colombo et al. 2011: 39).

multi-level steering efforts and their impact on eldercare service development, we gathered national-level and local statistics, policy documents, blue-books, local case-study reports, and fieldwork (interview) data.[3] In the following, we first examine the central steering efforts of local governments through policy analysis and descriptive statistics of national-level statistical data. We then examined each case study by coding information according to the three areas of the welfare mix: regulation, finance, and provision to comparatively assess how local government steering efforts in both cities have impacted the welfare mix in each case respectively.

3 Central Steering of Eldercare Service Development in China

China's rapid population aging has increased demand for eldercare services at a time when China is facing prospects of lower economic growth. The China Aging Longitudinal Social Survey from 2014 estimated that by 2030 around 27 million elderly residents will need long-term care (LTC) (Sun and Du 2017: 10–11, 27). It finds that 8.54 percent of elderly respondents, equivalent to 18.8 million persons, already require ADL assistance.[4] The on-going family and household-related changes mean that this rising demand cannot be met by traditional family-based care. To be sure, families are still the locus of eldercare. Yet increasing numbers of elderly people cope alone—whether by choice or necessity. While in 2000, 2.0 percent of urban and 0.8 percent of rural respondents were self-dependent, in 2010 the figures rose to 9.2 and 19.5 percent respectively. Especially for rural residents this tremendous increase points to a looming care crisis (Sun and Du 2016: 101–105). Chinese people are increasingly concerned about eldercare provision and expect the government to provide it publicly (Chen and Yang 2012: 148).

[3] Our fieldwork was undertaken in the summers of 2018 and 2019, when we held semi-structured qualitative interviews with government officials, eldercare providers and academics. In each interview we inquired about government regulation and strategies, financial responsibilities as well as the development and coordination of public and private care provisions.

[4] ADLs include walking, feeding, dressing, and grooming, toileting and bathing, while IADLs comprise managing finances, transportation and communication, shopping and meal preparation, housecleaning and home maintenance.

China's population aging thus creates a significant social and economic problem for Chinese people across the country.

Since the late 1990s, the central government has tried to address this problem by steering local eldercare development. During the socialist era and early reform period the Chinese party-state only provided eldercare to the "Three Nos" (those who lack financial resources, have no children, are incapacitated and/or very old) as a form of social assistance, relying on families (particularly women) to provide care (Harper 1992). However, this changed with the adoption of the PRC's Law on Protecting the Rights and Interests of Older Persons in 1996 (revised in 2012 and amended in 2015 and 2018). In doing so, the center intervened in eldercare provision, on the one hand, by using soft steering to create a discourse of individual and family responsibility to care, and on the other hand, by using steering instruments, enshrined in national laws, policies, and FYPs, to steer its steering objects—local governments in charge of regulating, financing and providing care.

In spite of crumbling informal care arrangements,[5] the party-state repeatedly emphasized that caring responsibilities lie with the families and elderly themselves. Firstly, the 1996 Law (and later revisions of the Law) as well as the 12th and 13th FYPs draw on Confucian values such as filial piety (孝) to demonstrate the family's moral responsibility to provide care. If this care is not provided, it can be legally sanctioned. The party-state's first response to the increase in demand for eldercare services thus was to firmly place the responsibility for care on families and to establish that the state only provides publicly funded eldercare in the form of social assistance as a last resort.

Although national legislation emphasizes family caring responsibilities, the center has simultaneously issued various policies and action plans to increase eldercare service provision on the ground (Feng et al. 2012: 2764–2773). Since 2011, social services such as eldercare are moreover included in national Five-year-plans, such as the 12th FYP (2011–2015) (Du 2013). National legislation and plans use various policy instruments

[5] According to a nationally representative panel study the share of elderly receiving informal care declined from 90 percent in 2000 to 75 percent in 2010, while more elderly relied on themselves or formal arrangements (Sun and Du 2016: 105).

to steer eldercare development: First, the center has defined a development model local governments need to use based on a three-tier system of eldercare provision. This includes home-based care as the "basis", community-based services as "backing", and institutional care as "supplement" (Feng et al. 2012: 2767). Since 2000, the center has moreover set clear numerical targets, such as increasing the supply of beds from 10 beds (10th FYP) to 30 beds per 1000 urban citizens (12th FYP) or determining that 90 percent of villages and townships are to establish old people's homes (10th FYP). Subsequently, targets were aligned with the three-tier development model by establishing the 90-7-3 framework. In this new target formula, local governments are to ensure that 90 percent of Chinese elderly receive family caregiving at home (supported by home-based care), 7 percent needing additional care are supported by community-based care, and the 3 percent who cannot rely on family caregiving receive institutional care (see Chen and Han 2016: 294). Home-based care includes services such as food delivery, in-house social and health care services as well as improvement of home facilities (Shang and Wu 2011: 128). Steering its steering objects via models and targets, central pressure on local governments to enhance eldercare supply has increased tremendously over the last decade (Alpermann and Zhan 2019: 359).

Finally, the center has drafted two-pronged development strategies which local governments are to employ to increase care provision on the local level. Firstly, starting in 2012 and intensifying since, local governments are to foster commercialization of eldercare services by establishing an "elderly industry" (养老产业).[6] According to the 13th FYP on aging, they are to encourage any kind of private investment in the sector, opening up the market completely. Other areas of this commercialization strategy include to "corporatize" public care institutions or set up Private–Public-Partnerships (PPPs). More recently, the State Council (2019) clarified, however, that reformed (semi-)public institutions are to primarily cater to the neediest cases. While commercialization of public

[6] While privatization includes shifting to for-profit and non-profit service providers, commercialization only pertains to strengthening the role of the former. As we argue, local governments differ in their emphasis on either strategy. The term marketization, as used by Luo and Zhan (2018), does not distinguish between for- or non-profit participation and, thus more generally refers to introducing non-public providers and competitive mechanisms.

care providers is to benefit the needy, enhanced provision through the "private" care industry is to provide families with the opportunity to purchase care.

Secondly, in line with the objective to enhance "private" provision, the central government has sought to encourage social organizations (社会组织) and—thus the third sector—to provide eldercare services. To support them, central legislation states that local governments are to grant social organizations subsidies, tax levies, access to land, and lottery funds in return for eldercare service provision at government-set prices (Alpermann and Zhan 2019: 359–361). To fund this, the Ministry of Civil Affairs called for extensively mobilizing "idle capital in society" (For Book Health Research Centre 2018: 53). According to Alpermann and Zhan, the aim of this strategy, "is to reach the high targets for beds in old-age care facilities, while ensuring at the same time that the share of government-run institutions accounts for less than 50 percent" (Alpermann and Zhan 2019: 361). Driven by central steering efforts local governments are thus to initiate a shift in the welfare mix characterized by a move from public to greater commercial and third sector provision.

As Alpermann and Zhan note "commercialization is not to be confused with a retreat of the state, instead competition in the 'shadow of hierarchy' is at work" as a specific mode of policy steering (Alpermann and Zhan 2019: 361). Governmental subsidies in various forms (construction land, tax holidays or reductions, direct pay-outs etc.) play an important role in steering industry development. These subsidies increased by almost 10 percent from 2014 to 2015, reaching Renminbi (RMB) 40.5 billion. The subsidies are supposed to "crowd in" private-for-profit and non-profit investors.

In addition to soft steering via promoting a public discourse of filial piety and steering local development via policy instruments, the center moreover encourages competition between localities to develop a long-term care (LTC) insurance which can be upscaled for national implementation. In 2016, 15 pioneering municipalities were selected to develop an LTC insurance pilot scheme (Zhu and Öesterle 2019). Due to the great variety of schemes,[7] there is no consensus as to which model

[7] See Yang, Wei and Jingwei He, Alex and Fang, Lijie and Mossialos, Elias (2016) Financing institutional long-term care for the elderly in China: a policy evaluation of new models. *Health Policy and Planning*, for a comparison of the LTC insurance schemes in Shanghai, Nanjing, and Qingdao.

to follow. Consequently, the central government has further increased the number of local governments participating in the competition over time. Currently, there are 49 LTC pilot insurance schemes (Xinhua 2022).

An analysis of national-level statistics shows that the various central hard steering efforts have been able to achieve central objectives—thus demonstrating implementation effectiveness. Comparing the 11th and 12th FYPs, infrastructure investments in eldercare more than doubled and reached RMB 13.1 billion in 2014. Yet, facing vacancies in some cities' newly established care homes, investments dropped to RMB 12.4 billion in 2015 (Task Force 2017: 97–98). Despite slowing growth in eldercare beds in 2016 and 2017, in late 2017 China's total number of care beds stood at 29.7 beds per 1000 elderly—thus just falling short of the center's target of providing institutional care for 3 percent of Chinese elderly people.[8]

Overall, the central party-state seeks to meet the rise in demand by implementing a multipronged hard steering approach to eldercare service development based on fostering private and third sector engagement in the eldercare industry, while using a soft steering approach to emphasize self-reliance and family support and providing public resources only for those in dire need. Yet, to understand how local governments respond to central steering efforts, we need to turn to the local level.

4 Local Government Steering Efforts—Influence on Welfare Mix Development

Local governments respond to central steering efforts, while simultaneously developing ways to steering local steering subjects such as businesses, social organizations, and consumers to pursue their own interests. The following two case studies demonstrate how, on the one hand, local government has responded to central steering and, on the other hand, what these changes in local government behavior have meant for the development of the local welfare mix in the sector of eldercare service provision. To assess the emerging welfare mix, the case studies examine regulation, financing, and provision respectively.

[8] This had been achieved while reducing the national number of care providers from 43,000 in 2013 to just 29,000 in late 2017—a significant concentration of providers (Han et al. 2018: 50–51).

4.1 Case 1: Shanghai

Shanghai responded to central steering efforts in the late 1990s by fully embracing eldercare service development. Shortly after 1996, Shanghai released its "Measures on Administering Eldercare Homes" in 1998 (revised in 2010; Shanghai Municipal Government 1998) to follow up on central regulation. Shortly after, it adopted regulations on establishing a local "Starlight Project" in 2001 (Shanghai Municipal Government 2001). In these early policies, Shanghai pursues the strategy to "socialize social welfare" (Wong and Li 2012: 237)—a slogan of the central government—to involve social organizations in welfare service provision. In its 2001 policy, for instance it states it will "expand mobilizing the participation of social forces", and support non-governmental institutions such as social groups and civil non-enterprises and individuals to become service providers and administrators, as well as to explore models such as "society builds and administers", "government builds, society administers" and "civilian-operated, government supported" (广泛动员社会力量参与，并扶持社会团体、民办非企业单位等非政府机构和个人成为服务者和管理者，探索"社会建社会管"、"政府建社会管"和"民办公助"的模式) (Shanghai Municipal Government 2001). Shanghai thus responded to the center's first hard steering effort by complying with top-level regulation and development models.

The extent to which Shanghai pursued the goal of developing eldercare services in practice is evident in its increase in eldercare facilities and policies in the coming years. Starting off with 358 eldercare institutions in 2000 (Zhang 2007: 43), the municipality increased this number to 615 in 2009 and 712 in 2019 (Shanghai Municipal Government 2009, 2018), demonstrating the municipality's eagerness to develop eldercare services locally. Shanghai's rapid eldercare service development could thus be explained by its response to central steering efforts. However, as the municipality is home to a rapidly aging population (see Fig. 1), it might have targeted development earlier than other municipalities due to its comparatively larger number of older people in need of care (Di and Rosenbaum 1994). Therefore, central steering efforts might have coincided with local development interests. In any case, as a result of Shanghai's comparatively early promotion of eldercare services in China, it became a forerunner in Chinese eldercare (Chen and Han 2016: 292–307), prompting other Chinese cities to copy Shanghai's development approaches (Harper 1992; Chen and Han 2016).

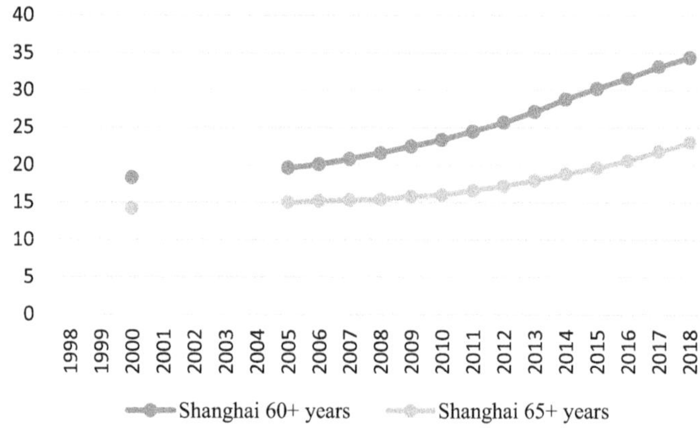

Fig. 1 Population aging in Shanghai

Regulation. While Shanghai has followed central guidelines by adopting local legislation and government programs such as the Starlight Project, it subsequently used its leeway in policy formulation and implementation to develop a distinctive steering approach of its own. Firstly, the municipality prioritized community-based services in establishing its three-tier system. After Shanghai had already heavily invested into community-*funded* care homes since the 1980s (371 in 1987) and had turned its focus to community-based systems in the 1990s to support family caregiving[9] (Di and Rosenbaum 1994: 105–107), it prioritized this tier during the 2000s (Chen and Han 2016: 293). According to one expert interviewee, Shanghai municipality adopted this approach after learning from the Japanese eldercare service development.[10]

Secondly, Shanghai's steering approach was distinct since this community-care development was to be spearheaded by the third sector, including social organizations, civilian-run non-profit operators (民办非企业单位), non-governmental institutions (非政府机构) and individuals, who became care providers and administrators—as the short excerpt

[9] Shanghai's greater focus on strengthening community-based care in the 1990s was later promoted by the central as a part of the three-year "Starlight" Plan (2001–2003)—mentioned above—which sought to increase means-tested eldercare service provision at the community-level across the country.

[10] Interview with expert, September, 2018.

above demonstrates. This decision could have been made, since including social organizations in public service provision has a long history in Shanghai (Hsu and Hasmath 2014: 517), particularly in the area of eldercare (Wong and Li 2012: 241).

To set its own targets on how many older persons would be serviced by which tier, in 2007, it developed the 90-7-3 framework mentioned above. Eventually, this target framework was adopted nationally (Chen and Han 201). Starting in the mid-2000s, the further expansion of these three tiers was to be funded by targeting more private-for-profit commercialization. This is exemplified by its 2008 policy, which mentions promoting brands and letting enterprises reduce profits to ensure greater access to provision (Shanghai Municipal Government 2008). While selectively developing certain tiers and "social forces" at different times, Shanghai on the one hand, stayed within the central's development modes and objectives, yet laid the foundations for the development of a distinctive welfare mix.

A second steering "push" from the center occurred in 2011 with the 12 FYP. Although Shanghai had already developed service provision much further than other municipalities, the 12th FYP resulted in a massive increase in new municipal initiatives to further extend and professionalize eldercare service provision. Shanghai municipality responded to central steering efforts by, for instance, expanding service coverage and improving service quality of community-based care (Chen and Han 2016: 296–297). However, one key reform sticks out, the new focus on further developing home-based care, as outlined in a bulk of policies since 2014 (Shanghai Municipal Government 2014). Although local governments such as Shanghai could have pointed to previous accomplishments, it not only felt the need to actively respond to central steering by adopting a wave of new regulation (see Table 1, Appendix) but to do so in a way that would strengthen the one tier—of the officially promoted three-tier system—which it had not developed as much before: home-based care. The second central steering push thus resulted in a move toward "filling the gaps" in Shanghai's implementation of central models and plans.

Financing. In line with central policy instruments, a key method to develop eldercare services has been the use of tax levies and subsidies. Whereas Shanghai's community-based care providers were the first to enjoy government subsidies, the same strategy was soon used to enhance profit-for-profit provision of eldercare—although commercial sector subsidies are lower than those of the third sector.[11] In 2014, for instance, the municipal government spent 92.12 million RMB on eldercare infrastructure investment, spending on average 21.26 RMB per elderly. While the use of subsidies is in line with central policy objectives, Shanghai municipality decides which provider type (non-for-profit) receives higher subsidies (for-profit), which impacts eldercare service development on the ground. In terms of subsidies, in 2015 the Shanghai government in total spent 8.35 billion RMB in subsidies, which constitutes 13.25 million RMB per care institution. Finally, in 2015 Shanghai's 112,249 eldercare beds were on average subsidized with 74,388 RMB (Task Force 2017: 109).

In line with Shanghai's overall steering approach, the municipality contracts out a significant amount of services to third sector providers. To do so, the government commences a tendering process by publishing information online. Social organizations then compete to receive government funding. According to a local expert, since social organizations compete over government contracts, there is strong pressure to offer low-price services to obtain government funding, suggesting a partial transfer of financial pressure from local governments to the third sector.[12] Chen and Han explain the contracting out process as follows: "The Office on Aging in each district, under the Shanghai Civil Affairs Bureau, contracts out government services to non-profit civilian providers. These providers then collaborate with resident neighborhood associations to deliver services. The Office on Aging in each district oversees services and contracts" (Chen and Han 2016: 299). The government thereby sets service charges for third sector providers. Yet as for-profit providers sell their services on the market, they determine their own price (Wong and Li 2012). As observed in the analysis of Shanghai's regulation, the municipality steers the development of eldercare service providers ultimately impacting the local welfare mix: whereas social organizations need to adhere to government-set prices and are dependent on the tendering process, private-for-profit set their own prices and work according to market-based principles.

To further support the financing of eldercare services and to take part in the central government's promotion of pilot studies on long-term

[11] Interview with expert September 12, 2018a.

[12] Interview with expert September 12, 2018a.

care insurance, the municipality formally launched its eldercare insurance in 2016. Due to successful results, the LTC insurance has been extended from 3 districts (普陀区，徐汇区，金山区) to all 16 districts in 2018, which is likely to place it in a good position in the national-level competition for LTC pilot programs.

Provision. Shanghai's regulatory and financial approach has resulted in a rapid increase in eldercare service provision. Shanghai, in 2015, had 699 residential care homes offering 126,000 beds. Eighty-nine percent of these homes were in eldercare institutions of various ownership forms, while 11 percent were operated by neighborhoods (社区) (Shanghai Civil Affairs Bureau 2016). Thus, Shanghai is already close to fulfilling the political goal of offering 30 beds per 1000 elderly residents. By 2017, the number of residential care homes increased to 702, providing 132,800 beds.

On the one hand, this still falls short of demand given that in a 2016 Shanghai survey 57 percent of elderly respondents said they would consider moving to a care home (Shi et al. 2017: 21). On the other hand, a different set of official statistics highlights another challenge. Of 120,000 beds in eldercare institutions some 34 percent remained unoccupied in 2017 (Shanghai Statistical Yearbook 2018). This surprising finding of high vacancy rates points at misguided investments in high-priced facilities that are unaffordable for ordinary households, as discussed in the literature (DBS Insight 2016: 14–15), or in outskirts where supply exceeds demand, whereas the opposite is true for inner city districts (Data Journalism Centre 2019).

Community-based care has similarly increased significantly over the last two decades. While Shanghai did not have any community-based care in the 1990s, by 2015 it had opened 224 community-based elder support stations (社区助老服务社) and 488 elder day-care centers (老年人日间服务中心) (Chen and Han 2016: 296).

The increasing diversification in the welfare mix is moreover evident in the diverse ownership types. Shanghai has sought to increase the number of "civilian built and operated" (民建民营) care facilities to reduce "publicly built and operated" (公建公营) care facilities. Other models to enhance the welfare mix include PPPs, such as "publicly built, civilian-run" (公建民营) or "civilian-run, with public support" (民办公助).[13] As

[13] Interview with expert September 12, 2018a.

noted in the welfare mix literature, welfare rescaling has thus involved "hybridization" (Evers 2005).

This is particularly evident in the terminology employed, blurring the distinction between commercial and third sector provision. Due to hybridization and the Chinese use of the term "civilian-run" in official statistics which includes both for-profit and non-profit providers, the exact distribution of the ownership structure in Shanghai's eldercare service provision is difficult to assess. As some interviewees argue, Shanghai's residential eldercare is largely civilian-run, while public provision is means-tested.[14] This conforms with public policy stating that public homes should primarily supply the "Three Nos". Specifically, incapacitated residents should make up 70 percent in "practical and not luxurious" public homes (Shanghai Municipal Government 2014).

Moreover, the municipality appears to diversify eldercare services on the market—more upscale services are run by for-profit providers and cheaper services are provided by the third sector—to enable families of different income levels to purchase care. Shanghai's privatization strategy encourages both larger eldercare homes with "economies of scale" and smaller, more "family-like" care homes (家庭化，小型养老机构). In comparison, community-based care is largely run by the public or third sector.[15] Non-profit community-based services are based on Shanghai's strategy to contract services out to social organizations whose numbers have multiplied[16]: Pudong New Area alone boasts more than 240 eldercare social organizations (NDRC et al. 2018: 370).

The resulting welfare mix has created diverging access to eldercare among local citizens. On the one hand, commercial sector provision is often more expensive than public or third sector provision, although service quality is not necessarily higher. Therefore, one eldercare expert argued that low and middle-income residents, ineligible for means-tested eldercare, have difficulties finding affordable care and wait several years before being institutionalized.[17] Commercial ones are open to anybody and include various price ranges, while public institutions, and many

[14] Interview with government official September 11, 2018; Interview with expert September 12, 2018a.

[15] Interview with expert September 12, 2018.

[16] Interview with expert September 12, 2018.

[17] Interview with expert September 12, 2018b.

beds in third sector facilities, are reserved for means-tested elderly with Shanghai *hukou* (household registration). However, elderly receiving social assistance cannot freely choose but are assigned to a public or third sector care facility in their district.[18] The differing service availability across districts results in an uneven geographical access to care.[19] In addition to income and *hukou*, the location of residents thus significantly impacts access to eldercare. However, the situation is even more complex. Some experts argued that some commercial eldercare providers cater more exclusively to lower-income elderly, particularly non-*hukou* holders (Chen 2016: 66). Others stated that there are commercial residential homes at the city's outskirts which are more affordable but less attractive due to their remoteness and inconvenient access to public transport.[20] While state-led marketization thus seemingly bifurcates service provision along income levels, it in fact creates more complex arrangements on the ground.

Shanghai's steering approach suggest that the municipality directs investment into the more lucrative residential care sector providing services to the elderly ineligible for subsidized care, whereas the third sector caters to means-tested clientele (see also Chen and Han 2016). Shanghai's approach has thus resulted in the welfare mix in which the private-for-profit and the third sector play a greater role, while residential care is predominantly provided by the former and community care by the latter.

4.2 Case 2: Beijing

Beijing responded to national-level initiatives of the late 1990s by adopting its own legislation[21] in 1995 (Beijing Municipal Government 1995), regulations for eldercare residential institutions in 2000 (Beijing Municipal Government 2000) and establishing a "Starlight Project" for means-tested urban elderly in 2001 (Beijing Municipal Government

[18] Interview with government official September 11, 2018.

[19] Interview with government official September 11, 2018, see also Chen and Han 2016: 302, Data Journalism Centre 2019.

[20] Interview with expert September 12 2018b.

[21] In addition to the municipality, each district also develops its own regulation and development strategies (Interview with expert August 21, 2018).

2003). While enterprises and social groups were allowed to set up eldercare homes and provide financial assistance through donations (Art. 3), Beijing's early policies foresaw a major role of the local government in managing and financing eldercare institutions (Art. 6). (Beijing Municipal Government 2000). Similarly, the municipality took the promotion of rural eldercare into its own hands by financially supporting grassroot-level governments in its rural districts and counties to set up a "Starlight Plan" there (Beijing Municipal Government 2006).

From the late 1990s to mid-2000s, Beijing thus did not engage much in the "socialization of care" but—as in previous decades—preferred to continue its position in financing and administering means-tested care. Perhaps for the same reason, the number of eldercare homes did not increase as rapidly during the 2000s. While Beijing already had 319 residential homes in 2001 (Zhang 2006, 2007), this number "only" increased to 366 in 2009 but then rapidly increased to 534 in 2018 (Beijing Disable Person's Federation 2011; Beijing City Report 2018).[22] While it adopted legislation, Beijing, however, rather shirked away from allowing large-scale "socialization" of eldercare until the mid-to-late 2000s.

While Beijing might have wanted to shirk away from following central steering as much as, e.g., Shanghai, to direct investment elsewhere, it also did not face as much demographic pressure as Shanghai. As shown in Fig. 2, Beijing's population aging is lagging behind that of Shanghai by around 6 years.

Regulation. While adopting regulation as a response to the first central steering effort in the late 1990s, it was not until the late 2000s that Beijing commenced to develop its own development approach to eldercare services. Since 2009, an increase in policies and strategies suggests that Beijing started to pay the issue of eldercare service development more attention. In comparison to Shanghai, Beijing's 2009 policy explicitly targets home-based care by developing delivery services, in-home care workers, and doctor visits (Beijing Civil Affairs Bureau 2009). While this is in line with the central strategy of developing a three-tier care system, local decision-makers have opted for developing home-based care institutions before moving to community-based care, which was the starting

[22] Other sources report a much lower number of care homes in Beijing, such as Feng et al. (2011: 740) who state the municipality was home to 150 care homes in 2000 and only reached 331 in 2009.

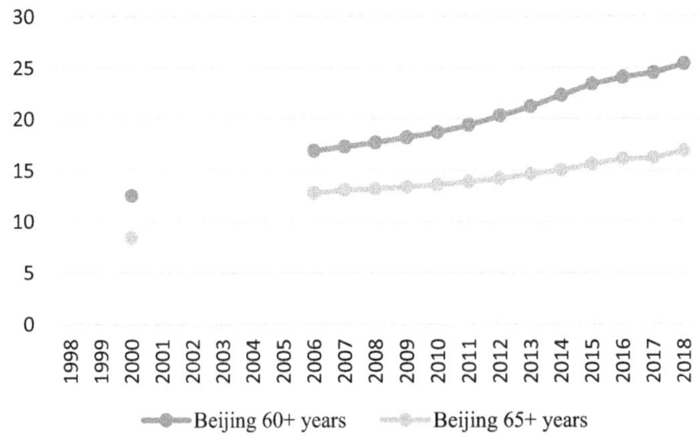

Fig. 2 Population aging in Beijing (*Source* Beijing Municipal Government Reports, 2006–2018)

point for Shanghai. This could be explained by the preference of many Chinese older persons in Beijing to age at home (Yu and Rosenberg 2017) and the greater move toward deinstitutionalization and home-based care across the world, particularly in industrial countries (Tarricone and Tsouros 2008).

In addition, Beijing created its own version of the 90-3-7 framework. In 2009, Beijing's policy articulated its local "90-6-4 strategy": 90 percent of elderly should receive family care; six percent are to be supported by community-based care and four percent to be placed in residential care—slightly altering the nation-wide 90-7-3 strategy. While following national initiatives, Beijing thus used its leeway in policy formulation to focus on a certain tier and reframe national development strategies.

While Beijing had started to develop a local approach to eldercare service development much later than Shanghai, it similarly received a boost after the second central steering "push" in 2011. In response to the central-level 12th FYP, Beijing municipality launched an impressive array of new policies, ranging from standardizing eldercare, an eldercare insurance system, an insurance for care providers against accidents, and streamlining governmental subsidies. Moreover, Beijing started to focus on further developing the community-based services as well—and thereby moving to a full three-tier system. While community-based care services have been mentioned in early policies in relation to home-based services, Beijing's first specific policy on community-based care was adopted in 2015 (Beijing Municipal Government 2015). That year, community-based care homes only accounted for a minuscule 1.2 percent of all eldercare beds in Beijing (Task Force 2017: 120–125). Similar to Shanghai, Beijing thus commenced the selective development of certain tiers after the first central steering push (residential and home-based care) but then moved to consolidate the three-tier system by developing community-care.

Financing. Similar to Shanghai, Beijing's local approach to eldercare service development would be based on the "socialization" of eldercare provision. Starting with its 2009 policy mentioned above, the municipality has attempted to promote the "participation of social forces" via providing subsidies to older persons themselves or eldercare providers (providing land, financial support for establishing facilities, utility or running costs, subsidies per bed, and by contracting out services) (Task Force 2017: 29). In addition, Beijing offers in-kind support such as public housing to run eldercare services (公建民办).[23]

Beijing's use of financial incentives to steer eldercare service development has resulted in large-scale public investment. In 2014, for instance, the Beijing government spent 105.17 million RMB on eldercare infrastructure investment, 12 million more than Shanghai. However, in contrast to Shanghai its expenditure on subsidies is lower. In 2015, Beijing spent 3.49 billion RMB on subsidies, constituting 5.84 million RMB (in comparison to Shanghai's 13.25 million RMB) per institution. The same year, Beijing spent an average of 26,309 RMB on subsidies for its 132,574 beds—about a third of Shanghai's subsidies per bed (Task Force 2017: 109). This could be due to the fact that Beijing provides 59 percent of its oldest old (高龄) with financial aid, while Shanghai's coverage rate is only 21 percent. In contrast, Shanghai provides "nursing" (护理补贴) or "eldercare"-related subsidies (养老补贴) to a larger

[23] In an Interview on September 19, 2018, an expert from Beijing stated that Beijing municipality does provide the subsidies mentioned Taskforce 2015 as well as in-kind support.

number of people[24] (Task Force 2017: 91). It thus appears that Beijing municipalities grant subsidies to older persons directly which they can spend on eldercare services of their choosing, while Shanghai ties its subsidies more to certain service types, which are often to be redeemed at certain types of providers.

In addition to the individualized financial aid, Beijing's level of subsidies suggests that its financing strategy is strongly geared toward promoting private-for-profit commercialization. Firstly, private-for-profit providers receive the same level of subsidies as non-profit providers (Wu 2019: 32). Secondly, Beijing tries to steer this development via special funds according to "critical success factors". Comparatively high subsidies for for-profit providers demonstrate a strong push for private-for-profit commercialization. This is moreover evident in its promotion of eldercare "products" and private insurances (Zhou and Kang 2019). In contrast to Shanghai's early embrace of social organizations to provide eldercare, Beijing's financial incentive structure thus suggests a greater reliance on spurring for-profit investment.

To support individual purchasing power of elderly, and perhaps receive central-level recognition for policy innovation, Beijing municipality moreover participated in experimenting with a long-term care insurance system. This LTC insurance again reflects Beijing's more individualistic and commercial approach. According to Beijing demographers involved in evaluating the insurance experiment in 2017, the commercial LTC insurance was unsuccessful. Therefore, Beijing is now considering a social LTC insurance instead.[25]

Provision. As a result of Beijing's efforts, there has been a steady growth of eldercare homes over time. In 2006, for instance, Beijing was home to 324 eldercare residential institutions of which 214 were public and 110 were civilian-run (Beijing Municipal Government 2006)—again reflecting the rather late incorporation of "social forces" in comparison to Shanghai. By 2016, this number had increased by 65 percent, mostly in the form of commercial providers. Among the 534 residential institutions, 180 are fully public institutions—"publicly administered, publicly run" (公办公营) providing 25,953 beds. Eighty are "publicly administered,

[24] Whereas in 2015, Beijing municipality offered 1880 residents a "nursing subsidy" and 128,046 residents an "eldercare subsidy", in Shanghai these subsides were offered to 48,390 and 186,243 residents respectively (Task Force 2017: 91).

[25] Interview with Beijing experts October 31, 2017.

civilian run" (公办民营) offering 16,527 beds, mirroring the hybridization of welfare provision among the public and third sector. The majority, however, are the 274 "civilian administered, publicly supported" (民办公助) holding a total capacity of 68,942 beds (Beijing City Report 2018).[26] These residential homes offer a variety of services, which differ depending on the care facility, but commonly include: social and health care-related activities, physical exercise, socio-cultural activities, and education (Cheng et al. 2011: 1280).

Beijing's approach to commercialization via for-profit providers is again visible when examining eldercare provision according to ownership type. Firstly, Beijing is home to more for-profit providers than third sector providers. In 2017, there were 1329 private enterprises compared to 600 social organizations (Beijing City Report 2018). Secondly, the municipality appears to be pursuing a "big is beautiful" strategy resulting in the skewing of distribution of eldercare facilities toward larger providers. In March 2017 it decided to "completely open up the market for eldercare" by 2020, including pushing for "franchises" (连锁化) by allowing one market actor (both for-profit and non-profit) to establish several subsidiaries within one city district with just one registration (Zhou and Kang 2019: 30–34). Although service providers involve a network of decentralized community-level "care stations" (see below), the municipality's idea is to foster "large eldercare companies or social organizations" with competitive power through mergers and acquisitions. This has resulted in a major increase in eldercare provision. In 2015, Beijing therefore had the second-highest share of eldercare beds per capita of the local aged population in the country (Task Force 2017: 120–125). With its franchising model and easier registration across jurisdictions, Beijing has set a trend. In March 2019 the State Council (2019) published a policy document that made this the new national standard.

While Beijing is pursuing its local eldercare steering approach based on for-profit commercialization, it is nonetheless using this approach to meet central-level plans. To establish a comprehensive three-tier system, Beijing started to promote community-based care more strongly. A 2016–2017

[26] Yet, the same paradox of high vacancy that we observed in Shanghai also pertains to Beijing, and even more glaringly. Here, the vacancy rate of eldercare beds according to the Beijing Statistical Yearbook (2019, Table 21–29) was 58 percent in 2018. While we again suspect affordability and location to be the prime reasons, more research is needed to confirm this.

report states that there are 350 community-level eldercare stations (社区养老服务驿站) and 208 eldercare centers (养老照料中心). While the report does not reveal whether community-based care is run by public, for-profit, or non-profit providers, evidence suggests that community-based care is largely civilian-run. As a local expert explained, "stations" are commonly run by social organizations, suggesting greater third sector involvement in community-based care. In any case, these community-based care stations are to foster aging at home, and thus support home-based care services.

Most recently, Beijing has commenced an ambitious plan to increase community-based eldercare stations to 1000 by the end of 2020, of which 542 are to be built in urban and 458 in rural areas (Zhou and Kang 2019). To achieve this goal, between 2014 and 2016 the government invested 500 million RMB public funds in community care, while attracting four times as much investment from the third or commercial sector (Beijing City Report 2018). As evident in its policies, financial incentives, and provision, Beijing has focused more on the development of home-based care and for-profit commercialization and is now expanding community care by allowing a greater role for social organizations.

The ways in which Beijing's local approach to eldercare services has developed over time, has clear implications for the welfare mix on the ground. First of all, as in the case of Shanghai, Beijing's efforts to develop eldercare services have resulted in a massive increase of diverse eldercare services. Due to Beijing's local steering approach, this expansion was based on a shift from largely public means-tested provision to largely private-for-profit provision, running on a franchise model. Social organizations do play a role, to a much smaller extent than in Shanghai. Private-for-profit providers dominate, offering a broad product portfolio for elderly able to purchase these services (Zhou et al. 2013: 540). As private-for-profit services are more expensive than public services, and more likely to be located at the outskirts of the city (Zhou et al. 2013: 539, 546; Yu and Rosenberg 2017: 195–196), the increase in services demonstrate a growth in services for older persons who are ineligible for public means-tested care provision (for Beijing *hukou* holders) and who can afford the comparatively higher prices. In addition, since Beijing's local steering approach has had a clear focus on home-based care, community-based care was only targeted later and seems less developed in comparison (Cheng et al. 2011: 365). Since the 12th FYP, however, Beijing has made greater efforts to fill in this gap in its three-tier system by more strongly investing and promoting community-based care stations.

Similar to the case of Shanghai, Beijing's steering approach seems to have resulted in a bifurcation of services, in which means-tested local *hukou* holders can access public and third sector service provision, while the rest purchases services from private-for-profit providers, many of which are located in the outskirts of the city. However, in contrast to Shanghai, there are fewer social organizations which could support the public sector in providing means-tested care for eligible older persons. In addition, private-for-profit provision is found across all tiers, particularly in home-based and residential care, as third sector providers are largely operating in support of home-based care in community-based "stations". Beijing's welfare mix is thus less diversified in terms of provider types and tiers at which these operate than Shanghai, due to the larger private-for-profit-based expansion of eldercare services.

5 Comparative Discussion

With rapid population aging and demand for eldercare services, the Chinese party-state is scaling up its efforts to foster eldercare service provision on the ground, particularly by devolving the responsibility to establish a three-tier service system to local governments. Local governments, such as Shanghai and Beijing examined in this study, need to complying with central steering efforts. This compliance is clearly observable in the spur of development of eldercare policies and eldercare facilities after central pushes in 1996 and 2011, which as seen below, over the subsequent years produce the desired effect: an increase in eldercare services across the country (see Fig. 3).

However, due to decentralization, Beijing and Shanghai have leeway to adopt their own steering approaches as long as they are within acceptable limits of central steering instruments such as development models and strategies. On the face of it, Shanghai and Beijing's local steering efforts diverge mainly in terms of timing, prioritization of tier level and support for the third sector. Shanghai embraced the first central steering effort, moving on to play a national forerunner role. It concentrated efforts on developing community-based care centers, primarily by letting the third sector take over community-care provision. In contrast, Beijing's municipal government at first shirked central steering efforts and then developed a different development approach. It has opted to foster large

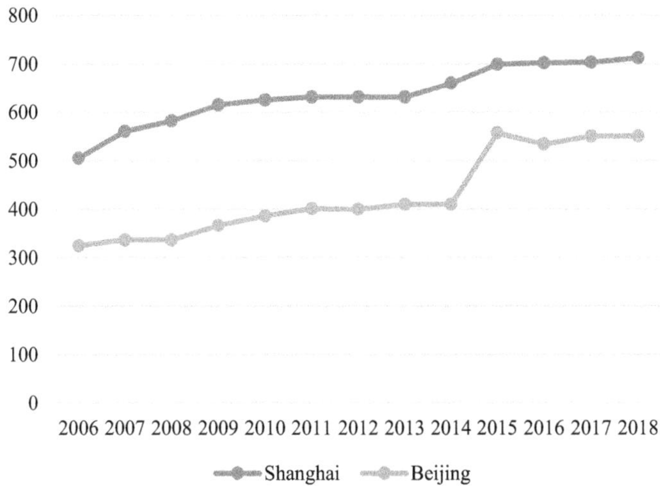

Fig. 3 Comparing eldercare service development in Shanghai and Beijing (*Source* Shanghai Municipal Government Reports 2006–2018, Beijing Municipal Government Reports 2006–2018)

franchises of residential care suppliers and support home-based care provision, while allocating a smaller role to social organizations in comparison to Shanghai. Although one can find large eldercare franchises and social organizations offering community-based elder care in both cities, their relative role differs.

After the first central steering "push" opened the floor to selectively develop elements of central development models and plans, both municipalities again responded to the second steering push by fostering underdeveloped tiers in their eldercare service system and thereby seemingly reducing cross-municipal divergences somewhat. Central steering efforts thus work as a streamlining effort which reign in on decentralized approaches by making sure localities adhere to central policy instruments.

While the national-level stipulation and local utilization of central policy instruments such as the three-tier system, the 90-70-3 framework and the two-pronged "socialization" strategy could be regarded as a sign of recentralization of social welfare, a closer look at steering *tactics* points to a more complex picture. In fact, Beijing and Shanghai do not just differ in terms of which tier or service provider are prioritized and when, but their entire steering approaches are based on fundamentally different logics and tactics. For instance, while using the same policy instruments, inherent financial incentives often differ markedly. Beijing's logic is based on for-profit commercialization and the support of individual purchasing power since it provides the same subsidizes for private-for-profit and third sector providers, as well as promotes franchises, commercial insurances, and individual-based financial aid. Shanghai's tactic, in contrast, steers development toward a greater welfare mix and socialization of risk, for instance by providing comparatively larger financial support to the third sector than to the private sector, spending more on institutional and service-based subsidies which directs financial resources across the sector rather than fostering individual choice, and by developing a social insurance-based LTC insurance pilot. Despite central steering efforts, eldercare service provision in China thus differs across space due to different local government responses, creating different local welfare mixes.

The underlying logic of and steering tactics behind policy instruments create different welfare mixes on the ground which have significant implications for older person's access to eldercare. On the one hand, the local adoption of central policy instruments has created comparable trends in both localities under study: Both cities have experienced a rapid increase in services by letting private-for-profit and third sector providers offer eldercare services. This increase in services is mainly to the benefit to older persons who can afford such services. Means-tested provision for local *hukou* holders has not seen a marked increase, in fact, service provision is often taken over by the third sector. However, on the other hand, the relative role of different providers is markedly different across both cases. Whereas in Beijing private-for-profit providers dominate all three tiers, in Shanghai provision is more mixed, as third sector dominates community-based care, while the private sector is more invested in residential care. In addition, older people's experiences of the eldercare sector will differ. In Beijing an older person is more likely to reside in a very large, franchised residential homes, and receive financial aid when they reach the age of "oldest old", whereas in Shanghai eldercare home size strongly differ and older people are more likely to receive vouchers for certain service types or providers. Local steering approaches thus create very different experiences for older people's access to and experience of eldercare provision.

6 Conclusion

Is social welfare still largely decentralized or is it experiencing a new wave of recentralization? Based on our analysis of eldercare service development in Shanghai and Beijing, we do not find sufficient evidence to support the claim of large-scale recentralization in this sector. Out of the three recentralization instruments Zhu (2016) has identified, (1) binding targets, (2) upscaling of transfer payments and centrally guided regional pilot projects as well as (3) strengthening of line management and power concentration in provincial governments, only binding targets and centrally guided regional pilot projects seemed to play a role in local eldercare development. This is because service provision has been largely taken over by private-for-profit and third sector providers and most welfare recipients need to purchase eldercare services from the market. Moreover, even where the center stipulates binding targets or development models and strategies, local governments in Beijing and Shanghai use their leeway to develop their own local steering approaches which determine the nature of eldercare provision on the ground, thus reducing central control and steering of day-to-day experiences of social welfare recipients.

In line with Mok (2004) and Chien (2007), we find a coexistence of recentralization and decentralization processes. On the one hand, the center periodically launches central steering efforts to re-centralize and streamline social welfare development, which forces local government compliance. On the other hand, the latter still have sufficient leeway in selectively prioritizing and implementing certain central policy instruments as well as to develop their own local versions of steering instruments and tactics.

Basing our analysis on "political steering theory", we were able to demonstrate that it is the interplay between these two steering efforts at the central and the local level which shape policy implementation on the ground. Depending on local government response, central steering efforts can be met by full embrace, shirking, negotiation or counter-steering, which can set social welfare development off on different development paths. In addition, local governments may face social problems or may be influenced by alternative policy solutions at different points in time. Both the interplay between central and local steering efforts as well as the timing and sequence of events thus has an impact on how recentralization and decentralization processes play out locally.

In order to understand the implications of top-level steering efforts on social welfare provision, it is necessary to include an analysis of the welfare mix. As we have shown, central recentralization efforts in the form of the 12th FYP have led to reducing the selective implementation of central development models and strategies in both cities, to pave the way for a more comprehensive development of the three-tier system. Nevertheless, as local steering efforts have pursued a different logic, the municipalities' welfare mix, differs strongly in terms of ownership structure and degree of service provision per tier, influencing older persons' access to eldercare services differently across cities.

This study has certain limitations. First, due to its research design it has focused on two "special cases" of highly developed local eldercare regimes. To test this study's argument, more cases from more diverse geographical regions would need to be assessed. However, as Beijing and Shanghai can be seen as forerunners in eldercare service development, this study's findings may point to certain directions that Chinese eldercare service development is taking in developed regions. In addition, the analysis was not able to cover service delivery and quality of care. However, an interested reader will find existing pieces in the literature which focus more on delivery in both cities, including quality of care (see Cheng et al. 2011 for Beijing; Chen and Han 2016 for Shanghai). More research is needed to make sense of the link between central and local steering approaches and their practical implications on the ground.

Bibliography

Alpermann, B. and Zhan, S. (2019). Population planning after the one-child policy: Shifting modes of political steering, *Journal of Contemporary China, 28*(117), 348–366.

Ascoli, U. and Ranci, C. (2002). *Dilemmas of the welfare mix: The new structure of welfare in an era of privatization.* New York: Springer

Andreotti, A., Mingione, E. and Polizzi, E. (2012). Local welfare systems: A challenge for social cohesion, *Urban Studies, 49*(9), 1925–1940.

Beijing City Report. (2018). 北京市老龄事业和养老服务发展报告 (2016 年—2017 年) (Beijing city report on the elder age industry and eldercare service development (2016–2017)), *Beijing Civil Affairs Bureau*, http://mzj.beijing.gov.cn/attached/file/20180515/20180515155035_570.pdf (accessed June 30, 2019).

Beijing Civil Affairs Bureau. (2009). 关于贯彻落实《北京市市民居家养老(助残)服务("九养")办法》的意见 (Opinions on the Implementation of the "Measures for Home-based Elderly Care (Disabled Assistance) Services for Citizens in Beijing ("Nine Care")"), https://www.beijing.gov.cn/zhengce/zhengcefagui/qtwj/201106/t20110610_567111.html

Beijing Disable Person's Federation. (2011). 以需求为导向 建立和完善残疾人托养服务体系 (Using a demand-oriented approach, establish and improve the care service system for disabled people), https://www.bdpf.org.cn/n1544/n1689/n1766/n1808/c56380/content.html (accessed 1 May 2024).

Beijing Municipal Government. (1995). 北京市老年人权益保障条例 (Beijing Municipality's Regulations on the Protection of the Rights and Interests of the Elderly), http://www.bjrd.gov.cn/rdzl/dfxfgk/dfxfg/202101/t20210106_2200152.html (accessed 13 September 2022).

Beijing Municipal Government. (2000). 北京市养老服务机构管理办法 (Beijing Municipality's Measures for Managing Elderly Care Institutions), https://www.beijing.gov.cn/zhengce/zfwj/zfwj/szfl/201905/t20190523_75715.html (accessed 13 September 2022).

Beijing Municipal Government. (2003). 关于抓紧做好第三批"社区老年福利服务星光计划"设施建设工作的通知 (Notice on Speeding up the construction of the third batch of "Community Elderly Welfare Service Starlight Plan" facilities), http://www.bjmzj.gov.cn/news/root/llgz/2011-10/101035.shtml (accessed 13 September 2022).

Beijing Municipal Government. (2006). 关于资助山区村建设老年福利服务设施的意见 (Opinions on subsidizing the construction of elderly welfare service facilities in mountainous villages), http://www.bjmzj.gov.cn/news/root/gfxwj_llgz/2011-10/101030.shtml (accessed 13 September 2022).

Beijing Municipal Government. (2015). 北京市民政局、北京市老龄工作委员会办公室关于依托养老照料中心开展社区居家养老服务的指导意见 (Guiding Opinions of the Beijing Municipal Civil Affairs Bureau and the Office of the Beijing Municipal Aging Commission on the Development of Community Home-based Elderly Care Services Based on Elderly Care Centers), https://mzj.beijing.gov.cn/art/2015/4/17/art_413_314702.html (accessed 13 September 2022).

Beijing Statistical Yearbook. (2019). 北京统计年鉴 2019 (Beijing statistical yearbook), *Beijing Statistical Bureau*, http://202.96.40.155/nj/main/2019-tjnj/zk/indexch.htm (accessed April 4, 2020).

Cai, H. and Treisman, D. (2006). Did government decentralization cause China's economic miracle?, *World Politics, 58*(4), 505–535.

Chen, L. and Yang, D. L. (2012). Old age care concerns and state–society relations in China: Public anxiety and state paternalism, *Journal of Asian Public Policy*, *5*(2), 136–154.

Chen, L. (2016). *Evolving eldercare in contemporary China: Two generations, one decision*. New York: Palgrave Macmillan.
Chen, L. and Han, W. (2016). Shanghai: Front-Runner of community-based eldercare in China, *Journal of Aging & Social Policy, 28*(4), 292–307.
Chen, G. C. and Lees, C. (2018). The new, green, urbanization in China: Between authoritarian environmentalism and decentralization, *Chinese Political Science Review, 3*, 212–231.
Cheng, Y., Rosenberg, W., Wang, W., Yang, L. and Li, H. (2011). Aging, health and place in residential care facilities in Beijing. China, *Social Science & Medicine, 72*, 365–372.
Chien, S.-S. (2007). Institutional innovations, asymmetric decentralization, and local economic development: A case study of Kunshan, in Post-Mao China, *Environment and Planning C: Government and Policy, 25*(2), 269–290.
Cho, S. (2020). The Fang-Shou cycle in Chinese politics. In *Hindsight, insight, foresight: Thinking about security in the Indo-Pacific,* Chapter 18, 269–281.
Colombo, F., Llena-Nozal, A., Mercier, J. and Tjadens, F. (2011). *Help wanted? Providing and paying for long-term care*. Paris: OECD Publishing.
Data Journalism Centre. (2019). 我们解读了上海 733 家养老机构的数据,发现养老问题没这么简单 (We analysed data from 733 Shanghai eldercare institutions and realised that things aren't so simple), *Shanghai Observer*, May 31, 2019, https://www.jfdaily.com/news/detail?id=154517 (accessed April 4, 2019).
DBS Asian Insights. (2016). Eldercare in China: A sunrise industry, *Sector Briefing*, 33. Asian Insights Office, DBS Group.
Di, J. and Rosenbaum, E. (1994). Caregiving system in transition: An illustration from Shanghai, China, *Population Research and Policy Review, 13*, 101–112.
Du, P. (2013). Intergenerational solidarity and old-age support for the social inclusion of elders in Mainland China: The changing roles of family and government, *Aging & Society*, *33*, 44–63.
Evers, A. (2005). Mixed welfare systems and hybrid organizations: Changes in the governance and provision of social services, *International Journal of Public Administration*, *28*(9-10), 737–748, https://doi.org/10.1081/PAD-200067318
Feng, Z., Liu, C., Guan, X. and Mor, V. (2012). China's rapidly aging population creates policy challenges in shaping a viable long-term care system, *Health Affairs, 31*(12), 2764–2773.
Feng, Z., Zhan, H.J., Feng, X., Liu, C., Sun, M. and Mor, V. (2011). An industry in the making: The emergence of institutional elder care in Urban China, *International Health Affairs, 59*, 738–744.
ForBook Health Research Centre (Ed.) (2018). *中国养老产业政策大全 (Complete collection of policies on the eldercare industry in China)*. Beijing: China Labour and Social Security Press.

Han, X., Bo, W. and Chi, Y. (2018). 我国城市养老机构发展研究◦基于北京，上海等九地养老机构服务状况调研 (A study of Chinese urban old-age care institutions development: Based on nine care institutions in Beijing, Shanghai and other localities). *社会福利 (China Social Welfare), 4*, 50–54.

Harper, S. (1992) Caring for China's aging population: The residential option—A case study of Shanghai. *Aging and Society, 12*, 157–184.

Hipgrave, D., Guo, S., Mu, Y., Guo, Y., Yan, F., Scherpbier, R. and Brixi, H. (2012). Chinese-style decentralization and health system reform, *PLOS Medicine, 9*(11), e1001337, https://doi.org/10.1371/journal.pmed.1001337

Hong, Y., Li, W. and Jerry, Z. Z. (2018). Central–provincial sharing of financial responsibilities for China's social safety-net, *Public Money & Management, 38*(6), 427–436.

Hsu, J. and Hasmath, R. (2014). The local corporatist state and NGO relations in China, *Journal of Contemporary China, 23*(87), 516–534.

Kostka and Nahm. (2017). Central–local relations: Recentralization and environmental governance in China, *The China Quarterly, 231*, 567–582.

Lee, S. (2017). An institutional analysis of Xi Jinping's centralization of power, *Journal of Contemporary China, 26*(105), 325–336.

Leung, J. C. B. and Xu, Y. (2015). *China's social welfare: The third turning point*. Cambridge: Polity.

Li, Y., Wang, C. and Wong, H. (2018). The role of the private sector in China's senior care industry. In: Elena G. and Feng, Z. (Eds.), *Options for aged care in China: Building an efficient and sustainable aged care system* (pp. 155–189). Washington, D.C.: World Bank.

Longo, F., Notarnicola, E. and Tasselli, S. (2015). A framework to assess welfare mix and service provision models in health care and social welfare: Case studies of two prominent Italian regions, *BMC Health Services Research, 15*(152), 1–12.

Luo, B. and Zhan, S. (2018). Crossing the river by feeling for stones: Contesting models of marketization and the development of China's long-term care services, *Journal of Chinese Governance, 3*(4), 438–460.

Maags, C. (2021). Hybridization in China's elder care service provision, *Social Policy and Administration, 55*(1), 113–127.

Mayntz, R. (2003). New challenges to governance theory. In: Henrik, B. (Ed.), *Governance as social and political communication* (pp. 27–40). Manchester: Manchester University Press.

Mayntz, R. (2009). *Über governance. Institutionen und Prozesse politischer Steuerung*. Frankfurt a. M.: Campus.

Mayntz, R. and Scharpf, F. (2005). Politische Steuerung—Heute? (Political steering—Today?). *Zeitschrift für Soziologie, 34*(3), 236–243.

Mok, K.-H. (2004). Centralization and decentralization: changing governance in In Education. In Mok, K.-H. (Ed.), *Centralization and decentralization: Educational reforms and changing governance in Chinese societies* (2nd edition). Comparative education Research Centre, The University of Hong Kong.

Mok, K.-H. and Han, X. (2017). Higher education governance and policy in China: Managing decentralization and transnationalism, *Policy and Society, 36*(1), 34–48.

Naughton, B. (2018). *The Chinese economy. Adaptation and growth* (2nd edition). MIT Press.

NDRC et al. (国家发展改革委社会发展司等) (2018). *走进养老服务业发展新时代.养老服务业发展典型案例汇编 (Towards a new era for elderly care services. Compilation of case studies)*. Beijing: Social Sciences Academic Press.

Ngok, K. (2007). Chinese education policy in the context of decentralization and marketization: Evolution and implications, *Asia Pacific Education Review, 8*, 142–157.

Qian, J. and Mok, K.-H. (2016). Dual decentralization and fragmented authoritarianism in governance: Crowding out among social programmes in China, *Public Administration and Development, 36*(3), 185–197.

Ramesh, M., Wu, X. and He, A. J. (2014). Health governance and healthcare reforms in China, *Health Policy and Planning, 29*(6), 663–672.

Powell, M. and Barrientos, A. (2011). An audit of the welfare modelling business, *Social Policy & Administration, 45*(1), 69–84.

Powell, M. (2014). 'A re-specification of the welfare state': Conceptual issues in 'The three worlds of welfare capitalism', *Social Policy & Society, 14*(2), 247–258.

Sarkar, M. G. (2020). Xi Jinping and the administrative hierarchy and subdivisions in China, Focus Asia, *Institute for Security and Development Policy*, August 2020.

Schubert, G. and Alpermann, B. (2019). Studying the Chinese policy process in the era of 'top-level design': The contribution of 'political steering' theory, *Journal of Chinese Political Science, 24*, 199–224.

Shang, X. and Wu, X. (2011). The care regime in China: Elder and child care, *Journal of Comparative Social Welfare, 27*(2), 123–131.

Shanghai Civil Affairs Bureau. (2016). 解读上海养老服务发展报告(白皮书) (Report explaining Shanghai's eldercare service development (white book)), http://www.shmzj.gov.cn/gb/shmzj/node687/u1ai41785.html (accessed June 30, 2019).

Shanghai Statistical Yearbook. (2018). 上海统计年鉴2018, http://tjj.sh.gov.cn/tjnj/nj18.htm?d1=2018tjnj/C2115.htm (accessed June 30, 2019).

Shanghai Municipal Government. (1998). 上海市养老机构管理办法 (Shanghai Municipal Measures for Managing Elder Care Institutions), https://www.shanghai.gov.cn/nw26170/20200820/0001-26170_27335.html

Shanghai Municipal Government. (2001). 上海市民政局关于实施"社区老年福利服务星光计划"的意见 (Opinions of the Shanghai Municipal Civil Affairs Bureau on the Implementation of the "Community Elderly Welfare Service Starlight Plan"), https://mzj.sh.gov.cn/MZ_zhuzhan279_0-2-8-15-55-231/20200519/MZ_zhuzhan279_7874.html

Shanghai Municipal Government. (2008). 关于继续开展2008年度"银发无忧"保障工作的通知 (2008 Notice on the Continued Development of the Old-Age Security Work), http://www.shmzj.gov.cn/gb/shmzj/node8/node15/node55/node231/node279/userobject1ai16226.html

Shanghai Municipal Government. (2009). 2009年上海市老年人口和老龄事业监测统计信息 (Monitoring the 2009 Shanghai elderly population and aging statistical information), http://www.shweilao.cn/cms/cmsDetail?uuid=c0da78d4-7179-45a5-b343-7d78759d9b4b

Shanghai Municipal Government. (2014). 市政府关于加快发展养老服务业推广社会养老服务体系建设的实施意见 (Opinions on the implementation of advancing the expansion of the eldercare services sector and constructing a social eldercare services system). Document 28 (2014), http://www.shanghai.gov.cn/nw2/nw2314/nw2319/nw10800/nw11407/nw31810/u26aw38830.html (accessed April 1, 2019).

Shanghai Municipal Government. (2018). 2018年上海市老年人口和老龄事业监测统计信息 (Monitoring the 2018 Shanghai elderly population and aging statistical information), https://shyl.mzj.sh.gov.cn/elderly_care_policy/policy_details?uuid=5615186e-685f-4003-bbc2-09454a4f7736&title=2018%E5%B9%B4%E4%B8%8A%E6%B5%B7%E5%B8%82%E8%80%81%E5%B9%B4%E4%BA%BA%E5%8F%A3%E5%92%8C%E8%80%81%E9%BE%84%E4%BA (accessed 13 September 2022).

Shi, S.-J. (2017). Social decentralization: exploring the competitive solidarity of regional social protection in China, *Journal of Asian Public Policy, 10*(1), 74–89.

Shi, Y., Qian, Z. and Pu, G. (2017). 上海公办养老机构定价问题及其对策探讨 (Service pricing of public nursing homes in Shanghai and its countermeasures), *智慧健康 (Smart Healthcare), 10*, 21–23.

Solinger, D. and Hu. (2012). Welfare, wealth and poverty in Urban China: The Dibao and its differential disbursement.

State Council. (2019). 国务院办公厅关于推进养老服务发展的意见 (State council opinions on advancing the development of eldercare services), State Council Document No. 5 (2019), http://www.gov.cn/zhengce/content/2019-04/16/content_5383270.htm (accessed November 1, 2019).

Sun, J. 孙鹃娟 and Du, P. 杜鹏 (Eds.) (2017). *中国人口老龄化和老龄事业发展报告 2016 (Report on China's population aging and the elderly welfare facilities 2016)*. Beijing: 中国人民大学出版社 (China Renmin University Press).

Sun, J. 孙鹃娟 and Du, P. 杜鹏 (Eds.) (2016). *中国人口老龄化和老龄事业发展报告 2015 (Report on China's population aging and the elderly welfare facilities 2015)*. Beijing: 中国人民大学出版社 (China Renmin University Press).

Tarricone, R. and Tsouros, A. D. (2008). *Home care in Europe: The solid facts*. World Health Organization. Regional Office for Europe, https://iris.who.int/handle/10665/328766

Task Force 课题组. (2017). *中国城市养老指数蓝皮书2017 (Blue book on China's urban endowment index 2017)*. Beijing: China Development Press.

Taylor-Gooby, P., Heuer, J., Chung, H., Leruth, B., Mau, S. and Zimmermann, K. (2019). Regimes, social risks and the welfare mix: Unpacking attitudes to pensions and childcare in Germany and the UK through deliberative forums, *Journal of Social Policy*, https://doi.org/10.1017/S004727941800079X

Teets, J. (2013). Let many civil societies bloom: The rise of consultative authoritarianism in China, *The China Quarterly, 213*, 19–38.

Tsui, K.-y. and Wang, Y. (2004). Between separate stoves and a single menu: Fiscal decentralization in China, *The China Quarterly, 177*, 71–90.

Wong, L. and Li, N. (2012). Changing welfare institution and evolution of Chinese nonprofit organizations: The story of eldercare homes in urban Shanghai. In: Chen, S. and Powell, J. L. (Eds.), *Aging in China: Implications to social policy of a changing economic state* (pp. 237–259). New York: Springer.

Wu, W. 吴 为 (2019). 北京: 营利性与非营利性养老机构享受同等运营补贴政策 (Beijing: For-profit and non-profit eldercare institutions enjoy same operational subsidy policy). *参观 (Visit)*, *1*, 32–34.

Xinhua. (2022). *China focus: China expands long-term care insurance coverage for disabled, 22 July 2022*, https://english.news.cn/20220722/4e87d181241e4774a869ac99f3e92d9b/c.html (accessed 1 May 2024).

Yu, J. and Rosenberg, M. W. (2017). "No place like home": Aging in post-reform Beijing, *Health & Place, 46*, 192–200.

Zhang, H. (2006). Family care or residential care? The moral and practical dilemmas facing the elderly in urban China, *Asian Anthropology, 5*(1), 57–83. https://doi.org/10.1080/1683478X.2006.10552560

Zhang, H. (2007). Who will care for our parents? Changing boundaries of family and public roles in providing care for the aged in Urban China, *Care Management Journals, 8*(1), 39–46.

Zheng, Y. (2007). *De facto federalism in China: Reforms and dynamics of central-local relations*. Singapore: World Scientific Publishing.

Zhou, S., Cheng,Y., Xiao, M. and Bao, X. (2013). Assessing the location of public-and-community facilities for the elderly in Beijing, *China GeoJournal*, *78*(3), 539–551.

Zhou, J. 周佳佳 and Kang, Y. 康越 (2019). 北京市养老驿站的政策演变及发展趋势分析 (An analysis of the policy evolution and development trends of Beijing's eldercare stations), *北京化工大学学报 (Journal of Beijing University of Chemical Technology)*, *106*(1), 30–34.

Zhu, X. (2016). Dynamics of central–local relations in China's social welfare system, *Journal of Chinese Governance*, *1*(2), 251–268.

Zhu, Y. and Österle. A. (2019). China's policy experimentation on long-term care insurance: Implications for access. *International Journal of Health Planning and Management*, *34*(4), 1661–1674.

CHAPTER 3

China's Population Change and Its Geopolitical Impact

Xu Zhu, Shuzhuo Li, and Zhongshan Yue

1 Introduction

Population issues, as one of the most significant social issues globally, have long received extensive attention from countries around the world. In the era of globalization, the transnational movement of capital and talent has become more frequent, and the interaction between population and geopolitics has become a new academic research topic following

The research was supported by National Natural Science Foundation of China (No. 72174165).

X. Zhu · S. Li · Z. Yue (✉)
Xi'an Jiaotong University, Xi'an, China
e-mail: zhshyue@xjtu.edu.cn

X. Zhu
e-mail: xu_zhu@xjtu.edu.cn

S. Li
e-mail: shzhli@mail.xjtu.edu.cn

A. Aliu (ed.), *Complexity Thinking and China's Demography Within and Beyond Mainland China*,
https://doi.org/10.1007/978-981-97-0172-8_3

the rise of a series of demographic issues, such as international migration and population ageing.

As a large country with a population of more than 1.4 billion people, China sees the population as a global, long-term, and strategic issue. A low fertility rate, low population growth, and population ageing will become the main trends in China's demographic change in the coming period. What kind of interaction mechanism exists between demographic change and geopolitics? What kind of demographic changes are taking place in China? How will China's demographic changes affect geopolitics? These are the main questions explored in this chapter.

Research on the topic of population and geopolitics in recent years has focused on the following aspects:

1. The relationship between population size and structure and geopolitics. He XY (2016) noted that the population is the primary carrier of economic and social development and the basic source of national strength. Trends in population size, structure of the population, the size of the labour force, and structure of the labour resources are the core elements that determine the demographic power of large countries.[1] Chu XB (2011) argues that countries with relatively low levels of population ageing that also happen to be located in historically and geopolitically sensitive regions, which are usually those that have essential energy resources, also have sensitive fuses such as religious or ethnic tension, which raise the likelihood of conflict.[2] According to Bao YP (2013), transnational marriages caused by a structural imbalance in gender are likewise geopolitical issues that cannot be ignored.[3] Cincotta, R., Engelman, R., and Anastasion, D. (2003)

[1] He XY. (2016). 国际关系视角下的美国少数族裔人口政治学 [Political Demography of U.S. Ethnic Minority in the Perspective of International Relation]. *国际论坛* [*International Forum*] (03), 67-72+81. https://doi.org/10.13549/j.cnki.cn11-3959/d.2016.03.012.

[2] Chu XB. (2011). 人口老龄化与国际安全战略 [Population Ageing and International Security Strategy]. *中国国际战略评论* [*China International Strategy Review*] (00), 378–393.

[3] Bao YP. (2013). 选择与困境:云南边境跨国婚姻的社会学分析 [Choice and Dilemma: Sociological Analysis of Cross-border Marriages in Yunnan Border Area]. *北方民族大学学报 (哲学社会科学版)* [*Journal of North Minzu University* (Philosophy and Social Science)] (04), 5–12.

find that the population of a country is a major factor that influences its geopolitics. The nation's geopolitical position is influenced by demographic factors such as population size, age distribution and ethnic makeup as well as by other national factors such as economic strength, military power, and political stability. Additionally, population growth or decline can affect resource demands, migration patterns, and regional power dynamics, influencing a country's role in international relations.[4] Jane Golley and Rod Tyers (2012) argue that China's rapidly ageing population is one of the most visible consequences of the One-Child Policy. The number of older adults is growing as health care improves and life expectancy rises. This shift has a variety of economic and social consequences, including increased demand for health care services and social welfare for elderly individuals. It also poses difficulties in maintaining economic growth in the face of a shrinking workforce.[5]

2. International population migration and geopolitics. An N and Zhang B (2022) explore the issue of cross-border migration and ethnic communities from a geopolitical perspective, pointing out that population mobility has a high degree of geopolitical significance, and migration is an essential manifestation of population mobility.[6] Huang YH and Chen HS (2022) discuss the geopolitical issues arising from uneven transnational flows in population mobility concerning the U.S.-Mexico migration history and policies. Mexican immigrants have provided sufficient labor but also exacerbated racial conflict and prompted the United States to continuously introduce policies to restrict Mexican immigrants.[7]

[4] Cincotta RP, Engelman R, Anastasion D. (2003). The Security Demographic: Population and Civil Conflict After the Cold War. *Population Action International*, 12.

[5] Golley J, Tyers R. (2012). Demographic Dividends, Dependencies, and Economic Growth in China and India*. *Asian Economic Papers*, 11, 1–26.

[6] An N, Zhang B. (2022). 地缘政治视角下的跨境移民和族裔社区研究 [The research of transnational migration and ethnic communities from the perspective of geopolitics]. *世界地理研究* [*World Regional Studies*] (06), 1119–1129.

[7] Huang YH, Chen HS, Li ZG. (2022). 不均衡的跨国人口流动:对美墨移民历程与政策的思考 [Unbalanced transnational population mobility: Reflections on the history and policy of US-Mexico immigration]. *世界地理研究* [*World Regional Studies*] (06), 1204–1214.

Zhang ZY (2017) conducts field research on illegal transnational migration in the border cities of Yunnan, pointing out that a harmonious and stable geopolitical environment is a prerequisite for governing illegal transnational migration.[8] Hou DQ (2013) argues that geopolitical changes often cause cross-border migration among certain ethnic groups, thus creating the phenomenon of transborder ethnicities.[9] Ali Fakih and May Ibrahim (2016) argue that the movement of Syrian refugees to neighbouring nations brought about notable consequences for the geopolitical situation in the Middle East, impacting diplomatic ties and regional power dynamics.[10] Hein, Jeremy (1993) finds that more people are coming across the border, which is happening when there is not enough money for public services, such as those offered in schools and hospitals. When the number of people increases, the economy does not grow well, the government struggles, and the places where people live become more tense and damaged. Additionally, there's more crime and people feel unsafe.[11] Borjas, G.J. (2003) discusses in his study that cross-border migration can carry noteworthy economic consequences for both the countries of origin and destination. The arrival of labour has the potential to enhance economic growth in receiving nations; however, it may also result in wage disparities and pose employment challenges for the local population. These economic imbalances have the capacity to impact trade relations and shape the broader landscape of economic cooperation between

[8] Zhang ZY. (2017). 云南及周边国家跨国非法移民的治理 [The governance of transnational illegal immigrants in Yunnan and its neighboring countries]. *云南行政学院学报* [*The Journal of Yunnan Administration College*] (04), 25–31. https://doi.org/10.16273/j.cnki.53-1134/d.2017.04.005.

[9] Hou DQ. (2013). 从地缘政治视角看中国朝鲜族跨界民族的形成 [Formation of the Cross-border Koreans in China in the Geopolitical Perspective]. *云南民族大学学报 (哲学社会科学版)* [*Yunnan Minzu University* (Philosophy and Social Sciences Edition)] (04), 20–26. https://doi.org/10.13727/j.cnki.53-1191/c.2013.04.019.

[10] Fakih A, Ibrahim M. (2016). The impact of Syrian refugees on the labor market in neighboring countries: empirical evidence from Jordan. *Defence and Peace Economics*, 27, 64–86.

[11] Hein J. (1993). Refugees, Immigrants, and the State. *Annual Review of Sociology*, 19, 43–59.

> countries, which can have a significant impact on their geopolitical relations.[12] Chiswick (1978, 1986) argues that it is difficult for noneconomic migrants to demonstrate their abilities simply because they lack proper education and work experience. In addition, these workers are perceived as being less skilled and driven than economic migrants, which hinders their capability to compete successfully in the job market. Thus, it is less likely that they possess transferable talent inside the job market. He further describes the potential outcome if these challenges are not adequately addressed: unresolved issues in migration may lead to social tensions and economic strains and potentially impact geopolitical relations.[13] Nichols Eberstadt (2019) finds that changes in the population of China and the US affect their geopolitics. China's ageing population and sex imbalance might impact its global status. The US's diverse and growing population contributes to its economic strength and cultural influence. These demographic shifts influence how both countries make decisions in global affairs.[14]

These studies analyse the relationship between demographic change and geopolitics from different perspectives, still, none of them profoundly analyses the pathways of the interaction between demographic change and geopolitics or the systematic impact of China's demographic change on geopolitics. Based on the existing research, this chapter provides a comprehensive overview of China's demographic changes, including an overview of China's demographic trends, population ageing, the sex structure of China's population, and China's international migration patterns over the years; it also provides a detailed discussion of the interactions between China's demographic changes and geopolitics, including the mechanisms guiding the interactions between demographic changes and geopolitical changes, and the impact of China's demographic change on geopolitics at the global, regional and neighbouring levels.

[12] Borjas GJ. (2003). The Labor Demand Curve Is Downward Sloping: Reexamining the Impact of Immigration on the Labor Market. *The Quarterly Journal of Economics,* 118(4), 1335–1374.

[13] Chiswick BR. (1978). The Effect of Americanization on the Earnings of Foreign-born Men. *Journal of Political Economy,* 86(5), 897–921.

[14] Eberstadt N. (2019). With Great Demographics Comes Great Power: Why Population Will Drive Geopolitics. *Foreign Affairs,* 98(4), 146–157.

2 Demographic Change in China

The most fundamental demographic shift has been taking place in modern China. This shift moves towards permanently low fertility, population ageing, and eventual depopulation. Furthermore, China's sex structure and immigration patterns deserve close attention. The deep-rooted son preference in traditional concepts has also exacerbated the sex imbalance towards more males than females, making this shift a significant demographic feature in Chinese society. China has been a net exporter of international immigrants over the past few hundred years, but in recent years, an increasing number of residents from other developing countries have started to take China as a new destination for immigration.

This section introduces China's population shift and trends since 1949 in terms of four aspects: China's demographic transition, population ageing, sex structure, and China's international migration.

2.1 China's Demographic Transition

Since 1949, China's total fertility rate (TFR) has changed from a steady high level to a brief decline, a rapid rebound and then a continuous fluctuating decline to negative growth.

In the first ten years (1949–1958) after the founding of the People's Republic of China (PRC), the country pursued a liberal fertility policy. China's TFR was high at approximately 6.0,[15] and the birth rate stayed at a high level of approximately 35‰ for nine years.[16] China witnessed the first baby boom in its history during this period. The population size grew from 540 to 660 million in only a decade.

During the Great Famine from 1959 to 1961, China experienced the first episode of population shrinkage after the founding of the PRC. The TFR fell to 3.29, the birth rate dropped to 18‰, and the population size decreased by 13.48 million over these three years. As a result of post-disaster compensatory childbearing, China's TFR peaked at 7.51[17]

[15] Source of data: Department of Development Planning of the National Family Planning Commission, China Population and Development Research Center, ed.: Handbook of Commonly Used Data on Population and Family Planning (2003).

[16] Unless otherwise specified, data for China in this article come from the National Bureau of Statistics.

[17] *Data source* World Bank.

in 1963 and remained at approximately 6.2 during 1962–1975. The total population was 920 million by the end of 1975. During the same period (1971), China's TFR began to be lower than that of India and has never since been (nor will it be, for the foreseeable future) greater than that of India (see Fig. 1[18]).

With the implementation of family planning policies in the late 1970s, China's TFR dropped to below 3.0 and then fluctuated downwards. In the early 1990s, it fell below the replacement level of 2.1. China's TFR became lower than that of the US and gradually approached that of Japan and South Korea. Since then, China has entered an era of low fertility, while India consistently maintained a high fertility level of approximately 3.6 throughout the 1990s.

According to China's seventh population census, China's TFR fell to 1.3 in 2020 and ranked second to last globally just before South Korea

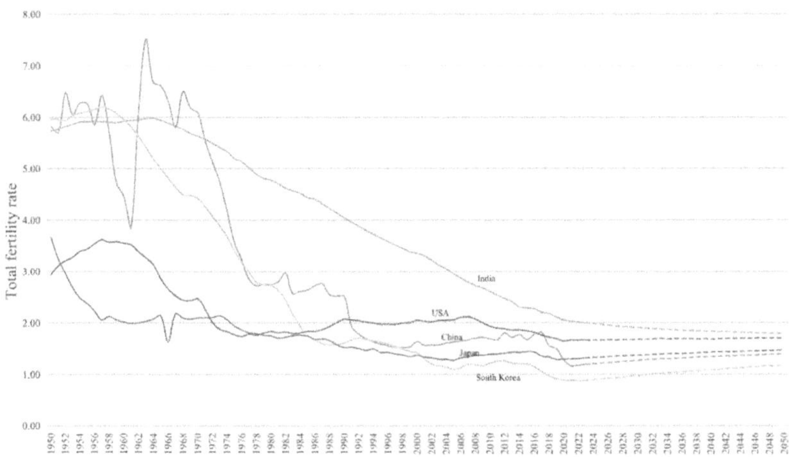

Fig. 1 Trends in total fertility rates of China, the USA, India, Japan, and South Korea, 1950–2050 (*Data source* United Nations Department of Social and Economic Affairs, United Nations World Population Prospects 2022, https://population.un.org/wpp/ [2024–2050 are projected])

[18] The data in Figs. 1–3 are all sourced from the United Nations World Population Prospects 2022.

(0.84), which is obviously below the international alert level of 1.5.[19] On May 31, 2021, the Chinese government held an important meeting on population policies and decided to permit couples to have up to three children and initiate more measures to support family planning and birth rates. However, China's TFR did not rise but fell to 1.07 in 2022. With only 9.56 million births (less than half of those in India in the same period) and 10.41 million deaths, China's population decreased by 0.85 million, and the natural population growth rate (PGR) dropped to −0.60‰. China has thus experienced the second episode of negative population growth since 1949.[20] According to the latest UN statistics,[21] India's population was expected to surpass China's 1.41 billion by mid-2023, making India the world's most populous country. By 2050, India's population (1.67 billion in total) will be approximately 300 million more than China's population (1.32 billion in total). As the world's second most populous country, China will still have a much larger population than the United States, the third most populous country in the world. This new shift in world population trends might result in a new global geopolitical landscape.

2.2 *Population Ageing*

Population ageing is a product of the modern population growth model of "low birth rate, low mortality rate, and low natural growth rate". Data from China's fifth census show that China's proportion of elderly people (65 plus)[22] reached 7% in 2000. According to World Health Organization standards, China has already qualified as an ageing society, nearly 30 years after Japan. As the "baby boomer" generation enters old age,

[19] *Data source* World Bank, Population Reference Bureau (PRB).

[20] *Data source* United Nations Department of Social and Economic Affairs, United Nations World Population Prospects 2022, https://population.un.org/wpp/. Unless otherwise specified, international data in this article are derived from this source.

[21] United Nations Population Fund, Report on the State of World Population 2023, April 19, 2023.

[22] Proportion of elderly individuals: the proportion of the population aged 65 and over to the total population. According to the international standard, if proportion of the elderly >7%, it means that the country has become an ageing society; if it is >14%, the country has become a deeply ageing society; if it is >21%, the country has become a severely ageing society; and if it is >28%, the country has become an extremely ageing society.

China's population ageing has accelerated, and the proportion of elderly individuals rose to 8.9% by 2010. Over the past 10 years, China's population ageing process has further accelerated under the combined effect of a persistently low TFR and increasing life expectancy. By 2021, the proportion of elderly individuals climbed to 14.2%, formally moving from ageing to a stage of deep ageing in just 21 years, faster than Japan's transition between the same stages, which took 24 years.

According to the United Nations WPP 2022, China will enter the stage of severe ageing before 2035 and extreme ageing before 2050 (see Fig. 2). Japan's Ministry of Internal Affairs and Communications' latest data show that Japan's proportion of elderly people reached a high value of 29.1% in 2023, officially entering the extreme ageing stage. The number of elderly people aged 80 plus increased to 12.59 million, accounting for more than 10% of the total population and ranking Japan first in the world by demographic weighting. During the same period, the proportion of elderly individuals in the United States was 16.9%, while India's population structure is still relatively young, with a median age of 28. WPP 2022 predicts that the median age in Japan will reach 53.6 by 2050, and in China, it will rise to 50.7, significantly higher than that of the United States, Europe and India, thus constraining China's international competitiveness.

Population ageing is an important trend in economic and social development and has become a common phenomenon around the world. Figure 2 illustrates the proportions of elderly people in China, the USA, Japan, and India from 1950 to 2050. In comparison, China's population ageing has the trends and characteristics of a large scale, a rapid speed, many individuals at a high age, unbalanced regional development (urban–rural inversion), and ageing before becoming rich.[23,24] Therefore, China will face many challenges, such as a heavy financial burden supporting old age pensions, high pressure on social security and public services (especially medical services), and a shrinking working-age population.

[23] Du P. (2023). 中国人口老龄化现状与社会保障体系发展 [The Status Quo of Population Aging and the Development of the Social Security System in China]. *社会保障评论* [*Chinese Social Security Review*] (02), 31–47.

[24] Tang J. (2022). 世界和中国的人口老龄化及其原因 [Population Aging in the World and China and Its Causes]. *社会政策研究* [*Social Policy Research*] (03): 3–18.

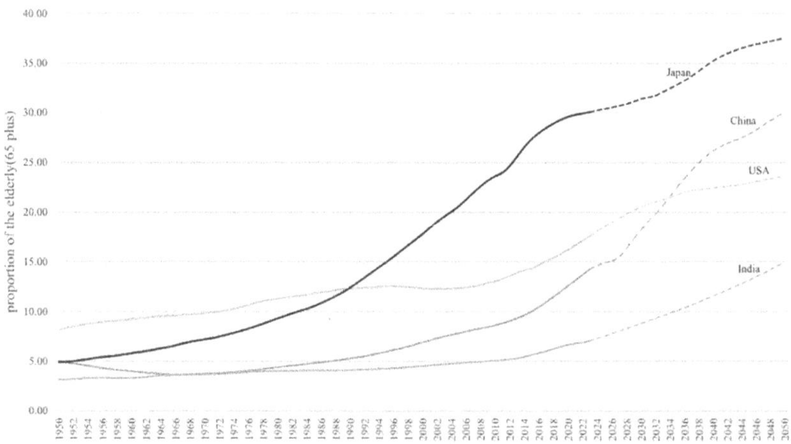

Fig. 2 Percentages of population above 65 in China, the USA, India, and Japan in 1950–2050 (*Data source* United Nations Department of Social and Economic Affairs, United Nations World Population Prospects 2022, https://population.un.org/wpp/ [Data for 2024–2050 are projected])

2.3 *Sex Structure*

The sex structure of China's population is prominently characterized by a sex imbalance, with "more males than females"[25] (as shown in Fig. 3). As of 2022, there were 33.26 million more males than females. The reason for this is the cumulative effect of the persistently high sex ratio at birth (SRB) in China since the 1980s.[26] In 1982, China's SRB (108.5) exceeded the natural level (103–107) for the first time, and it has continued to climb since then. By 2004, it reached a peak of 121.2 and then began to decline. Although the SRB fell back to 111.3 in 2020, it was still well above the normal level (103–107).

[25] LI SZ, Wang XX. (2022). 社会可持续发展下性别失衡社会风险治理 [Social Risk Governance of Gender Imbalance under Social Sustainable Development]. *中国特色社会主义研究* [*Studies on Socialism with Chinese Characteristics*] (01), 86–94.

[26] Li SZ, Guo Z, Shang ZJ. (2014). 中国性别失衡与社会可持续发展的理论、实践与政策创新—国家社科基金重大攻关课题 "中国人口性别结构与社会可持续发展战略研究" 成果概述 [Gender Imbalance and Sustainable Social Development of China: Theory, Governance Practice and Policy Innovation—A summary of results of the Strategy Research on China's Population Structure and Sustainable Social Development]. *西安交通大学学报（社会科学版）* [*Journal of Xi'an Jiaotong University* (Social Science)] (06), 1–13.

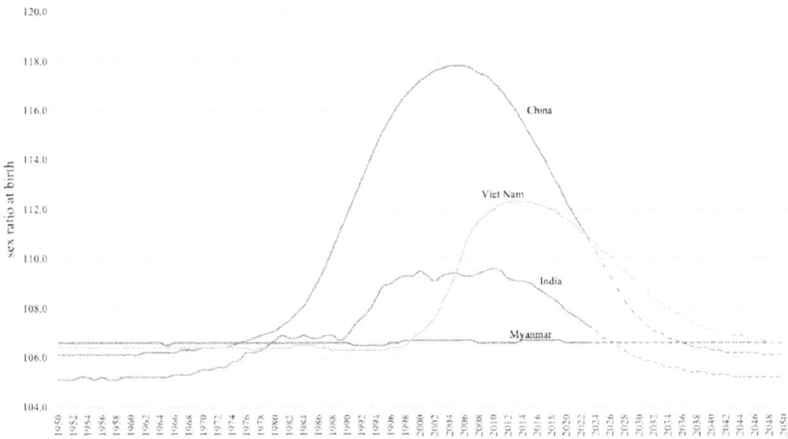

Fig. 3 Sex ratios at birth of China, India, Myanmar, and Vietnam in 1950–2050 (*Data source* United Nations Department of Social and Economic Affairs, United Nations World Population Prospects 2022, https://population.un.org/wpp/ [Data for 2024–2050 are projected])

Most researchers believe that the main reason for the increase of the SRB in China is the comprehensive effect of declining fertility, son preference and the popularization of abortion technology since the implementation of family planning policies (1979).[27,28,29,30] Family planning policies in China strictly limit the number of children a couple can have, which undoubtedly leads to fewer opportunities for childbearing. At the same time, China's traditional patriarchal family system and son preference are deeply rooted. Along with the popularization of prenatal sex

[27] Guilmoto CZ. (2009). The Sex Ratio Transition in Asia. *Population and Development Review*, 35, 519–549.

[28] UNFPA. 2012. Sex Imbalances at Birth: Trends, Consequences, and Policy implications. http://www.documentation.ird.fr/hor/fdi;010060220. August.

[29] Gu BC. (2011). 关于出生性别比问题: 成因与反思 [On Sex Ratio at Birth: Causes and Reflection]. *福建江夏学院学报* [*Journal of Fujian Jiangxia University*] 2011, 1(02): 11–16.

[30] Chen YH. (2007). 出生性别比偏高的治理对策研究—以广东省为例 [A Study of Solutions to High Sex Ratio at Birth: A case study of Guangdong Province]. *人口与经济* [*Population Economics*] (02), 60–65.

determination and abortion technology, families tend to fill the demand for sons through sex-selective abortion.[31]

Son preference undoubtedly constitutes the most important reason for the long-term sex imbalance in Chinese society. However, with the advancement of China's governance on the sex imbalance, the deepening of the concept of gender equality and the liberalization of fertility policies, this gap is expected to gradually dissolve.[32] According to the prediction made by the United Nations, China will reverse the SRB in approximately 2035, while Chao et al. (2021) are more optimistic. They believe that China's SRB will drop to approximately 106 in 2045–2050 and remain there until 2100.[33]

Although the SRB is gradually returning to normal levels, the problems of astronomical bride prices and the loss of marriage opportunities among older rural youths caused by the sex imbalance will continue for a long time in the future. This may even give rise to new social consequences and social phenomena. For example, the sex gap may reduce matchmaking and fertility, affect family and population reproduction,[34] and then exacerbate low fertility rates and population ageing. In serious cases, the sex gap may even lead to human trafficking, violence, and sexual crimes,[35,36,37] thereby threatening social stability. At the same time, the

[31] Zhen Z, Ma X. (2022). 中国出生性别比转变的人口老龄化后果:前景与对策 [Impact of the Transition of Sex Ratio at Birth on Population Ageing in China]. *人口研究* [*Population Research*] (01), 3–18.

[32] Kang CK, Wen Q, Chu TS. (2020). 房子还是儿子?—房价与出生性别比 [House or Son?—Housing Price and Sex Ratio at Birth]. *经济学(季刊)* [*China Economic Quarterly*] (03), 913–934.

[33] Chao F, Gerland P, Cook AR, Guilmoto CZ, Alkema L. (2021). Projecting sex imbalances at birth at global, regional and national levels from 2021 to 2100: scenario-based Bayesian probabilistic projections of the sex ratio at birth and missing female births based on 3.26 billion birth records. *BMJ Global Health*, 6.

[34] Yang B, Meng Y. (2016). 性别失衡社会的家庭发展分析框架与实践 [Framework and Practice of Family Development Analysis in Gender Imbalanced Society]. *西安交通大学学报 (社会科学版)* [*Journal of Xi'an Jiaotong University* (Social Science)] (06), 119–122.

[35] South SJ, Trent K, Bose S. (2014). Skewed Sex Ratios and Criminal Victimization in India. *Demography,* 51, 1019–1040.

[36] Kisekka MN. (2007). Addressing Gender-Based Violence in East and South-East Asia.

[37] Schacht R, Tharp D, Smith KR. (2016). Marriage Markets and Male Mating Effort: Violence and Crime Are Elevated Where Men Are Rare. *Human Nature* 27(4): 489–500.

gap also contributes to the rise of transnational marriages. In recent years, due to geographic proximity, complementary sex structure, and China's relative economic advantage,[38] a large number of "Vietnamese brides" and "Myanmar brides" have entered China. Although this has alleviated the squeeze in the domestic marriage market, these marriages have also objectively increased the likelihood of illegal cross-border marriages,[39,40] bringing new challenges to China's international migration and national border management.

2.4 International Migration in China over the Years

Along with the advancement of globalization, the scale of international migration is rapidly expanding. By 2020, the number of international migrants globally increased to 281 million, accounting for 3.6% of the world's total population.[41] At the same time, the number of international migrants[42] in and out of China increased to 7.75 million people. The number of international migrants in China is 846,000, which is only 0.3% of the global migrant stock and less than 0.06% of China's total population. Clearly, China has still not become a major destination for international migrants. The number of migrants leaving China was 6.904 million, accounting for 89.1% of China's international migrant stock. This made China the fifth largest migrant-sending country in the world.

For China's international migrants, the gravity centre of migration has gradually shifted from East and Southeast Asian countries to developed countries in Europe and especially North America. In 1990, the

38 Cao Y. (2015). 从 "越南新娘" 现象看大龄青年婚姻现状 [From the "Vietnamese Brides" Phenomenon to See Older Youth's Marital Status]. *当代青年研究* [*Contemporary Youth Research*] (05), 105–109.

39 Qiu GP. (2020). 被拐来的"越南新娘"—犯罪学的分析 [The Abducted "Vietnamese Brides"—Criminological Analysis]. *警学研究* [*Police Science Research*] (03), 7–19.

40 Shang Zj, Liu Z. (2019). 中国性别失衡背景下婚姻挤压问题的治理研究—基于 "越南新娘" 现象的思考 [Research on the Governance of Marriage Squeezing Problems in the Context of Gender Imbalance in China—Thinking Based on the Phenomenon of "Vietnamese Brides"]. *武汉科技大学学报 (社会科学版)* [*Journal of Wuhan University of Science and Technology* (Social Science Edition)] (06), 633–637.

41 *Source of data* United Nations International Organization for Migration (2021).

42 *Data source* National Bureau of Statistics (NBS) 7th Census data, China's international migrants in this article only include international migrants from mainland China.

United States began to become the top destination for China's international migrants. By 2020, the number of Chinese immigrants in the United States reached 2.18 million, accounting for nearly 30% of all Chinese migrants worldwide. Among the top ten destinations, the only three countries left in Asia are Japan, South Korea, and Bangladesh.[43]

In terms of countries of origin, since 1960, international migrants in China have mainly come from Asia, Africa, and Latin America. Among them, Asia has a significantly higher share, with North Korea and South Korea always sitting at the top of migrant-sending countries. After 1980, the attractiveness of China as a destination spread to other continents, with the most obvious changes in Africa and Latin America.[44] In addition, after 2010, Vietnam became China's top source of international migrants. At present, China has become a new gathering place for Africans globally,[45] but it is still not attractive enough for developed countries in Europe, North America, Australia, and other continents.

With the global decline in fertility rates and shrinking population size, attracting international migrants, especially highly skilled migrants, to move in and settle down will be a common policy goal for all countries.[46] To prevent further population shrinkage and domestic brain drain, less developed countries, such as China, will introduce more open immigration policies to attract international migrants[47] and limit

[43] Qiu YD, Duan CR. (2023). 1960 年以来中国国际移民的变迁—以移民存量与目的地为主的分析 [The Changes of China's International Migration since 1960: An Analysis of Migration Stock and Destination]. *华侨华人历史研究* [*Journal of Overseas Chinese History Studies*] (01), 13–22.

[44] Duan CR, Qiu YD. (2023). 1960~2020 年在华国际移民变动情况研究 [The Changing International Immigration in China: 1960–2020]. *南方人口* [*South China Population*] (02), 1–11.

[45] Liang YC. (2013). 在广州的非洲裔移民行为的因果机制—累积因果视野下的移民行为研究 [African Immigration in Guangzhou China: A cumulative causation perspective on immigration behavior]. *社会学研究* [*Sociological Studies*] (01), 134–159 + 243–244. https://doi.org/10.19934/j.cnki.shxyj.2013.01.007.

[46] Lv LD, Wang H, Duan CR. (2021). 国际移民最新趋势和政策应对 [Review of International Immigration Trends and Policies]. *人口学刊* [*Population Journal*] (06), 68–84. https://doi.org/10.16405/j.cnki.1004-129X.2021.06.006.

[47] Mathews G, Lin, LD, Yang Y. (2017). The World in Guangzhou: Africans and Other Foreigners in South China's Global Marketplace.

their own population's out-migration. In 2018, China formally established the National Immigration Administration.[48] The aim is to manage the country's immigration affairs, integrate the functions of international migration governance and serve the country's overall development strategy.

In the context of the Belt and Road Initiative (BRI), China is expected to become an emerging international migrant-importing country.[49,50] This is the combined effect of China's rising international status with immigration restrictions in traditional migrant-receiving countries. Unlike in the past, future Chinese international migrants will break the unidirectional flow from developing countries to developed countries, showing instead mutual migratory flows among multiple countries.[51] This provides an opportunity for China to further absorb foreign business investors, international students, and high-skilled talent. The opportunity will help China occupy the global talent plateau and more leisurely cope with negative population growth and ageing. However, this opportunity also brings certain pressure and challenges to China's economic development and the government's migration management policies.

3 Geopolitical Implications of Demographic Change in China

Demographic change is a complex social phenomenon that can profoundly impact geopolitics. The geopolitics referred to in this paper refers to geopolitical reality, drawing on the views of American scholar Zbigniew Brzezinsky, who argues that "geopolitics refers to the interplay of those geographic factors that determine the situation of a country

[48] Official website: https://www.nia.gov.cn.

[49] Li SZ, Xue L, Song RX. (2022). 新时代在华国际移民的融合、发展与治理 [Integration, Development and Governance of International Migrants in China in the New Era]. *北京工业大学学报(社会科学版)* [*Journal of Beijing University of Technology* (Social Science Edition)] (04), 16–28.

[50] Duan CR, Xie DH, Wang H, et al. (2020). 从新冠肺炎疫情防控看国际人口迁移: 三论人口迁移转变 [International Migration in the Era of COVID-19 Prevention and Control: Remarks on Migration Transition in China]. *人口研究* [*Population Research*] (05), 33–43.

[51] Liang Z, Wang N. (2021). 中国和 21 世纪的国际移民研究 [Studies on China and the 21st Century International Immigration]. *学术月刊* [*Academic Monthly*] (08), 123–134. https://doi.org/10.19862/j.cnki.xsyk.000250.

or region, emphasizing the influence of geography on politics."[52] This shows that geopolitics is a relational category. The relationship between geography and politics can be extended to three kinds of relationships, namely, geographic spatial location relationships, the relationship of power and national strength or weakness, and the relationship of intertwined interests in strategy, which constitute the three basic elements of geopolitics.

From the perspective of changes in population size and structure, this paper explores the changes in geospatial relations, state power relations, and interest-intertwined relationships triggered by demographic changes, which in turn lead to the evolution of geopolitical patterns in neighbouring countries, regions, and the globe (see Fig. 4).

3.1 The Impact Mechanism of Demographic Change on Geopolitics

3.1.1 The Impact of Population Size Changes on Geopolitics

The changes in the population size of a country are mainly determined by the natural population growth rate and international migration. Population change first manifests as a change in the size of a country's population. Under the condition that all other countries have the same or similar elements of power, population size is positively correlated with state power.[53] Population growth brings more labours and talent to the country, expands the domestic market and enhances its capacity for military mobilization. Under the guidance of appropriate policies, population growth can develop into a population-scale benefit, enhance the strength of national power, and give the country to have an advantage in competition over power. When population growth keeps pace with economic and social development, a country's capacities for cross-border processing and trade, foreign investment attraction, military mobilization, and even influence in international education will all improve. When the population decreases, it can increase the per capita possession of natural resources in

[52] Zbigniew Brzezinski. 竞赛方案—进行美苏竞争的地缘战略纲领 [Game Plan: A Geostrategic Framework for the Conduct of the US-Soviet Conflict]. Beijing: China Translation & Publishing Corporation. *Beijing: China Foreign Translation Company*, 1998. p. 6.

[53] Hans J. Morgenthau. 国家间政治:权力斗争与和平 [Politics Among Nations: The Struggle for Power and Peace]. Peking University Press, 2006, pp. 162–165.

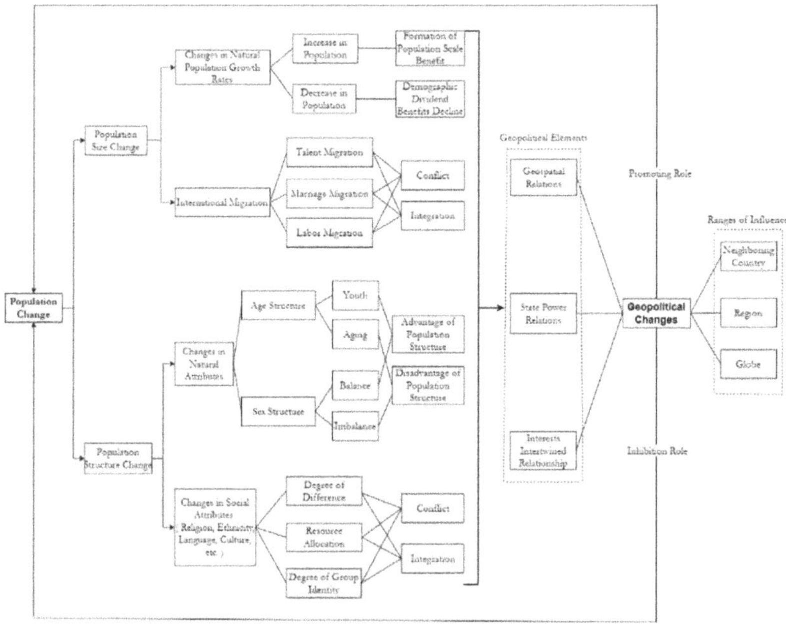

Fig. 4 Mechanisms of the effect of demographic change on geopolitics

the country in the short term, reducing resource and environmental pressures. However, in the long run, population reduction will inevitably lead to problems such as a shortage in the labour force, a decrease in talent, a shrinking domestic demand market, and insufficient defence spending and defence forces, weakening national power and inducing a weak board effect. When the population of a country with vast land decreases, especially when the border population decreases significantly, the power over the border held by the country will inevitably decline, and there will be potential border security risks. If the national strategy and policies are inappropriate and overlap with the trend of population ageing, it may lead to issues such as adjustments to the import and export structure, decreases in the attractiveness of the nation to foreign enterprises, declines in national military strength, and insufficient influence in international education. These issues, through the strength and weakness effects of state power, trigger profound adjustments in geographical spatial relationships, state power relationships, and intertwined interests, thereby triggering the evolution of geopolitical patterns.

The international migration of the population is an essential reason for changes in population size and a key factor in promoting the adjustment of geopolitical patterns, mainly including talent migration, marriage migration, and labour migration. The international migration of the population brings uncertainty over border control, social stability, regional conflicts, and transnational crime, especially in the complex and acute issues of racial conflicts and discrimination caused by migration. Environmental degradation, the spread of infectious diseases, and tensions in international relations are also potential risks for international migrants.[54] For the countries experiencing a migration outflow, the direct result is similar to a decrease in population size. In the long run, although population outflow can alleviate the country's resource burden, it can easily lead to a decrease in the international capital and technological competitiveness of migrants and a slowdown in improving productivity levels. When the outflow is too large, it can even lead to a decrease in the labour force, a narrowing of the domestic demand market, a decrease in military mobilization capacity, and a weakening of the country's population power. In particular, the "wealth loss" and "talent loss" caused by the international migration of highly educated groups can produce talent security issues for countries with migrant outflows. The frequent waves of emigration, especially with large numbers of highly skilled immigrants, have caused an increasingly severe "brain drain" in developing countries, exacerbating the risk of global political and economic imbalance and polarization. Investment run, these flows pose a challenge to the comprehensive national strength of the countries with large relocated populations.[55] The emergence of a large number of "investment immigrants" during the third wave of immigration in the early twenty-first century has become the main path for

[54] Li FT. (2009). 国际移民及其对国际政治经济的影响 [International Migration and Its Impact on the International Political and Economy]. *齐鲁学刊* [*Qilu Journal*] (01), 99–104.

[55] Zhang JJ. (2010). 探讨保护和发展城市移民文化多样性的经验和政策—"中国与亚洲的移民:实践与政策" 国际会议综述 [Exploring the Experience and Policies of Protecting and Developing the Cultural Diversity of Urban Immigrants: A Review of the International Conference on "Immigrants in China and Asia: Practice and Policy"]. *国外社会科学* [*Social Sciences International*] (06), 149–154.

wealth loss.[56] For destination countries, under the conditions of social and economic stability, reasonable resource allocation, vital social and cultural inclusiveness, and reasonable immigration policies, immigrants can integrate with permanent residents,[57] thus bringing positive impacts to politics, economy, culture, and society. A large number of immigrants can not only strengthen the population and power of the country, expand population dividends, enhance labour advantages, and expand military mobilization capabilities but also profoundly affect the social, economic, and cultural structural systems of the immigrant export and import regions.[58] In contrast, if the country's socioeconomic instability, uneven resource allocation, weak cultural inclusivity, restrictive or exclusionary immigration policies, serious cultural identity differences and religious conflicts brought by foreign immigrants exacerbate the conflicts with local residents, the result may include psychological barriers and opposition between foreign immigrants and local residents with an increasing risk of social conflict.

3.1.2 The Impact of Population Structure Changes on Geopolitics

Population structure is the distribution of the population and its movements.[59] The natural population structure attributes include age and sex structure. The age structure of the population mainly affects the country's economy, politics, culture, military, and other fields through the dependency coefficient of the elderly and young populations. On the one hand, the age structure of the population directly affects the proportion of the domestic population eligible to work and mobilize for military service,

[56] Li ZY. (2012). 21 世纪初中国国际移民与国家安全 [International Migration and National Security in China in the Early 21st Century]. 国际关系学院学报 [*Journal of International Security Studies*] (04), 111–118.

[57] Wu XM, Xue Lin, Fang WJ, et al. 中国国际移民的社会融合与发展: 分析框架的构建与应用 [Social Integration and Development of International Immigrants in China: Construction and Application of a Theoretic Framework]. *西安交通大学学报 (社会科学版)* [*Journal of Xi'an Jiaotong University* (Social Sciences)] (05), 115–122. https://doi.org/10.15896/j.xjtuskxb.202205012.

[58] An N, Zhang B. (2022). 地缘政治视角下的跨境移民和族裔社区研究 [The research of transnational migration and ethnic communities from the perspective of geopolitics]. *世界地理研究* [*World Regional Research*] (06), 1119–1129.

[59] Chen YP. (1999). 论人口变动对政治发展的影响 [On the Impact of Population Changes on Political Development]. *中国人口科学* [*China Journal of Population Science*] (03), 59–64.

and the age structure can also affect the geopolitical field. When the dependency ratio of the elderly and young populations is too high, the social burden is too heavy, which will challenge the political system to encourage economic development. It will significantly affect the country's geopolitical strength and strategic goals, thereby affecting neighbouring countries, triggering adjustments in spatial interests and even conflicts, exacerbating regional tensions, and changing the geopolitical pattern of relationships. On the other hand, the age structure of the population is related to the formulation of domestic policies and political culture. Due to differences in social experience among different age groups, there is a generation gap in political consciousness, and their attitudes, beliefs, values, political skills, and behavioural patterns towards the political system are also different. Therefore, the population's age structure can affect the geopolitical system's social environment, resulting in a correlation between the mainstream political culture of a country and the type of population age structure.[60] The age structure of the population can affect a country's political and cultural structure, as well as its foreign policy. If there is a sudden change in the population age structure of a country in a short period of time, the result is often a change in strategic goals and an adjustment in the interest structure, which will introduce many uncertainties into geopolitics. Although the sex structure is not directly related to geopolitical issues, cross-border marriage rates caused by sex imbalance are a geopolitical issue that cannot be ignored. The data show that countries with imbalanced sex structures, especially in border areas such as Yunnan, China, have more frequent cross-border marriages.[61] Moreover, illegal cross-border marriages among border residents provide breeding grounds for traffickers to kidnap and sell women, increasing pressure on law enforcement in border areas. For foreign nationals who "marry into" China, the complex foreign-related governance issues are constituted collectively by the lack of valid documents, lack of marital legal relationships, and new burden of elderly care, thereby increasing the

[60] Lu JH, Wang XF. (2022). 人口结构变化对美国政治格局的潜在影响探究—基于多数据源的考察 [Exploring the Potential Impact of Population Structure Changes on the Political Pattern of the United States: A Study Based on Multiple Data Sources]. *学术研究* [*Academic Research*] (12), 72–78.

[61] Bao YP. 选择与困境:云南边境跨国婚姻的社会学分析 [Choice and Dilemma: Sociological Analysis of Cross-border Marriage in Yunnan Border Area]. *北方民族大学学报（哲学社会科学版）* [*Journal of North Minzu University* (Philosophy and Social Science)] (04), 5–12.

difficulty of border governance. It can be said that the imbalance in population sex structure brings new challenges to international migration and national border management.

The social attributes of population structure include race, culture, language, ethnicity, and religion. The changes in population structure and social attributes may directly lead to the redistribution of social and political resources, resulting in ideological and identity conflicts between different groups. When the domestic economic and social developments are relatively stable, the heterogeneity of ethnic cultures and racial differences is not significant, the level of group identification is high, the distribution of social and political resources is relatively balanced, population policies are appropriate, and different ethnic, cultural, linguistic, and religious groups integrate with each other, then domestic economic and social development can be promoted and the country's geopolitical influence enhanced. In North America, while providing political, economic, and military material assistance to allies, the United States also incorporates cultural and educational exchanges between Asian countries and regions into its diplomatic strategy, making it the preferred destination for studying abroad.[62] In the Asia–Pacific region, international migration has brought about the integration of different civilizations, which in turn has become an important driver of international migration in the Asia–Pacific region. This circular connection promotes relations between relevant countries and the stability and development of regional situations.[63] However, changes in population structure may also have adverse geopolitical impacts. Excessive differences in population structure, the uneven distribution of social and political resources, rampant xenophobia, and lagging population policies can also easily lead to conflicts between various ethnic groups and trigger geopolitical instability. From a regional and global perspective, changes in the population structure of one or more countries often lead to changes in national strength, affecting the spatial distribution of national interests, promoting cultural exchange, and increasing the possibility of conflicts. In Asia, since the start of the twenty-first century, the issue of population migration caused by the water

[62] Liang MX, 美国移民史新论 [New Studies on U.S. Immigration History]. Beijing: social sciences academic press, 2019, pp. 279–280.

[63] Karl H. (2021). 太平洋地缘政治学: 地理与历史之间关系的研究 [Geopolitics of the Pacific Ocean: Studies on the Relationship between Geography and History]. Beijing: Huaxia Publishing House, 2021.

resource issue of the "Asian Water Tower" has led to multiple violent conflicts.[64] In Europe, Muslim communities express their dissatisfaction with society through negative means such as car burning and anti-Semitic activities, which have raised concerns among local governments.[65] In Africa, cross-border ethnic groups have had many negative impacts on the politics, economy, and society of relevant African countries. In some regions, they have even sparked serious conflicts.[66]

In short, population is an important variable in the evolution of geopolitics, and the impact of population changes on geopolitics is complex. In contrast, geopolitics can also have impacts on population changes, particularly in promoting or inhibiting population migration. First, geopolitics can be a driver of population migration under certain circumstances. Some countries, taking into account geopolitical considerations such as increasing national strength, optimizing population structure, and reaping economic development benefits, will formulate geopolitical policies that are conducive to population migration, encouraging immigrants, especially highly skilled talent and labour, to come. To achieve their geopolitical goals, some countries provide refuge for reactionary forces or "dissidents" from hostile countries. These countries may arbitrarily apply the category "refugees" to certain immigrant groups based on their national interests; in this way, countries can interfere in the internal affairs of other nations under the guise of "humanitarianism". The adoption of various social policies can in turn actively encourage illegal immigration. At the same time, intense geopolitical conflicts such as war and political persecution in some countries and regions can create a large number of "refugees", who have to leave their homes to survive, resulting in a large amount of international migration.

[64] Du DB, Liu CL, Hu ZD, etc. (2020). "亚洲水塔"变化对中国周边地缘政治环境的影响 [The impact of "Asian Water Tower" change on the geopolitical environment around China]. *世界地理研究* [*World Regional Studies*] (02), 223–231.

[65] Luo AL. (2009). *存在与冲突—试论穆斯林移民对欧洲政治与社会的影响* [Existence and Conflict—On the Impact of Muslim Immigrants on European Politics and Society]. *世界民族* [*Journal of World Peoples Studies*] (03), 62–71.

[66] Liu WC. (2012). "跨界民族—国际移民综合症"与非洲国家冲突—以科特迪瓦为中心 ["Cross Border Ethnic Groups—International Migration Syndrome" and Conflicts in African Countries—Centred around Côte d'Ivoire]. *世界民族* [*Journal of World Peoples Studies*] (06), 49–55.

However, geopolitics can sometimes hinder population migration. Some destination countries are concerned that the influx of many immigrants will lead to changes in their population structure and racial proportions, resulting in adverse political consequences. Worrying about the gradual increase in the number of immigrants, these countries will engage in political power struggles with local people. If local people fail to gain the upper hand in politics, they will inevitably become the object of immigration control. To prevent immigrants from becoming a political threat to local people in the future, various political strategies are adopted to vilify the image of immigrants and restrict their naturalization; some of these strategies include border walls to prevent immigrants from entering, restrictions on their employment scope, and even political persecution, thereby hindering population migration. In addition, the host country also hinders immigration through economic repression, cultural discrimination, and other means. For emigration, many countries are concerned that net population outflow will weaken their national strength, putting them at a disadvantage in geopolitical competition, and thus these countries may adopt various restrictive measures on population migration. These factors will have a hindering effect on immigration.

3.2 *The Geopolitical Impacts of China's Demographic Changes at the Global Level*

The distribution and changes in demographic factors have a significant impact on national strength and even on global economic, political, and military affairs, which in turn have a profound influence on the formulation of geopolitical strategies and participation in global affairs. The internal operating mechanism for how demographic change affects the global geopolitical landscape is intricate and complicated. To put it simply, this mechanism mainly manifests in the fact that changes in the size and structure of the global population have a direct impact on the global economy, politics, culture, environment, and security, accelerating the evolution of the global geographic space, the power of individual states and the interwoven relationship of interests. Thus, these mechanisms bring about both integration and conflicts of civilizations at the global level.[67]

Over the past century, the global population has gone through development stages, including mortality declines, rapid growth, declining fertility and slowed growth. As a populous country, China has experienced demographic change that is broadly consistent with the general trend of global demographic change, including multiple demographic changes, especially low fertility, population ageing, and population migration.[68] From the geopolitical point of view, since China occupies an important position in the international community, China's demographic changes will have an enormous and far-reaching impact on the evolution of the global geopolitical pattern, which is manifested in the following aspects.

First, China's demographic changes have profoundly affected the world economic landscape. As the world's second most populous country, the world's second-largest economy, the second-largest consumer market and the largest goods-trading country, China has used its sustained and stable economic development as a stabilizing force and a source of power in the global economy. At present, China's early descent into negative population growth will directly result in the ageing of the country's population, and the ensuing impacts include improved human capital, declining effective demand, reduced consumption spending, slower economic growth, decreased corporate profits, and reduced savings and investment, which will have a knock-on effect on the global supply chain. The shrinking market brought about by the declining population will depress Western companies that have long reaped the benefits of sales to China. At the same time, as China's demographic dividend is gradually weakening as a driver of the global economy, it is likely to accelerate the global economic declining, indirectly leading to a revision of the international community's expectations and confidence in global economic growth.

Second, China's demographic changes will intensify the long-term competition between China and the United States. At present, the most significant challenge China faces is from the hegemony of the United States. On October 12, 2022, the United States officially released the

[67] Dai CZ, Wang HB. (2009). 国际人口流动中的反恐问题探析 [An Analysis on Anti-terrorism Issue of International Population Floating]. *中国人民大学学报* [*Journal of Renmin University of China*] (02), 107–113.

[68] Zheng ZZ. (2023). 从全球人口变化看中国人口负增长 [The Population Decline in China: A Global Perspective]. *人口研究* [*Population Research*] (02): 3–10.

first National Security Strategy under the Biden administration, which said that China is the only competitor that has both the intention to reshape the international order and the growing economic, diplomatic, military and technological power to do so.[69] The United States has regarded China as its primary strategic competitor, and in the Sino-US strategic game, the technology field has become an important field of competition. The competition to seize the commanding heights of science and technology is becoming increasingly fierce. With the increasing ageing of China's population, to overcome the adverse impact of the weakening of demographic dividends on economic development, China actively promotes the transformation of demographic dividends into talent dividends and accelerates the establishment of competitive advantages in human resources. In this process, Western countries led by the United States have taken advantage of technological advantages in the name of safeguarding national security and set strict technological and security thresholds to contain China in high-tech fields. Economic sanctions or even maritime blockades against China, which will directly endanger China's core national interests, will not be ruled out in the future. This geopolitical position brings great uncertainties and risks to China's economic, social development and the process of opening up to the outside world and participation in economic globalization.[70]

Third, China's demographic changes are accelerating the uncertainty of the international order. The foundation of the strategic landscape of the major powers is the balance of international power, which largely determines international stability or disorder. A large population is a crucial premise for a major power, and a reasonable population size and structure are essential prerequisites for national power and strategic capability.[71]

[69] Fact Sheet: The Biden-Harris Administration's National Security Strategy [EB/0 L]. [2022-10-17]. https://China.usembassy-China.org.cn/fact-sheet-the-biden-harris-administrations-national-security-strategy/.

[70] Liu SL, Hu AG. (2023). 中国经济发展趋势：机遇与挑战（2021–2035）China's Economic Development Trend: Opportunities and Challenges (2021–2035). *甘肃社会科学* [*Gansu Social Sciences*] (01), 195–207. https://doi.org/10.15891/j.cnki.cn62-1093/c.20230117.002.

[71] He XY. (2016). 国际关系视角下的美国少数族裔人口政治学 [Political Demography of U.S. Ethnic Minority in the Perspective of International Relations.] *国际论坛* [*International Forum*] (03), 67–72 + 81. https://doi.org/10.13549/j.cnki.cn11-3959/d.2016.03.012.

Since the mid-1990s, China's demographic dividends have led to continuous economic growth and an increase in national strength, propelling China's influence and discourse power on the international stage. With the advancement of globalization and multipolarity, the confrontation between major power groups has slowed down during this period, and there has been an increasing willingness among world powers to cooperate. During the Trump administration symbolizing a shift in policy, the United States has vigorously promoted political opposition, security confrontation, military standoff, economic decoupling, and technological disengagement between major powers. The COVID-19 pandemic and the conflict between Russia and Ukraine have become two driving forces accelerating competition between major powers. In the context of great power competition, some regional powers are seizing opportunities to expand their influence. Taking the fluctuation of power within the United Nations Security Council as an example, with the population of China and India changing directions, India is more active in striving to become the sixth permanent member of the Security Council, fighting for a greater voice and influence in international affairs to establish a new international order that can maximize its national interests. The United States is constantly recruiting India to contain China. This not only accelerates major power competition but also brings greater uncertainty to the international order.

3.3 *The Geopolitical Impacts of China's Demographic Changes at the Regional Level*

The changing pattern of population power in major countries can be divided into two spatial categories: the change in population systems within sovereign states, and the change in the distribution of population ratios in different regions. In terms of its content, the core driving force of patterns of population power in large countries includes two aspects, the change in population size and the change in population structure. Specifically, the main driving factors affecting the population power of large countries include the trend in population size, the change in population structure by age, the change in labour force population size and the change in labour resources.[72]

[72] He XY. (2016). 国际关系视角下的美国少数族裔人口政治学 [Political Demography of U.S. Ethnic Minority in the Perspective of International Relations International relations

China is located on the eastern edge of the Eurasian continent, with a vast territory and a large population. It is a large country with advantages in both sea and land power.[73] Superior geographical conditions are the cradle of Chinese civilization and the basis for China to become the centre of East Asian civilizations and a leader in world politics.[74] Under the condition that all other elements of state power constitute the same or similar levels of influence, there is a positive correlation between the change in population size and the change in state power.[75] First, population size and resource demand can both lead to conflicts. The scarcity of resources can spark competition and tensions that eventually escalate into bigger issues. Second, population size has a profound impact on trade patterns in East Asia. As China's population has grown, it has become one of the world's largest consumer markets, fueling a rapid expansion of trade in East Asia and beyond. If China's demoghrapic shift might lead to a slowdown, it will effect its exports to East Asia. The change in the size of China's population has not only affected China's own economic development but also shaped the trade pattern of the entire East Asia region to a large extent. Issues such as unemployment rates can cause geopolitical shifts. Finally, resource scarcity and environmental security issues have seriously threatened the sustainable development of the planet and induced geopolitical conflicts caused by environmental or resource issues.[76]

As China's population ages, it may lead to pressure on the labour market, which may affect labour supply in East Asia. Ageing population might lead to subtle changes in international strategic approaches.

(IR).]. *国际论坛* [*International Forum*] (03), 67–72 + 81. https://doi.org/10.13549/j.cnki.cn11-3959/d.2016.03.012.

[73] Hu ZD, Ge YJ, Du DB et al. (2021). 走向伟大复兴的中国地缘战略: 国家周边论 [China's geopolitical strategy on the way to the great rejuvenation: The National Neighborland Theory.]. *世界地理研究* [*World Regional Studies*] (03), 443–453.

[74] Hu ZD, Ge YJ, Du DB et al. (2021). 走向伟大复兴的中国地缘战略: 国家周边论 [China's geopolitical strategy on the way to the great rejuvenation: The National Neighborland Theory.] 世界地理研究 [*World Geographical Studies*] (03), 443–453.

[75] Hans J. Morgenthau. (2022). 《国家间政治: 权力斗争与和平》 [Politics Among Nations: The Struggle for Power and Peace]. 北京大学出版社 [Peking University Press], 2006, pp. 162–165.

[76] Xiong CR, Wang LM, Qu QS et al. (2020). 地理学之地缘政治学与地缘经济学: 学科之争抑或学科融合? [Paradigms between geopolitics and geoeconomics: Controversy or integration]. *世界地理研究* [*World Regional Studies*] (02), 296–306.

At the level of competition over comprehensive national strength, mere comparison of gross national product might no longer be enough, and the focus may need to be more inclined towards sustainable development, competition for advanced and sophisticated fields, and control of institutional power and voice. Major powers with central global influence may be forced to adjust their security strategies to rely more on alliances and emphasize the role of regional and international organizations. China's ageing population may lead to increased demand for foreign labour, triggering population movements from other countries. Especially in the neighbouring East Asia region, demographic change will have an impact on the local labour supply.

The impact of migration on geopolitics is mainly reflected in the following three aspects: international relations, the importing countries' political ecology and policies, and geopolitical security.[77] China faced demographic pressures and environmental degradation long before Europe did. Different from Europe, China did not experience large-scale overseas migration, except for the migration from the southeast coast to Southeast Asia, nor did it experience an industrial revolution like the one in Europe. Demographic changes in China are likely to affect migration trends.

In China, the main economic hub is located in the southeastern coastal areas, which means that China's economic ties with East and Southeast Asian countries are far greater than those with North, Central and West Asian countries and regions.[78] The influx and distribution of Chinese immigrants have shaped the geopolitical relations of East Asian countries to a considerable extent. Some countries face social tensions due to migration, which can lead to ethnic, religious, or economic conflicts or even transnational conflicts. At the same time, the resettlement and integration of Chinese immigrants in East Asia are also challenges to the political stability of the region. Therefore, countries in the region need to strengthen cooperation and develop common migration policies and social integration strategies to ensure the stability and sustainable development of geopolitical relations.

77 中央民族大学

78 Xie BJ, Zhu XM. 地缘经济研究进展 [The Research Development of Geo-economic]. 社会科学 [*Journal of Social Sciences*] (10), 29–41. https://doi.org/10.13644/j.cnki.cn31-1112.2019.10.003.

3.4 *The Geopolitical Impacts of China's Demographic Changes on the Neighbouring Countries*

Demographic changes, especially transnational population movements, have profound impacts on the development of bilateral relations with the neighbouring countries. The impacts of demographical changes are two-sided, with positive impacts linked to labour force and economic development, as well as conflicts stemming from national identities, cultures, and values. Racial discrimination caused by migration is an important factor contributing to tensions in relations between neighbouring countries.

The complexity and international nature of the floating population in the southwestern border area of China are very extreme. In the areas bordering Myanmar, Laos, and Vietnam, there are a large number of special migrant groups, including cross-border ethnic migrants, war refugees, and cross-border marriage migrants. These floating populations can lead to nontraditional security threats such as cross-border crime, drug trafficking, AIDS, illegal immigration, ethnic separatism, and challenges to geopolitical stability. The issue of cross-border marriages in the China-Vietnam and China-Myanmar border regions has become a crucial concern for population management and social governance. In recent years, the influxes of Vietnamese young women marrying into local Han Chinese families in provinces such as Guangxi and Yunnan have become part of China's population. However, many "Vietnamese brides" staying in China due to cross-border marriage relationships often enter the country through illegal means such as abduction, increasing the difficulty of population management along the China–Vietnam border. This, in turn, poses risks and challenges to social order and security, fostering illegal activities such as human trafficking, marriage fraud, and illegal marriage intermediaries. Similar to Vietnamese brides, "Myanmar brides" entering China through cross-border marriages face marginalization in the labour market and social connections. Their lower access to social welfare in areas such as health care, child education, and women's rights protection creates concerns about the social integration of these brides and the implications for the security and stability of the Yunnan border region and even the entire country. In recent years, due to the political turmoil in Myanmar, Chinese residents who migrated into Myanmar from border areas during the special period of the last century have gradually returned to their homeland, forming a new problem of a "returning population", constantly changing the population spatial pattern of the southwestern border.

The ageing trend of China's population is similar to that of Japan, and there are significant similarities in the temporal and spatial evolution of ageing between the two countries. Therefore, addressing the social pressure brought about by the ageing population has become an important dimension of Sino-Japanese cooperation. The Chinese government has gradually established a long-term strategic plan for eldercare policies by summarizing Japan's experience and providing response reserves for the period when the elderly population peaks. China continuously strengthens policy exchanges with Japan in terms of financial support, management, and risk response in the eldercare industry, and it also improves policy and regulatory requirements in relevant fields. Simultaneously, China is also leveraging its geographical and cultural advantages to cater to the needs of Japan's elderly population, absorb the emerging consumer markets brought by the potential influx of the Japanese elderly population, and transform the heavy burden of public support for elderly people into human capital to promote social development and international cooperation.

As a vital channel and hub to the Asia–Pacific region, the Far East region is geostrategically advantageous for Russia to integrate into the shared development of the region. However, in recent years, the Far East region has also faced economic threats resulting from a sharp population decline. To enhance Russia's influence in the international community, particularly the national security of the Far East region, and to connect with the rapid economic development of the Asia–Pacific region, Russia has implemented a series of outlines and strategies to support the development of the Far East and signed cooperation treaties with China. The border area of Heilongjiang in China provides important labour and population support for the development of the Far East region. The two nations rely on "two resources" and "two markets" to integrate regional elements and provide an economic foundation for geostrategic cooperation. Governments in both border regions focus on long-term planning, emphasizing on the establishment of border cooperation systems and starting with infrastructure investment, collaborating to construct major transportation channels, including sea transportation, land transportation, and airport transportation. This effort aims to build a cooperative exchange platform that meets international needs, fostering regional geopolitical strategic cooperation.

India's vast consumer market and labour resources have gradually become vital in international competition, and its young population structure is more suitable for innovation and learning. Compared with China and its reduced age advantage and increased public burden for supporting the elderly community, India may gradually replace China's position as the "world factory". Due to its consistent emphasis on education and the cultivation of scientific and technological talent, India has abundant talent reserves both domestically and internationally. Relying on the development of its information technology industry, India has created enormous wealth and identified unparalleled international advantages.[79] Therefore, from the perspective of population factors, India's population strength will surpass that of China in the future. Faced with the trend of a gradual decline in relative population strength, China is also actively transforming its population development model, placing greater emphasis on "population quality" and increasing financial support for industries such as health care, education, and eldercare. China is also committed to improving the quality of its labor force and population. The industrial transformation and new consumption growth points brought about by China's demographic transformation will also create opportunities for China-India cooperation. China is also actively exploring dialogue on the population issue between China and India to promote mutual learning between the world's first and second most populous countries on improving the level of population governance. China and India are also committed to promoting dialogue on global population issues within the SCO, BRICS cooperation mechanism, G20 and other frameworks.

With the frequent flow of people brought about by the "Belt and Road Initiative" international cooperation, such population influx due to the change of geographical relations will form new accumulations in China's border areas, which will gradually change the population structure of the border areas and cause more and more frequent ethnic, religious and stability problems in the border areas.[80] The China-Pakistan Economic Corridor starts from Kashgar in Xinjiang Province in the east,

[79] Li JX. (2004). 中国与印度未来人口实力比较研究 [Comparative Study on the Future Population Strength of China and India]. *人口学刊* [*Population Journal*] (06), 8–14. https://doi.org/10.16405/j.cnki.1004-129x.2004.06.002.

[80] Zhou Q, Yang Y, Liu Y, et al. (2018). 中国"一带一路"地缘政治研究进展与展望 [Basic public service evaluation of resource-based cities in Northeast China]. *世界地理研究* [*World Regional Studies*] (03), 1–10 + 64.

passes through Pakistan, and finally reaches Gwadar port in southwest Pakistan. The ethnic composition of Kashgar area is complicated, and with the increase of population mobility after the opening of the port, Kashgar area and its surrounding areas are more strongly influenced by the "three forces",[81] which poses a threat to the population and environment security in China's border and corridor areas.

4 Conclusion

This paper explores the interaction mechanism between demographic change and geopolitical change, analyses the impact of China's demographic change on geopolitics, and draws the following conclusions. First, demographic change is a complex social phenomenon that can have a profound impact on geopolitics. Population change drives changes in the geopolitical landscape by affecting geospatial relations, state power relations and intertwined interests among countries. Geopolitical changes also have an impact on demographic changes, which is highlighted in the promotion or restriction of population migration. Second, China's population is undergoing irreversible and historic changes in both quantity and structure, especially in terms of low fertility, population ageing and migration. As a large country with an important geopolitical position and influence in the world, China and its demographic changes will have far-reaching and lasting impacts on the geopolitical landscape of neighbouring countries, regions and even the globe. Third, China's demographic changes will profoundly affect the world's economic landscape at the global level, intensify the long-term competition and strategy games between the major powers of China and the United States, and accelerate the uncertainty of the international order. Fourth, the outflow and distribution of Chinese immigrants have shaped the geopolitical relations of East Asian countries to a considerable extent. The geopolitical impact of China's demographic changes at the regional level is mainly

[81] On June 15, 2001, the SCO signed the Shanghai Convention on Combating Terrorism, Separatism and Extremism, which for the first time gave a clear definition of terrorism, separatism and extremism. The so-called three forces refer to violent terrorist forces (such as Al Qaeda under Osama-bin-Laden), ethnic separatist forces (such as the illegal armed groups in Chechnya, Russia), and religious extremist forces (such as the Islamic Movement in Uzbekistan).

concentrated in East Asia. Issues such as the resettlement and integration of Chinese migrants in East Asia, trade with East Asian countries, and labour supply all have an impact on regional geopolitics. Fifth, China's demographic change also affects the development of bilateral relations with neighbouring countries, with positive impacts linked to labour and economic development, as well as conflicts from national identity, culture, and values. This paper only provides a preliminary framework for exploring China's demographic change and its implications for geopolitical realities. What factors influence and constrain changes in geopolitical relations? How should China adjust its geostrategic and population policies to accommodate future demographic changes and their geopolitical implications? These questions still need to be further explored and researched.

CHAPTER 4

The PRC Belt and Road Initiative: An Accelerator to Achieve the United Nations Sustainable Development Goals?

Yin Liu and Jonathan Harrington

1 Introduction

On September 25, 2015, the United Nations General Assembly adopted 17 goals encompassing 169 targets as part of a new sustainable development agenda. The accompanying document is entitled *Transforming our world: the 2030 agenda for sustainable development* (2030 Agenda, 2015). *The 2030 Agenda* is a plan of action for people, the planet, and prosperity. It seeks to end poverty, protect the biosphere, and ensure prosperity for all. It resolves to take bold and transformative steps to promote global sustainable development (2030 Agenda, 2015).

Y. Liu (✉)
Huaqiao University, Xiamen, China
e-mail: liuyin@hqu.edu.cn

J. Harrington
Troy University, Troy, AL, USA

A. Aliu (ed.), *Complexity Thinking and China's Demography Within and Beyond Mainland China*,
https://doi.org/10.1007/978-981-97-0172-8_4

The SDGs, both global and universally applicable, are viewed by their proponents as integrated and indivisible (2030 Agenda, 2015). The three SDGs pillars—economic growth, environmental stewardship, and social inclusion—carry across all geographic, demographic, public policy, and private sectors, from cities facing rapid urbanization to agriculture, fossil-fuel extraction, infrastructure, energy, water availability, and transportation (China Development Bank and UNDP 2019; World Bank 2015). Developing countries and middle-income countries are encouraged to participate in international economic decision-making, norm-setting, and global economic governance (2030 Agenda, 2015).

The SDGs project and the BRI share specific broad goals. Like the 2030 Agenda, the BRI is a vast international infrastructure and development plan that its framers' state will help reduce poverty, encourage balanced economic growth, promote social inclusion, and foster environmental protection. The "Belt" refers to the land-based "Silk Road Economic Belt" which starts in Xi'an, Shanxi Province, and extends to Europe via Central Asia. The "Road" refers to the "Maritime Silk Road," which begins in Quanzhou, Fujian Province, and runs through the South China Sea, Indian Ocean, Red Sea, and the Mediterranean Sea to Europe. The BRI aims to promote connectivity among the Asian, European, and African continents and their adjacent seas, and establish and strengthen partnerships among countries situated along the Belt and Road (CNDRC et al. 2015). The total area is home to more than 60% of the world's population and represents over one-third of the global gross domestic product (GDP). Also, the BRI is not exclusive to the rest of the world but open to all other countries and organizations interested in participating.

To date, more than 3400 projects have been launched by 81 Chinese SOEs under the BRI banner.[1] According to PRC policymakers, the BRI and SDGs share a supremely ambitious and transformational vision, to promote a world of increasing prosperity and plenty free from poverty and hunger where humanity lives in harmony with nature (*Universal Declaration of Human Rights* (UNGA 1948); UN, International Covenant on Economic, Social and Cultural Rights 1967). It proposes a wide range of economic, social, and environmental objectives that promise to nurture

[1] The State Owned Assets Supervision and Administration Commission of the State Council (SASAC), *More Than 3,400 BRI Projects Undertaken by 81 SOEs*, http://news.cctv.com/2021/01/19/ARTItgNze0cQPMm5cmkNw1ur210119.shtml, posted January 19, 2021, accessed April 8, 2021.

more peaceful, inclusive, and sustainable societies. Its supporters view the BRI as a global "sustainable development plan" that can act as a powerful catalyst to achieve multiple SDGs within a given timeframe (DPAD 2017; Hong 2017; Lajčák 2018).

Despite the stated grand vision of BRI, many scholars and policy-makers have offered wide-ranging critiques of the Initiative. First, some question China's commitment to international law in general and global environmental governance in particular (Rolland 2017). They note the PRC's emphasis on its Five Principles of Peaceful Coexistence (hereinafter refered to as the "Five Principles" for short) over the UN Charter and relevant international laws and norms. They add that while PRC officials insist that BRI projects should be harmonized with the United Nations Sustainable Development Goals, many ventures aim to expand fossil-fuel intensive industries such as mining and coal-fired electric plants (Dollar 2017; Hillman 2017; Xue and Wang 2018). Second, they assert that the BRI framework emphasizes bilateral rather than multilateral cooperation, especially in finance and trade (Heiduk and Sakaki 2019; Sarangi 2020). They also express concern about China's lack of commitment to good governance, social and environmental safeguards, and human rights in recipient states (Presbitero 2016). Third, some are concerned that large debt-funded projects may be too costly for some recipient countries to sustain (Heydarian 2017; Zhang and Miller 2017; Hurley et al. 2018). Fourth, critiques note that the BRI lacks conceptual and policy clarity and transparency at all levels, including domestic institutions (Rolland 2017; Hameiri & Jones 2018).

2 Potential Links Between the SDGs and BRI: Shared Purposes, Principles and Priorities

The next section of this analysis presents arguments made by defenders of the BRI and the Initiative's stated congruence with the UN Charter, international law, SDGs, win–win outcomes for BRI partners, and human rights. They also assert that the BRI promotes free trade, provides capital for critical development objectives, and fosters peace and harmony among all stakeholders.

2.1 *Purposes and Principles*

According to PRC policymakers, the BRI is guided by the purposes (UN Charter, art.1) and principles (UN Charter, art. 2) of the UN Charter. It is also concurrently consistent with China's Five Principles, namely, mutual respect for state sovereignty and territorial integrity, mutual non-aggression, mutual non-interference in the internal affairs of others, equality and mutual benefit, and peaceful coexistence.

The BRI currently focuses on westward cooperation from China, connecting Asia, Europe, and Africa. But it is not necessarily limited to those current land routes and sea lanes. It may also extend eastward from China, Northeast Asia, Australia, Oceana, and the Americas. The BRI is viewed as an international development cooperation platform, open to all countries, and international and regional organizations (CNDRC et al. 2015).

Chinese development officials insist that the BRI is harmonious and inclusive. It respects a variety of development approaches and supports dialogues among different nations and civilizations based on the principles of seeking common ground while shelving differences and drawing on each other's strengths so that all countries can coexist in peace and enjoy mutual prosperity (Xi 2017).

BRI provisions pledge to abide by market rules and international norms, give play to the decisive role of the market in resource allocation and the primary role of enterprises, and allow governments to perform their due functions (Wei 2018).

BRI objectives call for promoting mutual beneficial outcomes by accommodating the interests and concerns of all parties involved, seeking common interest, and giving full play to the wisdom, creativity, strengths, and potential of all parties (CNDRC et al. 2015).

2.2 *Framework*

Chinese policymakers believe that the BRI can promote win–win cooperation, encourage engagement in all fields, and build a community of shared interests, destiny, and responsibility featuring mutual political trust, economic integration, and cultural inclusiveness (Xi 2017).

The Belt and Road spans the continents of Asia, Europe, and Africa by connecting the vibrant East Asia economic circle on one end and developed European economic ring on the other. It includes less developed regions in Africa and South Asia. The sea lanes of the Belt and Road run from China's coast to Europe through the South China Sea, Indian Ocean, and the South Pacific. There are five economic corridors along or close to the Belt and Road, including the China-Mongolia-Russia Economic Corridor, China-Central Asia-West Asia Economic Corridor, India-Indochina Peninsula Economic Corridor, China-Pakistan Economic Corridor, and the Bangladesh-China-India-Myanmar Economic Corridor (China Development Bank and UNDP 2019).

2.3 BRI Five Cooperation Priorities (Wu Tong)

The BRI identifies five cooperation priorities, including policy coordination, facilities connectivity, unimpeded trade, financial integration, and people-to-people exchanges (CNDRC et al. 2015).

Policy coordination is critical to promoting global macroeconomic stability. BRI proposals call for multi-level intergovernmental macro policy exchanges, enhanced mutual political trust, and the development of common growth strategies. Countries and international organizations engaged in the BRI are encouraged to harmonize and coordinate their economic development strategies and policies and jointly develop cooperative approaches (CNDRC et al. 2015). Facilities connectivity is a top BRI priority. The BRI aims to expand, transform, and advance all types of infrastructure along the Belt and Road. It will integrate infrastructure both within and among sub-regions in Asia, Asia, Europe, and Africa, increase investment in energy infrastructure, and advance telecommunications infrastructure (CNDRC et al. 2015).

Up to the end of September 2023, China Railway Express (CR Express) have extended to 217 cities in 25 European states and run 78 thousand times.[2]

The Regional Comprehensive Economic Partnership Agreement has gone into force binding 15 contracting states. Also, China has concluded 21 free trade agreements with 28 BRI partner states and territories, 107

[2] *BRI Grate Achievements in the Past Decade: Statistics*, https://news.cctv.com/2023/10/11/ARTIa03H9zKZns1WPHJwVrSA231011.shtml, posted October 11, 2013, accessed November 9, 2023.

standardization agreements with 65 BRI partner states, and double tax agreements with 112 BRI partner states and territories.[3]

Free trade and investment is another BRI priority. BRI supporters assert that international trade is an engine for inclusive economic growth and poverty reduction and can contribute to sustainable development (UN 2015). It supports trade facilitation that is consistent with the WTO. Cooperation in environmental infrastructure sectors such as renewable energy and energy efficiency and agriculture are prioritized.

In the past decade (2013–2022), the trade in goods between China and the BRI partner states valued $19.1 trillion with an average increase by 6.4%. Meanwhile, the investment between China and the BRI partner states amounted to $0.38 trillion. The BRI partner states have invested more than $0.14 trillion in China and established nearly 67 thousand enterprises.[4]

Financial integration is encouraged by significant and coordinated investments from multilateral institutions, national governments, and private entities. The Asian Infrastructure Investment Bank (AIIB), BRICS New Development Bank (NDB), and the Silk Road Fund were established to provide funding for BRI projects. Also, the harmonization of financial systems will help to address potential financial risks and crises. Both public and private financial resources are welcome.

People-to-people exchanges help to build public support both at home and abroad. The BRI pledges to foster cooperation in media, public health, traditional medicine, science and technology, vocational training, entrepreneurship, social security management, public administration, media, tourism, etc.

To date, China has signed agreements of mutual recognition of higher education degrees with 45 BRI partner states and territories, as well as those of cultural and tourism cooperation. Also, China grants the Silk Road Scholarship, and launches small but nice projects, e.g., Luban Workshop, *Juncao*, etc.[5]

[3] *Ibid.*

[4] *Ibid.*

[5] *Ibid.*

3 How Strong Are the Links Between the BRI and the SDGs: Arguments Promoting Unity Between the BRI and International Actors and Institutions

On June 13, 2018, a high-level symposium on "*Belt and Road Initiative and 2030 Agenda for Sustainable Development*" was held at the UN Headquarters in New York. It was jointly sponsored by the Chinese mission to the UN, UNDESA, World Health Organization (WHO), and UNDP. Addressing the gathering, UN General Assembly President Miroslav Lajčák thanked China for translating the SDGs into action on the ground by promoting the Belt and Road Initiative.

He noted that both the BRI and SDGs have a supremely ambitious and transformational vision; to build a world of prosperity and plenty, free from poverty and hunger, and humans live in harmony with nature. He believes that the BRI is highly compatible with the 2030 Agenda in that they share a common commitment to sustainable development.

BRI sponsors pledge to foster synergy with the development strategies of other countries and international organizations. They intend to deepen cooperation in infrastructure connectivity, facilitate trade through investment, and promote ecological and environmental protection, finance, culture, media, and tourism. The BRI is not only China's development strategy. Instead, it is global—rooted in cooperation, trade, and geography. From Montenegro to Kenya, the BRI includes over 100 countries and international organizations. The AIIB provides funding, which is critical for achieving the SDGs. In just its first year, the AIIB lent 1.73 billion US dollars to support sustainable infrastructure and other projects (Lajčák 2018).

3.1 Shared Purposes and Principles: Articles 1–2, the UN Charter

BRI proponents insist that the BRI and 2030 Agenda are both guided by the UN Charter. The main objectives of the Charter are to maintain international peace and security, develop friendly relations among nations, and achieve international economic, social, cultural, and humanitarian cooperation. Both encourage harmonization of countries' actions to attain these joint ends (UN Charter, art. 1). It conforms with a fundamental principle of international law, that sovereign states are equal and independent (UN Charter, art. 2).

3.2 *Shared Commitment: Sustainable Development*

Policymakers state that sustainable development principles should guide infrastructure construction, trade, and investment (China Ministry of Foreign Affairs—CMFA 2017). Economic theories and empirical studies attest the importance of infrastructure, trade, and investment to promote economic growth and employment and reduce poverty (Cockburn et al. 2013). According to McKinsey Global Institute (MGI) estimates, a dollar of infrastructure investment can raise GDP by 20% in the long run by boosting productivity (MGI 2016). However, our world is facing huge gaps in infrastructure investment. The world needs to increase its infrastructure investment by around 60% by 2030. More than $49 trillion is required over the next 15 years (MGI 2016). Asia alone needs to invest $26 trillion by 2030 to resolve serious infrastructure gaps to maintain growth, cut poverty, and deal with climate change. Fully two-thirds of that sum targets the transport and power sectors (Hasan et al. 2017; China Development Bank and UNDP 2019).

Recent spending trends reveal that infrastructure is a top recipient of BRI funding. Since 2013, Chinese enterprises have won $208 billion in infrastructure construction contracts (Joy-Perez & Scissors 2018), primarily financially supported by the Chinese government and private sector investment. The 2030 Agenda recognizes that good infrastructure helps achieve SDGs 1 No Poverty (1.b), 2 Zero hunger (2.a), 5 Gender Equality (5.4), and 7 Affordable and Clean Energy (7.a & b).

BRI supporters further assert that expanding trade is a primary BRI objective. International trade can be an engine for inclusive economic growth and poverty reduction and can contribute to the promotion of sustainable development. Both the BRI and the SDGs pledge to promote a WTO-consistent universal, rules-based, open, and equitable multilateral trading system (China Development Bank and UNDP 2019). The BRI calls for joint action of those countries along the Belt and Road to ensure the WTO Trade Facilitation Agreement's acceptance and enforcement. According to recently published statistics, Chinese enterprises have built 56 economic and trade cooperation zones in more than 20 countries along the Belt and Road, with an accumulated investment of over $18.5 billion, creating nearly $1.1 billion in tax revenue and 180,000 local jobs in host countries (B&R by Numbers 2017). Fostering an equitable multilateral trading system can help to achieve SDGs 2 Zero Hunger (2.b), 8

Decent Work & Economic Growth (8.a), 10 Reduced Inequalities (10.a), and 17 Partnership (17.5).

3.3 Shared Means of Implementation: Partnership

Chinese policymakers believe that the SDGs and BRI should work in concert with other relevant strategies and action programs. These, among others, include the *Istanbul Declaration and Program of Action* (UN 2018), the *SIDS Accelerated Modalities of Action (SAMOA) Pathway* (UN 2014), the *Vienna Program of Action for Landlocked Developing Countries for the Decade 2014–2024* (UN 2014), the *African Union's Agenda 2063* (AU 2015), and the program of the *New Partnership for Africa's Development* (NEPAD).

The BRI policymakers identify five cooperation priorities. The 2030 Agenda addresses numerous concrete steps required to achieve the Goals. These include the mobilization of financial resources, capacity-building, and transfer of environmentally sound technologies to developing countries. In particular, public finance is slated to play a vital role in providing essential services and public goods and catalyzing other finance sources (UN 2015).

BRI policies prioritize the poorest and most vulnerable needs, which are underscored as high priorities in the 2030 Agenda Preamble. China funds two multinational financial institutions, the Asian Infrastructure Investment Bank (AIIB) and BRICS New Development Bank (NDB) to achieve these objectives. It also created a domestic financial corporation, the Silk Road Fund.

Finance. The AIIB began operations in 2016. Its three thematic priorities include sustainable infrastructure, cross-border connectivity, and private capital mobilization. In 2017, the AIIB approved 15 projects totaling $2.5 billion (Lajčák 2018; AIIB 2018). Nowadays, the AIIB member states amount from to 106. By the end of 2022, it has had 202 lending projects valued $38.8 billion.[6]

[6] Shangjie Zheng, *Great Achievements By China and BRI Countries Shared Future and Better Advancement of the BRI* (十年共建结硕果 携手共向未来 扎实推进高质量共建 "一带一路" 行稳致远), the Journal of Xi Jinping Economic Thoughts, No. 6, 2023, available at https://www.ndrc.gov.cn/xwdt/ztzl/srxxgcxjpjjsx/xjpjjsxjyqk/202309/t20230908_1360478.html, posted September 9, 2023, accessed November 2, 2023.

The NDB was established on July 15, 2014, by Brazil, Russia, India, China, and South Africa, collectively the "BRICS" countries. On August 17, 2017, the Bank officially opened the African Regional Center (ARC) in Johannesburg. Its purpose is to mobilize resources for infrastructure and sustainable development projects within BRICS and other emerging economies and coordinate, when possible, complement the existing efforts of multilateral and regional financial institutions (NDB 2017).

The Silk Road Fund, a medium to long-term development and investment fund, was established in Beijing on December 29, 2014, with investment from the State Administration of Foreign Exchange, China Investment Corporation, Export–Import Bank of China (hereinafter referred to as "EXIM" for short), and China Development Bank (hereinafter referrd to as "CDB" for short). It mainly provides funding and financing support for trade and economic cooperation and connectivity for BRI projects. The Fund prioritizes collaboration and integration of China and partner states' development strategies. By the end of 2022, it has promised to lend $20 billion to more than 60 countries and territories.[7]

By the end of 2021, China had signed bilateral currency swap agreements with 22 BRI partner states.[8] By the end of 2022, it has concluded RMB clearing agreements with 17 BRI partner states,[9] which would help improve its cooperation in international financial supervision and regulation.

[7] Shangjie Zheng, *Great Achievements By China and BRI Countries Shared Future and Better Advancement of the BRI* (十年共建结硕果 携手共向未来 扎实推进高质量共建 "一带一路" 行稳致远), the Journal of Xi Jinping Economic Thoughts, No. 6, 2023, available at https://www.ndrc.gov.cn/xwdt/ztzl/srxxgcxjpjjsx/xjpjjsxjyqk/202309/t20230908_1360478.html, posted September 9, 2023, accessed November 2, 2023.

[8] https://en.ndrc.gov.cn/netcoo/achievements/202210/t20221027_1341511.html#:~:text=The%20RMB%20settlements%20climbed%2014.7%20percent%20in%20trade,in%20eight%20countries%20along%20the%20Belt%20and%20Road, posted Oct. 27, 2022, accessed November 5, 2023.

[9] Shangjie Zheng, *Great Achievements By China and BRI Countries Shared Future and Better Advancement of the BRI* (十年共建结硕果 携手共向未来 扎实推进高质量共建 "一带一路" 行稳致远), the Journal of Xi Jinping Economic Thoughts, No. 6, 2023, available at https://www.ndrc.gov.cn/xwdt/ztzl/srxxgcxjpjjsx/xjpjjsxjyqk/202309/t20230908_1360478.html, posted September 9, 2023, accessed November 2, 2023.

Capacity building. The BRI has the potential to intensify China's efforts to enhance capacity-building by providing planning, technical assistance, and personnel training to multiple economic sectors including agriculture, aquaculture, technology, public health, water and sanitation, and education. China provides trade aid to BRI emerging economies to help them expand transportation, port, and customs inspection services. In 2016, China provided funding for around 250 engineering and material projects, trained 29,000 personnel, dispatched about 5,000 aid experts, and delivered benefits to 156 countries and regional/ international organizations. In collaboration with the OECD, China established the Multilateral Tax Centre to strengthen its taxation implementation capacity (CMFA 2017; CDB & UNDP 2019).

Policy cooperation. Finally, Chinese policymakers assert that the BRI will promote intergovernmental cooperation, build multi-level intergovernmental macro policy exchanges, and enhance communication systems. Countries are encouraged, but not obliged, to fully coordinate their economic development strategies and policies, negotiate cooperation-related issues, and jointly provide policy support to implement cooperation and large-scale projects. This aspiration is in line with SDG 17.13–15, policy coherence for sustainable development (CDB & UNDP 2019). Chinese policymakers also reiterate its adherence to the market economy in its latest five-year plan, the contemporary international order and international law. It's claimed that BRI is coupled with regional as well as global development agendas.[10]

[10] PRC's 14th Five-Year Blueprint and National Economic and Social Development and Its 2035 Agenda.

Part XII High Quality Openness & Win–Win Game Chapter 41 High-Quality Development Along Belt & Road Countries. China promises to negotiate and consult with BRI countries, co-build BRI projects, in an environmentally friendly and socially inclusive way, share in development benefits, to deepen international cooperation and to strengthen security.

Section 1 Link BRI with regional and global development agents with regards to cooperation in financing, trade, energy, customs, taxation, regulation, and supervision, etc.

Section 2 build BRI transportation infrastructure projects and information highway and facilitate cross-border trade.

Section 3 Deepen economic and trade cooperation. China has pledged to adhere to market economy standards, international practices and usages, and sustainable debt principles, and to help diversify investment and financing services. Multilateral and foreign financial institutions are welcome to invest in BRI projects.

President Xi reiterated his commitment to many of these issues in his keynote speech at the Boao Forum for Asia (BFA) 2021 Annual Conference Opening Ceremony (April 20, 2021). Xi calls for a closer cooperation in COVID-19 control and a better governance for a global community of shared future.

1. Equality, negotiation, and cultivation for a win–win future. It's pledged that China adheres to genuine multilateralism oriented to just global governance. The world needs justice, not hegemony. Major countries ought to act as they are supposed to and shoulder more responsibilities.
2. Openness, innovation, and prosperity. Trade and investment must be facilitated. The regional economy needs to be deepened. World economies ought to be open where goods, services, data, and people would freely flow. Acts that violate economic law and market rules like building walls and decoupling with certain countries hurt both the actors and their target victims.

Section 4 Expand cultural exchanges. China will deepen cooperation in public health, infectious disease control, digital economy, climate change, desertification control, green development, wild animal protection, science and education, culture and in the arts. It will strengthen contacts between parliaments, political parties, NGOs, women organizations, youth organizations, and organizations of the disabled, etc.

Chapter 42 China will take a more active role in shaping better global governance.

Section 1 Adherence to multilateralism. It will work to maintain the multilateral trade system, help reform the WTO, while also safeguarding China's status as a developing country. It will develop more economic initiatives and development programs from China's perspective. The AIIB and NDB are supported. China is committed to help keep global financial markets stable grow the world economy, and to take a more active role in rulemaking in emerging industries.

Section 2 High-standard global free trade networks. Free trade strategies are going to be implemented. China is going to help enforce the Regional Comprehensive Economic Partnership (RCEP) agreement, speed up free trade negotiations with South Korea and Japan, and be ready to join the Transatlantic Trade and Investment Partnership (TTIP) agreement, etc.

Section 3 Good relations with foreign countries. China is going to continue developing partnerships with foreign countries, promote coordination and cooperation with major foreign countries, and deepen neighborly relations with neighboring countries and developing countries. It's committed to multilateralism, maintain the contemporary international order and international law centered on the UN, and actively implement the UNSDGs Agenda 2030.

http://www.gov.cn/xinwen/2021-03/13/content_5592681.htm, posted March 13, 2021, accessed November 9, 2023.

3. Mutual aid, global safety, and security. Strengthen cooperation in covid 19 control and climate change.
4. Adherence to justice, mutual respect, and learning. China objects to a new cold war, whichever form it might take, and ideological confrontation. All human societies share values of peace, security, fairness, justice, democracy, and freedom. Cultural exchanges are encouraged.

Xi stresses that BRI is committed to global sustainable development. It's pledged that China will keep helping build global peace, contribute to global growth, and maintain the international order; China will never dominate the world but take a more active role in multilateral trade and investment, helping build a better open economic regime. Foreign actors are welcome to share considerable opportunities in the Chinese market.[11]

4 BRI and SDGs: Concerns About Theoretical and Policy Gaps

The next section of this analysis will try to answer the question: what are the prospects for the BRI to achieve its many lofty goals? BRI implementation is still in its early stages. However, a growing body of research asserts that most BRI projects have not met expectations. One study reveals that nearly 250 BRI projects have increased environmental pollution or violated human rights in host countries. Critics have identified multiple policy, legal, regulatory, and financial gaps between SDG and BRI goals and objectives (Sarangi 2020; Heiduk and Sakaki 2019).

Hillman (2018) asserts that the BRI differs from the SDGs in five main areas.

First (4.1), apart from Articles 1–2, the *UN Charter*, the BRI is committed to the Five Principles rather than fully conforming to international law, including international instruments of human rights and environmental protection.

Second (4.2), the BRI has the potential to promote multilateral cooperation (Lajčák 2018). The AIIB is a good example of this. However,

[11] *Xi Jinping's Keynote Speech at Boao Forum for Asia 2021 Annual Conference Opening Ceremony*, http://news.cnr.cn/native/gd/20210420/t20210420_525466571.shtml, posted April 20, 2021, accessed November 9, 2023.

so far, most funded projects are Sino-foreign bilateral trade deals that adhere to China's unilaterally imposed rules or actions (Hillman 2017).[12] A related concern (4.2.1) is whether the BRI projects integrate internationally accepted environmental and social safeguards or not.

Third (4.3), the BRI may provide what the Belt and Road countries desperately want, namely, financing for infrastructure. However, many have asked serious questions about how BRI financing strategies potentially promote unsustainable sovereign debt obligations and debt dependency.

Fourth (4.4), most BRI projects seem to lack transparency. Detailed project information is not generally publicly available. Nor is data on monitoring or accountability.

Fifth (4.5), while the BRI pledges to promote policy coordination, its emphasis on bilateral deals, combined with incoherent domestic rules

[12] Since the BRI was launched, China has made new outbound investment rules that take into account environmental protection. Those rules include *Measures for the Administration of Overseas Investment* (Ministry of Commerce, 2014), *Measures for the Administration of Overseas Investment of Enterprises* (National Development and Reform Commission, 2018); *Provisional Rules Governing Key Information Reporting of Registered (Approved) Outbound Investment Projects* (Ministry of Commerce, 2018); *Guidelines for Environmental Protection in Foreign Investment and Cooperation* (Ministry of Commerce and Ministry of Environmental Protection); *Provisional Rules for Bad Credit Records in Outbound Investment and Foreign Trade* (Ministry of Commerce, Ministry of Foreign Affairs, Ministry of Public Security, Ministry of Housing and Urban–Rural Development, General Administration of Customs, State Administration of Taxation, State Administration for Industry and Commerce, General Administration of Quality Supervision, Inspection and Quarantine, and State Administration of Foreign Exchange, 2018); *Guidelines to Build the Green Belt and Road* (Ministry of Environmental Protection, 2017); *Outbound Investment Codes for Private Enterprises* (National Development and Reform Commission, Ministry of Commerce, People's Bank, Ministry of Foreign Affairs, and All-China Federation of Industry and Commerce, 2017); *Green Credit Guidelines* (Banking Regulatory Commission, 2013), in addition to the *Regulations on Contracting Foreign Projects* (State Council, 2008).

It's worth noting that all these rules mentioned above are administrative rules rather than legislation. All the new rules formulated recently are made by the ministries of the Chinese central government instead of the government itself. They are very low priority in the hierarchy of Chinese law meaning that penalties are light for violating them. In practice, they are neither well followed nor enforced. Even if they were enforced, it would not have much impact. They fall short of relevant international norms or "best practices" only requiring Chinese companies abide by the host country's local laws and regulations. In case of the BRI, due to weak environmental and social governance in a majority of BRI countries, those rules are far from sufficient to safeguard local environment and human rights.

relevant to the BRI is not conducive to promoting policy coherence needed to achieve SDGs.

4.1 *Integration with Existing Global Governance Frameworks*

To what extent is BRI fully integrated with existing environmental global governance frameworks, and especially the Sustainable Development Goals initiative? SDGs are aligned with many *UN Charter* principles and related international laws and treaties. Some of these foundational documents include the *Universal Declaration of Human Rights* and other international human rights treaties,[13] the *Millennium Declaration* (UNGA 2000), and the *2005 World Summit Outcome* (UNGA 2005). They are informed by other instruments such as the *Declaration on the Right to Development* (UNGA 1986), and reaffirm all the principles of the *Rio Declaration on Environment and Development* (UNCED 1992). SDGs address numerous concrete steps required to achieve the Goals, supported by the concrete policies and actions outlined in the *Addis Ababa Action Agenda* (AAAA 2015).

The Chinese government states that it steadfastly adheres to the Five Principles. Those principles were first codified in the *Agreement between the Republic of India and the People's Republic of China on Trade and Intercourse between Tibet Region of China and India* (1954).[14] They are partly a response to the decolonization movement and were adopted to deal with international relations during the Cold War Era. They do not substantively address global governance or development while highlighting peaceful co-existence. The BRI is supposed to be "non-ideological" but underpinned by "equal negotiations and consultations, non-intervention and observance of international rules" (Jin & Jin 2018). In contrast, the SDGs acknowledge there can be no world peace without sustainable development. SDGs strengthen universal peace and human

[13] The core international human rights treaty collection can be accessed at, https://www.ohchr.org/EN/ProfessionalInterest/Pages/CoreInstruments.aspx.

[14] Preamble: The Government of the Republic of India and the Central People's Government of the People's Republic of China, have resolved to enter into the present Agreement based on the following principles: (1) mutual respect of each other's territorial integrity and sovereignty; (2) mutual non-aggression; (3) mutual non-interference in each other's internal affairs; (4) equality and mutual benefit; and (5) peaceful co-existence. (No. 4307 UN-Treaty Series, https://treaties.un.org/doc/publication/unts/volume%20299/v299.pdf).

rights. They fully respect international law, including best practices and codes relating to environmental and social safeguards. The 2030 Agenda emphasizes the responsibilities of all States, in conformity with the *UN Charter*, to respect, protect, and promote human rights and fundamental freedoms for all (UN 2015).

4.2 Multilateral Governance Norms, Laws, and Treaties Gap

Are the PRC and other national partners fully engaged and integrated with multilateral governance norms, laws, and treaties? Also, do BRI projects apply globally accepted environmental and social safeguards? As John Ikenberry and John Ruggie suggest, multilateralism forms the core of the current international order that the United States promoted after World War II (Ikenberry 2012; Ruggie 1992). Multilateral rules apply to all participant countries.[15] The UN President of the General Assembly says that multilateralism is a cornerstone of the BRI (Lajčák 2018). However, BRI projects rarely exhibit quantity-based or quality-based multilateralism. So far, most BRI agreements are bilateral rather than multilateral except for agreements involving the AIIB and/or NDB. Hameiri and Jones (2018) note that the AIIB is not deeply involved in BRI projects (Hameiri & Jones 2018). Jun and Zadec (2019) point out that China does not require BRI recipients to adhere to specific sustainable development standards or take the carbon intensity of projects into account. Since emerging economies are slated to grow more quickly in the coming years, promoting green investments will have a more significant impact in reducing future emissions (Jun & Zadec 2019).

[15] A Chinese law professor coins a new term "Chinese multilateralism." According to him, an agreement applicable to only three of all the BRI countries, e.g., China-Mongolia-Russia Economic Corridor Framework, would be a typical Chinese multilateral agreement. See GU Bin, Globalization and Governance of the Belt and Road Initiative: A Soft Law Approach, Foreign Affairs Review, Vol. 39, No. 4, 2022, pp. 1–28.

Up to date, China has concluded 205 BRI agreements with 152 countries and 32 international organizations.[16] All BRI agreements are bilateral. There is no single universal BRI rule that applies to all BRI countries. BRI rules are little more than a patchwork of various Sino-foreign bilateral regulations and China's unilateral policies. This is somewhat consistent from the perspective of the Five Principles. However, bilateral rules and/or unilateral policies will hardly help achieve SDGs, particularly SDG 17.10 (to "promote a universal, rules-based, open, non-discriminatory and equitable multilateral trading system under the WTO"), unless they adhere to contemporary international norms and standards (Tago 2017). Again, due to the Five Principles and weak governance of most BRI countries, BRI rules, bilateral and unilateral, will not help SDGs implementation. Instead, they fail to foster a better-integrated world market. They may disrupt the current international order and thus hamper SDG progress. Additionally, those various bilateral rules fall short of international norms, and standards work against the policy coherence needed to achieve the SDGs.

4.2.1 Global Governance and Environmental and Social Safeguards Gap

Private financial institutions from Western countries have generally subscribed to international environmental and social standards under the "Equator Principles" (EP).[17] China's BRI approach is more flexible, less bureaucratic. It includes less stringent requirements for meeting social and environmental safeguards included in relevant international instruments, like the *Guiding Principles on Business and Human Rights* and the labor

[16] Shangjie Zheng, *Great Achievements By China and BRI Countries Shared Future and Better Advancement of the BRI* (十年共建结硕果 携手共向未来 扎实推进高质量共建 "一带一路" 行稳致远), the Journal of Xi Jinping Economic Thoughts, No. 6, 2023, available at https://www.ndrc.gov.cn/xwdt/ztzl/srxxgcxjpjjsx/xjpjjsxjyqk/202309/t20230908_1360478.html, posted September 9, 2023, accessed November 2, 2023. This link deleted is not available any longer.

[17] The principles are: [A] risk management framework, adopted by financial institutions, for determining, assessing, and managing environmental and social risk in projects. It is primarily intended to provide a minimum standard for due diligence to support responsible risk decision-making. Currently, Equator Principles Financial Institutions (EPFIs) in 36 countries have officially adopted the EP, covering 70% of international Project Finance debt in emerging markets (Equator Principles Associate 2011).

standards of the International Labor Organization (ILO), the *Convention on the Rights of the Child* (CRC), and key multilateral environmental agreements (Hillman 2017).

In contrast, China is a significant funder of mining and energy infrastructure projects. Such projects typically carry substantial environmental risks and often involve the involuntary resettlement of large numbers of people (Chen et al. 2016). So far, China has been reluctant to accept international standards for social and ecological safeguards formally whereas Chinese investors are supposed to be subject to the host countries' institutional framework (Zhang 2021). Notwithstanding its recent "green" lending guidelines, China while investing outbound follows the laws and regulations of the host country rather than international norms. This position is consistent with the Five Principles. However over-reliance on investment recipient country domestic and regulations creates massive risks for poorly governed states (Hameiri & Jones 2018). Chinese government statistics reveal that half of the Chinese enterprises operating in BRI countries failed to conduct social impact assessments before commencing their projects, while over a third neglected environmental impact assessments. Ignorance of local regulations is rife, suggesting widespread violation of Chinese rules (Hameiri & Jones 2018). In Gabon, Sinopec was found exploring for oil in Loango National Park before any environmental impact study. There are other similar cases, including the Congou Dam in Gabon, the Bui Dam in Ghana, and the Lower Kafue Gorge Dam in Zambia. All of these cases call for a careful balance of development needs with environmental risks (Dollar 2017; Song et al. 2016; Xue and Wang 2018).

The AIIB has promulgated environmental and social policies that, on paper, are similar to the principles embodied in World Bank safeguards. These include environmental and social assessments to analyze risks, timely public disclosure of project information, consultation with affected parties, and decision-making that incorporates these risks.

Also, AIIB policies differ from World Bank standards in essential ways. The AIIB does not require detailed prescriptions for how to manage the project lending process but indicates that "the level of detail and the complexity of the ESMP (environmental and social management plan) should be proportional to the risks and impacts of the Project." (43 Proportionality, AIIB Environmental and Social Framework, as amended 2021). The AIIB's leadership aspires to meet international standards but prioritizes quick and cost-effective measures. If AIIB encourages the

World Bank and the Asian Development Bank (ADB) to streamline their procedures and speed up their infrastructure projects, it would positively change the global system built by Chinese investment and leadership (Song et al. 2016).

4.3 Financial and Trade Governance and Debt Sustainability

Gaps in multilateral coordination can be clearly identified in how BRI projects are planned and financed. Also, there are serious questions about whether the BRI funding arrangements safeguard recipients from taking on excessive debt obligations or not. If infrastructure is a critical engine of growth in developing economies, then debt financing is the fuel that keeps the machine going (Hurley et al. 2018). The BRI spans at least 68 countries with announced investments as high as $8 trillion to build a vast network of transportation, energy, and telecommunications facilities and services linking Europe, Africa, and Asia (Hurley et al. 2018). However, the empirical literature identifies serious economic, political, and social risks when governments incur too much debt (Presbitero 2016). Overbuilding can also slow economic growth (Warner 2014), which is particularly relevant in light of the BRI "big-push" approach to fund infrastructure investment (Hurley et al. 2018; Presbitero 2016).

Some experts and numerous press reports have expressed alarm about how the BRI may threaten debt sustainability (Heydarian 2017; Krakowska 2017; Zhang and Miller 2017). The primary concern is that an $8 trillion-dollar initiative may foster debt "overcharge," impeding sound public investment and economic growth. According to a recent analysis by the Center for Global Development (CGD), the BRI is unlikely to cause regional systemic debt problems (Hurley et al. 2018). However, researchers found that 23 BRI countries are currently at risk for debt distress. These states include Cambodia, Mongolia, Laos, Afghanistan, Bhutan, Kyrgyzstan, Maldives, Pakistan, Sri Lanka, Tajikistan, Djibouti, Egypt, Ethiopia, Iraq, Jordan, Kenya, and Lebanon, Albania, Armenia, Belarus, Bosnia and Herzegovina, Montenegro, and Ukraine. Eight states are of particular concern. They include Djibouti, Kyrgyzstan, Laos, the Maldives, Mongolia, Pakistan, and Tajikistan (Hurley et al. 2018). According to a recent Nikkei Asian Review and The Banker magazine report, the BRI has hit a roadblock in seven countries—Indonesia, Sri Lanka, Kazakhstan, Bangladesh, Poland, Laos, and Pakistan. The report details problems ranging from BRI projects' tendency to not provide enough jobs to local workers and excessive public debt (ET 2018).

Sovereign debt sustainability is a common concern of multilateral financial institutions like the International Monetary Fund (IMF) Sovereign Debt Restructuring Mechanism (SDRM) or multilateral mechanisms like the Paris Club[18] and the London Club.[19] However, China seldom participates in multilateral approaches to debt relief. Instead, the Chinese government provides debt relief in an ad hoc, case-by-case manner and does not disclose details about bilateral debt agreements (Hurley et al. 2018). China's policy banks, e.g. CDB, EXIM, etc., do not disclose the terms of their loans, making it difficult to assess the present value of the debt obligations accurately. Anecdotal evidence from media and IMF reports indicates that the terms of CDB and EXIM loans vary widely, from interest-free loans in some Pakistan projects to market-rate loans, e.g., Ethiopia-Djibouti railway project. More precisely, Peking University professor Muyang Chen finds out that the loans provided by Chinese policy banks are "a mixture of official aid and export credits" which "in most cases are non-concessional and surprisingly costly" (Chen 2020). Chen sings praises to this new means of development finance with Chinese characteristics ("state-supported, market-based") as well as its exportation to BRI countries, and looks forward very much to its reshaping of international development finance. However, he acknowledges that it is "peculiar," if not unique to China's own development experience, and whether it would be sustainable remains questionable (Chen 2020). While managing its bilateral debt problems, Chinese expectations in exchange for debt relief vary widely. Some are overtly political and infringe on the sovereignty of recipient nations. They

[18] The Paris Club is an informal group of official creditors whose role is to find coordinated and sustainable solutions to payment difficulties experienced by debtor countries. As debtor countries undertake reforms to stabilize and restore their macroeconomic and financial situations, Paris Club creditors are expected to ensure appropriate debt treatment. China appears to be an ad hoc participant that has never participated as a creditor in any Paris Club Agreements or Tours d'Horizon, http://www.clubdeparis.org/en/. This might help explain why some scholars say that China is an observer, not ad hoc participant, of the Paris Club (John Hurley, Scott Morris, and Gailyn Portelance, *Examining the Debt Implications of the Belt and Road Initiative from a Policy Perspective*, CGD Policy Paper 121, March 2018, p. 19).

[19] The London Club is a multilateral forum that assists with rescheduling sovereign debt to commercial banks.

include demands to return disputed territory (Hurley et al. 2018),[20] additional trade credits and financing for port rehabilitation (Hurley et al. 2018),[21] and demands for long-term leases for critical infrastructure such as ports, etc. (Hurley et al. 2018).[22]

4.4 *Transparency Gap*

Do BRI frameworks and related projects exhibit widespread transparency and public disclosure about their operations? SDGs supporters view transparent, adequate, and accountable institutions as central underpinnings of peaceful, just, and inclusive societies (UN 2015). BRI policymakers advocate openness and rule orientation (Wang Yi 2018). However, their actions eschew transparency and accountability. As has already been stated, BRI project information is seldom published or reported transparently. Projects funded by the AIIB and NDB are exceptions (Hameiri and Jones 2018). Basic project information is publicly available. The AIIB and NDB are multilateral development banks and follow MDB practices set by the World Bank. Most BRI projects are funded by Chinese banks and undertaken by Chinese State-Owned enterprises. CDB and EXIM are the largest among those Chinese lenders (CDB & UNDP 2019).[23] They are subject to Chinese and partner country domestic laws rather than international standards or norms.

Wang (2019) acknowledges that BRI projects need to be rule-based, open, and transparent in time. Sarangi (2020) points out that transparency is critically important to the implementation of BRI projects. Stakeholders need to have a reliable way to determine whether the BRI

[20] In 2011, China reportedly agreed to write off an unknown amount of debt owed by Tajikistan in exchange for some 1158 square kilometers of disputed territory).

[21] Also in 2011, China agreed to restructure between $4–6 billion of debt owed by Cuba in exchange for additional trade credits and financing for port rehabilitation.

[22] In 2017, in response to Sri Lanka's unwillingness to service an $8 billion loan at 6% interest used to finance the construction of the Hambantota Port, China agreed to a debt-for-equity swap accompanied by a 99-year lease for managing the port).

[23] According to E. Wragg's estimates, CDB and EXIM together provide more international development finance more than the World Bank (WB), the Asian Development Bank (ADB) and the Inter-American Development Bank (IADB) combined. E. Wragg, Analysis: From Belt and Rode to Stars and Stripes, Global Trade Review, December 17, 2018.

projects are achieving their stated objectives or not. Sustainable development can only be achieved through deeds (Sarangi 2020). Horvath (2016) adds that timely monitoring of relevant indicators is necessary to identify progress as well as shortcomings in project implementation.

4.5 Policy Coherence Gap

Does the BRI framework demonstrate effective multi-level policy coherence and coordination (global, national, and project level)? Policy coherence is one of the main objectives of SDG 17, Partnership. It is not included in crucial BRI documents. The BRI seeks, in principle, to promote policy cooperation but fails to identify any specific cooperation targets or outline any concrete steps to do so (Rolland 2017). BRI countries are encouraged but not obliged to cooperate or coordinate policymaking to achieve policy coherence. Under the Five Principles, all sovereign states technically do not need to adhere to international law when making their own policy choices. No clear definition of a BRI project is described in detail, so it is difficult to differentiate between BRI and other types of initiatives. These issues complicate policy implementation. The principles underpinning the BRI and various Sino-foreign bilateral agreements do not promote policy coherence (CNDRC et al. 2015; Haiduk & Sakaki 2019).

Even China's BRI domestic institutions, rules, and regulations lack coherence. Dozens of government departments are involved in policy formation and implementation. Although a State Council leading small group (LSG) for advancing BRI development was formed in late 2014 or early 2015, its membership appears small. It excludes key agencies, and its authority overlaps with several others, notably finance and foreign affairs LSGs. Accordingly, despite creating the AIIB, the BRI system will continue to be incoherent, even contradictory, far from a policy coherence perspective (Hameiri & Jones 2018).

Private business activity, investment, and innovation are significant drivers of productivity, inclusive economic growth, and job creation (Addis Ababa Agenda for Action 2015). Public–Private Partnerships are set to play an increasingly important complementary role in BRI projects. By the end of April 2017, 865 PPP projects had been implemented in 64 counties along the Belt and Road associated with a total investment of $509 billion (CDB & UNDP 2019). However, the BRI does not recognize a significant role for private sector actors. The Chinese government, through its SOEs, is heavily involved in business activities and mostly excludes partner country contractors. Suppose it recognized the importance of private sector players in the market and society. In that case, it might pay more attention to making coherent policies committed to fostering a dynamic and well-functioning market. It may also garner more public support in partner countries.

One strategy for encouraging private sector involvement while also increasing transparency is to put a price on carbon. Carbon pricing allows firms to integrate the cost of carbon pollution into their standard operating procedures while also revealing the financial status of firms along with their carbon emissions. Carbon pricing encourages firms to identify strategies that will increase resource efficiency, adopt renewable energy, and gain economic benefits from selling excess carbon offsets in public carbon markets (Horvath 2016).

5 Conclusion

The BRI, which officially commits China to sustainable development principles as stated in the 2030 Agenda, has the potential to act as a powerful catalyst to achieve SDGs. China has previously provided support to more than 120 developing countries to help them achieve the Millennium Development Goals (CMFA 2017). China has stated that the BRI should contribute to sustainable development (CNDRC et al. 2015)and will facilitate the implementation of the UNSDGs 2030 Agenda. In his keynote speech at the opening ceremony of the BRI International Collaboration and Cooperation Summit Forum, President Xi Jinping stated that Sino-foreign trades would be expected to amount to more than $37 trillion in five years (2024–2028), 32 trillion in goods and 5 trillion in services, that an extra 350 billion RMB lending instrument would be provided by each China Development Bank and the Import Export Bank of China, and 80 billion RMB capital increase would be made to the Silk Road Fund. According to him, more than $97.2 billion valued project agreements have been concluded during the Entrepreneurs Congress of the 3rd BRI Forum for International Cooperation; and China is going to implement 1000 well-being projects.[24]

[24] Xi Jinping, Keynote Speech at the Opening Ceremony of the 3rd BRI Forum for International Cooperation, https://news.sina.com.cn/gov/xlxw/2023-10-18/doc-imzrpcqp3164877.shtml, posted October 18, 2023, accessed November 9, 2023.

However, this analysis concludes that significant gaps remain between the BRI framework and its lofty objectives.

- The BRI is based on dozens of individual Sino-foreign bilateral agreements and PRC-mandated unilateral rules. BRI bilateral agreements and unilateral rules sometimes fall short of international standards and/or norms of environmental and social safeguards.
- The BRI framework does not include meaningful requirements for funding recipients to integrate sustainable development principles or carry out rigorous environmental assessments. Domestic recipient rather than international standards dictate how projects are planned and implemented.
- Debt sustainability and trade governance remain significant concerns. More than 20 BRI partner countries are at risk of financial hardship due to excessive debt service requirements. There is little coordination between Chinese funding entities and multilateral institutions.
- Inadequate policy and project transparency is an endemic problem. Public information about BRI projects is scarce. Financial metrics used to measure policy effectiveness are lacking. Stakeholders often lack meaningful strategies to evaluate how BRI projects affect their political, economic, and social lives. Internationally accepted human rights laws and norms are largely ignored.
- Promoting policy clarity and coordination are stated BRI objectives. However, China's BRI bureaucracy, rules, and regulations lack coherence. Also, the BRI does not recognize a significant role in private sector investment.

Going forward, the best strategy for achieving BRI success is to harmonize it more fully with the 2030 Agenda. Doing this will allow the BRI to sustain and be sustained by SDGs and promote global development. Harmonization will also reduce suspicions of strategic mistrust felt by some states and stakeholders in the international arena (Table 1).

Table 1 The seventeen sustainable development goals

Goal 1. End poverty in all its forms everywhere
Goal 2. End hunger, achieve food security and improved nutrition, and promote sustainable agriculture
Goal 3. Ensure healthy lives and promote well-being for all
Goal 4. Ensure inclusive and equitable quality education and promote lifelong learning opportunities for all
Goal 5. Achieve gender equality and empower all women and girls
Goal 6. Ensure availability and sustainable management of water and sanitation for all
Goal 7. Ensure access to affordable, reliable, sustainable, and modern energy for all
Goal 8. Promote sustained, inclusive, and sustainable economic growth, full and productive employment, and decent work for all
Goal 9. Build resilient infrastructure, promote inclusive and sustainable industrialization, and foster innovation
Goal 10. Reduce inequality within and among countries
Goal 11. Make cities and human settlements inclusive, safe, resilient, and sustainable
Goal 12. Ensure sustainable consumption and production patterns
Goal 13. Take urgent action to combat climate change and its impacts
Goal 14. Conserve and sustainably use the oceans, seas, and marine resources for sustainable development
Goal 15. Protect, restore, and promote sustainable use of terrestrial ecosystems, sustainably manage forests, combat desertification, and halt and reverse land degradation and halt biodiversity loss
Goal 16. Promote peaceful and inclusive societies for sustainable development, provide access to justice for all, and build effective, accountable, and inclusive institutions at all levels
Goal 17. Strengthen the means of implementation and revitalize the Global Partnership for Sustainable Development

Source The United Nations Department of Economic and Social Affairs, *The 17 Goals*, https://sdgs.un.org/goals, accessed January 12, 2019. Goals in bold type are directly linked to BRI objectives

References

Addis Ababa Action Agenda, 2015, endorsed by the UN General Assembly in its resolution 69/313 of July 27, 2015.

Africa's Agenda 2063, http://archive.au.int/assets/images/agenda2063.pdf.

AIIB 2018 Business Plan and Budget (Summary), January 2018, https://www.aiib.org/en/policies-strategies/_download/business-plan-2018/2018-Business-Plan-and-Budget.pdf.

Asian Infrastruction and Investment Bank. AIIB Environmental and Social Framework, 2021, website.

B&R by the Numbers: Enterprises Need to Be Prepared for B&R Projects, https://eng.yidaiyilu.gov.cn/jcsj/dsjkydyl/40513.htm, posted December 21, 2017, accessed August 4, 2018.

Chen, J., H. Shi, B. Sivakumar, and M.R. Peart, Population, Food, Water, Energy and Dams, *Renewable and Sustainable Energy Reviews* 56 (April 2016), 18–28.

Chen, M., Beyond Donation: China's Policy Banks and the Reshaping of Development Finance, *Studies in Comparative International Development* 55 (2020), 436–459.

China Development Bank & UNDP, Harmonizing Investment and Financing Standards towards Sustainable Development along the Belt and Road: Economic Development along the Belt and Road (2019), November 2019, http://www.un.org.cn/uploads/20191108/bbb5cee285b9e35d7de574f4e9e4f6df.pdf, accessed April 27, 2021.

China's Ministry of Foreign Affairs, *China's Progress Report on Implementation of the 2030 Agenda for Sustainable Development*, August 2017, p. 11.

China's National Development and Reform Commission, Ministry of Foreign Affairs and Ministry of Commerce, with the State Council authorization, *Vision and Actions on Jointly Building Silk Road Economic Belt and 21st-Century Maritime Silk Road*, https://eng.yidaiyilu.gov.cn/qwyw/qwfb/1084.htm, posted March 30, 2015, accessed July 31, 2018.

Cockburn, J., Y. Dissou, J. Duclos, and L. Tiberti, ed., *Infrastructure and Economic Growth in Asia*, Springer International Publishing, 2013, p. 6.

Development Policy Analysis Division (DPAD) of the UN Department of Economic and Social Affairs, *Strengthening National Policy Capacity for Jointly Building the Belt and Road towards the Sustainable Development Goals*, 2017, https://www.un.org/en/unpdf/sdg-2016-02.

Dollar, D., *China as a Global Investor*, 2017, p. 12, https://www.brookings.edu/wp-content/uploads/2016/07/China-as-a-Global-Investor_Asia-Working-Paper-4-2.pdf.

Economic Times, https://economictimes.indiatimes.com/news/international/world-news/chinas-bri-initiative-hits-roadblock-in-7-countries-report/articleshow/63771550.cms, updated April 15, 2018, accessed August 3, 2018.

Haiduk, F., and A. Sakaki, *Introduction to the Special Issue—China's Belt and Road Initiative: The View from East Asia,* East Asia 36 (2019) 93–113.

Hameiri, S., and L. Jones, China Challenges Global Governance? Chinese International Development Finance and the AIIB, *International Affairs* 94:3 (2018) 573–593; https://doi.org/10.1093/ia/iiy026, pp. 575–579.

Hasan, R. et al., *Meeting Asia's Infrastructure Needs*, Asian Development Bank, February 2017, https://www.adb.org/news/asia-infrastructure-needs-exceed-17-trillion-year-double-previous-estimates.

Heydarian, R. J. *China's Silk Road Project: A Trap or an Opportunity*, https://www.aljazeera.com/indepth/opinion/2017/05/china-silk-road-project-trap-opportunity-170514142652061.html, posted May 17, 2017, accessed August 18, 2018 ("China's trading partners are concerned that the new Silk Road project may get them stuck in 'debt-trap' diplomacy").

Hillman, J., *Belt and Road Summit: Beijing's Push on Trade*, The Cipher Brief, May 2, 2017, https://www.thecipherbrief.com/belt-and-road-summit-beijing-push-on-trade-2, p. 5.

Hillman, J., *China's Belt and Road Initiative: Five Years Later*, January 25, 2018, https://www.csis.org/analysis/chinas-belt-and-road-initiative-five-years-later-0, accessed August 3, 2018.

Hong, P., *Strengthening National Policy Capacity for Jointly Building the Belt and Road Towards the Sustainable Development Goals*, a Capacity Development Project Financed by UN Peace and Development Trust Fund (UNPDF), 2017, https://www.un.org/development/desa/dpad/wp-content/uploads/sites/45/publication/2017_cdas_beltandroadb.pdf.

Horvath, B., *Identifying Development Initiative along the BRI*, UNDP Scoping Paper, 2016, https://www.undp.org/content/dam/china/docs/Publications/UNDP-CH-BRI%202017%20Scoping%20Paper1%20%EF%BC%88Final%EF%BC%89.pdf, accessed February 4, 2019.

Hurley, J., S. Morris, and G. Portelance, *Examining the Debt Implications of the Belt and Road Initiative from a Policy Perspective*, CGD Policy Paper 121, March 2018, p. 3.

Ikenberry, J., *Liberal Leviathan: The Origins, Crisis, and Transformation of the World Order*, Princeton: Princeton University Press, 2012.

Jin, C., and J. Jin, *China's Criticial Task in its Peaceful Development and BRI's Role Therein*, 2018, http://www.people.com.cn.

Joy-Perez, C., & Derek Scissors, *The Chinese State Funds Belt and Road but Does not Have Trillion to Spare*, p. 2 (Source: American Enterprise Institute and Heritage Foundation, Chinese Global Investment Tracker), 2018, https://www.aei.org/research-products/report/the-chinese-state-funds-belt-and-road-but-does-not-have-trillions-to-spare/.

Jun, M., and Simon Zadec, *A Low-Carbon Belt and Road*, Project Syndicate, March 28, 2019.

Małgosia Krakowska's interview with Sijbren de Jong, a strategic analyst at The Hague Centre for Strategic Studies: China's One Belt One Road Initiative-A Push for Influence or Debt? http://neweasterneurope.eu/2017/09/27/china-s-one-belt-one-road-initiative-a-push-for-influence-or-debt/, posted September 27, 2017, accessed August 18, 2018 ("Countries with a poor trade balance … may benefit from the Chinese loans but also see their debt burden increase as result").

Mckinsey Global Institute, *Bridging Global Infrastructure Gaps*, 2016, p. 2.

Miroslav Lajčák, President of the 72nd Session on the UN General Assembly, at High-Level Symposium on "Belt and Road Initiative and 2030 Agenda for Sustainable Development", https://www.un.org/pga/72/2018/06/13/high-level-symposium-on-belt-and-road-initiative-and-2030-agenda-for-sustainable-development/, posted June 13, 2018, accessed July 30, 2018.

New Partnership for Africa's Development, https://www.nepad.org.

NDB 2017 Annual Financial Statement, https://www.ndb.int/wp-content/uploads/2018/06/NDB-2017-Annual-Financial-Statements.pdf.

Presbitero, A.F., Too Much and Too Fast? Public Investment Scaling-up and Absorptive Capacity, *Journal of Development Economics* 120 (May 2016), 17–31, pp. 17, 30.

Rolland, N., China's Belt and Road Initiative: Underwhelming or Game Changer, *The Washington Quarterly* 40:1 (2017), 127–142.

Ruggie, J., Multilateralism: The Anatomy of An Institution, *International Organizations* 46:3 (Summer 1992), 561–598.

Sarangi, U., Belt and Road Initiative and Transformation of Economies for Achieving Global Sustainable Development, *ABSM Journal of Management*, 13:1 (2020), 108–119.

Song, L., C. Fang Garnaut, and L. Johnston, *China's New Sources of Economic Growth*, Vol. 1, ANU Press, 2016, pp. 205–206, available at http://www.jstor.org/stable/j.ctt1rrdn9.16.

Tago, A., *Multilateralism, Bilateralism, and Unilateralism in Foreign Policy*, Oxford Research Encyclopedia of Politics, 2017, https://doi.org/10.1093/acrefore/9780190228637.013.449, p. 7.

UN, International Covenant on Economic, Social and Cultural Rights, 1967, https://treaties.un.org/doc/treaties/1976/01/19760103%2009-57%20pm/ch_iv_03.pdf

UN Charter, https://www.un.org/en/about-us/un-charter/chapter-1

UN, *Report of the Fourth UN Conference on the Least Developed Countries* (Istanbul, Turkey, May 2011), pp. 1–55, http://unohrlls.org/UserFiles/File/A-CONF_219-7%20report%20of%20the%20conference.pdf, accessed August 1, 2018.

UN, *Report on the Third International Conference on Small Island Developing States* (Apia, Samoa, September 2014), pp. 4–34.

UN, *Transforming our World: The 2030 Agenda for Sustainable Development*, 2015, http://www.un.org/ga/search/view_doc.asp?symbol=A/RES/70/1&Lang=E

UN, *Vienna Program of Action for Landlocked Developing Countries for the Decade 2014–2024*, http://www.lldc2conference.org/custom-content/uploads/2014/11/Vienna-Programme-of-Action1.pdf.

UNCED, *The Rio Declaration on Environment and Development*, June 14, 1992, http://www.unesco.org/education/pdf/RIO_E.PDF.

UNGA, *United Nations Universal Declaration of Human Rights*, 1948, http://www.un.org/en/universal-declaration-human-rights/index.html.

UNGA, *Declaration on the Right to Development*, December 4, 1986, https://www.ohchr.org/Documents/ProfessionalInterest/rtd.pdf.

UNGA, *United Nations Millennium Declaration*, September 8, 2000, http://www.un.org/millennium/declaration/ares552e.htm/.

UNGA, *2005 World Summit Outcome: A Resolution Adopted by the General Assembly*, October 24, 2005, http://www.un.org/womenwatch/ods/A-RES-60-1-E.pdf.

United Nations Department of Economic and Social Affairs, *The 17 Goals*, https://sdgs.un.org/goals, accessed January 12, 2019.

United Nations, *The Sustainable Development Goals Report 2018*, https://unstats.un.org/sdgs/files/report/2018/TheSustainableDevelopmentGoalsReport2018-EN.pdf.

Wang, Y., *The International Economic Order under BRI: Development-Based or Rule-Based*, North Eastern Asia Forum, No. 1, 2019, 78–91.

Wang Y., *Wang Yi On Sino-UK BRI Cooperation: Open, Inclusive & Rule-Based*, https://www.fmprc.gov.cn/web/zyxw/t1581380.shtml, posted July 30, 2018, accessed April 26, 2021.

Warner, A., *Public Investment as an Engine of Growth*, IMF Working Papers 14/148. International Monetary Fund, 2014, p. 8.

Wei, L., *The Belt and Road Initiative: A Bellwether of China's role in Global Governance*, Carnegie-Singhua Center for Global Policy, 2018, https://carnegietsinghua.org/2018/09/10/belt-and-road-initiative-bellwether-of-china-s-role-in-global-governance-pub-77204, accessed January 15, 2020.

World Bank, *Sustainable Development*, 2015, https://doi.org/10.1596/978-1-4648-0484-7_sustainable_development.

Xi, Jinping, Work Together to Build the Silk Road Economic Belt and the 21st Century Maritme Silk Road, Keynote speech at the opening ceremony of the Belt and Road Forum for International Cooperation, Xinhuanet, May 14, 2017. http://www.xinhuanet.com/english/2017-05/14/c_136282982.htm, posted May 14, 2017, accessed February 14, 2019.

Xue, L., and L. Wang, Thoughts on China's Belt and Road Initiative for Promoting UN 2030 Sustainable Development Goal, *Journal of Chinese Science Academy* 33:1 (2018), pp. 43–44.

Zhang, S., and M. Miller, *Behind China's Silk Road Vision: Cheap Funds, Heavy Debt, Growing Risk*, https://www.reuters.com/article/us-china-silkroad-finance/behind-chinas-silk-road-vision-cheap-funds-heavy-debt-growing-risk-idUSKCN18B0YS, posted May 15, 2017, accessed August 18, 2018.

Zhang, Y., Understanding China's Dam- Induced Resettlement under the Institutiionalised Governance Process of Policy Coevolution, *Journal of Environmental Management* 283 (April 2021), 111968.

CHAPTER 5

Creating Legitimacy and Exercising Political Power: An Analysis of the Functions of the Chinese Constitutional Preamble Based on a Linguistic Study

Kathrin Tremml

1 Introduction: Language as a Political Tool

Although many linguistically trained Sinologists show interest in the Chinese legal system, including the Constitution, it appears that a comprehensive linguistic study of the Chinese constitutional preamble has yet to be conducted. In articles where it is anticipated that such a study would be conducted due to their subject matter or scope, the preamble is merely examined as a speech act[1] or semantic analysis is limited to the

[1] *Cao*, Chinese Law: A Language Perspective, 2016, 122–140.

K. Tremml (✉)
Ludwig Maximilian University of Munich, Munich, Germany
e-mail: kathrin.tremml@jura.uni-muenchen.de

A. Aliu (ed.), *Complexity Thinking and China's Demography Within and Beyond Mainland China*,
https://doi.org/10.1007/978-981-97-0172-8_5

extent necessary to capture its legal content.[2] Alternatively, some articles concentrate on specific linguistic anomalies or consist of only very general observations and, quite often, praise such as: '*On the whole, the Preamble to our Constitution is concise in its choice of words, precise in its expression, solemn in its language and fluent in its writing*'.[3] The lack of thorough exploration of this subject is particularly surprising considering that Mao Zedong in particular, as well as many contemporary and subsequent leaders in China, were known to have relied on the power of words and language, employing linguistic devices in a deliberate and highly nuanced manner. Hence, it can be presumed that nothing was left to chance regarding the wording and style of such a pivotal text as the preamble of the Constitution.[4]

The language employed in preambles differs from that used in the substantive articles of the Constitution and other legal documents. Generally, the language of preambles is characterized by its ambiguity, vagueness, and a sense of grandeur and emotion. Constitutional preambles employ a variety of language styles, including solemn, celebratory, and simple, everyday language, rather than exclusively relying on technical, legal language.[5] This observation stems from the fact that preambles serve a wide variety of non-legal functions, which is reflected in their atypical use of non-legal language. There exists an interrelation between function and language, and the stylistic elements of preambles play a vital role in fulfilling these non-legal functions.[6] Preambles serve a wide range of non-legal purposes, including expressive, identifying, evocative, and educational functions.[7]

[2] *Chen Yushan* 陈玉山, 中国宪法序言研究 [A Study of the Chinese Constitutional Preamble], 2016, 30–50.

[3] *Yang Linhong* 杨临宏/*Liu Yamei* 刘亚梅, 宪法序言比较研究 [A Comparative Study on Constitutional Preambles], Guangdong xingzheng xueyuan xuebao 广东行政学院学报, Vol. 15, No. 5, 2003, 53 (57); similar also *Pu Zengyuan* 浦增元, 宪草序言的基本特点 [The Basic Characteristics of the Preamble of the Constitutional Draft], Zhengzhi yu falü 政治与法律, No. 1, 1982, 25 (26) and *Xu Chongde* 许崇德, 中华人民共和国宪法史 [The History of the Constitution of the People's Republic of China], 2003, 770.

[4] *Schoenhals*, Doing Things with Words in Chinese Politics, 1992, 3–4.

[5] *Häberle*, Präambeln im Text und Kontext von Verfassungen, in: FS Broermann, 1982, 211 (227–229); see also *Voermans/Stremler/Cliteur*, Constitutional Preambles, 2017, 81–83.

[6] See e.g., *Voermans/Stremler/Cliteur* (n. 5), 83–88, 151.

[7] *Voermans/Stremler/Cliteur* (n. 5), 91–94.

Considering this interplay between function and language, as well as the intentional use of language in the drafting of the Constitution and its preamble, this chapter adopts a linguistic analysis approach. By assessing how elements such as structure, style, and wording contribute to the fulfillment of certain non-legal functions of the Chinese constitutional preamble, this methodology enables drawing well-informed conclusions regarding its functions. Such an approach promises to provide valuable insights as it allows for a more scientifically and quantitatively rigorous examination of the non-legal functions that are otherwise challenging to study.[8]

2 The Preamble as a Central Component of China's Constitution (as a Political Document)

The relationship between law and politics, and between the political and the normative character of the Constitution, has been a central topic of discussion and dispute in Chinese constitutional theory.[9] After the emergence of a school of 'normative constitutionalism' (*guifan xianfa zhuyi*, 规范宪政主义), whose core is the preoccupation with the constitutional text and the independence of constitutional studies as an academic discipline,[10] 'political constitutionalism' (*zhengzhi xianfa zhuyi*, 政治宪政主义) soon emerged with the demand to shift the focus of constitutional studies to the actual political conditions and reality in which the constitution unfolds. Since politics in China is primarily shaped by the CCP, this approach means first and foremost accepting the reality of the party-state and recognizing party leadership as the starting point for studying

[8] On the challenges of making scientific assertions about non-legal functions of preambles: *Voermans/Stremler/Cliteur* (n. 5), 91.

[9] *Veg*, The Rise of China's Statist Intellectuals: Law, Sovereignty, and "Repoliticization", 82(1) China Journal 2019, 23 (25–28); *Zhang*, Stufenordnung und Verfahren der Setzung von Rechtsnormen in der Volksrepublik China, 2017, 95–96.

[10] *Lin Laifan* 林来梵, 从宪法规范到规范宪法 - 规范宪法学的一种前言 [From Constitutional Norms to the Norms of the Constitution: An Introduction of Normative Constitutionalism], 2001; on its development and proponents: *Xie/Patapan*, Contesting Legitimacy in China: The Politics of Law in Modern Chinese Jurisprudence, 46(3) HKLJ 2016, 991 (1004–1008).

the Constitution.[11] The different varieties of political constitutionalism amount to accepting and defending the current political system, which is decisively based on the leadership role of the CCP. The (written) constitution does not set limits on the CCP's actions; rather, the principle of party leadership is above the constitution, and the important position of the constitution is based on its political character.[12]

With political constitutionalism on the rise, the constitutional preamble has increasingly gained attention. It is the part of the Constitution that is most outspoken about the guiding ideology and fundamental policy issues and '*reveals the political nature of the Chinese Constitution*'.[13] Therefore, it is most suitable as the textual basis for the construction of a political theory of the Constitution. While entirely dismissing the Chinese Constitution as a political document with no legal significance whatsoever seems to be an overly simplistic approach,[14] it also holds true that it primarily fulfills non-legal functions.[15] Those political functions are clearly expressed in its preamble. It is generally accepted in constitutional theory that preambles are located at the intersection between law and politics and fulfill a variety of non-legal, especially political, functions in almost every constitutional order.[16]

[11] *Zhang*, Carl Schmitt in China: Why Is He Needed and How Is He Understood? 25(2) ZChinR 2018, 83 (92); *Xie/Patapan* (n. 10), 991; *Lin*, The 2018 Constitutional Amendments: Significance and Impact on the Theories of Party-State Relationship in China, China Perspectives, no. 1, 2019, 11 (19).

[12] *Xie/Patapan* (n. 10), 1014; *Zhang* (n. 9), 95.

[13] *Lin*, Idealism and Realism in Chinese Constitutional Theory and Practice, in: Adams/Meuwese/Hirsch Ballin (eds.), Constitutionalism and the Rule of Law, 2017, 294 (322).

[14] See also *Holbig*, Auf dem Weg zur konstitutionellen Einparteienherrschaft? Die Verfassungsänderungen vom März 2004, 33(3) China aktuell 2004, 259 (259–260); *Hsueh*, The New Constitution, 24(3) Problems of Communism 1975, 11 (11–12).

[15] On the observation that the political functions outweigh the legal functions of the Chinese Constitution: *Zhang*, The Leadership of the CCP, 12(1) Hague Journal on the Rule of Law 2020, 147 (157); *Peerenboom*, Social Foundations of China's Living Constitution, in: Ginsburg (ed.), Comparative Constitutional Design, 2012, 138 (139–140).

[16] *Frosini*, Constitutional Preambles, 2012, 22–23; *Addis*, Constitutional Preambles as Narratives of Peoplehood, 12(2) ICL Journal 2018, 125 (179); *Levinson*, Do Constitutions Have a Point? Reflections on "Parchment Barriers" and Preambles, in: Paul/Miller/Paul (eds.), What Should Constitutions Do? 2011, 150 (166, 177).

Given that the Chinese Constitution is primarily a political document with the preamble at its core, it is indeed worthwhile to examine the political functions of the preamble. Due to its political nature and significance, and the interconnectedness of politics and law, it becomes necessary to examine the political dimensions of the Chinese constitutional preamble as well.

3 Linguistic Characteristics of the Different Content Sections of the Preamble

The objective of this study is to investigate the linguistic and stylistic characteristics of the Chinese constitutional preamble and how they contribute to fulfilling certain, primarily non-legal, functions. This is accomplished through an analysis that focuses on the linguistic peculiarities unique to certain parts of the preamble. Consequently, the analysis that follows is limited to an internal examination of the Chinese preamble and does not involve a comparison with other constitutional preambles. This approach allows for clearer results, as it goes beyond the already relatively well-established observation that there is a connection between language and functions of constitutional preambles.[17] Instead, this study aims to provide an in-depth analysis of how specific linguistic features in the preamble of China's Constitution, which may vary from paragraph to paragraph, serve different purposes.

To achieve this, the thirteen paragraphs of the comprehensive preamble are divided into sections based on the distinct categories of content they cover. In Chinese constitutional studies, there is broad consensus regarding the division of the preamble according to substantive criteria: The first six paragraphs form the historical narrative, constituting the initial part of the Constitution. Following this, paragraph 7 contains the guiding ideology and basic tasks of the state. At times, paragraph 7 is treated as an independent section, while in other instances, it is regarded as part of a broader section on issues of national importance, along with paragraphs 8–12.[18] These five paragraphs outline basic state policies that are regarded as prerequisites for fulfilling the basic tasks outlined in

[17] *Häberle* (n. 5), 228; *Paydaş*, A Mythopoieic Analysis of Constitutional Preambles, 2021, 85–92.

[18] Paragraph 7 is treated as an independent part of the preamble for example by *Cai Dingjian* 蔡定剑, 宪法精解 [Commentary on the Constitution], 2004, 102 and

paragraph 7. For the purposes of the following study, paragraphs 7–12 are analyzed together, as they all relate to the ideological and political foundations of the state and constitutional order. However, when necessary, specific characteristics of paragraph 7 are highlighted. Finally, paragraph 13, which addresses the status and implementation of the Constitution, forms a distinct section.

In the following section, the 'historical part' (paragraphs 1–6), the 'political-ideological part' (paragraphs 7–12), and the 'legal part' (paragraph 13) will be examined with regard to certain linguistic peculiarities. The study begins with a primarily quantitative analysis of formal aspects of the preamble, followed by an examination of specific linguistic elements. Apart from syntax, the analysis focuses on examining specific semantic aspects, such as semantic fields, the use of *chengyus* (成语, Chinese idiomatic expressions), and the inclusion of proper names. These points of analysis are then compared for each part of the preamble to uncover differences in the language usage. Consequently, this study demonstrates that the language employed in different parts of the preamble varies, aligning with the different non-legal functions of the Chinese constitutional preamble.

3.1 Formal Aspects: Quantitative Analysis of Length, Structure, and Evolution of the Preamble

The Chinese constitutional preamble, in its current version from 2018, comprises 1,898 Chinese characters. The official English translation encompasses 1,185 words, rendering it the fifth longest preamble globally.[19] In terms of structure, it consists of 13 paragraphs, exhibiting noticeable variations in their lengths, as Fig. 1 illustrates.

Xie Weiyan 谢维雁, 论宪法序言 [On the Constitutional Preamble], Shehui kexue yanjiu 社会科学研究, No. 5, 2004, 76 (77).

[19] *Voermans/Stremler/Cliteur* (n. 5), 23. See also *Ginsburg/Foti/Rockmore*, "We the Peoples": The Global Origins of Constitutional Preambles, 46(2) GWashIntlLRev 2014, 305 (314–318); according to their analysis, the version of the Chinese preamble at that time is the eighth longest constitutional preamble throughout all time periods.

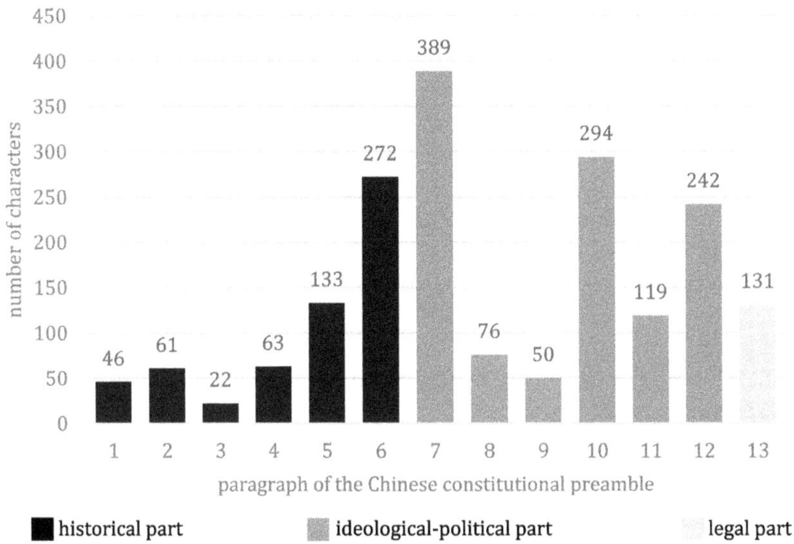

Fig. 1 Lengths of paragraphs

3.1.1 *Historical part: Short Paragraphs on Ancient and Pre-modern History, Longer Paragraphs on Modern History*

The Chinese preamble commences with six paragraphs that narrate specific events from China's history. This historical section, comprising 597 characters out of a total of 1,898, accounts for nearly one-third of the entire preamble. Within this historical narrative, there is a clear prioritization: The four paragraphs addressing China's ancient history and the modern times predating the establishment of the People's Republic consist of no more than two sentences each, averaging about 48 characters. In contrast, the two paragraphs on China's history since 1949 are notably lengthier, containing 133 and 272 characters respectively (see Fig. 1). The inclusion of references to the '*long history*' and '*glorious culture*' of ancient China in paragraph 1 is a novel addition introduced in the 1982 Constitution, setting it apart from previous constitutions. Recently, scholars have shown an increased interest in exploring these references.[20] While acknowledging the significance of China's historical and cultural continuity, it is evident that the primary focus of the historical narrative lies in modern history.[21] This can be seen from the allocation of space within the preamble, as the relatively short period since 1949 is given more prominence compared to China's long history preceding the establishment of the People's Republic. Numerically, this part of modern Chinese history encompasses more than two-thirds of the historical narrative.

The varying lengths of the paragraphs within the historical narrative reflect the significance attributed to the last two paragraphs. Notably, paragraph 6 places emphasis on the accomplishments attained under the leadership of the CCP. These achievements form the '*laws of historical development*' (*lishi fazhan guilü*, 历史发展规律)[22] from which subsequently ideological principles, especially the Four Cardinal Principles, are derived. The CCP's present rule is justified based on merits earned in the past.[23] Within this section, the legitimizing function is clearly pronounced, alongside the educational and identity-shaping aspects.[24]

3.1.2 Ideological-political Part: Extensive and Dynamically Revised and Amended Paragraphs

The section that follows the introductory part on national history focuses on ideological and political aspects. It consists of paragraph 7, which encapsulates the guiding ideology and the basic tasks of the state, as well

[20] *Yao Zhongqiu* 姚中秋, 从革命到文明 [From Revolution to Civilization], Falü pinglun 法学评论, No. 2, 2015, 45–56; *Qian Jinyu* 钱锦宇, 宪法序言、国家梦想与政制建构 [The Constitutional Preamble, the National Dream and the Political System], Falü luntan 法学论坛, Vol. 28, No. 4, 2013, 29–36; *Zhai Zhiyong* 翟志勇, 宪法序言中的国家观与世界主义 [Conceptions of State and Cosmopolitism in the Constitutional Preamble], Lishi faxue 历史法学, Vol. 10, 2015, 342–357.

[21] With this observation of the historical narration's selective character also *Yu Zhong* 喻中, 论宪法效力的终极依据 [On the Final Basis of the Binding Force of the Constitution], Zhengfa lun cong 政法论丛, No. 2, 2011, 79 (81).

[22] *Peng Zhen* 彭真, 关于中华人民共和国宪法修改草案的报告 [Report on the Revision of the Constitutional Draft of the PRC], Renmin Ribao 人民日报, 6/12/1982.

[23] *Qian Jinyu* (n. 20), 34, who speaks of a merit-based form of legitimacy; similarly also *Yu Zhong* (n. 21), 83.

[24] For further insights into the role of the preamble in the ideological education of the people, see *Xu Xiuyi* 徐秀义/*Han Dayuan* 韩大元, 宪法学原理 [Principles of Constitutional Law], 1993, 159 and 168–169.

as paragraphs 8–12, which establish fundamental national and international policies. Remarkably, this part is nearly twice as long as the historical part and significantly surpasses the length of any other section, constituting over 60% of the entire preamble's length. Furthermore, there is a discernible trend that this particular section has expanded in length over the course of time, progressively accounting for a greater proportion of the preamble's overall length: Starting out at 1,671 characters in 1982, the entire preamble has undergone a 13.6% increase in length up until the present day. The constitutional amendments carried out in 1993, 1999, 2004, and most recently in 2018 targeted paragraphs 7, 8, 10, and 12 and thus exclusively the ideological-political part of the preamble.

As Fig. 2 shows, paragraph 7 has experienced the most substantial growth among the paragraphs within this section. Since 1982, it has been amended four times to incorporate new strands of ideology, expanding from 250 characters to 389 characters. This signifies a percentage increase of 55.6%, making it now significantly longer than any other paragraph. The discrepancies in paragraph lengths and their subsequent growth indicate their significance within the Chinese legal and political system, as well as the sensitivity of the policy area they address. The significance of paragraph 7 as the embodiment of the ideological guidelines of the state, which is generally regarded as the most important content of the preamble and the entire constitutional order, is clearly evident from its share of the total length and the percentage increase it has experienced during constitutional amendments. The exceptional importance of this paragraph reflects the influential role of ideology, as its content holds high ideological value and is subject to changes that serve a signaling function for political developments and power dynamics.

3.1.3 Legal Part: Medium-Length and Unamended Paragraph

Last (and probably also least) is the final paragraph regarding the status and implementation of the Constitution. Spanning 131 characters, this medium-length paragraph has remained unamended since the Constitution was enacted in 1982. Notably, the legal part stands as a solitary paragraph, distinct from the other sections that comprise multiple paragraphs. This disparity underscores the subordinate importance assigned to legal aspects within the Chinese preamble.

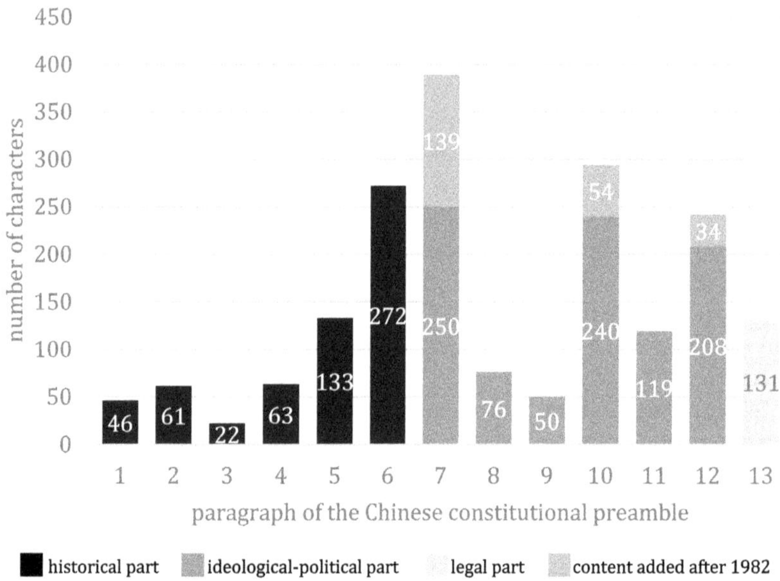

Fig. 2 (Change in) lengths of paragraphs (1982–2018)

3.2 *Syntax: The Level of Complexity*

The syntax of the preamble exhibits striking variations in the complexity of sentence structures. These differences become apparent when quantitatively analyzing the sentence length and the occurrence of complex sentence structures, particularly the increasing prevalence of enumerations with numerous items.

3.2.1 *Historical Part: Short and Concise Sentences that Convey Clear Interpretations on History*

In the historical part, the authors of the Constitution demonstrate a deliberate preference for accessible and comprehensible language. The sentences within this section are not very long, averaging around 37 characters. Figure 3 shows that apart from one exception (paragraph 5 Sentence 1, which contains 109 characters), all other sentences range between 15 and 54 characters. Moreover, the sentence structure is generally straightforward, often comprising only a single main clause without subordinate clauses or comma-separated enumerations. Furthermore, many of the sentences commence with a preceding year or other temporal reference, aiding readers in contextualizing the provided information.

The decision to employ simpler syntax in the historical section aims to reduce complexity and educate readers effectively. The first paragraphs of the Chinese preamble have been described to read like a '*little handbook on Chinese history*'.[25] Employing less complicated language, including syntax, serves the purpose of ensuring and facilitating the comprehensibility of the text for ordinary citizens, thereby aligning with the function of educating the general public about the country's history and achievements.[26] Consequently, enhanced comprehensibility strengthens the persuasive power of the text and contributes to its legitimizing function.

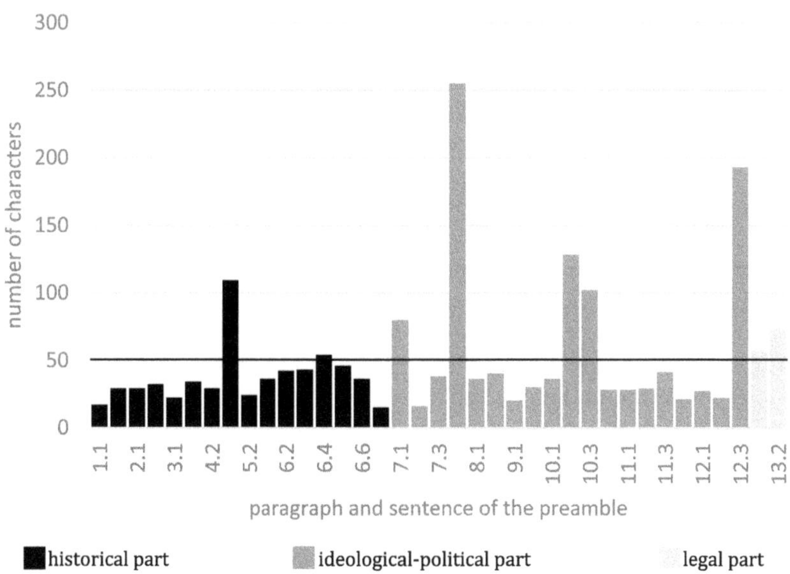

Fig. 3 Number of characters per sentence

[25] *Voermans/Stremler/Cliteur* (n. 5), 87.

[26] On the preamble's educative function *Xu Chongde* 许崇德, 许崇德自选集 [Selected Works of Xu Chongde], 2007, 48; *Xu Xiuyi/Han Dayuan* (n. 24), 168–169.

3.2.2 *Ideological-political Part: High Degree of Semantic Complexity and Increasingly Longer Enumerations*

Comparable patterns can be observed in the ideological-political part, where the drafters of the Constitution have also made a noticeable effort to maintain short sentences and simple syntax. Out of the 19 sentences in this section, the vast majority (14) are below the threshold of 50 characters per sentence marked in Fig. 3. Nevertheless, there are a few notable exceptions. Some sentences are exceptionally long, resulting in an average of 61.6 characters per sentence: almost twice as many as in the historical part. These lengthy and semantically complex sentences even pose challenges for legal interpretation.[27] Notably, the final sentence of paragraph 7 stands out with 255 characters, surpassing the length of ten out of the thirteen paragraphs. This sentence, which addresses the intricacies of the guiding ideology, is particularly semantically complex, not only due to its sheer length but also because it incorporates numerous parenthetical expressions, insertions, and enumerations. This sentence serves as a prime example of complex syntax within the Chinese preamble, a characteristic that has progressively intensified through more than ten revisions in four constitutional amendments.[28] For instance, the original phrase '*guided by Marxism-Leninism and Mao Zedong Thought*' has evolved into a six-part list ('*guided by Marxism-Leninism, Mao Zedong Thought, Deng Xiaoping's Theory, the important thoughts of the Three Represents, the scientific concept of development, and Xi Jinping's thoughts on socialism with Chinese characteristics in the new era*'). Each constitutional amendment only ever added new content, leading to the expansion of enumerations, longer sentences, and an overall increase in syntactic complexity.

The fact that certain sentences in the preamble gradually become longer and more complex can be attributed to the continuous addition of new ideologies and political guidelines by the political leadership. The level of complexity in syntax can therefore be interpreted as a peculiarity of the '*restricted code*'[29] utilized in Chinese political language. The preamble echoes the inclusion of political concepts in preceding party documents, effectively mirroring political transformations and shifts in

[27] See *Chen Yushan* (n. 2), 30.

[28] Paragraph 7 was amended through constitutional amendments 3 (1993), 12 (1999), 18 (2004) and 32 (2018).

[29] *Schoenhals* (n. 4), 1.

power. Thus, the increasingly complex syntax found in certain highly ideological parts of the preamble serves as both a signal for political change and a demonstration of the exercise of political power by the ruling authorities.

3.2.3 Legal Part: Slightly Increased Complexity as a Characteristic of Legal Language

The sentences in the last paragraph are of medium length and demonstrate a slightly elevated level of complexity, which is customary in legal language. Nevertheless, they are not overly intricate and remain comprehensible.

3.3 Semantics and Pragmatics: Certain Stylistic Features of the Different Parts of the Preamble

The following section investigates the semantic disparities across the different parts of the preamble. Noteworthy characteristics have been selected as examples that capture the reader's attention. These include the prevalence of certain semantic fields, frequent repetition of certain terms, the use of chengyus, and the inclusion of proper names. Through an examination of these aspects, broader conclusions about distinct peculiarities of the linguistic style of the preamble will be drawn.

3.3.1 Semantic Fields: Chrono-Ideological Narratives and Political Jargon

Historical Part: Expressions of Continuity and Revolution Within the Dominant Semantic Fields of 'Time' and 'History'

The initial six paragraphs of the Chinese preamble reveal a noteworthy abundance of words relating to the semantic fields of 'time' and 'history'. While the use of '*chrono-ideological narratives*' and '*vocabularies clustered around semantic fields of time*'[30] may not be surprising in a section dedicated to narrating history, what truly stands out is the prevalence of words within this lexical field expressing the passage of time, change, and transformation. The theme of 'revolution', symbolizing the most profound form of change and transformation, is notably prevalent. The observation that half of the occurrences of the term '*revolution/revolutionary*'

[30] *Holbig*, China after Reform, 47(3) JCurrChinAff 2018, 187 (189–190).

(*geming*, 革命) are found in the historical part of the preamble[31] suggests that revolution is part of the Chinese Constitution primarily as a historical and social phenomenon. The preamble invokes the revolutionary history and the founding of the Chinese state, but no longer advocates for a '*continuous revolution*' (*jixu geming*, 继续革命).[32] This is particularly evident when comparing it to the 1975 Constitution, where the term '*revolution*' appears nine times in the preamble alone and plays an important role in the normative provisions of the main text as well (with another 16 mentions).

When compared to the former Constitutions of 1975 and 1978, it is evident that references to '*revolution*' are less frequent in the present preamble. Furthermore, the overall tone of the preamble is less revolutionary, devoid of slogans associated with the Cultural Revolution. Nonetheless, the concept of revolution still plays a significant role in shaping the historical section of the preamble. Besides, a new kind of time-related vocabulary emerges, emphasizing historical continuities. This is particularly apparent in the first paragraph, which includes terms such as '*history*', '*culture*', and '*tradition*'. Overall, the dominant semantic field of history and time in the first part of the preamble signifies the dual basis of political power legitimacy in China: continuity and revolution.[33]

Ideological-Political Part: The Use of Political Vocabulary and Literal Incorporations from Political Documents

Michael Schoenhals's study on formalized language as an instrument of power in Chinese politics proves valuable in analyzing the language employed in paragraphs 7–12 of the Chinese preamble. Schoenhals's research reveals that political language in China operates under a '*restricted code*', which imposes severe restrictions on vocabulary, style,

[31] See *Ge Xianyuan* 葛先园, 我国八二宪法序言中历史叙事的法理与功能 [Legal Philosophy and Function of the Historical Narration in the Preamble of the 1982 Constitution of the PRC], Hainan daxue xuebao 海南大学学报(人文社会科学版), Vol. 33, No. 5, 2015, 91 (92–93).

[32] On Meo Zedongs "*Theory of the continuation of the revolution under the dictatorship of the proletariat*", see Advance Along the Road Opened Up by the October Socialist Revolution, 1967, 19–23.

[33] *Gao Quanxi*, Revolution, Reform & Constitutionalism, 2(1) PekingULJ 2014, 27 (31–32) on the '*dual idea of revolution*'; see also *Yao Zhongqiu* (n. 20), 45, 51.

and syntax, and has a negative impact on the overall linguistic richness. These restrictions on the formal level effectively constrain the scope of political discourse by impeding the creation of new political ideas and reinforcing the acceptance of existing concepts through constant repetition.[34] This phenomenon is most evident in the wording of the ideological-political part of the preamble. Paragraph 7, in particular, exhibits a distinct pattern where specific words and phrases are constantly reiterated to describe the guiding ideology, tasks, and policies of the state, such as the '*leadership of the CCP*' and the '*people's democratic dictatorship*'. The prevailing semantic field within paragraphs 7–12 clearly revolves around ideological and political concepts. An analysis of the frequency of certain characters or words indicates that the most commonly used words are those of high significance within Chinese political theory. Notably, the characters 主义 (*zhuyi*, doctrine/-ism) are mentioned 27 times, and 社会 (*shehui*, social/society) is mentioned 20 times in this section of the preamble. They occur a total of eighteen times in the composed noun or adjective 社会主义 (*shehui zhuyi*, socialism/socialist). Other frequently employed words, apart from 中国 or 我国 (*Zhongguo* or *woguo*, expressions for China) are also ones closely associated with Chinese political thought or ideology. These include 人民 (*renmin*, people, 12 times), 发展 (*fazhan*, development/to develop, 11 times), 民族 (*minzhu*, nationality/ethnic, 11 times), 坚持 (*jianchi*, to adhere to, used in connection with certain ideologies, 9 times), 文明 or 文化 (*wenming* or *wenhua*, culture or civilization, 7 times), 建设 (*jianshe*, construction/to build, 7 times), 统一 (*tongyi*, unity/unitary, 7 times), 党 (*dang*, party, 6 times), 民主 (*minzhu*, democracy/democratic, 6 times), 国家 (*guojia*, state, 6 times), 斗争 or 奋斗 (*douzheng* or *fendou*, struggle, 6 times), 领导 or 指引 (*lingdao* or *zhiyin*, leadership, 6 times), and 团结 (*tuanjie*, unity/to unite, 6 times).

A distinctive feature of the ideological-political part of China's constitutional preamble is the presence of words and characters that possess political connotations, often reiterated throughout the text. Considering that the Chinese Constitution is perceived, often primarily, as a political document, its language therefore carries political connotations in many instances.[35] However, it is important to note that the language of this part

[34] *Schoenhals* (n. 4), 1, 20–21; *Cao* (n. 1), 130–131; on the restrictive function concerning political discourse of authoritarian constitutions in general: *Ginsburg/Simpser*, Introduction, in: *Ginsburg/Simpser*, Constitutions in Authoritarian Regimes, 2014, 1 (14).

[35] *Cao* (n. 1), 130; *Zhang*, The Constitution of China, 2012, 65.

of the preamble not only belongs to the semantic field of ideology and politics but also adheres to a very specific and restricted political jargon. It follows that the expressions and phrases used in this section can be found in similar or identical forms within political documents. For example, large parts of the preamble are taken verbatim from the Party Constitution, the Statute of the CPC (*Zhongguo gongchandang zhangcheng*, 中国共产党章程). This is particularly true for paragraph 7, where the majority of phrasings are identical to those found in the Party Statute. Although the level of '*language formalization*'[36] is not as pronounced as during the Cultural Revolution, it remains a distinct characteristic of the ideological and political content of the preamble. This formalization serves to reinforce the exercise of political power through linguistic means.

Legal Part: Elements of Legal Language

The final paragraph of the preamble stands out as the section that contains elements of technical, legal language. It is notable that the word for Constitution (*xianfa*, 宪法) appears for the first time and exclusively in this final paragraph. Despite this, paragraph 13 references the '*legal authority*' of the Constitution and '*compliance*' with the Constitution. It employs the imperative verb 必须 (*bixu*), which is commonly utilized in regular Chinese legal language to express legal obligations.[37]

3.3.2 Idioms: The Use of Classical and Modern Chengyus

The Chinese preamble, similar to other legal documents in the Chinese context, primarily employs plain language.[38] This choice of accessible, everyday language aims to provide clarity and facilitate understanding by utilizing comprehensible words and concepts. However, an intriguing stylistic feature present in the preamble sets it apart from its usual linguistic framework: the inclusion of idiomatic expressions. Notably,

[36] *Schoenhals* (n. 4), 19.

[37] *Cao*, Chinese Language in Law, 2018, 134–138.

[38] *Cao*, Translating Legal Language Between Chinese and English, in: Ye, The Palgrave Handbook of Chinese Language Studies, 2022, 539 (542): The language of Chinese legal documents is generally known to be more modern and simplified, particularly when compared to Taiwan; see also *Voermans/Stremler/Cliteur* (n. 5), 87; *Huang Weiqin* 黄惟勤, 论我国宪法序言的法律效力 [On the Legal Effect of the Chinese Constitutional Preamble], Faxue zazhi 法学杂志, 2010, No. 2, 104 (105).

the use of chengyus, four-character idioms that are still common in Chinese language, displays variations between the historical and the ideological-political sections of the preamble.

Historical Part: Classical Chengyus Foster Historical Continuity and Elevate the Language Level

While especially the historical part of the preamble aims to be accessible to ordinary citizens, this part also incorporates more poetic and emotive language elements. One prominent feature in this regard is the use of chengyus that evoke the classical style and are rich in metaphors. Almost all chengyus used in the first six paragraphs of the preamble are derived from classical Chinese texts. This infusion of classical Chinese elements enriches the otherwise modern, socialist-style language of the preamble. For instance, in the first paragraph, Chinese culture is described using the chengyu 光辉灿烂 (*guanghui canlan*). This idiom originates from a historical work of the Song period and metaphorically conveys the idea of a grand, brilliant future or career. It can be translated as '*glorious*' or '*brilliant*'.[39] In the second paragraph, the heroic struggle for national independence and liberation waged by the Chinese people is depicted as '*wave upon wave*' (*qian pu hou ji*, 前仆后继). This idiom, derived from a prose text from the ninth century, carries the literal meaning of those in front falling and those behind taking up their positions. Figuratively, it conveys the notion of fighting bravely and fearlessly, without hesitation in making sacrifices.[40]

The use of the chengyu 翻天覆地 (*fan tian fu di*) in paragraph 3 of the Chinese constitutional preamble to depict the historical transformations of twentieth century China is particularly interesting. This phrase is usually translated as '*earth-shaking*' or '*world-shaking*' and literally means '*overturning heaven and earth*'.[41] Its origins can be traced back to the

[39] For translations of this chengyu see *Tan Song* 谭松/*Yao Xinxue* 姚新学, 中国成语汉英双解大词典 [A Dictionary of Chinese Idioms with English Translation], 1993, 328; *Qavuz,* A Chinese Idioms Dictionary with English and Uighur Translations (汉英维成语词典), 2003, 356.

[40] For translations of this chengyu see *Tan Song/Yao Xinxue* (n. 39), 645–646; *Heng/Zhang,* A Chinese-English Dictionary of Idioms and Proverbs, 1988, 255; *Huang Shengmin* 黃省民, 英譯漢語成語詞典[Chinese Idioms and Phrases], 1977, 156.

[41] For translations of this chengyu see *Tan Song/Yao Xinxue* (n. 39), 246; *Heng/Zhang* (n. 40), 89; *Huang Shengmin* (n. 40), 56.

Tang-era cycle of poems titled '*Eighteen Songs of a Nomad Flute*' (*Hu jia shiba pai*, 胡茄十八拍), where it is used to express the feeling of being overwhelmed when confronted with a foreign culture and environment.[42] In the context of the Chinese constitutional preamble, the utilization of this idiom holds a significant meaning. It references the notions of heaven (*tian*, 天) and earth (*di*, 地) that are central to Chinese political philosophy. The phrase immediately evokes associations with the concepts of the '*mandate of heaven*' (*tianming*, 天命), and of '*all that is under heaven*' (*tianxia*, 天下), which are closely linked to the claim of rule and legitimacy. Notably, the concept of *tianxia* has recently been revisited by contemporary political philosopher Zhao Tingyang as a foundation for the development of a new world order.[43] Against this backdrop, paragraph 3 goes beyond merely describing the transition from monarchy to democracy and eventually to the socialist system as '*revolutionary*'. Instead, it invokes classical imperial concepts of rule legitimacy to support the authority of the CCP.

Ideological-Political Part: Modern Instead of Classical Chengyus

The use of classical chengyus is primarily observed in the narrative section of the preamble, while chengyus derived from modern language usage can be found in the ideological and political sections. For example, the chengyu 独立自主 (*du li zi zhu*) used in paragraph 12 to describe Chinese foreign policy as '*independent and self-reliant*' originates from the works of Mao Zedong.[44] Similiarly, the chengyu 艰苦奋斗 (*jianku fendou*), which translates to '*hard working*', can be traced back to the writings of Tao Zhu, a comrade of Mao from the earlier generation of proletarian revolutionaries.[45] In the 2018 constitutional amendment, another idiom was added in paragraph 12 to describe the '*mutually beneficial*' nature

[42] Eighteen Songs of a Nomad Flute by Tang Dynasty poet Liu Shang tell the story of Han Dynasty poet Cai Wenji, who was kidnapped by Xiongnu nomads. The eighteen poems in this cycle tell of the time of her imprisonment and finally of her return to China. The mentioned chengyu is found in the sixth poem. For a translation of this poem see *Liu/Fong/Rorex*, Eighteen Songs of a Nomad Flute, 1974.

[43] *Zhao*, Redefining A Philosophy for World Governance, 2019.

[44] For translations of this chengyu see *Tan Song/Yao Xinxue* (n. 39), 227; *Huang Shengmin* (n. 40), 51; *Qavuz* (n. 39), 174.

[45] *Tan Song/Yao Xinxue* (n. 39), 411.

of international cooperation. The expression 互利共赢 (*huli gong ying*), closely associated with the Belt and Road Initiative strategy announced by Xi Jinping, represents a more recent addition.[46]

These modern chengyus, shaped by representatives of the socialist leadership while adhering to the classical Chinese style, intentionally blur the line between tradition and modernity. This deliberate fusion aims to place one's rule in a line of historical continuity, thereby contributing to the construction of political legitimacy and a cohesive ruling narrative.[47] On the other hand, these chengyus can also be understood as part of the political jargon within the language of the preamble, as they are closely associated with certain important political figures.

3.3.3 The Inclusion of Proper Names in Historical Context and Ideological Concepts

Another notable stylistic characteristic of the Chinese constitutional preamble is its incorporation of proper names. This particular feature sets it apart from international standards, as constitutional preambles typically adopt a more vague and aspirational approach in terms of both content and language, placing less emphasis on explicitly naming individuals or political parties.[48] However, in the Chinese preamble, proper names are mentioned in two distinct contexts.

Historical Part: The Mention of Modern Revolutionary Leaders

The historical part pays tribute to two significant figures, who played pivotal roles as revolutionary leaders in Chinese history: Sun Yat-sen (paragraph 4) and Mao Zedong (paragraph 5). This makes China one of the few countries that explicitly includes the names of political leaders

[46] This concept was employed by Xi Jinping to describe the spirt of the Silk Road Project in a speech delivered on September 7, 2013, titled 弘扬人民友谊 共创美好未来 [Promote People-to-People Friendship and Create a Better Future], available online at: http://politics.people.com.cn/n/2013/0908/c1001-22842914.html.

[47] On the fact that the constitutional preamble draws on both socialist constitutional traditions and traditional cultural traditions to demonstrate political legitimacy: *Tian Feilong* 田飞龙, 宪法序言: 中国宪法的 "高级法背景" [Constitutional Preamble: The "higher law background" of the Chinese Constitution], Jianghan xueshu 江汉学术, Vol. 34, No. 4, 2015, 31 (36).

[48] On the observation that the use of proper names of persons or parties is only common in authoritarian states, see *Frosini* (n. 16), 38–39.

within its constitutional preamble. The selection of these two historical figures is no coincidence and holds profound symbolic significance. It relates to the dual foundations of legitimacy of political power in China: continuity and revolution.[49] The inclusion of Sun Yat-sen's name serves to establish a sense of historical continuity, connecting the present era to the pre-People's Republic era. This choice holds significant meaning and represents an important and extensively debated innovation when compared to previous constitutional documents.[50] Then again, the decision to include two influential revolutionary leaders emphasizes the significance attributed to revolutionary movements in shaping Chinese history. This underscores the profound impact of revolution as a key aspect of China's political evolution.

Ideological-Political Part: The Deliberate Mention and Non-mention of Political Leaders As Expressions of Political Power

In paragraph 7, three political leaders since the founding of the People's Republic are explicitly referenced in relation to the ideological theories or political thinking they have shaped: Mao Zedong Thought (mentioned twice), Deng Xiaoping Theory, and Xi Jinping Thought. By examining the nuances in the utilization of proper names, several gradations can be identified. Firstly, not all political leaders are named explicitly; for example, Jiang Zemin and Hu Jintao are mentioned only by their political theories. Secondly, there are variations in the labeling of these concepts. The use of the term thought (*sixiang*, 思想) is considered more prestigious than the addition of theory (*lilun*, 理论).[51] Thirdly, certain individuals and their ideas have been incorporated into the preamble while they were still alive and held political power (such as Mao Zedong in the 1975 Constitution and Xi Jinping in the 2018 constitutional amendment), while others (such as Deng Xiaoping in the 1999 constitutional

[49] See above, n. 33.

[50] On the inclusion of Sun Yat-sen in the preamble: *Pu Zengyuan* (n. 3), 26; *Xu Chongde* (n. 26), 48; *Jones*, The Constitution of the People's Republic of China, 63(4) WashULQ 1985, 707 (726): '*new feature of the standard history*'.

[51] *Schurmann*, Ideology and Organization in Communist China, 1966, 24–25; *Holbig* (n. 30), 192; *Moody*, Some Reflections on the Functions of "Xi Jinping's Thought", in: Hua, Chinese Ideology, 2022, 218 (222).

amendment) have only been honored posthumously through their inclusion in the preamble.[52] Taken together, the employment of proper names reveals a clear gradation in the political power of the individuals being mentioned. Therefore, the inclusion of proper names in paragraph 7 serves a dual purpose. It not only serves as a means to educate the population about certain ideological principles but also symbolizes and thereby consolidates political power.

Similar patterns apply to the naming of the Chinese Communist Party (CCP). Four out of the five references in the preamble are situated within the political-ideological section, two of them in paragraph 7, which addresses the Party leadership as one of the Four Cardinal Principles at the core of Chinese ideology. Furthermore, two additional mentions are found in paragraph 10 on the united front and multi-party cooperation. The CCP is consistently referred to in the phrase '*under the leadership of the CCP*', which is a clear exercise of its political power.

4 Linguistic Variation Within the Chinese Preamble

The above analysis of linguistic peculiarities within the Chinese constitutional preamble demonstrates its linguistic variety, revealing substantial variations between the different sections of the preamble. Particularly with regard to the historical and the ideological-political part the linguistic analysis aids in understanding their underlying purposes and functions within the Chinese legal and political system. In contrast, regarding paragraph 13, there is relatively little to analyze. It primarily consists of a short and unobtrusive regulation on the position and implementation of the Constitution, written in a style that closely resembles the regular legal language used in Chinese (constitutional) law. However, the fact that there are fewer linguistic specifics to analyze is in itself an observation, which suggests that this paragraph is mostly intended to fulfill legal functions.

The introductory historical part can be characterized as a time-centered, carefully selected, and glorifying narration of national history. The analyses concerning this section have shown that in particular the

52 With the observations that the inclusion of individuals' names in the constitution while they are still alive is something almost unprecedented by international standards: *Elkins/Ginsburg/Melton*, The Endurance of National Constitutions, 2009, 175.

narration of historical achievements attained under the leadership of the CCP takes up significant amounts of space. The level of complexity is deliberately kept low to convey a clear and comprehensible narration and interpretation of history. This is primarily manifested in the use of relatively short sentences and syntactically uncomplicated structures. Semantically, the narration revolves around the topics of 'history' and 'time', conveying the narrative of continuity and revolution as the twin pillars of legitimacy in China. These overriding themes are also echoed in the use of primarily classical chengyus and selective mentions of political leaders. All in all, the use of narrative and evaluative language and the—also linguistically demonstrable—emphasis on continuity and revolution serve to create and demonstrate legitimacy.

The ideological-political part can be characterized as an ever-increasing enumeration of ideological and political guidelines and their change. By far the longest section of the preamble expanded even further in the wake of several constitutional amendments. These amendments mostly pertained to the guiding ideology and basic state tasks set out in paragraph 7, additionally contributing to convoluted sentences and ever-longer enumerations. Semantically, this section of the preamble is dominated by the use of a restricted code of political jargon with respect to style and wording. For example, there is limited variation in the vocabulary, and it predominantly consists of expressions and phrases mirrored in political documents, notably the Party Statute. Certain words, especially those pertaining to the political system and the fundamental ideological order of the state, are frequently reiterated. The use of chengyus that were coined by modern political leaders and the numerous mentions of proper names of individuals and the CCP can be understood as an exercise of political power and signals of political (power) shifts.

5 The Link Between Language and Function: Creating Legitimacy and Exercising Political Power Through Language

The understanding that the Chinese Constitution is primarily regarded as a political document is not a novel or surprising finding.[53] This becomes especially apparent in its preamble, where the ideological, political, and

[53] See above, 2. and esp. n. 15.

historical aspects far outweigh the legal references. Nevertheless, the linguistic analysis conducted in this study offers valuable insights into the non-legal objectives that the preamble effectively pursues. Instead of merely acknowledging the prevalence of political over legal functions, this analysis delves deeper into understanding the specific objectives the preamble aims to achieve. By comparing the linguistic characteristics of the different sections, it becomes evident that the preamble is not a homogenous text. Rather, there are clear variations in language usage that establish a connection between the employed language, the conveyed content, and the intended functions of the preamble.

Drawing from many small-scale research findings on specific aspects of language usage, an overarching trend can be discerned: The most significant disparities are observed between the historical part and the subsequent political-ideological section. Notably, paragraph 7 carries particular influence as the ideological framework of the Constitution. The language employed in the historical part indicates that its primary function is to establish the legitimacy of the Constitution, the state system, and the current government. This aligns with the Marxist belief that historical laws provide general legitimacy for action. In contrast, the ideological-political part serves a different purpose, focusing less on convincing and persuading and more on informing and educating the people about the fundamental ideological orientation and major policies of the state. Through this approach, the ruling party ensures that its core ideological and political beliefs are decisive. Thus, it exercises political power. Additionally, this section clearly reflects political developments and shifts in power.

The findings of the linguistic study, therefore, validate the assertions made regarding the objectives of the Chinese Constitution, which primarily center on ensuring CCP leadership and signaling political and ideological change within the system. Notably, the preamble plays a crucial role in fulfilling these purposes as it establishes the fundamental principles of China's ideology. Consequently, the preamble "*is key to understanding the character and function of the document*" and "*has the character of an ideological manifesto*".[54] Understanding the diverse effects intended by the preamble, as revealed through linguistic analysis, provides

[54] *Chang/Law*, Constitutional Dissonance in China, in: Jacobsohn/Schor (eds.), Comparative Constitutional Theory, 2018, 476 (492); see also *Xie Weiyan* (n. 18), 78 and *Huang Weiqin* (n. 38), 106.

valuable insights into the self-perception of those in positions of power. As a result, these insights should not be disregarded when examining Chinese constitutional law.

References

Addis, Adeno, Constitutional Preambles as Narratives of Peoplehood, 12(2) ICL Journal 2018, 125–181.

Cai Dingjian 蔡定剑, 宪法精解 [Commentary on the Constitution], 2004.

Cao, Deborah, Chinese Law: A Language Perspective, 2016.

Cao, Deborah, Chinese Language in Law: Code Red, 2018.

Cao, Deborah, Translating Legal Language Between Chinese and English, in: Ye, The Palgrave Handbook of Chinese Language Studies, 2022, 539.

Chang, Wen-Chen/Law, David S., Constitutional Dissonance in China, in: Jacobsohn/Schor (eds.), Comparative Constitutional Theory, 2018, 476–514.

Chen Yushan 陈玉山, 中国宪法序言研究 [A Study of the Chinese Constitutional Preamble], 2016.

Elkins, Zachary/Ginsburg, Tom/Melton, James, The Endurance of National Constitutions, 2009.

Frosini, Justin O., Constitutional Preambles: At a Crossroads between Politics and Law, 2012.

Gao Quanxi, Revolution, Reform & Constitutionalism: The Evolution of China's 1982 Constitution: An Interpretation Based on Political Constitutionalism, 2(1) PekingULJ 2014, 27–58.

Ge Xianyuan 葛先园, 我国八二宪法序言中历史叙事的法理与功能 [Legal Philosophy and Function of the Historical Narration in the Preamble of the 1982 Constitution of the PRC], Hainan daxue xuebao 海南大学学报(人文社会科学版), Vol. 33, No. 5, 2015, 91–97.

Ginsburg, Tom/Foti, Nick/Rockmore, Daniel, "We the Peoples": The Global Origins of Constitutional Preambles, 46(2) GWashIntlLRev 2014, 305–340.

Ginsburg, Tom/Simpser, Alberto, Introduction, in: Ginsburg/Simpser, Constitutions in Authoritarian Regimes, 2014, 1–17.

Häberle, Peter, Präambeln im Text und Kontext von Verfassungen, in: FS Broermann, 1982, 211–249.

Heng, Xiao-jun/Zhang, Xue-zhi, A Chinese-English Dictionary of Idioms and Proverbs, 1988.

Holbig, Heike, Auf dem Weg zur konstitutionellen Einparteienherrschaft? Die Verfassungsänderungen vom März 2004, 33(3) China aktuell 2004, 259–274.

Holbig, Heike, China after Reform: Th Ideological, Constitutional, and Organisational Makings of a New Era, 47(3) JCurrChinAff 2018, 187–207.

Hsueh, Chun-tu, The New Constitution, 24(3) Problems of Communism 1975, 11–19.

Huang Shengmin 黄省民, 英譯漢語成語詞典 [Chinese Idioms and Phrases], 1977.
Huang Weiqin 黄惟勤, 论我国宪法序言的法律效力 [On the Legal Effect of the Chinese Constitutional Preamble], Faxue zazhi 法学杂志, 2010, No. 2, 104–106.
Jones, William C., The Constitution of the People's Republic of China, 63(4) WashULQ 1985, 707–736.
Levinson, Sanford, Do Constitutions Have a Point? Reflections on "Parchment Barriers" and Preambles, in: Paul/Miller/Paul (eds.), What Should Constitutions Do? 2011, 150–178.
Lin, Feng, Idealism and Realism in Chinese Constitutional Theory and Practice, in: Adams/Meuwese/Hirsch Ballin (eds.), Constitutionalism and the Rule of Law, 2017, 294–325.
Lin, Feng, The 2018 Constitutional Amendments: Significance and Impact on the Theories of Party-State Relationship in China, China Perspectives, no. 1, 2019, 11–21.
Lin Laifan 林来梵, 从宪法规范到规范宪法 - 规范宪法学的一种前言 [From Constitutional Norms to the Norms of the Constitution: An Introduction of Normative Constitutionalism], 2001.
Liu, Shang/Fong, Wen/Rorex, Robert A., Eighteen Songs of a Nomad Flute, 1974.
Moody, Peter R., Some Reflections on the Functions of "Xi Jinping's Thought", in: Hua, Chinese Ideology, 2022, 218–232.
Paydaş, Eren, A Mythopoieic Analysis of Constitutional Preambles, 2021.
Peerenboom, Randall, Social Foundations of China's Living Constitution, in: Ginsburg (ed.), Comparative Constitutional Design, 2012, 138–163.
Peng Zhen 彭真, 关于中华人民共和国宪法修改草案的报告 [Report on the Revision of the Constitutional Draft of the PRC], Renmin Ribao 人民日报, 6/12/1982.
Pu Zengyuan 浦增元, 宪草序言的基本特点 [The Basic Characteristics of the Preamble of the Constitutional Draft], Zhengzhi yu falü 政治与法律, No. 1, 1982, 25.
Qavuz, Qadir, A Chinese Idioms Dictionary with English and Uighur Translations (汉英维成语词典), 2003.
Qian Jinyu 钱锦宇, 宪法序言、国家梦想与政制建构 [The Constitutional Preamble, the National Dream and the Political System], Falü luntan 法学论坛, Vol. 28, No. 4, 2013, 29–36.
Schoenhals, Michael, Doing Things with Words in Chinese Politics: Five Studies, 1992.
Schurmann, Franz, Ideology and Organization in Communist China, 1966.
Tan Song 谭松/Yao Xinxue 姚新学, 中国成语汉英双解大词典 [A Dictionary of Chinese Idioms with English Translation], 1993.

Tian Feilong 田飞龙, 宪法序言: 中国宪法的"高级法背景" [Constitutional Preamble: The "higher law background" of the Chinese Constitution], Jianghan xueshu 江汉学术, Vol. 34, No. 4, 2015, 31–38.

Veg, Sebastian, The Rise of China's Statist Intellectuals: Law, Sovereignty, and "Repoliticization", 82(1) China Journal 2019, 23–45.

Voermans, Wim/Stremler, Maarten/Cliteur, Paul, Constitutional Preambles: A Comparative Analysis, 2017.

Xie, Libin/Patapan, Haig, Contesting Legitimacy in China: The Politics of Law in Modern Chinese Jurisprudence, 46(3) HKLJ 2016, 991–1016.

Xie Weiyan 谢维雁, 论宪法序言 [On the Constitutional Preamble], Shehui kexue yanjiu 社会科学研究, No. 5, 2004, 76–81.

Xu Chongde 许崇德, 中华人民共和国宪法史 [The History of the Constitution of the People's Republic of China], 2003.

Xu Chongde 许崇德, 许崇德自选集 [Selected Works of Xu Chongde], 2007.

Xu Xiuyi 徐秀义/Han Dayuan 韩大元, 宪法学原理 [Principles of Constitutional Law], 1993.

Yang Linhong 杨临宏/Liu Yamei 刘亚梅, 宪法序言比较研究 [A Comparative Study on Constitutional Preambles], Guangdong xingzheng xueyuan xuebao 广东行政学院学报, Vol. 15, No. 5, 2003, 53–57.

Yao Zhongqiu 姚中秋, 从革命到文明 [From Revolution to Civilization], Falü pinglun 法学评论, No. 2, 2015, 45–56.

Yu Zhong 喻中, 论宪法效力的终极依据 [On the Final Basis of the Binding Force of the Constitution], Zhengfa lun cong 政法论丛, No. 2, 2011, 79–85.

Zhai Zhiyong 翟志勇, 宪法序言中的国家观与世界主义 [Conceptions of State and Cosmopolitism in the Constitutional Preamble], Lishi faxue 历史法学, Vol. 10, 2015, 342–357.

Zhang, Qianfan, The Constitution of China: A Contextual Analysis, 2012.

Zhang, Xiaodan, Stufenordnung und Verfahren der Setzung von Rechtsnormen in der Volksrepublik China: Eine historische und normative Studie, 2017.

Zhang, Xiaodan, Carl Schmitt in China: Why Is He Needed and How Is He Understood? 25(2) ZChinR 2018, 83–101.

Zhang, Xiaodan, The Leadership of the CCP: From the Preamble to the Main Body of the Constitution—What are its Consequences for the Chinese Socialist Rule of Law? 12(1) Hague Journal on the Rule of Law 2020, 147–166.

Zhao, Tingyang, Redefining a Philosophy for World Governance, 2019.

CHAPTER 6

Revisit Chinese Exceptionalism Through the Lens of New Foreign Relations Law

Zixuan Yang

1 Introduction

> Charges of international law exceptionalism betray an undefended assumption that one particular view of international law (for scholars, usually the European view) is universally valid.
> —Anu Bradford, Eric A. Posner, Universal Exceptionalism in International Law[1]

[1] Anu Bradford & Eric A. Posner, 'Universal Exceptionalism in International Law' (2011) 52 Harv Int'l LJ 1.

The chapter was written in 2022, when the Law on Foreign Relations of the People's Republic of China hasn't come out. This is a preliminary attempt to revisit some assumptions on foreign relations law. Sincere thanks go to the discussion participants in Heidelberg and Hamburg. Many thanks to Mr John Foulks for the linguistic polishing. All errors are mine.

Z. Yang (✉)
Hamburg University, Hamburg, Germany
e-mail: zixuan.yang@studium.uni-hamburg.de

A. Aliu (ed.), *Complexity Thinking and China's Demography Within and Beyond Mainland China*,
https://doi.org/10.1007/978-981-97-0172-8_6

Exceptionalism is a frequently used term in comparative law. To set something as an exception means it is distinct from others and needs to be treated differently. Previous discussions of the U.S. foreign relations law contain at least two trends of exceptionalism. Firstly, foreign relations exceptionalism from a domestic perspective means foreign relations law is 'functionally, doctrinally and even methodologically distinct' from domestic law and policy.[2] Secondly, American exceptionalism from a global perspective means America's distinctive approaches toward international law are based on its own values and interests.[3] However, as Bradford and Posner argue, 'all major powers are similarly exceptionalist in the sense that they take distinctive approaches to international law that reflect their values and interest.'[4] A more universal argument would be that, whether being a major power or not, every state has its distinctive approaches to international law that are consistent with its national interest. This universal exceptionalism lays the basis for the future prospect of comparative foreign relations law study.[5]

This article revisits Chinese exceptionalism through the lens of planned foreign relations law with a focus on the status of treaties in the Chinese domestic legal order. China's multiple identities, as a 'socialist state', a 'developing state', and a 'rising power',[6] have led to the discussion of

[2] Ganesh Sitaraman & Ingrid Wuerth, 'The Normalization of Foreign Relations Law' (2015) 128 Harv L Rev 1897, 1900.

[3] The term 'American exceptionalism' originated with de Tocqueville, in whose view the United States differs qualitatively from other developed nations because of its unique origin, national credo, historical evolution, and distinctive political and religious institutions. See in Hongju Koh, 'On American Exceptionalism' (2003) 55 Stan L Rev 1479.

[4] Anu Bradford & Eric A. Posner, n 1, p. 6.

[5] Knop, Karen, 'Foreign Relations Law: Comparison as Invention', in Curtis A. Bradley (ed.), The Oxford Handbook of Comparative Foreign Relations Law, Oxford Handbooks (2019; online edn, Oxford Academic, 13 June 2019), https://doi.org/10.1093/oxfordhb/9780190653330.013.3, accessed 18 Oct 2023.

[6] Cai, Congyan, 'State Identity and Legal Policies', The Rise of China and International Law: Taking Chinese Exceptionalism Seriously, Law And Global Governance (New York, 2019; online edn, Oxford Academic, 24 Oct 2019), https://doi.org/10.1093/oso/9780190073602.003.0003, accessed 18 Oct 2023) pp. 41–42.

Chinese exceptionalism in both a positive[7] and a negative light.[8] From its passive responses in the nineteenth century to its active participation post-World War II, China's attitude toward international treaties has undergone a huge transition. In my view, rather than exceptionalism or exemptionalism, the treaty practice in China has tended to demonstrate efforts to find common ground rather than difference.[9] It gives China a good opportunity to demonstrate its exceptionalism on the international level and normalize it along with other states. The old maxim of 'seeking common ground while reserving differences' may be the best way to rethink the nature of Chinese exceptionalism in the context of the new foreign relations law.

2 Identifying Exceptionalism

Bradford and Posner describe Chinese exceptionalism as 'minimalist developmentalism' with the two distinct characteristics of *strict sovereignty* and *developmentalism*.[10] Both characteristics can be identified in the theory and practice of international law in China.

As for the characteristic of strict sovereignty, the principle of sovereignty is the primary principle of Chinese international law. It both reflects and is a reaction to the long-standing Westphalian sovereignty principle.[11] For instance, the Five Principles of Peaceful Coexistence that first established a rapport between China and India in 1954 still remain the basic premise of Chinese international law. These five principles are mutual respect for territorial integrity and sovereignty, mutual nonaggression, mutual noninterference in internal affairs, equality and mutual benefit, and peaceful coexistence. In Ginsburg's view, the decolonization movements led to the export of the mode of territorial nation-state, and

[7] Zhang, F. (2013). The Rise of Chinese Exceptionalism in International Relations. European Journal of International Relations, 19(2), 305–328. https://doi.org/10.1177/1354066111421038.

[8] Pitman B. Potter, 'Globalization and Economic Regulation in China: Selective Adaptation of Globalized Norms and Practices' (2003) 2 Wash U Global Stud L Rev 119.

[9] Anu Bradford & Eric A. Posner, n 1, p. 9.

[10] Ibid.

[11] Tom Ginsburg, 'Eastphalia as the Perfection of Westphalia' (2010) 17 Ind J Global Legal Stud 27.

state-building therefore became the most important task for China and other Asian and African states after the war. This partly accounts for the silence of China's 1954 constitution on the status of international law, because the establishment of the constitution did not satisfactorily resolve the issue of the termination of unequal treaties, which themselves concerned the crucial question of territorial integrity and sovereignty for the new government.

Along with the strict sovereignty principle, the power to conclude treaties is considered to be an essential element of sovereignty that in China must be exercised under the unified leadership of the State Council. The 1990 Law of the People's Republic of China on the Procedure of the Conclusion of Treaties empowered the State Council (central government) to conclude treaties and agreements with foreign states, while the Standing Committee of the National People's Congress of the People's Republic of China (legislative branch) was to decide on the ratification and abrogation of treaties and other important agreements.[12] The president, pursuant to the decision of the Standing Committee, ratifies and abrogates treaties and important agreements concluded with foreign states.[13] In practice, the State Council plays the central role in concluding treaties (ninety-nine percent of treaties)[14] as it has the power to initiate the course of treaty-making and to conduct diplomatic negotiations under the constitution.[15] For a detailed introduction to this procedure, see Chaoyi (2021) and Yifeng (2009).[16]

In this sense, concluding international treaties and carrying out obligations under them is regarded as an important symbol of the identity and sovereignty of the state and one that is especially important for the People's Republic of China to be positively regarded and supported by

[12] Art. 7 of the Law of the People's Republic of China on the Procedure of the Conclusion of Treaties.

[13] Art. 3, 4, 5 of the Procedure Law of the People's Republic of China on Conclusion of Treaties of 1990.

[14] Chen Yifeng, 'The Treaty-Making Power in China: Constitutionalization, Progress and Problems' (2009) 15 Asian YB Int'l L 43, 46, 69.

[15] Art. 89 of the Constitution of the People's Republic of China.

[16] Chaoyi Jiang, 'The Deviations of China's Treaty-Making Practices from Its Constitutional and Statutory Provisions? An Interbranch Perspective' (2021) 9 (3) Chinese J Comp Law 387–417.

international society. However, the allocation of power among the executive and legislative branches of government to conclude treaties on behalf of China operates more on a procedure than a constitutional level, and it is not as important as under the US constitution, which mandates that treaties undergo complex checks and balances. The allocation of treaty-making power in China instantiates a unified outcome obtained through *cooperation and coordination* among these branches.[17] Deng Xiaoping argued that the greatest advantage of this system is its efficiency. This uniformity in treaty-making also reflects the strict sovereignty principle of domestic supremacy (unity) and international independence (autonomy).

3 Universalizing Exceptionalism

Turning now to the developmentalism, on the other hand, one can observe China's policy of maintaining 'common but differentiated responsibilities' depending on the different stages of development and unequal capacities of different states in complying with international law. I have introduced this form of exceptionalism under the title of 'universalizing exceptionalism' because it is a stance advocated not only by China, but by China on behalf of all developing countries.

China's approaches to and stances on the Kyoto Protocol and to special and differential treatment before the WTO furnish two distinctive examples of this developmentalism.[18] Indeed, this 'common but differentiated responsibilities' principle appeared even earlier, and elsewhere, namely in the Treaty of Versailles (1919)[19] and in the General Agreement on Tariffs and Trade (1979)'s differential and more favorable tariff treatment. Nowadays, Western scholars sometimes criticize this principle, arguing that the law should apply equally to the rich and poor. But we would question whether the divergence between developed and developing countries can be simplified into the economic status of the rich or poor in the first place. In this sense, Chinese exceptionalism should be integrated into the broad challenges of developing countries' exceptionalism in taking on certain international obligations.

[17] Cai C, 'Chinese Foreign Relations Law' (2017) 111 AJIL Unbound 336.

[18] Christopher D. Stone, Common But Differentiated Responsibilities in International Law (2004) 98 AM. J.INT'L L. 276, 279.

[19] Constitutional of the International Labour Organisation, June 28, 1919, Art. 427, 49 Stat. 2712, 2733–2734, 225 Consol. T.S. 188, 385.

Another frequent criticism of China's treaty practice is its approach to international human rights law.[20] In general, China has two methods for the application of international treaties, which are referred to as 'automatic incorporation' and 'transformation'.

For treaties that are automatically incorporated, such as the United Nations Convention on Contracts for the International Sale of Goods, there is an underlying principle that international treaties binding on China have a status lower than constitutional law but higher than that of ordinary legislation. A conflicts rule is commonly adopted in specific domestic legal provisions stating that 'if there is a difference between the relevant domestic law and the related treaty to which China is a party, the treaty provision shall prevail, unless China has made a reservation to that effect.' For example, Article 189 of the Civil Procedure Law of the People's Republic of China of 1982 provides, 'If an international treaty concluded or acceded to by the People's Republic of China contains provisions that differ from provisions of this Law, the provisions of the international treaty shall apply, except for those on which China has made reservations,' and Article 142 of the General Principles of the Civil Law of the People's Republic of China, promulgated in 1986, states that 'the application of law in civil relations with foreign elements shall be determined by the provisions of said chapter. If any international treaty concluded or acceded to by the People's Republic of China contains provisions differing from those in the civil laws of the People's Republic of China, the provisions of the international treaty shall apply, unless the provisions are ones on which the People's Republic of China has declared reservations.'[21] However, it should be noted that the abovementioned treaties are all in the areas of civil and commercial law dealing with relations between private actors and foreign elements. Chinese courts frequently apply these treaties without stumbling over their status as law. By one calculation, by 2016 Chinese domestic courts had invoked the CISG in 198 cases, the New York Convention in 66 cases, the Paris Convention for the Protection of Industrial Property in 381 cases, and the Berne Convention for the Protection of Liberty and Artistic Works in 622 cases.

[20] Anu Bradford & Eric A. Posner, n 1, pp. 25–31.

[21] Art 142 of the General Principles of the Civil Law of the People's Republic of China (2009 Amendment).

The transformation method requires specific national legislation to transform treaties into domestic law. Chinese stances on the protection of individual human rights are provided through national law,[22] though this method is not specifically used for human rights conventions. For WTO agreements,[23] the UN Convention on the Law of the Sea,[24] and the Convention against Terrorism,[25] China adopted the same method by amending or revising pre-existing national laws to ensure their conformity with these international treaties. What this transformation method actually demonstrates is how international treaties (foreign-related rule of law) promote the rule of law domestically in many areas. But the practice of this transformation method to domesticate international human rights law also has drawn doubts and attacks on China's understanding of human rights based on its own national traditions, which definitely falls under Chinese exceptionalism.

However, if we place Chinese approaches within the broad landscape of Asia, the exceptionalism one finds may turn out to play a more familiar, conservative role toward the Global North-led international order. The common absence of ICC membership or a regional human rights court among Asian countries, their reluctancy to establish a powerful regional organization, and their insistence on the non-intervention principle are subtly described by Ginsburg as 'Eastphalia as the perfection of Westphalia'.[26] Unlike the gradual weakening of Westphalian sovereignty, eroded by globalization and by the post-war UN system in the so-called

[22] Xue Hanqin & Jin Qian, International Treaties in the Chinese Domestic Legal System, 8 Chinese J. INT'l L. 299 (2009), listing that 'The Compulsory Education Law of 1986, the Law on the Protection of Disabled Persons of 1990, the Law on the Protection of Women's Rights and Interests of 1992 and the Labor law of 1994 all contain clauses implementing international obligation that China has undertaken under human rights treaties'.

[23] Ibid. p. 308, 'To fulfill the international commitment, China has repealed, abrogated, revised, enacted and promulgated more than 3000 domestic laws, administrative regulations and administrative orders to ensure compliance with WTO rules'.

[24] The Law of the People's Republic of China on the Territorial Sea and Contiguous Zone in 1992.

[25] Art 9 of the Criminal Law of the People's Republic of China, 'This law is applicable to the crimes proscribed in the international treaties concluded or acceded to by the People's Republic of China and over which the People's Republic of China exercises criminal jurisdiction in accordance with its treaty obligations.'

[26] Tom Ginsburg, n 11.

New World Order,[27] most Asian countries still rely on the traditional Westphalian to shore up the modern state and try to strike a balance between state traditions and universalism toward better participation in the international community.

Learning to speak in the tone of international law (although sometimes in an outdated way) has been an important method for China, other Asian countries, and almost all international Asian scholars who have been endeavoring to attain the recognition and respect of international society for the last hundred years. However, faced with the latest tendencies, led by the United States, of trying to open states to outside scrutiny (defined by Ginsburg as liberal internationalism) and of identifying human rights as the central goal of global institution,[28] even the most brilliant international scholars from Asia would hesitate before acquiring and hastily transplanting them, because it would lead to resistance, not only from those governments who emphasize noninterference and sovereign equality, but also from regular citizens who might have encountered these foreign concepts of Westphalian international law in the past few years (notwithstanding growing doubts and criticism of the U.S. double standard and inconsistent practices of humanitarian intervention).[29] While this may be a frustrating reality for scholars who argue in good faith for a New World Order, it is a necessary fact of being seen and considered. If the New World Order is 'networks of state bureaucrats and judges interacting with each other cross borders to make and enforce rules' (a very European landscape),[30] then, firstly, these scholars need to well understand and communicate with Asian bureaucrats and judges, because the latter are representatives of sovereign states with all their respective powers. Secondly, the various perspectives of the population in Asian countries should also be taken into consideration, most of whose concept of and enthusiasm toward international law are not as active or advanced as Western scholars may assume.

[27] Anne-Marie Slaughter, *The New World Order* (2004).

[28] Tom Ginsburg, n 11, p. 30.

[29] Harold Hongju Koh, 'On American Exceptionalism' (2003) 55 Stan L Rev 1479, 1485–1487.

[30] Anne-Marie Slaughter, n 26, p. 16.

4 Normalizing Exceptionalism

In the context of global constitutionalism, we are calling for 'normalizing' foreign relations law to construct a new foreign relations law.[31] This normalization can be realized in different dimensions and indeed has already gone through several waves in the United States.[32] Ultimately, this paper wishes to see Chinese exceptionalism normalized in the new foreign relations law agenda. Chinese scholars argue that we should take Chinese exceptionalism seriously.[33] But overemphasizing any exceptionalism would lead to undue exemptions and even to the exclusion of other interests. Together with other Chinese international law scholars, I am optimistic about the normalization of Chinese exceptionalism though the lens of a new foreign relations law. My optimism is based particularly on the following three grounds.

Firstly, China has been learning to speak the language of international law since the nineteenth century. China's transplantation of public and private international law from Western legal systems has been quite continuous and has been welcomed compared to other fields of law because foreign relations are crucial to sovereignty, independence, and state-building. Meanwhile, China's recent advocation of a foreign-related rule of law is not merely rhetoric but rather is supported by the active adoption and adaption of international treaties. Faced with allegations by the United States of permitting forced labor, the Standing Committee of the NPC on 20 April 2022 ratified the Forced Labor Convention of 1930 and the Abolition of Forced Labor Convention of 1957.[34] Further legislation and implementation can be expected to follow.

Secondly, Chinese scholars actively discussing foreign relations law will open up the channels for communication, understanding, and contributions from both sides. A review of the literature shows Chinese publications on foreign relations law by private international law scholars

[31] Peters A, 'Foreign Relations Law and Global Constitutionalism' (2017) 111 AJIL Unbound 331.

[32] Ganesh Sitaraman & Ingrid Wuerth, 'The Normalization of Foreign Relations Law' (2015) 128 Harv L Rev 1897, 1919–1930.

[33] Cai Congyan, *The Rise of China and International Law* (2019).

[34] Decision of the Standing Committee of the National People's Congress to Ratify the Abolition of Forced Labour Convention, 1957. Decision of the Standing Committee of the National People's Congress to Ratify the Forced Labour Convention, 1930.

dating back to 2009.[35] The current promotion of domestic and foreign-related rule of law standards has started a new wave of foreign relations law that actively reaches for dialogue with foreign scholars. For example, the Chinese Journal of Comparative Law Vol. 9(No.3) in 2021 gathered outstanding international law scholars to write in English on 'the Rule of Law in Chinese Foreign Relations'. These forward-thinking scholars can become bridges for demonstrating and normalizing Chinese exceptionalism in the new foreign relations law agenda.

Thirdly, current decolonial perspectives which revisit and rethink the Eurocentric approaches and standards give China good opportunities to make itself understood and achieve better inclusion for itself against long-lasting prejudices and distrust of Chinese institutions and approaches. It is indeed moving to read Ginsburg's argument that 'Eastphalia may be Westphalia without the universalism – a kinder, gender Westphalia'.[36] But the decolonial approach is not to create antagonism or seek to wrest hegemony from the other side, but to understand differences based on each state's historical and ideological context, which in the future will make foreign relations law much more inclusive and pluriversal.

[35] Liu Renshan, 'Chinese Foreign Relations law is Essential Part of Chinese Legal System' (2009) 15 Law and Social Development, p. 151.

[36] Tom Ginsburg, n.11, p. 45.

CHAPTER 7

Coordination and Interaction Between Intra-Party Regulations and National Laws in the Context of Supervision System Reform

Ma Sijie

1 Introduction

State institutions, political party, and other members of society are obligated to operate and engage in activities according to specific rules, this embodies the fundamental essence of the rule of law. Within the unique political developmental trajectory of China, characterized by a "Party-State" system, the interplay between Intra-Party Regulations and national laws jointly upholds the leadership of the Communist Party of China (CPC) and the governance order of the state. Due to the particular political reality, the principle that "Govern the country, one must first govern

S. Ma (✉)
College of Administrative Law, Northwest University of Political Science and Law, Xi'an, China
e-mail: sijie.ma@nwupl.edu.cn

A. Aliu (ed.), *Complexity Thinking and China's Demography Within and Beyond Mainland China*,
https://doi.org/10.1007/978-981-97-0172-8_7

the Party; and in governing the Party, strict discipline is essential" (治国必先治党、治党务必从严)[1] (Jiang 2006: 496) distinctly underscores the close interrelation and interdependence between party governance and national governance. Therefore, some legal scholars point out that in order to understand the Chinese party state and its governance practices, it is essential to delve deep into intra-party regulations, especially their position and role within the broader Chinese legal system (Samuli 2022).

In terms of the meaning of "law", in a narrow sense, "law" refers solely to behavioral rules that are established or approved by state authorities and are enforced under the state's coercive power, specifically meaning statutes and regulations. However, the system of social norms or the regulatory system is composed of rules of varying natures, scopes, and levels. Broadly understood, all these rules can be termed "law". Due to differences in form and methods of implementation, some scholars refer to legal norms enforced by state coercive power as "hard law", while behavioral rules that exist in reality, effectively constrain actions but are not primarily enforced directly through state coercive power, are referred to as "soft law".

The intra-party regulation is designed to regulate the behavior of the party organization, its activities, and its members. They do not inherently require the coercive power of the state for enforcement, thus falling under the category of "soft law."[2] However, doubts persist. A representative skeptical viewpoint questions whether intra-party regulations are indeed "law". If not, why are they termed as such? If they are, what is their relationship with national laws? Emphasizing the development and refinement of the intra-party regulation system could potentially diminish the authority of national laws, possibly leading to conflicts between the two normative systems, leaving society in uncertainty. These concerns are not unfounded. The matters adjusted by intra-party regulations and national laws are mostly clearly distinguishable, but there are also areas of overlap.

To address these concerns and bridge the gap between party regulations and national laws for a more coordinated governance approach, the

[1] This concept emphasizes the pivotal role of a strong and disciplined political party in ensuring the stability and prosperity of a nation.

[2] Most Chinese scholars support incorporating party regulations into the category of "soft law". See Song Gongde (2016), Qin qianhong (2016), Jiang mingan (2012) and Luo haocai and Zhou qiang (2013).

Chinese Communist Party's Decision Concerning Some Major Questions in Comprehensively Promoting the Rule of Law ("the Decision")[3] issued in 2014 has incorporated intra-party regulations into the socialist legal system with Chinese characteristics. It also put forth the proposition of "emphasizing the connection and coordination between intra-party regulations and national laws."[4] This step not only elevated the significance of intra-party regulations but also demonstrated the Party's determination to enhance governance through legal means. Over the last five years, with the progression of China's supervisory system reforms, the convergence and mutual reinforcement between intra-party regulations and national laws in the realm of party and national oversight have grown more pronounced. Especially when it comes to the tangible processes of party disciplinary reviews and state oversight, understanding the nuances between intra-party regulations and national laws, and discerning their synergistic relationship, demands thorough investigation and precise delineation. Determining how to seamlessly integrate both, and addressing potential disparities and overlaps in their application, stand as pivotal challenges in the ongoing efforts to enhance the rule of law.

This research aims to explore how intra-party regulations and national laws can effectively coordinate and interact with each other during the supervision system reform. To understand the origins, characteristics, and the role of intra-party regulations in China's rule of law journey more accurately and comprehensively, this paper adopts a systematic approach to delve into four progressively related questions. Firstly, we have explored the background, nature, and connotation of China's intra-party regulations from the dimension of historical origin, laying the foundation of understanding for a comprehensive discussion. Following this, the relationship between intra-party regulations and national laws is scrutinized to decipher their interplay and mutual implications. In the context of the state's supervision system reform, based on Intra-Party Supervision perspective, we further dissect how these two distinct systems can coexist

[3] English version of this Decision, see https://chinacopyrightandmedia.wordpress.com/2014/10/28/ccp-central-committee-decision-concerning-some-major-questions-in-comprehensively-moving-governing-the-country-according-to-the-law-forward/, assessed on June 12, 2023.

[4] The Decision concerning Some Major Questions in Comprehensively Promoting the Rule of Law with the proposition of "focusing on the convergence and coordination between the Party's internal regulations and national laws".

in a "dual-track" structure, effectively complementing and reinforcing one another. Concluding this exploration, the paper sheds light on the practical challenges and dilemmas posed by this dual system, aiming to offer insights into potential resolutions and forward-thinking strategies.

2 Understanding Intra-Party Regulations from a Historical Perspective

In China, following the establishment of the legal system of socialism with Chinese characteristics, the intra-party regulatory system has emerged as another significant normative framework. This framework is regarded as a core component of the socialist legal system with Chinese characteristics. This unprecedented innovation in the annals of global jurisprudence signifies the CPC centennial journey of exploration and adaptation, as it had no historical precedents to rely on. The formation of this system encountered unparalleled challenges due to its uniqueness and complexity.

Throughout the evolution of the intra-party regulatory system, the emergence of "intra-party regulations" can be traced back to the early twentieth century, undergoing a relatively prolonged period of gestation, growth, and systematization. There are two fundamental questions arise: What prompted the establishment of these intra-party regulations? And why was there a need to construct such a system? The answers to these questions are pivotal in understanding how the CPC has transformed into a modernized and institutionalized ruling party.

2.1 From 1921 to 1978: Emphasizing Strict Discipline Within the Political Party

The first program of the Communist Party of China, adopted at its first Congress in 1921, is retrospectively considered to be the inaugural intra-party regulation. However, in the nascent stages of the party's establishment, there were no formal intra-party regulations in the conventional sense. The party's operations and activities primarily relied on meetings and documents,[5] with the latter being central to the governance

[5] Documents, also referred to as 'official papers,' are categorized into official documents (abbreviated as 'official papers') and private documents. The party's documents

approach. Later, during the local governance period of the Communist Party of China in Yan'an district, Mao Zedong first introduced the term "intra-party regulations"*(党内法规)* in his report[6] at the Sixth Plenary Session of the Sixth "Central Committee".

> Mao Zedong proposed that in order to streamline the internal relations of the Party, in addition to the four most important disciplines of 'individuals obeying the organization, the minority obeying the majority, the lower levels obeying the higher ones, and the entire Party obeying the Central Committee', there was also a need to formulate a more detailed set of intra-party regulations to unify the actions of leadership organs at all levels.

At this plenary session, Liu Shaoqi delivered a speech titled 'Report on Party Rules and Party Laws', addressing the question of 'why there is a need for party rules and laws as well as organizational decisions'. He highlighted three primary reasons: firstly, the Party constitution was formulated quite early on and is not adaptable to many new situations; secondly, to ensure the unity and cohesion of the Party, there is a need for 'party rules and laws to educate comrades'; and thirdly, to 'ensure that our Party is built according to the principle of democratic centralism' (CPC Central Committee Literature Research Office and Central Archives 2011: 749). The concept of intra-party regulations and laws had emerged by this time, yet these regulations were still fundamentally considered a component of the Party's discipline.

fall under the category of official documents. After its establishment, the party organization formulated a plethora of documents. The names of these documents are numerous, including 'programs,' 'resolutions,' 'decisions,' 'regulations,' 'reports,' 'announcements,' 'notifications, ' 'bulletins,' 'propositions,' 'constitutions,' 'manifestos,' 'policies,' 'plans,' 'opinions,' 'suggestions,' 'requests,' 'resolutions,' 'directives,' 'methods, ' 'letters, ' and so forth. The content of these documents is also extremely rich, covering areas such as domestic politics, international situations, social movements, economic conditions, organizational development, disciplinary supervision, and propaganda education. For example, volumes 1 to 18 of the 'Selected Documents of the CPC Central Committee' edited by the Central Archives and published by the Publishing House of the CPC Central Party School, include various documents issued in the name of the CPC Central Committee prior to 1949.

[6] "In 1938, Mao Zedong presented his report titled 'The Role of the Chinese Communist Party in the National War' at the Sixth Plenary Session of the Sixth Central Committee".

2.2 From 1978 to 2012: Integrating Discipline with Party Building and Leadership

After the founding of the People's Republic of China, the development of intra-party regulations experienced various ups and downs. Following the end of the ten-year turmoil, Deng Xiaoping emphasized at the Third Plenary Session of the 11th Central Committee that "the nation needs national laws, and the Party requires intra-party regulations and laws". Although this session still considered intra-party regulations and laws as part of the Party's discipline, it marked the election of the Central Discipline Inspection Committee, ensuring a specialized mechanism for the implementation of intra-party regulations and laws.[7]

After the plenary session, there was an expansion in both the content and form of the intra-party regulations. In 1980, the Fifth Plenary Session of the 11th Central Committee passed the "Several Criteria on Intra-Party Political Life", which provided regulations on many matters related to party construction and leadership. From then on, the scope of intra-party regulations and laws was no longer limited to party discipline but extended to party construction and leadership.

After 1990, intra-party regulations became a specific category of party documents. In 1990, the CPC Central Committee issued the "Interim Regulations on the Formulation of Intra-Party Regulations of the Communist Party of China,"[8] which for the first time defined the concept of "intra-party regulations" and clearly stipulated their names, scope of application, formulation procedures, and other matters. In 1992, the 14th National Congress of the Communist Party of China (CPC) incorporated the term "intra-party regulations" into the Party Constitution, marking the official recognition of the vocabulary and concept

[7] The Communique of the Third Plenary Session of the 11th Central Committee stated, "The nation needs national laws, and the Party requires intra-party regulations and laws. All party members and officials must adhere to the Party's discipline; this is the basic requirement for restoring normal political life in the Party and the country. ... The fundamental task of the Discipline Inspection Committee is to uphold intra-party regulations and laws and to earnestly improve the Party's conduct". This was cited in Document Research Office of the CPC Central Committee. (2008). Selected Important Documents from Thirty Years of Reform and Opening Up: Volume I. Central Literature Publishing House.

[8] The "Interim Regulations on the Formulation of Intra-Party Regulations of the Communist Party of China" stipulates the seven names for intra-party regulations: Party Constitution, Guidelines, Regulations, Rules, Provisions, Methods, and Detailed Rules.

of "intra-party regulations" by the party's fundamental laws. Since then, "intra-party regulations" have become a standardized term and have entered the process of institutionalized construction. Meanwhile, the 1999 amendment to the Constitution of the People's Republic of China[9] clearly defined the basic principle and objective of "governing the country according to law". The CPC leaders and national leaders attach great importance to the construction of the legal system for people's livelihood. Against this backdrop, the experience of building a national legal system was introduced into the field of party construction. The coverage of the intra-party regulatory system has expanded to institutionalize all aspects of the party's work and intra-party life (Meng 2021).

2.3 Since 2012: Legalization, Systematization, and Standardization of Intra-Party Regulations

During this stage, both in form and content, the internal party regulations showed a clear distinction from the Party's documents. The internal party regulations not only possessed a complete set of formulation, implementation, and construction guarantee systems but also found a new affiliation: the legal system of socialism with Chinese characteristics. In November 2013, the Party Central Committee issued the Five-Year Plan Outline for the Formulation of Central Party Internal Regulations (2013–2017), explicitly proposing to strive to form a framework for the internal party regulatory system that covers the main areas of party construction and work and meets the needs of party governance. In October 2014, the fourth plenary session of the 18th Central Committee of the Party incorporated "forming a comprehensive internal party regulatory system" into the overall goal of comprehensively promoting the rule of law.

In December 2016, the Central Committee of the Communist Party of China held the first national internal party regulation work conference in the history of the Party. It introduced the "Opinions of the CPC Central Committee on Strengthening the Construction of the Internal Party Regulatory System", proposing the construction of the internal

[9] Zhonghua renmin gongheguo xianfa [PRC Constitution] PRC Constitution, as amended on 15 March 1999, article 13: "The Constitution's Article 5 adds a provision as the first clause, stating: 'The People's Republic of China practices the rule of law and builds a socialist rule of law country". See https://flk.npc.gov.cn/xf/html/xf5.html, accessed July 15, 2023.

party regulatory system with the "1 + 4" basic framework (as shown in Fig. 1). At the same time, it set the goal of forming a relatively comprehensive internal party regulatory system by the 100th anniversary of the Party's founding.[10] In October 2017, the 19th National Congress of the CPC emphasized the organic unity of governing the country by law and governing the party by regulation. In February 2018, the CPC Central Committee issued the second five-year plan for the formulation of the Central Party's internal regulations (2018–2022), further clarifying the task book, timetable, and roadmap for the construction of the party's internal regulatory system. In April 2023, the CPC Central Committee issued the latest five-year plan outline for the formulation of the Central Party's internal regulations (2023–2027). It can be said that since the 18th National Congress of the CPC, the importance attached to the party's internal regulations has further increased, the pace of improving the party's internal regulatory system has accelerated, and it is regarded as the key carrier for realizing the rule of law in party governance. This reflects the party's pursuit and determination for the modernization, standardization, and rule of law of internal governance.

In broad terms, the Communist Party of China (CPC) has experienced significant transformations in its role and internal governance as it transitioned from a revolutionary party to a ruling entity. Initially, the

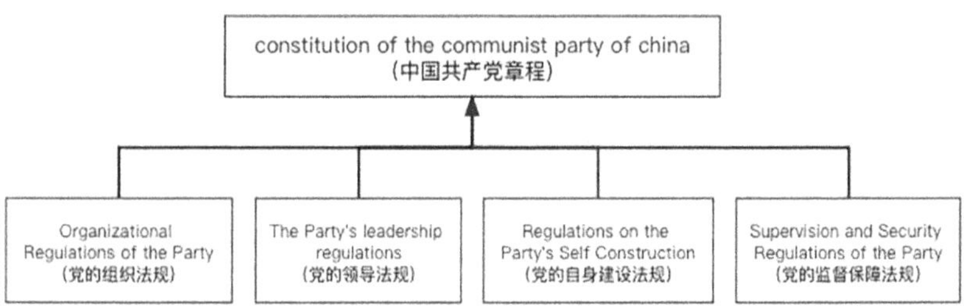

Fig. 1 The construction of the internal party regulatory system with the "1 + 4" basic framework

[10] CPC Central Committee. Zhonggong Zhongyang guanyu jiaqiang dangnei fagui zhidu jianshe de yijian [Opinions on Strengthening the Construction of the Internal Party Regulatory System] (2019), In Selected Internal Regulations of the Communist Party of China (2012–2017), edited by the Bureau of Legal Regulations of the CPC Central Office, Zhongguo Falü chuban she.

CPC predominantly utilized a document-centric governance approach to oversee party discipline and organization. However, with the initiation of the reform and opening-up policy, coupled with the establishment of the socialist market economic framework, there was a discernible shift toward a rule of law governance paradigm within the party's operations. It's imperative to recognize that political parties, as political establishments, possess vast autonomous rights within the legal parameters. They are expected to function according to their intrinsic rules and regulations, provided they don't contravene national laws. Yet, to foster exemplary intra-party governance, a comprehensive and standardized set of intra-party regulations is pivotal. This inherently suggests a move toward the codification of the party's governance structure. Every facet of intra-party activities, from decision-making, steering state institutions, and organizational management to safeguarding members' rights and conducting disciplinary inspections, necessitates a system that's institutionalized, standardized, and procedural.

History underscores that for the CPC's evolution from a revolutionary entity to a governing body, a meticulously crafted regulatory framework is irreplaceable. Sole reliance on charismatic leadership, paired with a fragmented document-based governance system, not only impedes the maturation of a ruling party but might also pave the way for potential abuses of power. Given the CPC's pivotal leadership stature, constructing a rule of law state and a contemporaneous national governance mechanism mandates the infusion of sophisticated intra-party regulations to ensure cohesive resonance. For the modernization of governance, both within the party and at the national level, intra-party regulations serve as the quintessential institutional conduit.

3 The Relationship Between Intra-Party Regulations and National Laws

Following the Fourth Plenum of the 18th Central Committee placed the "intra-party regulation system" and the "legal norm system" in parallel, making each an integral part of the "system of socialist rule of law", the relationship between intra-party regulations and national laws has been a continuous focus of academic discussion and exploration (e.g., Song and Zhang 2020: 22; Ou 2018: 40; Deng and Wu 2022: 80–90). Intra-party regulations and state laws should be two different rule systems, with different constraints, different normative affairs, different formulating entities, and different implementation methods. So far, almost all academic contributions in the Chinese scholarly community have enthusiastically embraced this change, recognizing its rationality and legitimacy. Mou Licheng and Xiao Jinming have conducted in-depth studies on the three paradigms of the relationship between intra-party regulations and national laws since the 1980s, clearly illustrating the developmental logic from a "dual" to a "systemic connection" (Mou and Xiao 2021: 62–72). Wu Xiaochuan, from a broader perspective, points out that intra-party regulations, as a product of history and society, do not necessarily conflict with national laws. Instead, they can play their rightful role through adjustments to their internal structure (Wu 2016: 14–23).

However, despite scholars agreeing on this transition, concerns have been raised about potential overlaps, conflicts, and insufficient integration between the two. For instance, Hou Jiabin believes that the intersections between intra-party regulations and national laws could result in these regulations impacting non-party members or the general public (Hou 2018: 98); Jiang Feng holds a similar view, suggesting that the boundaries between intra-party regulations and national laws are becoming increasingly blurred, with party regulations no longer solely governing intra-party behaviors but extending into a broader public space (Jiang 2019: 260); Qin Qianhong points out that the joint issuance of intra-party regulations by party and government agencies could lead to confusion in areas like record reviews, discipline enforcement, and even potential judicial applications and incidental reviews (Qin and Zhang 2021: 54–70). Zhang Qianfan argues that incorporating the party's disciplinary inspection committee into the state mechanism extends the applicability of party regulations beyond judicial constraints in criminal investigations (Zhang 2021: 595). International scholars, such as Acques deLisle, Holly Snape, and Samuli Seppänen, also indicate that the relationship between intra-party regulations and national laws presents contradictions and challenges on various levels, encompassing law, politics, and ideology (Holly 2019: 255–259; DeLisle 2017: 70; Seppanen 2019: 267). This paper contends that party regulations and national laws are two distinct normative systems in terms of their inherent nature and the boundaries of their authority, and they should not be indiscriminately equated. The co-governance relationship between the two manifests differently in terms of their formulation, implementation, and applicable subjects. The subsequent discussions will be organized into three sections.

3.1 *Intra-party Regulations and National Laws: Two Parallel and Non-contradictory Institutional Paths for Governance*

The relationship between law and politics has always been a fundamental category in the philosophy of law. With the establishment of the rule of law concept and the continuous advancement of legal system construction in China, the political system and the legal system are increasingly separated. Within the political system centered on the ruling party, a political normative system centered on the Party Constitution and intra-party regulations has emerged, while the national legal system continues to be refined. Currently, two of the most important normative systems have been formed in the national governance system, namely, the intra-party regulatory system as the core norm of the political system, and the national legal system as the external norm of the political system.

From a temporal perspective, the emergence of intra-party regulations predates the time when the Communist Party, after establishing its rule, led the people to formulate the constitution and laws. For a significant period after the founding of the People's Republic of China, intra-party regulations and national laws did not influence each other, nor was there a relationship of replacement or being replaced. Furthermore, after the twists and turns of the 1960s and 1970s, the Communist Party of China realized that party leadership and party construction must conform to the spirit of the rule of law. While intra-party regulations and national laws influence each other, they do not merge into one, nor do they replace each other, and they both play roles in their respective fields. Thus, Deng Xiaoping asserted:

> The Party should manage issues related to its internal discipline, while issues within the scope of the law should be overseen by the state and government. Excessive intervention by the Party is not conducive to establishing the concept of the legal system among the entire population. This is a matter concerning the relationship between the Party and the government, and it pertains to the political system. (Deng Xiaoping 2001: 163–164)

The current Constitution, adopted in 1982, confirms the leadership position of the Party, (Database of National Laws and Regulations 1982) and the basic guidelines for subsequent political system reforms emphasize the approach of promoting the "separation of the Party and the government" while adhering to the fundamental premise of the Party's leadership. This serves as practical evidence of the concept regarding the coexistence of the political system (means) and the legal system (means) and their interrelationship. However, critics argue that incorporating the Party's leadership into the Constitution is both theoretically and practically at odds with the rule of law.

Some criticized opinions suggest that "governing according to law" is rule by law, not rule of law, and that law is a tool to be wielded by the authoritarian state as it wishes without imposing meaningful constraints on state and Party power. Starting from the specific national conditions of China, Peerenboom elucidates that the Party and state systems in China are separate. Each has its own constitution, institutions, rules, and procedures, yet they operate in tandem. While the Party assumes a leadership role in China and steers the ideological realm, the state primarily shoulders the duties of governance and administration (Peerenboom 2015: 49–74).

3.2 *The Hierarchy of Efficacy: National Law Supersedes Party Regulations*

For a long time in China's national political life, there has been a "gray zone" in the connection between systems—the relationship between the Party and the law, which is the primary catalyst for metaphorical questions like "Is the Party superior or is the law superior?" (Tao 2015: 42). Some scholars believe that "the advanced nature of the CCP determines that the Party stands above the law" (Seppäne 2022: 128–139). In this regard, the author cites the views of Chinese legal scholar Professor Xu Xianming from the 2017 China Rule of Law Forum as a basis. The content of Professor Xu's speech is:

> The Party's leadership must be within the framework of the state's laws and constitution, hence the Party is below the law. The Party's ruling status and power are based on the constitution and laws, so the Party is within the law. The advanced nature of the Communist Party determines that it must grasp the laws of social development, propose amendments from outside the legal framework, and achieve legislative leadership, so the Party stands above the law. (See e.g., Xu Xianming 2017)

The paper believes that interpreting "the Party can stand above the law" might does not entirely align with Professor Xu's original intention. Professor Xu's viewpoint emphasizes the multiple roles of the Communist Party of China within the legal domain. The stance of being "above" stems from the fact that the Party is not only the maker and practitioner of the law but also its guardian. Furthermore, it possesses the ability to guide and reform the law. Such a multifaceted role allows the Communist Party to both adhere to and guide and reform the law, ensuring the Party's leadership and the continuous progress of society.

In terms of efficacy, national laws inevitably hold precedence over intra-party regulations, and legal authority naturally supersedes party authority. Firstly, Article 5, Clause 4 of the Constitution stipulates: "All state organs, armed forces, political parties, social groups, enterprises, and institutions must abide by the Constitution and the law". According to the requirements of the Constitution, just like other organizations, the Communist Party of China, as the ruling party, must also use the Constitution and laws as the guideline for its activities. The "Preamble" of the Party Constitution also stipulates: "The Party must operate within the confines of the Constitution and laws". The "Five-Year Plan for the Formulation of Central Party Internal Regulations (2013–2017)" also proposes that one of the basic requirements for the formulation of intra-party regulations is "the Constitution takes precedence, with the Party Constitution as the foundation".

Secondly, the CPC has already clearly differentiated the intra-party regulatory system from the national legal system, emphasizing their linkage and coordination. This distinctly conveys to both within and outside the party that there is no intention to mix or conflate the two. Otherwise, it would be a return to the tortuous old paths of "governing the country by the Party" and "indistinctness between Party and government", contradicting its proclaimed values of ruling the country according to law and governing by law (Li Shuzhong 2017: 65); Thirdly, the word "internal" in the term "intra-party regulations" distinctly delineates its scope of regulation, indicating that it serves as a fundamental guideline for the work and activities of the party organizations at all levels and all its members, without relying on the state's coercive power for enforcement. Therefore, intra-party regulations are "laws" in the sense of behavioral rules. They are behavioral norms within the party, falling under the category of "soft law" (Wu 2016: 18). They are not components of state law, which can be termed as "hard law", and do not rely on state coercive power for implementation. Hence, they naturally wouldn't conflict with state law (Qin 2016: 54).

Conflating intra-party regulations with state law or even placing them above state law essentially overlooks the differences in nature and effectiveness between different norms. Therefore, the "gray area" problem of the state system has been preliminarily resolved in theory and logic. The metaphorical relationship between the party and the law is no longer an issue. The focus has shifted to the institutional linkage between state law and party regulations within the legal system of socialism with Chinese characteristics.

3.3 Stringency and Standards: Intra-party Regulations Are Stricter Than National Law

As the ruling party, the Party must consistently maintain its vanguard nature and purity. This requires continuous reinforcement of constraints and norms on the ideologies and actions of its organizations and members. Relying solely on the law, which serves as the "basic moral standard", is insufficient. Instead, the Party should adopt disciplinary rules that are more stringent than the law. Party members are subject to stricter supervision and higher standards than ordinary citizens. A violation of national law by a party member is undeniably also a breach of party regulations. Such a member would face dual scrutiny under both legal responsibilities and party disciplinary actions. If a party member's actions breach party rules but not national law, they might be exempt from legal repercussions, but not from internal party reviews. They must shoulder the responsibilities stipulated by the party's regulations. This mechanism ensures that party members are consistently held accountable within the bounds of both 'law' and 'discipline', thereby maintaining the Party's vanguard nature and purity.

Simultaneously, Party regulations are stricter than national laws, which is not only reflected in the principle that Party discipline is stricter than state law but also in the notion that Party discipline precedes state law, embodying the idea that "discipline should be at the forefront" *(把纪*

律挺在前面).[11] This preemptive nature of Party discipline establishes a disciplinary baseline for Party members before any legal bottom line, intervening and addressing misguided behaviors in their infancy. This approach prevents minor transgressions from escalating into illegal activities, nipping any pathways for Party members' criminal conduct in the bud (Yao 2020: 68).

However, an important point to note is that the principle of 'Party regulations being stricter than national laws' does not necessarily conflict with the principle that 'national laws supersede Party regulations.' This is because being 'stricter' doesn't inherently mean being 'inconsistent.' For instance, while engaging in improper relationships with others may not be legally prosecuted, it is considered a violation of the Party's conduct and can result in disciplinary action. Ordinary citizens who do not assist others in danger may not face legal repercussions, being subject at most to moral condemnation and public criticism. However, Party members who, when faced with threats to state property or public life and assets, have the ability to help but choose not to, could face penalties ranging from warnings to expulsion from the Party, depending on the severity of the neglect.[12] Thus, it's evident that the "higher standards" of Party

[11] In the work report at the 6th Plenary Session of the 18th Central Commission for Discipline Inspection of the Communist Party of China, Wang Qishan, the former Vice President of the People's Republic of China, delivered a speech titled "Comprehensively Strictly Governing the Party, Putting Discipline at the Forefront, and Faithfully Fulfilling the Sacred Duties Endowed by the Party Constitution". He emphasized the importance of prioritizing strict political discipline and rules. General Secretary Xi Jinping also emphasized during the 2nd Plenary Session of the 20th Central Commission for Discipline Inspection that "discipline construction should be given a more prominent position" and made important deployments in this regard.

[12] Article 110 of the Regulations of the Communist Party of China on Disciplinary Actions states: "Anyone who engages in trading in power and sex, or gives property or goods for the purpose of trading in money and sex, shall be given a warning or a serious warning; if the circumstances are more serious, he shall be given the punishment of revocation of his post within the Party or put on probation; if the circumstances are serious, he shall be expelled from the Party"; Article 127 stipulates that: "Anyone who engages in improper sexual relations with another person, causing adverse effects, shall be given a warning or a serious warning; if the circumstances are more serious, he shall be given the punishment of revocation of his Party post or probation; if the circumstances are serious, he shall be given the punishment of expulsion from the Party".

regulations, in terms of behavioral benchmarks and disciplinary red lines, are stricter than national laws but don't inherently conflict with them.

4 Realizing the "Dual-track System" of Party Regulations and State Law: A Perspective on the Reform of the Supervisory System

In the realm of China's governance model, the interplay between Party regulations and state law represents a unique dynamic that has evolved alongside the nation's political and legal development. Given the Chinese Communist Party's predominant role in shaping and guiding the state's path, it's imperative to understand how Party regulations can coexist, intertwine, and at times, differentiate from state laws.

The recent reform of the supervisory system offers a fresh lens through which we can examine this relationship. This reform, the establishment of the National Supervisory Commission,[13] which operates in conjunction with the Party's Discipline Inspection Commission (colloquially known as "yitao banzi liangkuai paizi" or "one team, two badges"), underscores the deepening and conspicuous overlap and interplay between these two regulatory frameworks.

Academics commonly adopt this perspective to observe the coexistence, challenges, and integration issues between the two systems. Some scholars express concerns that the intensified reforms on the Party's discipline and its intra-party regulations will legitimize the intra-party regulatory framework. This effectively expands the purview of the Communist Party of China's disciplinary inspections into the Chinese state apparatus, thereby narrowing the scope of formal legal procedures (Zhang 2021: 580; Jiang 2019: 265). Additionally, some experts point out that, in the realm of anti-corruption, not only is there a disconnect between national laws and the intra-party regulatory system, but there are also issues of conflation, overlapping ambiguities, and insufficient continuity (Hu 2016: 15).

[13] In March 2018, the National People's Congress approved a constitutional amendment to establish the powerful National Supervisory Commission as a fourth branch of government, giving it the same constitutional status as the State Council, the Supreme People's Court, and the Supreme People's Procuratorate. The National Supervisory Commission answers to the National People's Congress and its standing committee.

The author posits that "coordination" and "integration" are distinct concepts in aligning intra-party regulations with national laws.[14] In essence, coordination avoids contradictions, while integration seeks seamless design alignment. A consistent legal status between Party rules and national laws is fundamental. Without such harmony, their alignment might be just theoretical (Li 2021: 45). Jurisprudentially, the integration of Party supervision with the state supervisory system depends on the consistent legal statuses of Party rules and national laws. If these legal entities are not harmonized or don't share a legal tier, their integration might merely be a theoretical construct (Ji 2020: 39).

4.1 *How Is Cooperation and Interaction Possible?*

Marked by the Decision, which clearly incorporated intra-party regulations into the legal system of socialism with Chinese characteristics, intra-party regulations have achieved a legal status that matches national laws, thoroughly eliminating the theoretical barriers to the integration of Party rules and national laws (Zhang 2021). At the same time, the establishment of the goals of comprehensively governing the country by law and governing the Party by rules in the new era has led to a deep and multifaceted overlap between Party and state governance. Therefore, China's political system dictates the coordinated application of Party discipline and national laws in anti-corruption efforts. Starting with this decision, the integration of intra-party supervisory regulations and the national legal system has been officially established. However, we should not simply conflate the two, they differ fundamentally in their theoretical bases and have distinct regulatory domains and theoretical features.

There are three mainstream views on the relationship between the two in the academic community: First of all, oppositional theory. Some scholars suggest that party regulations are not "laws" and that juxtaposing them with national laws will weaken the authority of national laws. This point of view is undoubtedly questionable. Until now the whole world has not yet reached a consensus on what is "law". Party regulations with

[14] "Coordination" grounded in the principle that "the Party must operate within the boundaries of the Constitution and laws", insists on the "legality" of intra-party regulations; "integration" stemming from the Party's leadership and governing position, underscores the systematic and cohesive adjustment between Party regulations and national laws.

the mandatory and sanction characteristics are very clear and cannot be simply defined does not belong to the category of "law". For example, as the internal management system of colleges and universities, the internal normative documents of grass-roots self-government organizations, etc., all have the characteristics of the law and coexist with the national law and complement each other to promote each other.

Secondly, some scholars have proposed that the legislative law should be amended as soon as possible so that the party regulations at all levels to become the main body of the national law-making in the name of the legitimate (Liu 2019; Wang 2016). This point of view only see the consistency of the two, and ignore the differences between the party regulations and national laws.

Thirdly, some may argue party regulations are a kind of advance law similar to natural law, and that when necessary, the national law, which is a kind of statutory law, needs to give way to the party regulations, which are a kind of advance law. Qiang Shigong proposes from the perspective of Western legal tradition that the relationship between party regulations and state law is similar to the relationship between natural law and statutory law. And in the Chinese context, the relationship between party law and state law is similar to the relationship between ritual and law under natural law (Qiang 2015). However, this viewpoint is clearly in conflict with the provision of the CPC Constitution that "the Party must act within the scope of the Constitution and the law", and also contradicts the principle of "supremacy of the Constitution and the law" that the CPC has always insisted on advocating.

All in all, party regulation and national laws have two sides, and there is both consistency and certain differences between them. The above three views either ignored the differences or discarded the consistency, did not comprehensively analyze, and observe this issue.

In terms of consistency, under the party-State political system of Chinese characteristics, CPC has no special interests of its own, and the Party's assertions are in fact transformed by the people's will, the two are organically unified rather than opposed. Thus, the will of the people, the interests of the state, and the party's claims are fundamentally the same, which determines the consistency between the party's intra-regulation and the state law, which are all important parts of the socialist rule of law system with Chinese characteristics. In the fundamental goal, the two are consistent, which is also determined by the ruling and leading position of the Communist Party of China. Whether it is the party regulations or national laws, are the bearer of the will of the party and the people, but also the defender of national interests. Specifically, the consistency of the two can be reflected from the three aspects of the normative object, adjustment content, and normative effect:

In terms of the normative object, the party regulations and national laws has a high degree of consistency. Party regulations to regulate party relations, focusing on regulating party organizations and party members in the exercise of public power. National laws, on the other hand, have a broader scope. However, in China's civil service, party membership accounts for the vast majority. The proportion of Party members among leading cadres above the county division level exceeds 95%.

Meanwhile, from the adjustment of the content, both intra-party regulation and national law are aimed at regulation of the behavior of the party and the government, making it predictable, stable, and procedural. For example, the CPC local committee work regulations (*中国共产党地方委员会工作条例*) and the People's Republic of China local people's congresses and local people's governments at all levels of the organizational law (*中华人民共和国地方各级人民代表大会和地方各级人民政府组织法*) in the granting of local party committees and local governments to decide on major issues in the region that reflects a high degree of overlap and consistency.

On the regulatory effectiveness side, Part two of this paper already lists and discusses some of the doubts and criticisms about that. It can be said that the effectiveness of the two has been highly concerned by the legal academia. The author argues that in discussing the differences in the effectiveness of the two, it is important to first recognize their internal consistency. It can be said that national law is the first adjustment of the behavior of all citizens, including party members, while party regulations are the second adjustment of party members' behavior. In some of the norms of the rights and interests of the target, the party regulations and the national law "conflict" is with the inevitability of the "norm", rather than accidental "accident". Because the party rules on the requirements of party members than the national law is more stringent. In the relationship between rights and obligations, the basic principle of party regulations is that obligations take precedence over rights (Liu 2023: 45–52).

In short, the consistency of the two can be reflected from the three aspects of the normative object, adjustment content, and normative effect. Therefore, it is necessary and feasible to promote the party regulations and national law in an integrated way and construct a socialist rule of law system with Chinese characteristics.

4.2 *What Issues Arise from Cooperation and Interaction?*

Under the supervisory reform, in the coexistence and joint governance of intra-party regulations and national laws, there are many issues, including the confusion between discipline and law, gaps in integration, lack of coordination, and the replacement of laws by discipline. For instance, before the amendments to the "Code of Conduct for Integrity and Self-Discipline of the Communist Party of China" (中国共产党廉洁自律准则) and the "Regulations on Disciplinary Actions of the Communist Party of China" (中国共产党纪律处分条例), the confusion between discipline and law was particularly severe. According to statistics, over half of the provisions in the old "Regulations on Disciplinary Actions" (纪律处分条例) duplicated those in relevant national laws. At the same time, a large number of joint legislative activities by the Party and the government in practice also easily led to the confusion between discipline and law.

Secondly, there's a gap in the alignment between national laws and intra-party regulations. As the comprehensive strengthening of party discipline continues to deepen, the construction of intra-party regulations has progressed rapidly, and the system of such regulations has become increasingly mature. However, on the other hand, the pace of state anti-corruption laws has noticeably lagged behind. Legal instruments that have been called for by experts for years, such as the "Anti-Corruption Law", the "Conflict of Interest Prevention Law", and the "Official Property Disclosure Law", have yet to materialize. As a result, there is a prevalent perception in anti-corruption practices that party rules and disciplines play a more significant role in combating corruption than national laws (Hu 2016: 14).

Moreover, there is insufficient coordination between the two in practice, leading to cases where discipline replaces law. For instance, in an incident where the Party Secretary of Xingtang Temple Township in Hongtong County, Shanxi Province, led a group of party members and officials to vandalize a restaurant after drinking, clear criminal offenses were committed. Yet, local authorities solely addressed the issue through party and government discipline, ignoring the criminal implications (Ma 2014).

Thirdly, there is an overlapping and intertwining between judicial procedures and discipline inspection and supervision procedures. The establishment of the Supervisory Committee embodies a dual nature (Liu 2019). Under the system of joint office operations, the Supervisory Committee is no longer just a pure state organ. Besides its state supervisory functions, it also encompasses the ruling party's disciplinary inspection duties (Qin and Li 2022). However, the challenge in their coexistence lies in maintaining a balance and independence between the party's disciplinary inspection structure and the state's supervisory structure. While the integration of disciplinary inspection and supervision is inevitable, the coupling of these entities in the "reformed constitution" poses risks. Specifically, the narrower political system to which the Discipline Inspection Committee belongs may risk overshadowing and instrumentalizing the administrative system of the Supervisory Committee (ibid.). When both the Discipline Inspection Committee and the Supervisory Committee handle cases concurrently, they may face dilemmas due to differing authorities and foundational bases for their actions, as well as distinct supervisory methods. This raises questions such as how to address conflicts in procedures like case jurisdiction, reviews, and investigations between the two bodies.

4.3 How Can Cooperation and Interaction Be Achieved?

In reality, the attributes of disciplinary inspection and state supervision are unified under the joint office system. Therefore, the party regulations and state laws that govern these two powers should also be interconnected.

Firstly, from a top-level design perspective, party regulations should be consistent with state laws. Additionally, national legislation should elevate effective rules from disciplinary inspection work to the status of law. For instance, the "Second Five-Year Plan for the Formulation of Central Party Regulations (2018–2022)" (*中央党内法规制定工作第二个五年规划 (2018—2022年)*) suggests the formulation of the "Regulations on the Work of the Communist Party of China's Discipline Inspection Committee". This regulation should be consistent with the "Supervision Law" (*监察法*) on common issues related to both disciplinary inspection and supervision. Similarly, a significant portion of the provisions in the "Supervision Law" refers to party regulations like the "Rules for Supervision and Disciplinary Execution by Discipline Inspection Organs of the

Communist Party of China (Trial) (*中国共产党纪律检查机关监督执纪工作规则(试行)*)".

Secondly, regarding the execution procedure, a clear intervention process needs to be established. On one hand, the criteria for determining instances of disciplinary violations, official misconduct, or official crimes should be made explicit (Zhu 2018: 24–37) On the other hand, the different modes of the "connection between discipline and law" should be clarified. Some scholars have proposed three procedural designs: "discipline before law", "law before discipline", and "discipline and law in parallel" (Meng and Xu 2019: 29). Each model has its advantages and disadvantages. Comparing the aforementioned three modes, it can be observed that all three have an unclear selection criterion. Currently, there is no authoritative official explanation, and there's no clear concept in academic theory either.

Thirdly, from the perspective of post-action remedies, we should strengthen the comprehensive assessment after legislative implementation, strict record review, and regular legal cleanup procedures. Doing so ensures that we can promptly identify and integrate discrepancies between intra-party regulations and national laws, thus ensuring their smooth integration and harmonious coordination (Ou 2018: 40). In the post-legislative record review of regulations, the existing approval process for party internal regulations uses the "degree of match" review based on national laws as the basis for legality. The legal compliance review of party internal regulations requires judging whether they are consistent with the constitution and laws and classifying the review results accordingly.[15] Therefore, looking at the spirit of the relevant review provisions, there is still a need to strengthen the coordination between various work institutions in practice. There should be a reasonable mechanism to promote effective coordination between the party committee, the National People's Congress, the government, and other record review institutions. In addition, besides formulating general and principled requirements, it is necessary to further refine institutional

15 <Regulations on the Review and Registration of the Communist Party of China's Internal Regulations and Normative Documents> Article 11 stipulates that the reviewing authority should register the Party's internal regulations and normative documents that meet the review requirements, and review them from political, legal and regulatory compliance, rationality, and normative perspectives. <Regulations on the Review and Registration of the Communist Party of China's Internal Regulations and Normative Documents> also provides detailed provisions for the handling of review results.

arrangements based on practical experience and the specific needs of the areas involved in specific affairs.

5 Conclusion

The intra-party regulatory system serves as an important pillar for the party's rule of law governance, while the national legal system is the cornerstone of governing the nation according to law. Both play an indispensable role in the construction of the rule of law with Chinese characteristics. The views of Qin Qianhong remind us that, for these two systems, we should not be confined to the traditional "state law centrism" perspective. Instead, from the height of China's modern state governance, we need to re-examine their relationship and interactions (Qin 2016: 52).

The reform of the supervision system provides us with an excellent perspective to observe the collision and integration of intra-party regulations and national laws in actual operation. Although there are phenomena of inconsistency, lack of connection, or even conflict between the two in some areas, this should be viewed more as a challenge we need to address and resolve in our rule of law construction. The author further points out that simplifying the relationship between party regulations and national laws to a mere demarcation of their respective scopes or merely converting one into the other in form is both superficial and insufficient. We should delve deeper into their inherent logic and regularities, seeking a linking mechanism that both aligns with objective laws and addresses actual challenges. Truly achieving a bidirectional connection and interaction between party regulations and national laws is key to ensuring the continuous improvement and advancement of the rule of law with Chinese characteristics.

Acknowledgements This academic research was supported by the China Scholarship Council (Grant No. 202008765004) and was conducted during my research visit to the Faculty of Law at the University of Helsinki, particularly within the auspices of the Finnish Center of Chinese Law and Chinese Legal Culture. I am grateful for the financial support and the conducive research environment provided, which were integral to the successful completion of this work.

References

CPC Central Committee Literature Research Office and Central Archives, eds. (2011). Selected Important Documents Since the Founding of the Party (1921–1949). (Vol. 15, p. 749). Central Literature Publishing House.

Database of National Laws and Regulations. (1982). The Constitution of the People's Republic of China (1982). Retrieved on July 10, 2023, from https://flk.npc.gov.cn/xf/html/xf1.html.

DeLisle Jacques. (2017). Law in the China Model 2.0: Legality, Developmentalism and Leninism Under Xi Jinping. J Delisle. Journal of Contemporary China, 26(103), 68–84.

Deng Bin & Wu Qian. (2022). xin shidai dangnei fagui yu guojia falv youji xianjie jizhi jiangou [Construction of a Mechanism for the Organic Connection Between Party Regulations and National Laws in the New Era]. Journal of Southwest University of Political Science & Law, 24(4), 80–90.

Deng xiaoping. (2001). Zai quanti renmin zhong shuli fazhi guannian [Establishing the Concept of Rule of Law among the Whole People]. In Selected Works of Deng Xiaoping (Volume 3, pp. 163–164). People's Publishing House.

Holly Snape (2019) Party Regulations: Changing the Rules of the Game? Chinese Law & Government, 51(5–6), 255–259.

Hou Jiabin. (2018). dangnei fagui yu guojia falu xianjie xietiao de shixian jizhi yanjiu [Study on the Implementation Mechanism of Coordination and Connection between Party Internal Regulations and National Laws]. Shehui Zhuyi Yanjiu, 1, 97–103.

Hu Dawei. (2016). yifa fanfu yu yigui zhigong zhi liangxing hudong tanlun [Discussion on the Positive Interaction Between Anti-Corruption by Law and Party Governance by Regulation]. Guangzhou Daxue Xuebao (Shehui Kexue Ban), 15(10), 12–17.

Hu Dawei. (2016). yifa fanfu yu yiguizhi dang zhi liangxing hudong tantao [Exploration on the Positive Interaction between Rule-by-Law Anti-corruption and Rule-by-Party Governance]. Guangzhou University Journal (Social Science Edition), 15(10), 12–17.

Ji Mingwu. (2020). lun dang nei jiandu fagui yu guojia fǎlǜ zhidu de xianjie—yi <zhongguo gongchan dang dangnei jiandu tiaoli> yu <jianchafa> wei shidian [On the Connection of Party Internal Supervision Regulations and National Legal System: Taking the "Regulations on Inner-Party Supervision of the Communist Party of China" and "Supervisory Law" as the Perspective]. Jianghan Xueshu, 39(2), 38–45.

Jiang Feng (2019) Party Regulations and State Laws in China: A Disappearing Boundary and Growing Tensions. Chinese Law & Government, 51(5–6), 260–276.

Jiang mingan. (2012). Lun Zhong guo Gong chan dang dang nei fa gui de xing zhi yu zuo yong [The nature and role of the internal party regulations of the Communist Party of China]. Journal of Peking University, 49(3).

Jiang, Zemin. (2006). Jiang Ze Min Wen Xuan [Selected Works of Jiang Zemin] (Vol. 2, pp. 496).People's Publishing House.

Li Shuzhong. (2017). Dang nei fa gui yu guo jia fa lu guan xi de zai chan shi [Reinterpreting the Relationship Between Party Regulations and National Laws]. Chinese Legal Review, 2017(2), 60–68.

Li Yao. (2021). "danxiang xietiao" yu "shuangxiang xianjie": danggui yu guofa guanxi de jiben zezhu yu shixian lujing ["Unidirectional Coordination" and "Bidirectional Connection": The Basic Compliance and Implementation Path of the Relationship between Party Regulations and National Laws]. Lilun DaoKan, 2021(7), 42–49.

Liu lianjun. (2023). Dangnei fagui xue jiangyi [Lecture Notes on Party Laws and Regulations]. Peking University Press, 45–52.

Liu songshan. (2019). Zhunque bawo dangzai xianfa fǎlǜ fanwei nei huodong de hanyi--jianlun dangneifagui yu guojia fǎlǜ de guanxi [Accurately Grasp the Meaning of the Party's Activities within the Scope of the Constitution and Laws—Another Discussion on the Relationship between the Party's Internal Regulations and National Laws]. Fazhi Yanjiu, 2019(2).

Liu Yida. (2019). lun jijian jiancha quan de er yuan shuxing ji qi danggui guofa gongzhi [On the Dual Attributes of Discipline Inspection and Supervision Power and the Co-governance of Party Regulations and National Laws]. Shehuizhuyi Yanjiu, 2019(1).

Luo haocai & Zhou qiang. (2013). Ruan fa yan jiu de duo wei si kao [Multidimensional Thought on Soft Law Research]. Zhongguo Faxue, 2013(5).

Ma Diming. (2014). yi ji dai fa de guanli geng yao feizhi [The Habit of Placing Discipline Above the Law Should Be Abolished]. Shenyang Ribao, 2014–11–26.

Meng Hui & Xu Zhuangzhuang. (2019). jiancha tizhi gaige beijing xia "liang wei" he shu bangong wenti yanjiu [Research on the "Two Committees" Joint Office Issue Under the Background of Supervision System Reform]. Henan Shehui Kexue, 27(2), 27–33.

Meng Tao. (2021). Dangnei fagui tixi de xingcheng yu wanshan [Formation and Perfection of the Intra-Party Regulatory System]. Chinese Journal of Law, 43(6).

Mou Licheng & Xiao Jinming. (2021). cong xingzhi "er yuan" dao xitong guanlian: dangnei fagui yu guojia falv guanxi yanjiu de fanshi zhuanhuan [From "Dual Nature" to Systematic Connection: A Paradigm Shift in the Study of the Relationship Between Party Regulations and National Laws]. Dangdai Shijie Shehui Zhuyi Went, 2021(2), 62–72.

Ou Aimin. (2018). dangnei fagui yu guojia falv guanxi lun [On the Relationship Between Party Regulations and National Laws] (p. 40). Shehui Kexue Wenxian Chu Ban She.

Peerenboom, R. (2015). Fly High the Banner of Socialist Rule of Law with Chinese Characteristics! What Does the 4th Plenum Decision Mean for Legal Reforms in China? Hague Journal on the Rule of Law, 7, 49–74.

Qiang Sigong. (2015). Dangzhang yu xianfa: Duoyuan yiti fazhi gongheguo de jiangou [The Party Constitution and the Constitution: The Construction of a Pluralistic and Integrated Rule of Law Republic]. Wenhua Zongheng, 2015(4).

Qin Qianhong & Li Shihao. (2022). jiwei yu jianwei hurlong de keneng yu xiandu [The Possibility and Limit of the Integration of the Discipline Inspection Commission and the Supervisory Commission]. Sichuan Shifan Daxue Xuebao (Shehui Kexue Ban), 2022(1).

Qin Qianhong & Zhang Xiaoyu. (2021). dui dangnei fagui xiaoli waiyi de shensi yu huiying [Reflections and Responses on the Spillover of the Effectiveness of Party Internal Regulations]. Dangnei Fagui Lilun Yanjiu, 2021(1), 54–70.

Qin Qianhong. (2016). Lun dang nei fa gui yu guo jia fa lu de xie tiao yu xian jie [On the Coordination and Connection Between Party Regulations and National laws]. Renming Luntan·Xueshu Qianyan, 5 50–66.

Seppanen, S. (2019). Interrogating Illiberalism Through Chinese Communist Party Regulations. Cornell International Law Journal, 52, 267.

Seppänen, Samuli. (2022). Turning the Party State Inside Out: CCP Intra-party Regulations as a Theoretical Challenge, The Chinese Journal of Comparative Law, 10(1), 128–139.

Song Gongde & Zhang Wenxian (Eds.). (2020). dangnei fagui xue [Studies on Party Regulations] (pp. 22–23). Gao Deng Jiao Yu Chu Ban She.

Tao qingde. (2015). danggui naru guofa tixi hou de dangfa guanxi xinge ju, xin wenti [The New Pattern and New Issues in the Relationship Between the Party and the Law After Incorporating Party Regulations into the Legal System]. Gansu Theory Research, 2015(6), 38–45.

Wang chunye. (2016). Lun Jiang dangnei fagui naru guojia fǎlǜ tixi [On Incorporating Party Regulations into the National Legal System]. Tianjin Shifan Daxue Xuebao, 2016(3).

Wu Xiaochuan. (2016). Dang nei fa gui de quan li gui xian lun — jian lun dang nei fa gui ruan fa lun de ying yong ju xian [On the Role of "Statute of Party" for Limitation and Normalization on PowerReflection on Limitation of the Application of Soft Law]. Journal of the Party School of the Central Committee of the Communist Party of China, 20(6), 14–23.

Wu Xiaochuan. (2016). "dangnei fagui" de quanli guixian lun — jian lun "dangnei fagui" ruanfa lun de yingyong juxian ["On the Power Limitation of 'Party Internal Regulations' — Also on the Application Limitations of 'Party

Internal Regulations' Soft Law Theory"]. Zhonggong Zhongyang Dangxiao Xuebao, 20(6), 14–23.

Xu Xianming. (2017) 'Gongchandang ji zai falü zhi zhong, ye zai falü zhi xia, hai zai falü zhi shang' [The Communist Party is in, Under and Above the Law]. Retrieved on July 15, 2023, from https://m.sohu.com/n/488744587/.

Yao Guojian. (2020). lun "danggui yan yu guofa" de zhengdangxing ji qi jieyu [On the Legitimacy of "Party Regulations are Stricter than National Laws" and Its Boundaries]. Lilun Shiye, 6, 64–70.

Zhang Qianfan. (2021) The Communist Party Leadership and Rule of Law: A Tale of Two Reforms. Journal of Contemporary China, 30(130), 578–595.

Zhang Wenxian. (2021). jianchi yifa zhiguo he yigui zhigong youji tongyi [Adhering to the Organic Unity of Governing the Country by Law and Governing the Party by Regulations]. Zhengzhi yu Fǎlǜ, 2021(5).

Zhu Fuhui. (2018). guojia jiancha fa dui gongzhi renyuan jilu chufen tixi de chonggou [Reconstruction of the disciplinary system for public officials by the National Supervision Law]. Xingzheng Faxue Yanjiu, 2018(4), 24–37.

CHAPTER 8

What Influences Fertility Plans of China's Migrant Populations? Mechanism Analysis Based on House Prices Perspective

Jingwen Tan, Shixi Kang, He Shi, and Qi Zhang

1 Introduction

Human capital is an important position in the process of economic development (Gennaioli et al. 2013). In recent years, the stock and increment of human capital in China have gradually shown a tendency to be insufficient, and the average age of the working population is 38.8 years old, with a significant aging phenomenon (CUFE 2021). During the period, China's total fertility rate was between 1.5 and 1.6, significantly lower than the level of generation re-placement needed to achieve population

J. Tan (✉) · H. Shi · Q. Zhang
University of Copenhagen, Copenhagen, Denmark
e-mail: tjw@henu.edu.cn

H. Shi
e-mail: bhn423@alumni.ku.dk

A. Aliu (ed.), *Complexity Thinking and China's Demography Within and Beyond Mainland China*,
https://doi.org/10.1007/978-981-97-0172-8_8

stability (Yang et al. 2022). One of the reason for this phenomenon is China's long-standing family planning policy (Wang et al. 2017). In 2021, China's natural population growth rate is only 0.34 per 1000 and enter negative growth in 2022 (Lian and Xu 2023). At the same time, China's expanding economy and market size still have high labor demand (Wu and Zhang 2020). The potential structural imbalance of human resource supply arising from low fertility rate and high labor demand in China is a matter of concern.

Migrant is an important part of China's labor supply. Since the reform and opening up of China resolved the institutional barriers to population mobility, the size of the migrants has been expanding, reaching 375.82 million by 2020, an increase of 69.73% in 10 years (Cai 2018; Wang 2023). China's rural outflow population provides an important human resource for urban development and plays a huge role in the urbanization process (Zhang and Song 2003). Improving the fertility intention of the migrants, alleviating the structural imbalance of human resource supply, and providing a stable labor supply for economic development are important conditions for promoting China's sustained economic growth.

There are special policy and cultural contexts for exploring the fertility intention of China migrants from the perspective of house price. High house price can have an impact on families' financial situation, housing conditions, and employment opportunities, which can affect their fertility decisions, causing some families to give up or postpone having children for financial, housing, and employment reasons (Pan and Xu 2012). In addition, due to China's long-standing dualistic urban–rural household registration system, migrants are often unable to receive local medical and educational resources from the inflow cities, making social integration difficult from an institutional perspective (Hao and Tang 2015). China household registration is highly tied to housing, and high house price makes it impossible for the migrant laborer to settle down and obtain

Q. Zhang
e-mail: pvs237@alumni.ku.dk

S. Kang
University of Wisconsin-Madison, Madison, WI, USA
e-mail: ksx@henu.edu.cn

household registration in the inflow cities, which also affects their willingness to have children (Wang 2006). Moreover, traditional Chinese culture views housing as a necessity for marriage and children (Liu et al. 2020).

Based on the above background, this paper constructs the house price to household income ratio as the core explanatory variable using the China Migrants Dynamic Survey (CMDS) and empirically examines the impact of urban house price on the fertility plan of migrants. The results show that the higher house price in the inflow cities, the less likelihood female migrants have fertility plan; if the housing pressure of the migrants is low, their fertility plan is less affected by house price. The sensitivity of the migrants' fertility plan to house price is also influenced by the cultural infrastructure development in the inflow city. Heterogeneity analysis shows that the fertility plan of female migrant with larger family size, higher education level and younger age is more sensitive to house price.

The paper is structured as follows: Sect. 2 conducts a literature review, Sect. 3 presents the research methodology, Sect. 4 presents the empirical results, and Sect. 5 concludes.

2 Review of the Literature

The study of fertility is important in demography. Some research has examined the factors affecting the fertility intention of the population from a multidimensional perspective. For example, (Kim and Yeo 2019) focus on the low fertility in Korea about how socio-environmental factors can influence fertility plan through individual environmental factors. Arai (2007) argues for the indirect role of social relationships on fertility intention through an empirical analysis of the potential impact of community on fertility intention. It is worth noting that many scholars believe that high house price affects people's willingness to have children. Such as (Dettling and Kearney 2014) define fertility price as housing cost and argue that the real estate market has a more direct effect on fertility plan. (Lino 2002) finds a significant negative relationship between house price and fertility intention, suggesting that housing cost is the largest expense of raising children, and high house price is overwhelming many families, resulting in negative fertility behavior.

In studies about the effect of house price on the migrants in China, (Liu et al. 2020) confirmed the negative effect of high house price on fertility among the household population in China using census data. (Clark et al. 2020) analyzed the negative relationship between house price and fertility in China using data from the China Household Finance Survey and using land premiums as an instrumental variable for house price, and group tests were conducted for different levels of cities.

Regarding the mechanism of the effect of house price on the fertility plan of the migrants, the existing studies focus on both the willingness to integrate and the financial ability. On the one hand, the high or low house price is related to the strength of the social integration intention of the migrants. When house price is higher, the migrants' willingness to integrate socially decreases and the likelihood of having fertility plan subsequently decreases. According to (Entzinger and Biezeveld 2003), social integration includes psychological integration, cultural integration, economic integration, and political integration. House price as a specific quantification of property rights is an important indicator of the migrants' integration into the society of the place of migration in many ways, which in turn affects the willingness to stay. Since the migration of the migrants is a short-term decision-making behavior (Du et al. 2014), lowering the threshold of ownership of their property rights is a key initiative to promote long-term residence of the migrants and thus increase the likelihood of having children. High house price means that it is more difficult for the migrants to integrate subjectively into the local area, and accordingly, their willingness to have children decreases.

On the other hand, house price is also a test of the economic capacity of migrants. In China, housing is highly tied to household registration. The series of thresholds imposed by the household registration system makes the migrants relatively less able to afford house price and leads to a greater reluctance to bear the various cost arising from childbearing. The direction of population movement is mainly from rural to urban areas (Lewis et al. 1954). However, under the influence of China's dual economic structure between urban and rural areas and the household registration system, the migrants are not only disadvantaged in the job market but also suffer from financial constraints and a lack of public protection. The household registration system provides a natural barrier to entry into the job market, and self-employment is the rational choice for this group to deal with employment discrimination as opposed to wage employment (Banerjee 1983; Roberts 2001; Song and Appleton 2008). However, the precariousness of self-employment reduces migrants' ability to take economic risks and reduces their willingness to have children. (Oates 1969) highlights the role of public services in the utility model of population migration, arguing that a good social security system reduces expenditure in a number of ways. As the migrants do not benefit from the range of social security that comes with a household registration system, they have higher security expenditures relative to the local population, further reducing the ability to bear the potential economic risks associated with childbearing.

Although studies have been conducted to analyze the relationship between house price and fertility, there is no detailed analysis of the mechanisms. Also, there are gaps in research on samples of China migrants, and this paper will add to the existing research from these two perspectives.

3 Data Sources and Variables

3.1 Data Sources

This study uses data from the 2018 China Migrants Dynamic Survey (CMDS). The survey was conducted by the National Health Commission of China and adopted the stratified, multi-stage, large-scale PPS sampling method, covering 31 provinces (municipalities and autonomous regions) in mainland China. The average age of the sample used in this paper is 16–50 years old, and the sample size was 45,593 (married female migrant populations). The data relating to urban control variables are obtained from the statistical yearbooks of various cities.

3.2 Variable Selection

The dependent variable of this paper is the fertility plan of the sample, which is estimated using the CMDS questionnaire "Do you plan to have children in the near future?". The core explanatory variable in this paper is the house price, which is the ratio of the house price in the sample inflow area to the sample average monthly household income. Household income is measured by the CMDS questionnaire "What is your total monthly household income", which is a clearer indicator of the difficulty of access to urban property right for the migrant populations than the house price constructed from urban per capita disposable income.

The control variables in this paper include urban control variables and individual control variables. In existing empirical studies of fertility, indicators such as years of education, family size, age, employment situation, and health status are usually set as demographic control variables. In

Table 1 Variable description

Variables	*Description*
fertility	Planing to have children = 1, No = 0
hp	Inflow city house price/individual household income
job	Civil service career = 2, Other career = 1, Unemployed = 0e
health	Unhealthy = 1, Fair = 2, Fairly healthy = 3, Healthy = 4
age	Age of sample
family	Number of family members
edu	Years of education
hukou	Urban household = 1, Agricultural household = 0
tgdp	Share of tertiary sector in total GDP (%)
green	Percentage of green space in the city (%)
book	Book collection per capita
teacher	Number of primary school teachers per 10,000 population
medical	Number of physicians per 10,000 population

addition to the above variables, this paper also chooses household registration (hukou) as the control variable, based on the unique context of China's dualistic urban–rural household registration policy. This paper also selects industrial structure (share of tertiary sector in GDP), urban green space, education, and medical resources as control variables. A detailed description of the variables is in Table 1.

3.3 Descriptive Statistics

The descriptive statistics are reported in Table 2. As can be seen from the table, female migrants with fertility plan (fertility) for approximately 12% of the total sample. The mean value of the core explanatory variable, the ratio of the house price in the sample inflow city to the sample average monthly household income (hp) is 1.635, and its economic significance is that the average household income of the respondents needs 1.6 months to buy one square meter of property. In the hypothesis of this paper, high house price significantly reduce the fertility intention of female migrants. The average household (family) size of the sample is 3.479, and the smaller household size is related to the long-standing family planning policy in China. The average years of education (edu) of the sample are around 10 years, and the average age (age) is about 34 years. The majority

Table 2 Descriptive statistics results

Variables	*N*	*Mean*	*SD*	*Min*	*Max*
fertility	45,355	0.120	0.325	0	1
hp	45,355	1.635	1.506	0.0169	140.6
job	45,355	0.747	0.557	0	2
health	45,355	1.118	0.359	1	4
age	45,355	34.70	7.436	16	50
family	45,355	3.479	0.878	2	11
edu	45,355	10.32	3.482	0	19
hukou	45,355	0.323	0.468	0	1
tgdp	45,355	55.00	11.59	26.54	80.98
green	45,355	41.81	3.465	23	93.81
book	45,355	1.607	1.510	0.0793	8.742
teacher	45,355	42.96	8.907	18.54	85.70
medical	45,355	64.64	21.62	19.69	128.2

of the respondents were in agricultural household registration (hukou), a dualistic household registration system that divided Chinese citizens into agricultural household registration and non-agricultural household registration until 2015, and the large differences in the rights and benefits attached to the two types of household registration have had a profound impact on the regional labor endowment allocation in China.

4 Methodology

4.1 Research Hypotheses

This paper proposes the following hypotheses on the mechanism by which house price affects the fertility intention of the migrants.

Hypothesis 1 The probability of having fertility plan among the migrants and urban house price is negatively correlated.

High house price will not only bring huge economic pressure to the migrants but also affect the social integration of the migrants in the inflow city, leading to a decrease in their fertility intention. House price as a quantitative indicator of the difficulty of acquiring residential property rights, is an important indicator of whether the migrants can be institutionally integrated into the place of migration. In China, housing ownership is linked to household registration and children's eligibility for schooling, medical insurance, and other related social benefits. High house price mean that it is more difficult for the migrants to integrate economically and institutionally into the incoming region, leading to a decrease in fertility intention.

Hypothesis 2 The sensitivity of migrant fertility plan to house price is influenced by the availability of culture infrastructure in inflow cities.

The preference of the migrants for local property rights depends on the economic environment and infrastructure development of the inflow city. When making fertility decisions, the migrants will consider the impact of local culture resources on the future life of their children. This is also reflected in their willingness to have children, i.e., there are moderating effects between the construction of culture infrastructure services on the willingness to have children and the sensitivity to house price.

Hypothesis 3 The sensitivity of fertility intention to house price is influenced by the amount of housing pressure on the migrants.

High house price imposes a huge financial burden on the migrants. The huge financial pressure of housing expenses on the migrants will squeeze their ability to bear various costs arising from childbirth and affect their fertility intention, but this mechanism is affected by the housing pressure of the migrants. That is, the fertility intention of the migrants with housing pressure is vulnerable to house price, and the fertility intention of the migrants without housing pressure is not necessarily sensitive to house price.

Among them, hypothesis 1 can be proved by the results of the baseline regression. For hypothesis 2, this paper examines the possible moderating effects by using the interaction term between culture infrastructure variable and house price.

To address hypothesis 3, this paper regresses all samples in groups according to housing pressure status. The CMDS questionnaire does not contain questions about the housing pressure status of housing for the migrants, and this paper uses the sample household housing expenditure as a proxy variable for housing pressure status—the group with zero household housing expenditure is regressed in a separate group to examine the effect of migrants housing pressure on the mechanism.

4.2 Baseline Model

In this paper, the explanatory variable "fertility plan of migrants" is a dummy variable, and the models available include Linear probability model (LPM), Logit model, and Probit model. This paper chooses to use the Probit model for the empirical analysis, while reporting the estimation results of the Logit model for robustness check. The expression for the Probit model is.

$$\Pr\left(F_{ij} = 1|hp,\ X\right) = F(hp, \beta_1) = \frac{\exp\left(\beta_0 + \beta_1 hp_{ij} + \beta X + \varepsilon_{ij}\right)}{1 + \exp\left(\beta_0 + \beta_1 hp_{ij} + \beta X + \varepsilon_{ij}\right)} \quad (1)$$

In Eq. (1), F_{ij} is the fertility plan of the migrant. If the migrant i has fertility plan in the j inflow city, the value is 1, otherwise it is 0. Pr $(F_{ij} = 1 \mid hp, X)$ is the probability that the migrant i has fertility plan in the inflow city j. hp is house price to income ratio, X are other control variables, ε_{ij} are random disturbance term.

4.3 Robustness Checks

4.3.1 Instrumental Variable

Fertility intention is influenced not only by house price in the inflow cities, but also by other potentially influential factors. The paper screens variables at the variable selection stage, but it is still difficult to control for all potential influencing factors. Additionally, the high fertility intention of the migrants in a region may increase house price, thus creating a reverse causality, i.e., house price may be an endogenous variable. Considering potential problems of missing control variables and causal inference, it is necessary to find a instrumental variable (IV).

Research on instrumental variables for house price is well established. Common instrumental variables include land development area (Peng and Du 2016; Zhang et al. 2018), the product of long-term interest rate and land supply elasticity (Chaney et al. 2012), and land concession price (Waxman et al. 2020). In this paper, the lagged land concession price is chosen as the instrumental variable for house price. Land concession prices directly affect house price, which is consistent with the instrumental variable correlation hypothesis; at the same time, the migrants do not actively consider addressing land concession prices in previous years when considering childbearing, which is consistent with the instrumental variable exogeneity hypothesis. In order to conform to the data structure of house price, this paper constructs the ratio of lagged land price to lagged city disposable income per capita as an instrumental variable.

4.3.2 *Propensity Score Matching*

Although the baseline model controls for personal characteristics and regional factors, the fact that the fertility plan of individual female migrants is not necessarily randomly determined, e.g., those with higher economic and social status are usually more likely to stay in the city and thus have higher fertility intention, leads to the fact that when estimating the effect of house price on the fertility plan of the sample, direct use of a binary choice model may lead to serious sample bias due to 'self-selection'. Therefore, this paper matches the untreated sample with the treated sample based on propensity score matching (PSM) to balance the data so that the personal characteristics of the matched treated group (above-median house price to income ratio group) and the control group (below-median house price to income ratio group) remain the same and statistical differences are reduced.

The first step was to estimate the propensity score P (X) for each female migrants' fertility plan through logit regression, expressed as:

$$P(X_i) = Pr\,(Fertility_i = 1|X_i) \tag{2}$$

where X is a set of factors affecting female migrants' fertility plan, also known as matching variables. The average treatment effect on the treated (ATT) is calculated by matching the treatment and control groups according to the common support region of the propensity score, followed by the corresponding matching method, and the expression is:

$$ATT = E\,Y_i^T - Y_i^C \Big| Fertility_i = 1 = E\,Y_i^T | Fertility_i = 1 - E\,Y_i^C | Fertility_i = 1 \tag{3}$$

The ATT is designed to compare the difference in fertility plan between high and low housing pressure migrants who are equally likely to have fertility plan, and to derive a specific effect of house price on the fertility plan of migrants.

5 Regression Results and Discussion

5.1 *Baseline Regression*

Table 3 shows the results of the baseline regression. Models (1) to (5) are the stepwise regression results of the Probit model. Model (1) shows that, conditional on the exclusion of control variables, the coefficient of the house price to income ratio on fertility intention is −0.0437, which is significant at the 99% level, indicating that there is a significant negative relationship between house price and the fertility plan of the migrants. The higher the house price to household income ratio in the inflow cities, the lower the probability of having fertility plan among the female migrants. Model (5) includes city and individual control variables, along with provincial fixed effects. The coefficient increases slightly (−0.0522) compared to the results without including the control variables. The Logit model has similar estimation results. Model (6) shows the regression coefficient of −0.0858 for the house price to income ratio on fertility intention when no other control variables are included. Model (7) includes urban and individual control variables, with the coefficient −0.0927.

High house price can put enormous financial pressure on migrants, while home ownership is a necessary condition for childbearing in Chinese culture. Higher house price to income ratios makes it difficult for the migrants to obtain housing ownership and the various social security entitlements represented by household registration in the city to which they move, leading to a decline in their fertility intention.

5.2 *Robustness*

Table 4 depicts the results of instrument variable. It can be seen from the first-stage regression results that the regression result of instrumental variables on endogenous variables is significant at the 99% confidence level (Model 9), proving that instrumental variables have strong explanatory power on endogenous variables and there is no weak instrumental variable problem. Compared to the baseline results, the absolute value of the coefficient on the instrument variable in the Model (8) increases, indicating that the endogeneity problem tends to underestimate the effect of house price on the intention to have children among the migrants.

The sample size of the data used in this paper is large, and to avoid endogeneity issues due to potential sample selection bias, this paper uses

Table 3 Baseline results

	(1) *Probit*	(2) *Probit*	(3) *Probit*	(4) *Probit*	(5) *Probit*	(6) *Logit*	(7) *Logit*
hp	−0.0437***	−0.0394***	-0.0866***	−0.0475***	−0.0522***	−0.0858***	−0.0927***
	(0.00728)	(0.00906)	(0.00951)	(0.0109)	(0.0118)	(0.0142)	(0.0203)
job		−0.0205		−0.0270*	−0.0294*		−0.0521*
		(0.0161)		(0.0162)	(0.0163)		(0.0295)
health		−0.0107		−0.0139	−0.0165		−0.0437
		(0.0293)		(0.0294)	(0.0296)		(0.0553)
old		−0.0684***		−0.0680***	−0.0681***		−0.119***
		(0.00140)		(0.00141)	(0.00143)		(0.00258)
family		−0.658***		−0.673***	−0.687***		−1.400***
		(0.0173)		(0.0177)	(0.0181)		(0.0342)
edu		0.0376***		0.0389***	0.0393***		0.0706***
		(0.00316)		(0.00330)	(0.00341)		(0.00597)
hukou		0.0410**		0.0398**	0.00973		0.0690*
		(0.0195)		(0.0196)	(0.0217)		(0.0357)
green			0.000645	0.000200	−0.000957		0.00217
			(0.00230)	(0.00276)	(0.00424)		(0.00511)
book			0.00283	-0.0125	−0.0201		−0.0244
			(0.00713)	(0.00828)	(0.0176)		(0.0153)
teacher			0.00394***	0.0112***	0.00778***		0.0214***
			(0.000882)	(0.000999)	(0.00169)		(0.00183)
medical			−0.000128	−0.00214***	−0.0021**		−0.0038***
			(0.000468)	(0.000561)	(0.000874)		(0.00103)
tgdp			0.00840***	0.00334***	0.000931		0.00542**
			(0.00101)	(0.00119)	(0.00171)		(0.00220)

	(1) *Probit*	(2) *Probit*	(3) *Probit*	(4) *Probit*	(5) *Probit*	(6) *Logit*	(7) *Logit*
constant	−1.106***	2.796***	−1.696***	2.324***	2.452***	−1.857***	4.623***
	(0.0137)	(0.0924)	(0.104)	(0.150)	(0.217)	(0.0262)	(0.276)
Urban variables	No	No	Yes	Yes	Yes	No	Yes
Individual variables	No	Yes	No	Yes	Yes	No	Yes
Regional FE	No	No	No	No	Yes	No	No
N	45,355	45,355	45,355	45,355	45,355	45,355	45,355
Pseudo R^2	0.0013	0.1434	0.1867	0.2489	0.2860	0.0013	0.2576

Note Standard errors in parentheses; $^{***}p < 0.01$, $^{**}p < 0.05$, $^{*}p < 0.1$. The following tables are the same

Table 4 Instrumental variable regression results

	(8) *IVProbit*	*(9)* *First-Step Result*
Instrument variable	−0.204**	0.137***
	−(0.0918)	(0.00924)
Control Variables	Yes	Yes
N	45,355	45,355
Pseudo R^2	–	0.1866

propensity score matching for robustness check. Kernel density plots before and after using propensity score matching are reported in this paper (Figs. 1 and 2). The quality of the data is significantly higher after matching compared to before matching.

In the PSM dummy variable setting, this paper chose to use the median grouping of house price to income ratio. Table 5 shows the results of the PSM estimation, with the treatment effect for the four matching methods being approximately −0.025 after matching the characteristics of the sample and significant at the 99% statistical level. This is the same conclusion as the baseline regression results and the IV regression results that there is a negative effect of high house price on the fertility intention of the migrants. In summary, Hypothesis 1: "The probability of having

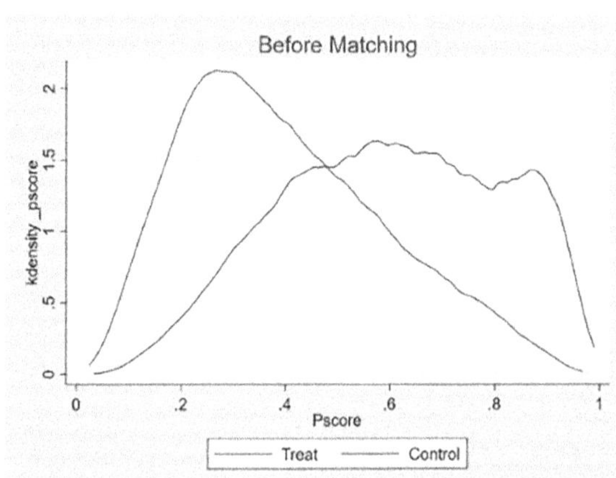

Fig. 1 Before-matching kernel density

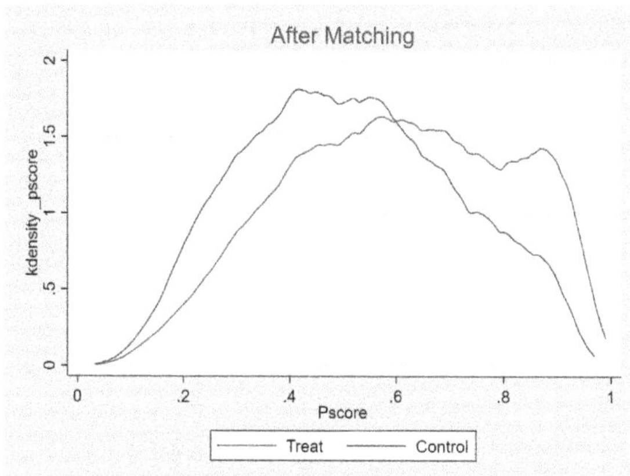

Fig. 2 After-matching kernel density

fertility plan among the migrants and urban house price is negatively correlated." is confirmed.

5.3 *Analysis of Mechanism*

5.3.1 *Moderating Effects of Infrastructure*

The effect of house price on the fertility plan of migrants is estimated above, Table 6 reports the moderating effects of culture infrastructure on the relationship between house price and the fertility decisions of migrants.

Model (10) is the result of the interaction between book collection per capita and house price, the interaction term is significant at the 95% level, demonstrating that the level of culture infrastructure has a moderating effect on house price affecting the fertility plan of the migrants. The coefficient of the main effect is negative, proving that the housing-income ratio has a negative impact on the migrant's fertility intention. The coefficient of the interaction term is negative, which is the same as the main effect, proving that cultural infrastructure strengthens the main effect. The preference of the migrants for local property rights also depends on the culture infrastructural development of the inflow city. When making

Table 5 Propensity score matching results

	1:1 Matching		*1:2 Matching*		*Radius Matching*		*Kernel Matching*	
Matching Status	*ATT*	*t*	*ATT*	*t*	*ATT*	*t*	*ATT*	*t*
Pre-match	−0.016***	−5.26	−0.016***	−5.26	−0.016***	−5.26	−0.016***	−5.26
Post-match	−0.025***	−4.08	−0.023***	−4.36	−0.022***	−4.25	−0.022***	−4.35

Table 6 Moderating effect of culture infrastructure

	(10) *Probit*
hp	−0.00593
	(0.00831)
hp*book	−0.00851**
	(0.00391)
pbook	0.000259
	(0.0109)
Control Variables	Yes
N	45,355
Pseudo R^2	0.2509

fertility decision, migrants consider the impact of local culture resources on the future lives of their children.

5.3.2 *The Effect of Housing Stress*

In the hypothesis of this paper, house price is negatively related to the fertility intention of the migrants. Another intuitive manifestation of this logic is that when the migrants are not under housing pressure, their fertility plan will no longer be influenced or less influenced by house price.

This hypothesis is analyzed in this paper using sample housing expenditure as a proxy variable for housing stress. In the CMDS questionnaire, the sample's household housing expenditure consists mainly of rent and housing loans. The paper runs a subgroup regression on the sample based on whether the sample's housing expenditure is zero. Table 7 reports the results of the subgroup regressions, Model (11) and Model (12) for the group without housing stress, and Model (13) and Model (14) for the group with housing stress. The coefficients for the group with housing stress are significantly higher than those for the group without housing stress, demonstrating that the fertility plan of the migrants with household housing expenditure is more likely to be influenced by house price.

Table 7 The effect of housing stress

	(11)	(12)	(13)	(14)
	With Housing Expenses		*Without Housing Expenses*	
hp	−0.0258**	−0.0467**	−0.0514***	−0.0503***
	(0.0115)	(0.0188)	(0.00900)	(0.0135)
Control Variables	No	Yes	No	Yes
N	10,965	10,965	34,390	34,390
Pseudo R^2	0.0007	0.2457	0.0016	0.2553

5.4 *Heterogeneity Analysis*

To further understand the sensitivity of fertility intention to house price among the migrants with different characteristics, this paper conducts a heterogeneity analysis of the sample. Table 8 reports the regression results based on household size, education level, and age grouping of the sample.

Model (15) shows the regression results for the sample with household size less than or equal to 3 persons, and its regression coefficient is smaller than that of the sample with household size greater than 3 persons (Model 16). Reasons for the larger household size in the sample may include supporting the elderly or already having children, both of which place a burden on the household economy, and the willingness to have a second child is also significantly lower than that of the first child. The fertility plan of female migrants with larger families are therefore more sensitive to house price.

Model (17) shows the regression results for the sample with no tertiary education, whose regression coefficients are smaller than those for the sample with tertiary education (Model 18). In general, highly educated female migrants tend to have higher income levels and lower fertility intention, and willing to purchase their own housing. They are more affected by changes in house price and have more sensitive fertility plan to house price.

Model (19) shows the regression results for the sample aged less than 30 years, and its regression coefficient is larger than the results for the sample aged more than 30 years (Model 20). The risk of childbearing increases with female age, so when women are older, their desire to have children is lower and fertility plan is not susceptible to house price.

Table 8 Heterogeneity analysis

	(15) *Family size*	*(16)*	*(17)* *Education*	*(18)*	*(19)* *Age*	*(20)*
hp	−0.0269**	−0.0562**	−0.0403***	−0.0881***	−0.0593***	−0.0394***
	(0.0111)	(0.0241)	(0.0129)	(0.0214)	(0.0148)	(0.0140)
Control Variables	Yes	Yes	Yes	Yes	Yes	Yes
N	24,530	20,825	36,126	9229	13,189	32,166
Pseudo R^2	0.1240	0.1534	0.2387	0.1916	0.1826	0.1370
Differences	0.029		0.048		0.020	

6 Conclusion

This paper uses Probit model to estimate the impact of house price on the fertility plan of the migrants based on data from the 2018 China Migrants Dynamic Survey. The results show that the higher house price in the inflow city, the less likelihood female migrants have fertility plan; when the housing pressure of the migrants is low, their fertility plan is less affected by house price; the sensitivity of the migrants' fertility plan to house price is also influenced by the moderating effect of culture infrastructure development; the fertility plan of female migrants with larger family size, higher education level, and younger age are more sensitive to house price. Although China's economic growth has slowed down in recent years, the country's expanding economy and market size still require a large labor force. Migrants is a non-negligible group in China's labor endowment structure, and increasing the fertility intention of migrants is an important way to optimize China's labour force structure and mitigate aging. According to the empirical results of this paper, the government can improve the fertility intention of the migrants by improving the housing policies of the migrants and reducing housing costs. Addressing the institutional barriers to the education of the children of the migrants and guaranteeing the right to education for school-age children. Deepening the reform of the household registration system and guaranteeing basic public service resources to increase the fertility intention of migrants.

References

Arai, L. (2007). Peer and neighbourhood influences on teenage pregnancy and fertility: Qualitative findings from research in english communities. Health & Place, 13(1):87–98.

Banerjee, J. (1983). An experimental study on the cold rolling of strips.

Cai, F. (2018). Perceiving truth and ceasing doubts: What can we learn from 40 years of china's reform and opening up? China & World Economy, 26(2):1–22.

Chaney, T., Sraer, D., and Thesmar, D. (2012). The collateral channel: How real estate shocks affect corporate investment. American Economic Review, 102(6):2381–2409.

Clark, W. A., Yi, D., and Zhang, X. (2020). Do house prices affect fertility behavior in China? an empirical examination. International Regional Science Review, 43(5):423–449.

CUFE (2021). China human capital report 2021(in chinese. Central University of Finance and Economics Press.

Dettling, L. J. and Kearney, M. S. (2014). House prices and birth rates: The impact of the real estate market on the decision to have a baby. Journal of Public Economics, 110:82–100.

Du, Y., Cai, F., Qu, X., and JieChen (2014). Continuing the chinese miracle: Reaping the dividends of the household registration system reform. Economic Research, 8:4–13.

Entzinger, H. and Biezeveld, R. (2003). Benchmarking in immigrant integration.

Gennaioli, N., La Porta, R., Lopez-de Silanes, F., and Shleifer, A. (2013). Human capital and regional development. The Quarterly Journal of Economics, 128(1):105–164.

Hao, P. and Tang, S. (2015). Floating or settling down: The effect of rural landholdings on the settlement intention of rural migrants in urban china. Environment and Planning A, 47(9):1979–1999.

Kim, J. S. and Yeo, Y. H. (2019). The relationship between family-friendly policy and intention of childbirth. International Journal of IT-based Social Welfare Promotion and Management, 6:1–6.

Lewis, W. A. et al. (1954). Economic development with unlimited supplies of labour.

Lian, Y. and Xu, W. (2023). Analysis of information technology management development in the context of population aging–based on gray prediction algorithm.

Lino, M. (2002). Expenditures on children by families. Family Economics and Nutrition Review, 14(2):3.

Liu, J., Xing, C., and Zhang, Q. (2020). House price, fertility rates and reproductive intentions. China Economic Review, 62:101496.

Oates, W. E. (1969). The effects of property taxes and local public spending on property values: An empirical study of tax capitalization and the tiebout hypothesis. Journal of political economy, 77(6):957–971.

Pan, L. and Xu, J. (2012). Housing price and fertility rate. China Economic Journal, 5(2–3):97–111.

Peng, D. and Du, Y. (2016). Do high housing prices inhibit firms' exports—A theoretical and empirical analysis from chinese manufacturing firms. China Economic Issues, 5:3–15.

Roberts, K. D. (2001). The determinants of job choice by rural labor migrants in shanghai. China Economic Review, 12(1):15–39.

Song, L. and Appleton, S. (2008). Social protection and migration in china: What can protect migrants from economic uncertainty. Migration and social protection in China, 14:138.

Wang, C. (2006). Study on the "semi-urbanization" of rural migrant population. Sociological Research(Chinese), 5(7):107–122.

Wang, F., Zhao, L., and Zhao, Z. (2017). China's family planning policies and their labor market consequences. Journal of Population Economics, 30(1):31–68.

Wang, S. (2023). Constructing children's psychological well-being: Sources of resilience for children left behind in northeast china. International Migration.

Waxman, A., Liang, Y., Li, S., Barwick, P. J., and Zhao, M. (2020). Tightening belts to buy a home: Consumption responses to rising housing prices in urban china. Journal of Urban Economics, 115:103190.

Wu, J. and Zhang, J. (2020). Barriers to school education for migrant children being left behind and urban labor supply. Economic Research Journal(Chinese), 11:138–155.

Yang, S., Jiang, Q., and Sánchez-Barricarte, J. J. (2022). China's fertility change: an analysis with multiple measures. Population Health Metrics, 20(1):1–14.

Zhang, K. H. and Song, S. (2003). Rural–urban migration and urbanization in china: Evidence from time-series and cross-section analyses. China Economic Review, 14(4):386–400.

Zhang, W., Xu, J., and Yang, Z. (2018). House price, wage and resource allocation efficiency—an empirical analysis based on micro household data. Financial Research, 458(8):69–84.

CHAPTER 9

The BRICS are 'Getting Old Before Getting Rich': Trends and Prospects

Lauren A. Johnston

1 Recent Historic Demographic Transitions

The world saw the passing of two independent demographic milestones in recent years. First, China, the country with the world's highest population since at least 1950, in 2022, saw its population peak at around 1.43 billion. Second, in 2023, China ceded its world's most populous country crown to India. Median total population estimates for China and India from 1950 to 2021 and projections from 2022 to 2100 suggest that India's population will peak in the early 2060s, at around 1.67 billion, a level more than 200 million people higher than China's demographic peak, while China's will decline into the foreseeable future (Figs. 1 and 2).

Those changes reflect the demographic transition, the process characterised by falling death rates and increasing life expectancy combining to set off a population boom that continues until fertility rates decline, in turn, producing a gradual shift in the population ageing structure toward

L. A. Johnston (✉)
University of Sydney, Sydney, Australia
e-mail: lauren.johnston@sydney.edu.au

A. Aliu (ed.), *Complexity Thinking and China's Demography Within and Beyond Mainland China*,
https://doi.org/10.1007/978-981-97-0172-8_9

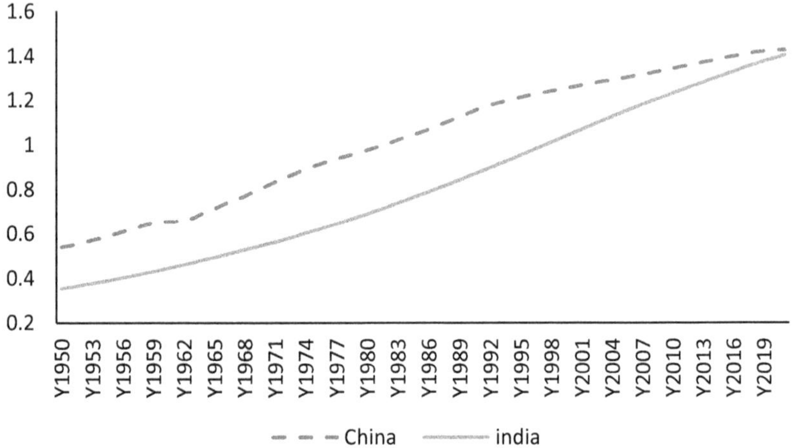

Fig. 1 Population estimates, China and India (1950–2021) (*Source* DESA [2022])

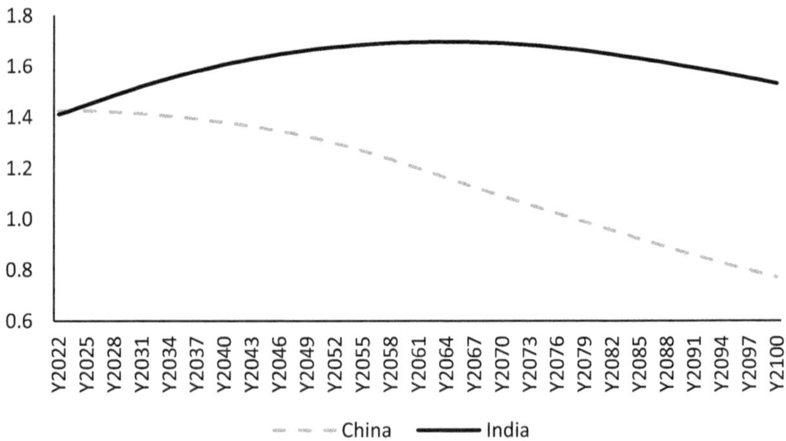

Fig. 2 Population forecast (medium estimates), China and India (2022–2100) (*Source* DESA [2022])

an increased share of elders (Zaiceva and Zimmermann 2016). Thus far, no country has developed socioeconomically without proceeding into the demographic transition (Bloom et al. 2007).

What has changed more recently, however, is that across countries and time, the demographic transition is speeding up and also beginning at lower per capita incomes than in earlier times. This is leading to not only a greater intensity of population ageing—a rising population share of seniors—across countries but in developed and developing countries alike (Unger 2022).

Empirically a population is classed as 'ageing' when at least 7% of the total population are aged 65 or older; 'aged' when 14% or more of the population are aged 65 and over; and 'super-aged' when that population share reaches 21% (National Bureau of Statistics 2023). France and Sweden both entered the demographic transition in the 1800s—and had more than 7% of population aged 65 and over before 1900. In that era, the demographic transition moved relatively slowly: it took them 114 years and 82 years respectively to transition from the 7% 'ageing' threshold to reach the 'aged' population threshold of 14% or more of population aged 65 and over (Messkoub 1999). Japan, a later developer, made the same transition over just 24 years, from 1970 to 1994 (Mirkin and Weinberger 2001). For later developers again, the process is often happening even more quickly, thanks to 'advantages of backwardness' gains being made in education and health at lower levels of per capita income than in the past (Gerschenkron 1962).

The speed of the demographic transition has important implications. A fast demographic transition impels that governments and entrepreneurs capture a compressed period of the demographic dividend potential. The demographic dividend is offered when a country has an elevated working-age population share and is powerful in a development context especially when combined with a Lewisian transfer of labour from the informal to the formal labour market and rural to the industrial sector (Gollin 2014).

The economic development level timing of the demographic transition matters too. Where the onset of population ageing arrives 'early'—that is population ageing onsets in a developing country context—countries are, in principle, less likely to have prepared sustainable pension schemes, affordable seniors housing, or a shift in healthcare capacity from communicable to chronic disease, let alone adapted economic policy approaches that can accommodate a larger pool of dependent seniors and a smaller population share of workers. Figure 3 highlights that the population ageing phase of the demographic transition is emerging over time at lower per capita incomes. By 2022, the average share of elders in even lower-middle-income countries is nearing the 7% 'ageing' threshold, and for upper-middle-income countries, the same average share is 12%, which is closer to the 14% 'aged' threshold than to the 7% 'ageing' threshold.

Finally, the cointegration of the demographic transition and the process of economic development, the 'economic demography transition' also has important implications (Johnston 2012, 2019a, 2021). For example, where in the case of a developing country with a rapidly ageing population, it is likely that pensions are inadequate in level, coverage, and payment reliability, in contrast in rich countries that got old after getting rich, there is on average a higher risk that at least a sizeable share of pension and other elder benefit promises in rear view appear generous and may bring a significant—productivity adverse—cost to current workers and future generations.

The political grouping of countries known as the 'BRICS'—Brazil, Russia, India, China, and South Africa—is the demographic giants of middle-income development. Moreover, those broader demographic

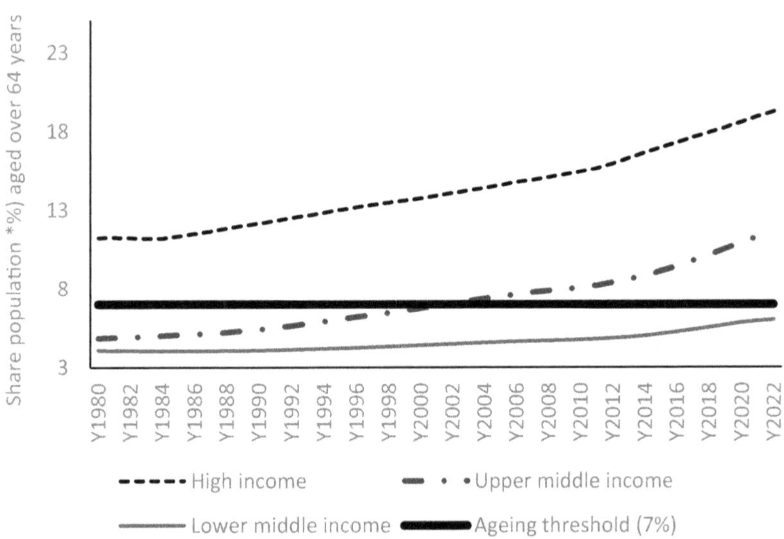

Fig. 3 Senior population share average by income group (*Source* The World Bank [2023])

trends and the epochal population transition of its two demographic giant members, China and India in 2022–2023, appear to have focused their high-level attention in 2023 on demographic issues too. Where Declaration of the XIV BRICS Summit hosted by Beijing in August 2022 had an almost exclusively health focus to its demographic reference, in contrast, the August 24, 2023, issued Johannesburg II Declaration of the XV BRICS Summit explicitly stresses cooperation in population matters:

> Beijing, 2022: 'We support continuing to hold the BRICS TB Research Network Meetings, which will contribute to achieving the WHO goal of ending TB by 2030. We support the early signing of the Memorandum of Understanding on Cooperation in the Field of Regulation of Medical Products for Human Use among our drug regulatory authorities and welcome the holding of a BRICS Seminar of Officials and Experts in Population Development in the second half of 2022'. (Ministry of Foreign Affairs 2023)
>
> Johannesburg, 2023: 'We remain committed to strengthening BRICS cooperation on population matters, because the dynamics of population age structure change, and pose challenges as well as opportunities, particularly with regard to women's rights, youth development, disability rights, employment and the future of work, urbanisation, migration and ageing'. (XV BRICS Summit 2023)

Thanks mostly to the rate of population growth in Africa and South Asia, since 1960 the BRICS' share of the total population of low- and middle-income countries combined has fallen 58 to 49% (The World Bank 2023). Led mainly by the growth of China's economy this century (Fig. 4), however, since 1990, the five countries' equivalent share of gross domestic product (GDP) has increased from less than half to some two-thirds of developing country GDP today (World Bank 2023; Johnston 2023a). This economic demography weight alongside recent epochal demographic inflection points makes the study of development and demographic change in the five BRICS countries important.

In that context, this chapter draws extensively from Johnston (2023b) and uses the 2022 Revision of World Population Prospects, the 27th edition of the United Nations' official population estimates and projections and World Bank World Development Indicators data to survey the related population and age structure trends. With focus on China's experience and the trend of population ageing, survey of demographic data, and forecasts draws attention to dramatic population structure dynamics

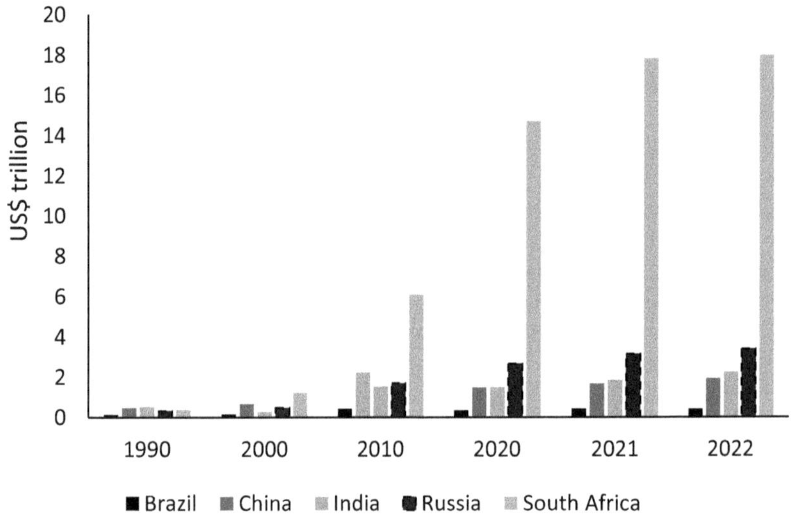

Fig. 4 Aggregate GDP, selected years, BRICS countries (*Source* The World Bank [2023])

taking place in the BRICS countries, Russia, China, and Brazil in terms of population ageing and decline especially. In this context, China's unique population structure dynamics-weighted approach to development since the 1980s provides a reference point of relevance for the other four of the first five BRICS.[1] Relevance to global development more generally is drawn in the conclusion for further research offered.

2 Demographic Change and the BRICS

An early signal of the arrival of the demographic transition is falling death rates. Since 1960, from when most cross-country international data sets begin, among the BRICS India experienced particularly dramatic gains in

[1] With Egypt, Ethiopia, Iran and United Arab Emirates having joined the BRICS grouping in January 2024, the group is now more diverse in economic demography context with most of these countries being demographically relatively young, and United Arab Emirates also being high-income country.

the under-five mortality rate. The child mortality rate (referring to children up to their fifth birthday), for example, fell from 243 deaths among every thousand children to 32 by 2020 (Fig. 5), though the decline in rural decline has been lower than that in urban regions (Kumar et al. 2022). Russia's relatively marginal falls in the infant mortality rate over the last half-century relate to the fact that it had entered the demographic transition much earlier than other BRICS countries. All BRICS countries have an under-five mortality rate below the average for middle-income countries of 26.8 deaths per 1000 live births, and well below the low-income country average rate of 47.4 deaths. But Russia alone among the BRICS has a rate that is on par with the high-income country average, of 4.1 deaths per 1000 live births (World Bank 2019).

A falling under-five mortality rate in the early phase of development in turn supports a steady reduction in the total fertility rate (TFR), the number of births a woman is expected to have in her lifetime. That arises partly owing to parents becoming more confident that children already born will survive into adulthood. Later, where the TFR falls below the

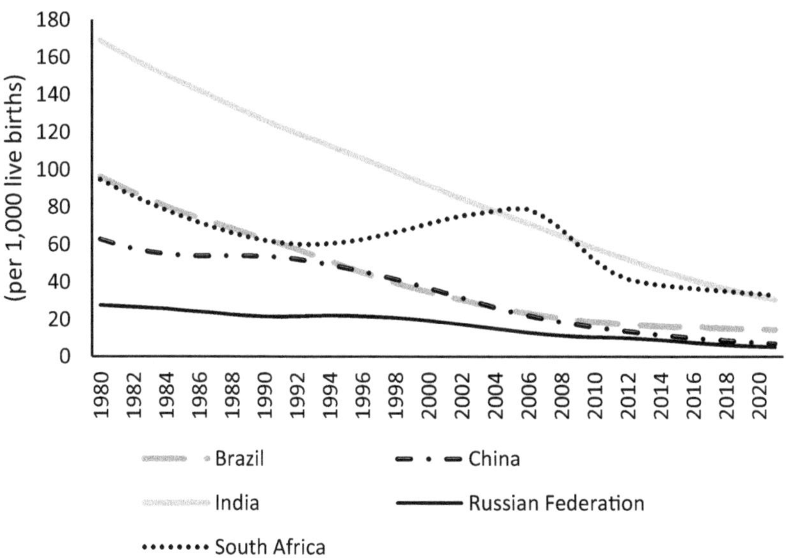

Fig. 5 Under-Five Mortality Rate, BRICS (1960–2021) (*Source* The World Bank [2023])

population replacement rate—of 2.1 births per woman—this signals a more advanced phase of the demographic transition, a probable intensive population ageing period, and even possible population decline in the future too. Among the BRICS, only South Africa had a TFR that was above 2.1, at 2.4 births per woman. India's TFR was 2.0, while Brazil, Russia, and China had TFRs of 1.6, 1.5, and 1.2 respectively (Fig. 6). Russia's population has been in decline since 1993, and China's peaked in 2021.

Recent gains in income, education, and healthcare, where applied to women especially, have also helped to drive up life expectancy (Fig. 7). Among BRICS countries, China stands out over the last four decades in having experienced a dramatic increase in life expectancy, adding years to average retirement length. Brazil and India have seen rapid life expectancy

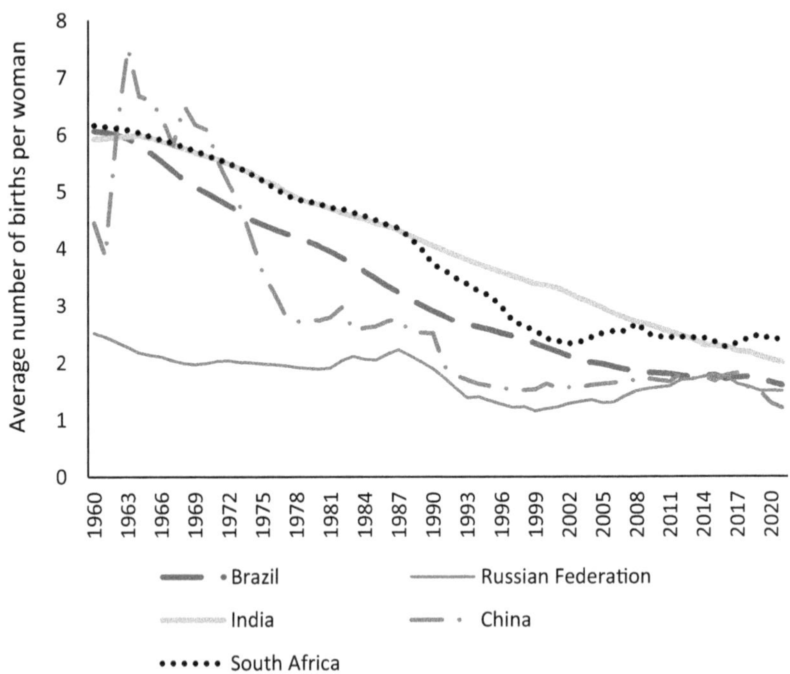

Fig. 6 Total Fertility Rate, BRICS countries (1961–2021) (*Source* The World Bank [2023])

gains too. In both Russia and South Africa, however, a challenging set of economic and institutional reforms, and in South Africa's case a medical crisis around HIV/AIDS, also impacted life expectancy trends. Overall, until the COVID-19 pandemic, however, all BRICS had enjoyed a decade of life expectancy gains, with only China impacted little by the life expectancy implications of the pandemic (Bo Hu and Liu 2023).

Recent falls in birth and death rates mean that today all BRICS countries over the last few decades are home to populations with both a rising and relatively elevated median age and population share of seniors (Figs. 8 and 9). Alongside its unusually rapid development and more rapid TFR decline, China has seen the greatest increase in the median age of its citizens over recent years, with the median age up from below twenty as recently as the 1970s to being around 40 years today. In other words, in China's case, a dramatic doubling of the median age in just half a century. Other BRICS too have seen striking rises in the median age, with Brazil's median age rising by nearly two decades (Fig. 8).

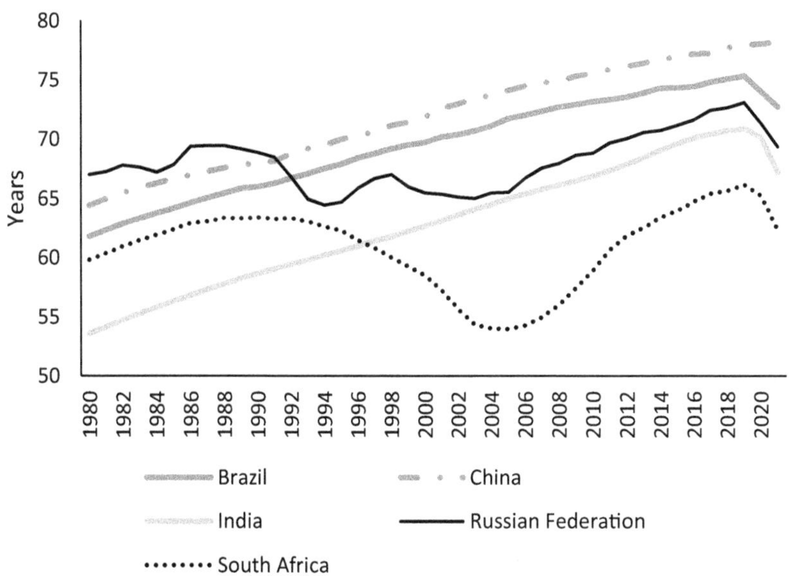

Fig. 7 Life Expectancy (years), BRICS countries (*Source* The World Bank [2023])

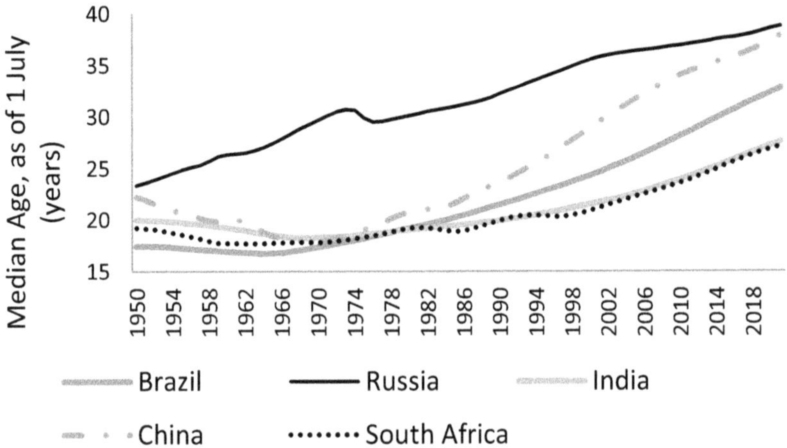

Fig. 8 Median population age, BRICS countries (years of age) (*Source* The World Bank [2023])

The speed of the demographic transition has major socioeconomic implications and hence implications for policy. For example, not only does it impact the working-age population share and size but also the dependency burden in fiscal resources and aged care context. In healthcare, there is a shift from communicable to chronic illness as populations age. Lack of ongoing preparedness during a process development for the demographic transition risks economic stagnation and elder poverty, especially among women who tend to accumulate a lower level of savings of their lifetime and also to live a few years longer than males (Priebe 2017).

Table 1 presents BRICS' country data around the year in which each reached the 'ageing' (7%) and 'aged' (14%) population share of seniors. Russia, the 'oldest' of the BRICS and the first to embark on the demographic transition, enjoyed a 50-year 'ageing' transition and adaption period. Younger BRICS, however, are lucky to have half this timespan to accommodate the equivalent population structure-related socioeconomic changes. China, alongside Russia, is the only BRICS country to have already reached the second threshold. Brazil is predicted to reach the second threshold within a decade, and like China hence to need to accommodate the necessary socioeconomic changes in just over two decades, while India will have little over a quarter-of-a-century.

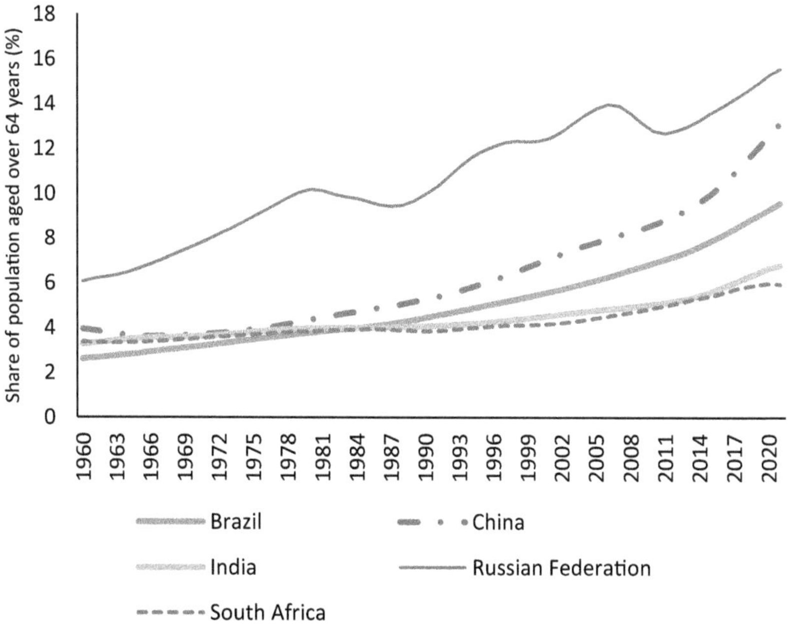

Fig. 9 Share of Population Aged 65 and over (%) (*Source* The World Bank [2023])

Table 1 Year of BRICS Country Reaching 'Ageing' Thresholds

	Year reaching 7% aged 65 years and over	*Year reaching 14% aged 65 years and over*	*Time Gap (years)*
Brazil	2011	2033	22
Russia	1967	2017	50
India	2023	2048	25
China	2001	2023	22
South Africa	2030	2059	29

Source For dates before 2021, the figure is taken from the World Bank, World Development Indicators; for dates after 2021, the figure is an estimate taken from the UN, World Population Prospects

What Table 1 also points to is that Russia and China, alone among BRICS members today, are already amid a sustained and projected long period of population decline. Russia's population peaked around 1993, at 148.59 million (World Bank, 2022). The UN forecasts that the trend of population decline is set to continue, reaching an estimated 112 million by the end of the century (Fig. 10). From the benchmark of estimates for 2023, over those years, Russia's working-age population share will fall from two-thirds to some 57.6%, and the dependent share of population (young and old combined) will increase one-third to 42.4%. To manage this shift, Russia must ensure that, led by its working-age population, it is able to retain sufficient productivity levels per capita, and hence policies must become increasingly focused on supporting areas of productivity to compensate for the weightier dependency burden over time.

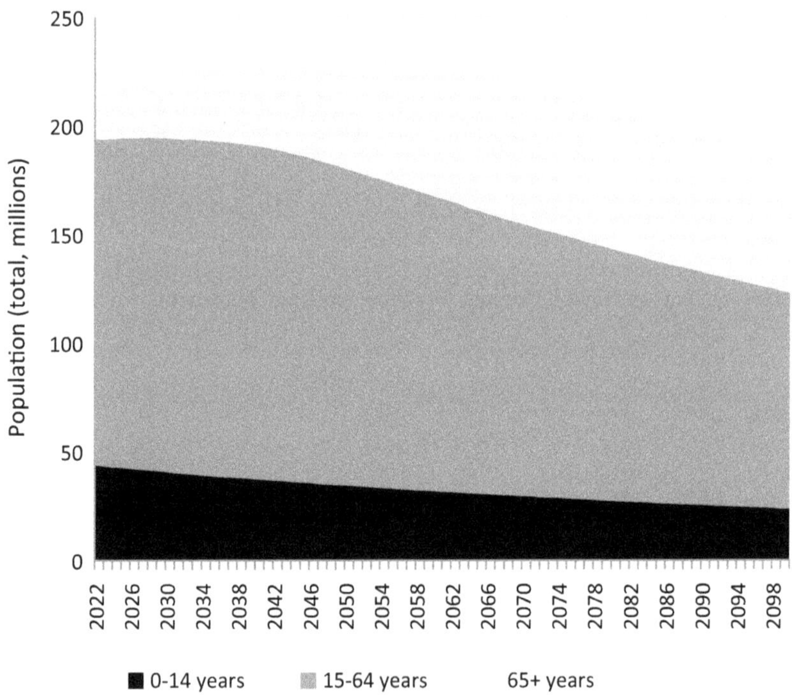

Fig. 10 Projected Population Structure, Brazil (millions of people, estimates) (*Source* The World Bank [2023])

In line with Russia, China (Fig. 11) has passed its contemporary demographic peak, though much more recently—in 2021. China's total population, according to UN estimates, is expected to gradually decline over the rest of the century, falling to some 771.3 from a peak of 1.413 billion, according to medium variant estimates. From the benchmark of estimates for 2023, by 2100, the working-age population share is expected to fall from 69% of the population to 49.3%, and the dependent share of population rises accordingly.

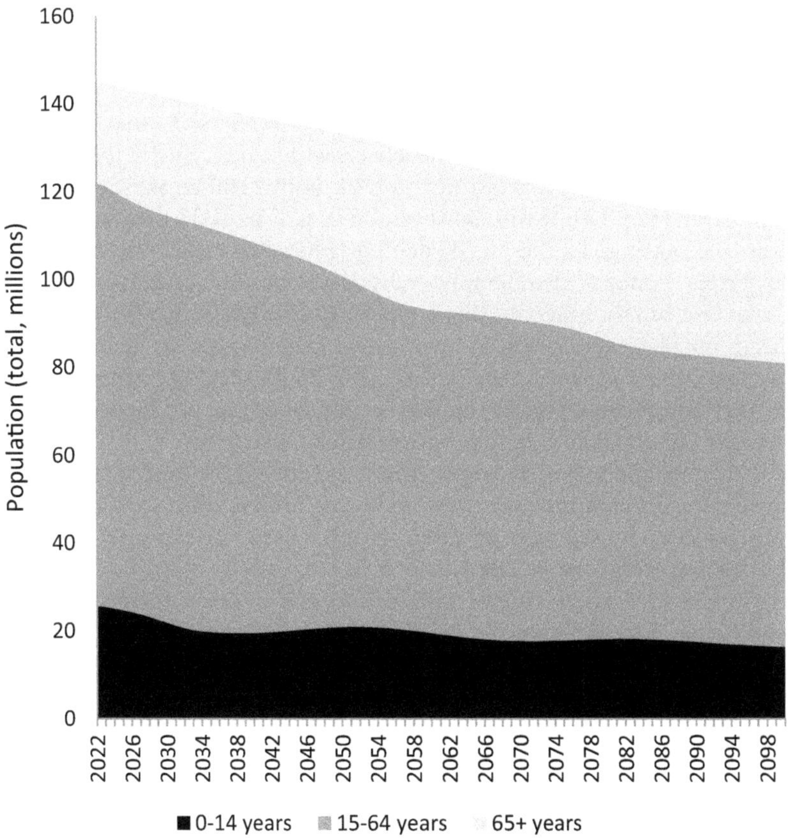

Fig. 11 Projected Population Structure, Russia (millions of people, estimates) (*Source* DESA [2022])

In population structure context, where in 2023, 16.8% of China's population were aged 0–14 years, and a further 14.3% were aged 65 and over, by 2100 accordingly to medium population forecasts that the balance will shift from 14.3% to 41.0%. Such a shift in favour of a seniors-heavy population, if it emerges, is unprecedented in human history and calls for dexterous policy-making to ensure that this large 'grey' population both has its basic needs met and also does not ultimately serve to stagnate productivity akin to a high youth share in the Malthusian case. Arguably navigating these related risks and opportunities of changing population structure over coming decades is what the BRICS have committed to cooperating to do.

Like China, Brazil (Table 1 and Fig. 12) is ageing relatively rapidly, but unlike China or Russia, Brazil's population is quarter-of-a-century away from reaching a total peak. According to the UN, that peak will arrive around 2046–2047, and moreover, within the century the population share of elders is forecast not to peak until 2100 at one-third of the population (Fig. 12). It will, however, be as early as 2033 that Brazil shifts from the 'ageing' to the 'aged' demographic class, and must prepare a dexterous economic demography transition approach accordingly. Unlike China and Russia, however, this is especially true of Brazil which must do this in the context of being an open democracy where there is an elevated risk that older voters will vote in their own policy-making interests and so sacrifice later-born cohorts—right at a time when the productivity of the younger cohorts is in fact disproportionately important.

The remaining two 'younger' BRICS, India and South Africa, have more demographic time on their side—but no less need to adopt? relevant policies. In the case of India, its population is expected to enter the 'ageing' category in 2023, and it has an estimated 25 further years to prepare to become 'aged': India is forecast to reach the 14% seniors population share threshold in 2048 (Table 1). Looking further forward, India's population is forecast to peak in the early 2060s, and the share of elders will have reached a century peak of some 30% by the end of the century (Fig. 13). India retains—some—demographic dividend time and must urgently optimise capture of the potential of its working-age population at the same time as preparing for when they are older and comprise a larger share of the population than in the past.

According to United Nations estimates, by 2024, South Africa (Fig. 14) is the sole BRICS country to be home to a population that remains 'non-ageing' as defined by having a population share of seniors

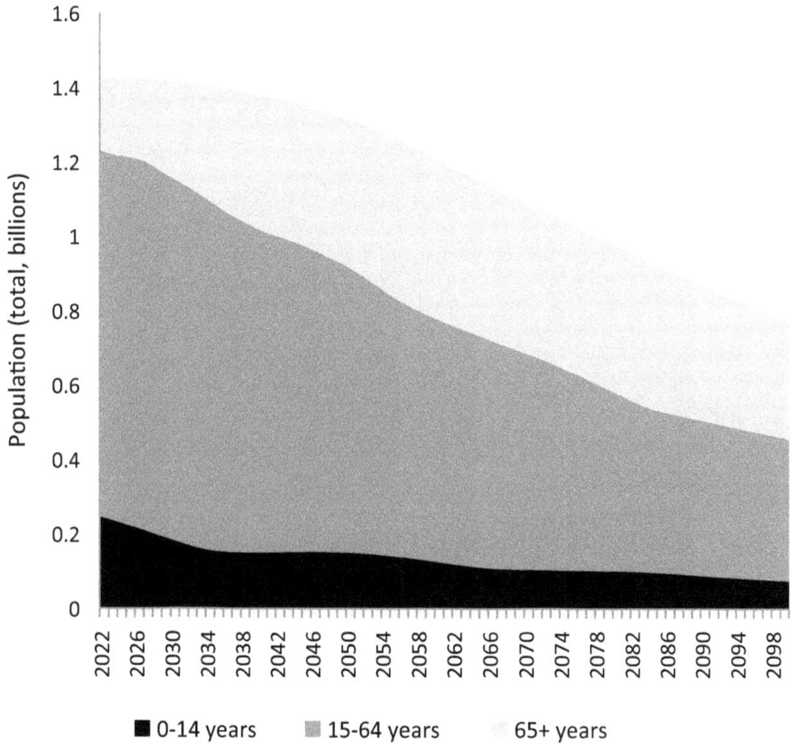

Fig. 12 Projected Population Structure, China (billions of people, estimates) (*Source* DESA [2022])

below the 7% ageing threshold. South Africa too, however, is forecast to join the 'population ageing' club around 2030 and by around 2060 become home to an 'aged' population (Table 1 and Fig. 14). With a population peak predicted for 2074, South Africa's senior share is expected to reach only 21% by the end of the century (Fig. 14)—a level Russia is expected to reach in the mid-2030s (Fig. 8). Importantly, however, Russia had 50 years between reaching the two thresholds, where South Africa will have under 30 years to adjust socioeconomically.

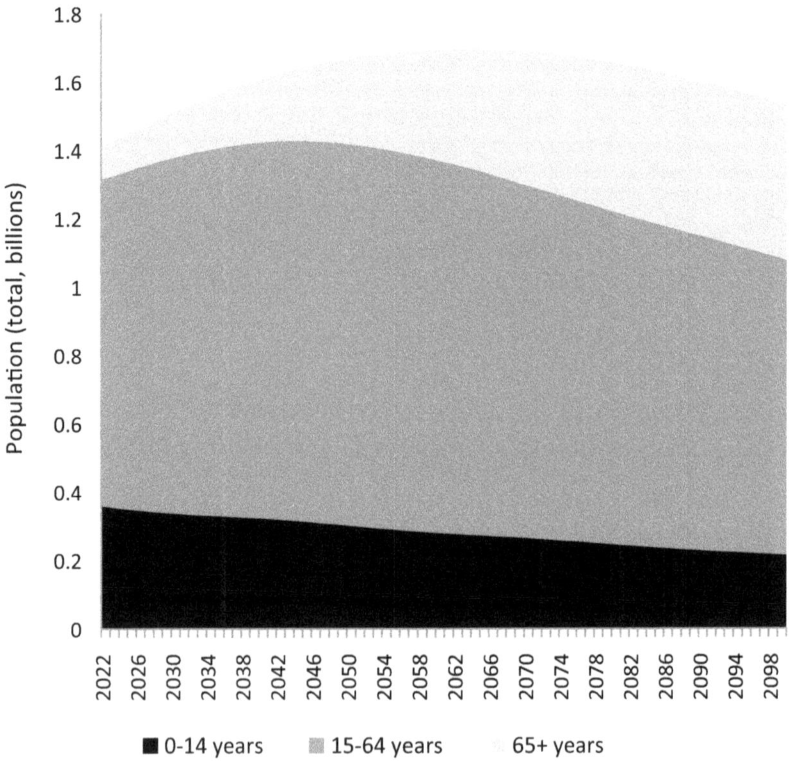

Fig. 13 Projected Population Structure, India (billions of people, estimates) (*Source* DESA [2022])

3 A Prescient Forecast of and Response to 'Getting Old Before Getting Rich'

China is a BRICS outlier not only for GDP size—greater than other BRICS combined—but also given its interventionist population policy (Ghosh 2019). Most infamously in that context for the fact that a unique set of circumstances in China in 1980, including recent famine and political turbulence, led to the introduction of the One Child Policy. The implementation came less than two years after paramount leader Deng Xiaoping implemented a process of policy reform and economic

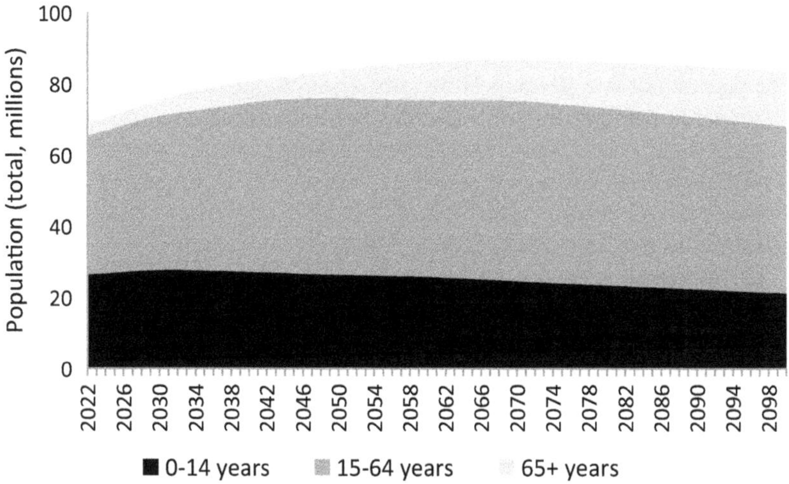

Fig. 14 Projected Population Structure, South Africa (millions of people, estimates) (*Source* DESA [2022])

opening that was intended to foster China's socioeconomic modernisation following several decades of domestic changes under the leadership of Mao Zedong.

'Emancipate the mind, seek truth from facts, and unite as one to face the future' was the December 13, 1978, speech by paramount leader Deng Xiaoping that launched a dramatic turn from economic isolation in international trade and investment (Naughton 1993). The goal was to drive economic modernisation and to elevate per capita income levels—as well as to create jobs for the hundreds of millions of Chinese born in the 1950s and 1960s (Fig. 6) (United Nations 2023). In fact, at that time China's population growth rate was already in decline thanks to the TFR having peaked in the late 1960s, but officials are said to have worried that if the large generation born in the 1950s and 1960s had large families themselves that China's total population would reach a level that was hard to sustain at all, let alone to sustain while improving living standards (Wu, 1980).

The draconian implementation of a One Child Policy from 1980 hence created not only the world's greatest-ever demographic dividend prospect—in terms of scale and the rapidly declining parallel birth rate—but also a unique and parallel effort to understand the consequences. The research of late Renmin University demographer Cangping Wu had a particular impact around a forecast the imposed decelerated rate of population growth meant that China had no feasible growth path to become a rich industrialised country before the onset of population ageing. China's destiny was to become old but not yet rich or to be '(economically) prematurely old', according to Wu (1986).

It was feared that getting old while still being a developing country might prevent China from ever attaining 'rich economy' status. For example, while still a developing country China would eventually need to re-direct scarce human and financial resources to 'unproductive' areas like elderly care. In addition, to remain competitive once the working-age population began to fall, evidently even then a drop that would be relatively precipitous from the 2020s, China would need to have acquired relatively elevated frontier capital-intensive competencies for a then middle-income country. These could replace China's low-wage labour-intensive advantages but would need to be acquired within just a few decades when China overall was still a developing country.

In the background, meantime, Chinese policymakers understood that neighbouring economies Japan, Taiwan, Singapore, and Hong Kong had all become rich economies when still home to young populations. This pathway of getting rich after getting old may not even be possible, yet China had no choice but to seek to inspire a development pathway that would follow this economic demography sequence (Johnston et al. 2016). China's apparent and experimental economic demography weighted approach to development since has been called an economic demography transition strategy (Johnston 2021). Summarised in Table 2, such a strategy consistently endogenises the cointegration of economic and demographic change and is summarised in Table 2.

The economic demography policy approach presented in Table 2 can be simplified as a two-tier approach. The first tier comprises identifying and implementing policies to ensure China captured its low-wage demographic dividend period for rapid economic development. The second tier concerned early incremental preparations, both direct and indirect, for the later period of intensive population ageing—economic and health and welfare-related. That is, when China would be 'old' but not yet 'rich' and need to cater for large numbers of elderly at the same time as continuing

Table 2 Overview of China's economic demography transition strategy

1980–1990s	Capture demographic dividend (labour-intensive investment incentives) Better educate the next (smaller) cohort to ensure later elevated productivity potential Create a population aging commission to lead the instigation of a population aging-preparedness agenda
2000s	Focus on preparations for elevated human welfare and elevated population dependents such as rising numbers of pensioners (e.g., health, social security, and pensions) Scale up investment in science and technological capacity (to support later more capital-intensive over labour-intensive-led growth)
2010s	Promote capital-intensive investment; investment in universities, science, and technology Develop active aging-industries strategy and incentivisation (e.g., equipment and services needed by the elderly; pension and wealth management industry incentives)
2020s	Push for social and economic aging-related tech and industry innovation; push up technology value chain; foster economic drivers to shift from labour- to capital-related factor advantages
2030s	Ensure each cohort is progressively richer and more educated than the last—i.e.,a constant if not rising effective labour supply—so as to accommodate older population's needs without derailing national development

Source Johnston (2020), Lauren (2021)

the economic development process (Johnston 2019a). Johnston (2019a, 2021) outlines the greater details of each phase in the unique case of China. In terms of the second tier, Appendixes A and B outline some relevant policy chronology information and details looking both forward and back.

An important nuance in those preparations in a developing country context—and in BRICS population structure change cooperation context—is that maintaining constant output with a declining working-age population share, all else constant, requires elevated productivity per worker. Since this is driven by either elevated human capital or technology improvements (Maestas and Zissimopoulos 2010), preparing to become 'old before rich' in other words requires that developing countries disproportionately invest in the education of (smaller) younger cohorts during the earlier phases of demographic transition—despite that resources available for educating what is even a falling youth population share may be limited.

Since 'most investments in human capital raise observed earnings at older ages, because returns are added to earnings then, and lower them at younger ages, because costs are deducted from earnings then', there is a high chance that fiscal revenues and household income are instead allocated to immediate needs and not toward long-run national economic demography needs (Becker 1962). Later, however, when population ageing intensifies and there is a smaller working-age cohort without sufficient human capital or available technology to drive a rate of technological progress that accommodate the whole population's needs and continue growing the economy, there lies an increased risk of stagnating or decreasing per capita living standards (Johnston 2021).

Are China's Productivity-Related Human Capital Investments Sufficient?

Contrary to having managed a perfect economic demography transition strategy over time, a well-cited contemporary text on China's very uneven human capital investments in its citizens under the age of 40 years, let alone 25 years, is Invisible China, by Stanford-based researchers Scott Rozelle and Natalie Hell. Their conclusion starts as follows:

> In the next several years, China either will prove itself the inevitable superpower some have predicated and reach the top of the development game board, or it will succumb to the invisible challenge described in this book, ending in economic downturn and stagnation or even in collapse. (p.153)

The essence of Invisible China is that while China may have managed to produce world-leading scientists and an elite next generation along its urban coast especially, the majority of its next generation citizens—those from rural and hinterland China—are often barely able to read, let alone forge a new scientific frontier or even be functional workers in a high-tech production plant. Rozelle and Hell (2020) compare China's educational success per capita compared with nations that have successfully entered the high-income group, such as South Korea and Poland, and find that China's educational per capita achievements more closely resemble those of countries that have failed to enter the high-income group, including Mexico and Brazil. On the other hand, Johnston et al. (2016) compared China's manufactured exports with countries in Eastern Europe and elsewhere that had successfully entered the high-income group and found China to be well-positioned.

Whether or not China's smaller cohort of future workers is well-prepared to not only carry the burden of hundreds of millions of pensioners but also to continue to push the economic frontier within China toward the global frontier, in population-ageing context comes down to whether those workers are well-positioned to productivity compensated for the adverse change in the dependency ratio. China's government's approach to achieving a 'Youth Education Effect' that in turn produces a 'Cohort Replacement Effect' (Jordon et al. 2014; Lin and Long 2020). The broad aim is to realise a constant level of effective labour—even as the number and population share of workers fall. This underpins a targeted change from the demographic dividend and unit of labour growth increment, that is, a Solow Model type growth increment to a human capital or labour quality (Romer Model) growth increment as population ageing intensifies. That in turn requires that China has made appropriate educational investments over recent decades, despite so many other priorities and scarce resources per capita.

China's socioeconomic development and poverty alleviation agenda over recent decades included extensive educational reforms (e.g., Tan 2013; Guo et al. 2019; Freije-Rodriguez et al. 2019) and had many layers to the extensive if uneven educational investments, Tan (2013) and Guo et al. (2019) elaborate. One estimate suggests that China's human resources-adjusted population will rise in 2020 population equivalent terms from 1.43 billion persons to 1.64 billion persons by 2050 (Pettis 2022). This equates with an average annual rate of growth of China's human resources stock of 0.48%—anticipated despite a broader trend of population decline.

In fact, it is difficult to forecast whether China has made 'enough' human capital investments, as much as it is to be sure that China's socioeconomic context will shape its next decades. One reason for that is seemingly ever-more limited educational and human capital data, let alone across the whole population by cohort and schooling year level and post-secondary education type and major. Moreover, it is also challenging to understand how automation, and artificial intelligence also, will shift the employment frontier. Finally, it is also challenging to understand what China's agenda for utilising might be what is of the productivity potential of its lesser-educated younger population share.

Moreover, China, also has a plan to tap productivity low-wage demographic dividend potential abroad, under the umbrella of the flagship Belt and Road Initiative (Johnston 2019b, 2019c). The plan overall is that

China moves into higher-value-added less labour-intensive manufacturing and becomes an outbound investor in the Global South in terms of its earlier lower-quality industries. Today, China is a net outbound investor and targets its infrastructure and investor-based manufacturing in today's poorer and younger countries, mainly along the Belt and Road (Johnston and Onjala 2022; Johnston 2019c). China has also, as an example in trade with richer ageing countries, captured a dominant position in manufacturing coffins for export to the world's 'oldest' country, Japan (Johnston 2020).

Alongside having prepared to shift from a high-speed growth phase to a lower-speed growth higher-quality development agenda, China has also emphasised sustainable improvement in the social welfare system for all residents across the whole life cycle and in line with economic demography change (Daokui 2018). Pension promises have mostly been kept minimal to ensure these would not later be extremely difficult to sustain as compared to difficult to sustain; the healthcare system, including health insurance, and aged care fundaments have been gradually evolved over time (Appendix A). Today China seeks to turn ageing into a 'silver economy' boom for entrepreneurs and the elderly alike, with a set of incentives for investing in aged care products and services, including technologies that can cut related costs and foster independence. The national policy umbrella that mainstreams the agenda in China is the 'mid- and long-term plan for proactively responding to population ageing' (Appendix B).

That China has foresightful plans does not itself imply it will succeed in getting rich after getting old. Yet, arguably at least it is better positioned to do so than developing countries getting old before rich—without having any such long-term preparations in train. The unbalanced geographic and demographic reality of China's investments, as Rozelle and Hell (2020) and others have detailed, confirms that whatever emerges over coming years will itself also be reflectively lumpy. That alone, however, does not imply China will fail to lumber along toward the high-income group. Indeed, some of China's coastal provinces are established high-income provinces, including Guangdong, Zhejiang, and Jiangsu, as well as Beijing, Shanghai and Tianjin. To that point, China is arguably in a long drawn-out high-income turning period, as compared to the turning point, reflecting the sheer scale of its geography and population. Unlike countries such as Poland and South Korea, it now also faces geoeconomics headwinds for its next phase of ascent also.

4 The BRICS, and Ageing and Development

For all countries, rich and poor, and young and old, a similar—but unique to local conditions,—economic demography-weighted approach, across countries and time, is a rational socioeconomic policy approach. The BRICS countries especially face rapid population ageing as middle-income countries and have agreed to deepen collaboration in this area. Moreover, among developing countries, the BRICS countries are home to the potential to use the benefits of economic and demographic scale to better position them to proactively respond to the related economic and public welfare challenges than can smaller developing countries. Members of BRICS have also earlier set a related precedent in terms of producing generically branded medicinal products. Affordable aged care may be a new such frontier.

The reality is that the ageing of populations is not a trend now limited to high-income countries but one that is also common to middle-income economies, on average (Fig. 3). Among middle-income countries, the economic and demographic giants include but are not limited to the BRICS countries, Brazil, Russia, India, China, and South Africa. That combination alongside recent attention to demographics with India taking China's place as the world's most populous country makes it fortunate that an outcome of the BRICS Summit of 2023 was the announcement of cooperation 'on population matters, because the dynamics of population age structure change, and pose challenges as well as opportunities, particularly with regard to women's rights, youth development, disability rights, employment and the future of work, urbanisation, migration and ageing' (XV BRICS Summit, 2023).

Since the BRICS are already 'old', ageing relatively rapidly, and not yet rich, if not on track to be so in future decades, this commitment is essentially a commitment to working together in the arena of navigating a 'getting old before rich' economic demography transition toward continued development. Thanks to an unusual population policy intervention in the 1980s, China in fact has been broadly testing methods of navigating this circumstance for four decades already. To this point, its approach at least offers a benchmark upon which all the other BRICS and China themselves can improve their efforts to successfully navigate a newly 'ageing'-rich economic development process. In doing so, as developing countries 'heavy' in weight in terms of their economic and demographic scale, the BRICS may help to set new development policy precedents for all developing countries, as well as help to make aspects of ageing more affordable, such as medicines and other ageing-related technologies. In this respect, it is expected that the BRICS may deepen their population age structure dynamics and research cooperation in the area of the BRICS Academic Forum, the BRICS Think Tank Forum, and other long-standing platforms.

A focus of that research and policy attentiveness may and should also be gender—females tend to live longer than males; earn less income; and accumulate less wealth and pension entitlements over their lifetime than males. This becomes a double whammy and livelihood risk in old age when women hence become at much greater risk of slipping into poverty, in some contexts leading to elevated risk of violence against them too. As BRICS populations age, it would be a tragedy if they also became home to large populations of under-supported, impoverished, and at-risk elder females. It would, equivalently, also be a disaster for families if population ageing is managed badly across generations and timing—resulting in diminished fiscal resources for younger households and children too.

Women and children have a deeply vested interest in BRICS countries' successfully concurrently navigating population change and economic development. The BRICS thinktanks community and academic forum should be able to tap related policy, civil society, and academic networks to mainstream these interests directly into any BRICS socioeconomic agendas. This may also offer leadership and practical policy lessons on population and development more widely among developing countries, too. Future research would be of service if shedding light and policy usefulness in any of these related areas, as well as following the outcomes of this area of BRICS cooperation.

Appendix A: Selected Population-Ageing Related Policy Initiatives, China (1982–2020)

Year of issuance	*Policy/Issue*	*Description*
1982	Committee on ageing was formed to participate in the First World Assembly on Ageing	The first group of officials dedicated to ageing issues

(continued)

(continued)

Year of issuance	*Policy/Issue*	*Description*
1983	National Working Commission on Ageing formed	Commission was charged with identifying important issues and laying the foundation for national ageing-related architecture and implementing or overseeing the related work
1991	UN and China adopt the Principles for Older Persons	On 16 December 1991, the UN General Assembly adopted the UN Principles for Older Persons (Resolution 46/91)
1994	Seven-Year Development Outline on China's Work on Aging (1994–2000)	Proposed the general objectives of China's work on ageing, defined by ageing-related items for national economic and social development
1996	Law of Safeguarding Rights and Interests of the Elderly	The state is responsible for establishing an old-age insurance system, safeguarding the basic livelihoods of the elderly (the first legal recognition of elderly rights)
1999	Year of the Elderly; China reaches ageing milestone	The General Assembly (Resolution 47/5) decided to observe the year 1999 as the International Year of Older Persons—the same year, China's share of population aged 60 and above reached 10%, which is the threshold of 'ageing'
1999	World Health Organisation proposed 'Active Ageing'	Policy framework for informing discussion and action plan formulation that promotes healthy and active ageing. By definition, 'active ageing is the process of optimising opportunities for health, participation and security to enhance quality of life as people age'. †
2000	The Communist Party of China (CPC) Central Committee and the State Council Decision on Strengthening Work on Ageing	Safeguard elderly rights and interests; develop the service sector for the elderly; ensure related funding and infrastructure; carry out advocacy for the elderly

(continued)

(continued)

Year of issuance	*Policy/Issue*	*Description*
2001	Outline of the 10th Five-Year Plan for China's Work on Aging (2001–2005)	Establish an urban–rural old-age security system; establish a community-based elderly management and service system; expand the activities for the elderly; advocacy; establish a normal investment mechanism for work on ageing; and improve the overall ageing-related system
2001	Decision to Strengthen the Work on Ageing issued by Central Committee of the CPC and the State Council	A policy system built on the Elderly Law, guided by the five-year plan goals for ageing and socioeconomic development, with emphasis on active response to population ageing. The system covers policy-making of elderly welfare in various aspects such as social security, elderly health, services, education, social participation, and age-friendly environment construction
2006	The 11th Five-Year Plan for China's Work on Aging (2006–2010)	Establish an elderly social security system compatible with the economy and society, and as with other security systems; establish a comprehensive system of policies and regulations on ageing; and actively promote the construction of elderly-friendly infrastructure
2011	The 12th Five-Year Plan for China's Work on Aging (2011–2015)	Establish a basic strategic framework centring on ageing; improve the urban–rural social old-age security system; improve basic elderly medical care system; enhance home-based and community-based care networks; promote planning and construction standards for elderly-friendly infrastructure; and increase amenities for elderly culture, education, and fitness activities
2013	Opinions on Supporting Development of Elderly Services Industry of Health Services	Opinions issued by the State Council which called for deeper all-round investment in direct and indirect areas that underpin the development of a modern and sustainable elderly services industry and related health services

(continued)

(continued)

Year of issuance	*Policy/Issue*	*Description*
2015	Opinions on Encouraging Private Capital to Participate in the Development of Pension Services	Opened the aged care sector to greater private investment, including foreign investors. Marked the beginning of a greater role for private investors in areas such as operating residential homes, pension funds, and establishing links between the medical sector and medical training sector and aged care services
2016	13th Five-Year Plan includes a section on 'actively responding to population ageing'	Emphasise the need to shift to new growth drivers; optimise human capital development; expand the scientific and innovative frontier in China; and actively respond to population ageing
2017	The 13th Five-Year Plan for National Work on Ageing and Elderly Care System Construction	Improve the multifaceted, inclusive, fair, and sustainable social security system; improve home care, community support, institutional backup, and medical nursing care integration; enable institutional structure to facilitate government and market roles; and create a social environment that is congenial to work on ageing and old-age care system
2017	Several Opinions of the General Office of the State Council on Fully Liberalising the Elderly Service Market and Improving the Quality of Elderly Service	Establish a subsidy system for financially strapped and incapacitated seniors; develop home-based old-age care services; enforce the migration of household registration of the elderly who move to their children's place; promote the construction of elderly-friendly communities and cities; further expand coverage of legal aid; and increase integration of medical and nursing care
2019	Opinions on Promoting the Development of Aged-care Services	Comprehensive agenda for advancing every aspect of aged care, from staffing to granting land for age-related infrastructure, and bond-related and foreign investment in pension-related financial services

(continued)

(continued)

Year of issuance	*Policy/Issue*	*Description*
2019	The mid- and long-term national plan for actively responding to population ageing (November)	States the related challenges and opportunities; a proactive national response is a requirement for achieving high-quality development and for maintaining social harmony and stability in this context
2020	Guiding Opinions on Promoting the Development of the Aged Products Industry	Encourage all economic sectors to be innovative and productive in sectors of importance to older populations, e.g., mobility-related technology products, healthcare products, and related communication-facilitating technologies
2021	14th Five-Year Plan (2021–2025) (March), and the 14th Five-Year Plan for the National Ageing Industry Development and Elderly Care Service System (Dec)	Further promote ageing-related infrastructure, including smart products that facilitate real-time usage data and equipment that helps with elder safety. China will also work toward creating an integrated nursing home and health care facilities service. A focus on disabled elders living with the least means was announced
2022	Report of the State Council on the Progress of Strengthening and Promoting Aging Work (Aug.)	China's highest policy-making body, the State Council, published a comprehensive review of preparations for intensive population ageing, with recommendations for how to improve progress
2022	20th National Congress of the Communist Party of China (October)	Promise to continue proactively responding to population, including via constructing a family-friendly society that may boost birth rates

Source Johnston (2021, 2023a), Wu (2022), China National People's Congress (2022)

Appendix B: Medium- and Long-term Plan for the State to Actively Respond to Population Ageing (2019)

Goal	*Agenda*
1. Consolidate the social wealth reserves to cope with the aging of the population	1.1. Expand the whole, optimise the structure, improve efficiency; and adapt economic development to the aging of the population
	1.2. Improve the system of national income distribution and optimise distribution patterns among government, enterprises, and residents; steadily increase the old-age wealth reserves; and create a fairer and more sustainable social security system
	1.3. Continue to improve the well-being of all people
2. Improve effective labour supply in the context of an aging population	2.1. Improve the overall quality of human resources by improving the quality of population policies and improving the quality of the labour force pipeline, and by building a lifelong learning system for the elderly to continue to learn
	2.2. Promote the development and utilisation of human resources; achieve higher-quality and full employment; and ensure a sufficient total level and quality of human resources is actively responding to the aging of the population
3. Create a high-quality supply system for elder services and products	3.1. Actively promote the construction of a healthy China; establish and improve a comprehensive and ongoing health service system for the elderly including health education, preventive health care, disease diagnosis and treatment, rehabilitation care, long-term care, and hospice care

(continued)

(continued)

Goal	*Agenda*
	3.2. Improve the multi-level elderly care service system based on the home, community reliance, fully developed institutions, and organically integrated medical care; expand the supply of products and services suitable for the elderly in multiple channels and fields and improve the quality of products and services
4. Strengthen scientific and technological innovation capabilities in response to the aging of the population	4.1. Implement the innovation-driven development strategy; take technological innovation as the first driving force and strategic support for actively responding to population ageing
	4.2. Comprehensively improve the intelligence level of the national economic industrial system
	4.3. Improve the level of technology and informatisation of services for the elderly
	4.4. Increase health technology support for the elderly
	4.5. Strengthen research and development and application of assistive technologies for the elderly
5. Build a social environment for providing for the elderly, filial piety, and respect for the elderly	5.1. Strengthen the legal environment in response to the aging of the population and protect the legitimate rights and interests of the elderly
	5.2. Build a family support system, build an elderly-friendly society, and form a good atmosphere for the participation of the elderly, family, society, and the government

Source Government of China (2022)

References

Becker, G. S. (1962). Investment in human capital: A theoretical analysis. Journal of Political Economy, 70(5), 9–49. https://www.jstor.org/stable/1829103

Bloom, D. E., Canning, D., Fink, G., & Finlay, J. E. (2007). Does age structure forecast economic growth? International Journal of Forecasting, 23(4), 569–585. https://doi.org/10.1016/j.ijforecast.2007.07.001

Bo Hu, Y. Y., & Liu, X. (2023). Life expectancy trends in China in the post-covid-19 era, Life expectancy trends in China in the post-COVID-19 era. https://www.thelancet.com/journals/lanpub/article/PIIS2468-2667(23)00074-9/fulltext

Cangping, W. (1986). The aging of population in China. http://www.cicred.org/Eng/Publications/pdf/c-d16.pdf

China National People's Congress. (2022, August 30). Report of the state council on the progress of strengthening and promoting aging work, August 30, 2022. Gy.china-Embassy.gov.cn.

Daokui, L. (2018). Sina News. Sina.com.cn; 新浪首页. https://finance.sina.com.cn/tech/roll/2023-02-12/doc-imyfnefq9410757.shtml.

Freije-Rodriguez, S., Hofman, B., & Johnston, L. A. (2019). China's economic reforms, poverty reduction, and the role of the World Bank. https://papers.ssrn.com/sol3/papers.cfm?abstract_id=3501983

Gerschenkron, A. (1962). Economic backwardness in historical perspective: In Harvard University Press Books. Belknap Press.

Ghosh, J. (2019). A brave new world, or the same old story with new characters? Development and Change, 50(2), 379–393. https://doi.org/10.1111/dech.12485

Gollin, D. (2014). The Lewis Model: A 60-year retrospective. The Journal of Economic Perspectives, 28(3), 71–88. https://www.jstor.org/stable/23800576

Government of China. (2022, November 21). 中国政府网_中央人民政府门户网站. www.gov.cn. https://www.gov.cn/

Guo, L., Huang, J., & Zhang, Y. (2019). Education development in China: Education return, quality, and equity. Sustainability, 11(13), 3750.

Johnston, L. A. (2012, December). Getting old after getting rich: Comparing China with Japan. In East Asia Forum (Vol. 22).

Johnston, L. A. (2019a). The economic demography transition: Is China's 'not rich, first old'circumstance a barrier to growth? Australian Economic Review, 52(4), 406–426.

Johnston, L. A. (2019b). The belt and road initiative: What is in it for China?. Asia & the Pacific Policy Studies, 6(1), 40–58.

Johnston, L. A. (2019c). An economic demography explanation for China's 'Maritime Silk Road' interest in Indian Ocean countries. Journal of the Indian Ocean Region, 15(1), 97–112.

Johnston, L. A. (2020). China's economic demography transition strategy: A population-weighted approach to the economy and policy. SSRN Electronic Journal. https://doi.org/10.2139/ssrn.3639054

Johnston, L. A. (2021). "Getting old before getting rich" and Africa: Of what relevance is China's economic demography transition? Journal of African Development, 22(2), 249. https://doi.org/10.5325/jafrideve.22.2.0249

Johnston, L. (2023a). China's demographic peak: Lessons and prospects for Africa occasional paper 340. https://saiia.org.za/wp-content/uploads/2023/04/SAIIA_OP-340_ChinaDemographicPeak-2.pdf

Johnston, L. (2023b). 'Poor-Old' BRICS: Demographic Trends and Policy Challenges, South African Institute of International Affairs, November 15. https://saiia.org.za/research/poor-old-brics-demographic-trendsand-policy-challenges/

Johnston, L. A., & Onjala, J. (2022). The belt and road initiative's Eastern Africa node: Survey of economic, demographic and security motivations. SSRN Electronic Journal. https://doi.org/10.2139/ssrn.4000937

Johnston, L., Liu, X., Yang, M., & Zhang, X. (2016). 'Getting rich after getting old: China's demographic and economic transition in dynamic international context', in R. Garnaut, L. Song, C. Fang, & L. Johnston (editors), China's new sources of economic growth Vol. 1: Reform, resources and climate change. ANU Press, Canberra, 215–246.

Jordan, L. P., Ren, Q., & Falkingham, J. (2014). Youth education and learning in twenty-first century China: Disentangling the impacts of migration, residence, and hukou. Chinese Sociological Review, 47(1), 57–83.

Kumar, C., Piyasa, & Saikia, N. (2022). An update on explaining the rural-urban gap in under-five mortality in India. BMC Public Health, 22(1). https://doi.org/10.1186/s12889-022-14436-7

Lauren, J. (2021, May 14). Understanding demographic challenges of transition through the China lens. Springerprofessional.de. https://www.springerprofessional.de/en/understanding-demographic-challenges-of-transition-through-the-c/18869212

Lin, F., & Long, C. X. (2020). The impact of globalization on youth education: Empirical evidence from China's WTO accession. Journal of Economic Behavior & Organization, 178, 820–839.

Maestas, N., & Zissimopoulos, J. (2010). How longer work lives ease the crunch of population aging. Journal of Economic Perspectives, 24(1), 139–160. https://doi.org/10.1257/jep.24.1.139

Messkoub, M. (1999). Crisis of ageing in less developed countries: Too much consumption or too little production? Development and Change, 30(2), 217–235. https://doi.org/10.1111/1467-7660.00115

Ministry of Foreign Affairs, the People's Republic of China. (2023, November 11). XIV BRICS Summit Beijing Declaration. www.fmprc.gov.cn. https://www.fmprc.gov.cn/eng/wjdt_665385/2649_665393/202206/t20220623_10709037.html

Mirkin, B., & Mb, W. (2001). The demography of population ageing. Population bulletin of the United Nations.

National Bureau of Statistics. (2023, January 18). 国家统计局信息公开. www.stats.gov.cn. http://www.stats.gov.cn/xxgk/jd/sjjd2020/202301/t20230118_1892285.html

Naughton, B. (1993). Deng Xiaoping: The economist. The China Quarterly, 135(135), 491–514. https://doi.org/10.1017/s0305741000013886

Pettis, M. (2022, October 6). Michael Pettis. South China Morning Post. https://www.scmp.com/comment/opinion/article/3194792/china-must-sacrifice-gdp-growth-rebalance-its-economy

Priebe, J. (2017). Old-age poverty in Indonesia: Measurement issues and living arrangements. Development and Change, 48(6), 1362–1385. https://doi.org/10.1111/dech.12340

Rozelle, S., & Hell, N. (2020). Invisible China. In press.uchicago.edu. University of Chicago Press. https://press.uchicago.edu/ucp/books/book/chicago/I/bo61544815.html

Tan, G. Y. (2013). Higher education reforms in China: For better or for worse? International Education, 43(1), 101.

The World Bank. (2021). Population, total—China | Data. Worldbank.org. https://data.worldbank.org/indicator/SP.POP.TOTL?locations=CN

The World Bank. (2023). World Development Indicators | DataBank. The World Bank. https://databank.worldbank.org/source/world-development-indicators

UN DESA. (2022). United Nations Department of Economic and Social Affairs, Population Division (2022). World Population Prospects 2022: Summary of Results, 3, 2022–1.

UN Department of Economic and Social Affairs. (2022). World population prospects 2022: Summary of results | population division, United Nations. https://www.un.org/development/desa/pd/content/World-Population-Prospects-2022

United Nations. (2023). First world assembly on ageing, Vienna 1982. United Nations. Retrieved November 24, 2023, from https://www.un.org/en/conferences/ageing/vienna1982#:~:text=The%20UN%20General%20Assembly%2C%20in

Unger, B. (2022, November 14). India will become the world's most populous country in 2023. The Economist. https://www.economist.com/the-world-ahead/2022/11/14/india-will-become-the-worlds-most-populous-country-in-2023

World Bank. (2019). Mortality rate, infant (per 1 000 live births) | Data. Worldbank.org. https://data.worldbank.org/indicator/SP.DYN.IMRT.IN

World Bank. (2022). Population, total—Russian Federation, World development indicators 2016. The World Bank. https://data.worldbank.org/indicator/SP.POP.TOTL?locations=RU

Wu, C. (1980). The objective criterion to measure the adaptation of population development and economic development: The economic basis for advocating a couple to have only one child at the current stage in China. Population Research, 1, 32–38.

Wu, C. (1986). Population ageing discussion. Liaoning People's Publishing House, Shenyang (in Chinese).

Wu, Y. (2022). Retrospect and prospect of China's ageing policy in the past 20 years. China Journal of Social Work, 15(2), 193–200.

XV BRICS Summit—Johannesburg II Declaration 24 August 2023 | The Presidency. (2023, August 24). www.thepresidency.gov.za. https://www.thepresidency.gov.za/content/xv-brics-summit-johannesburg-ii-declaration-24-august-2023

Zaiceva, A., & Zimmermann, K. F. (2016). Migration and the demographic shift. Handbook of the Economics of Population Aging, 1, 119–177. https://ideas.repec.org/h/eee/hapoch/v1_119.htm

CHAPTER 10

Conclusion: Future of China's Demography—Legal, Social, Political, and Economic Reforms

Armando Aliu, Karolina Kaczmarczyk, and Jakub Stefanowski

1 Introduction

This study is a comprehensive collection of Chinese political demography, an under-researched field, through anthropological, multidisciplinary, and complexity approaches.

A. Aliu (✉) · K. Kaczmarczyk · J. Stefanowski
Centre for International Studies and Development (CISAD), Faculty of International and Political Studies, Jagiellonian University in Kraków, Kraków, Poland
e-mail: armando.aliu@uj.edu.pl

K. Kaczmarczyk
e-mail: karolina1.kaczmarczyk@uj.edu.pl

J. Stefanowski
e-mail: kuba.stefanowski@uj.edu.pl

A. Aliu (ed.), *Complexity Thinking and China's Demography Within and Beyond Mainland China*,
https://doi.org/10.1007/978-981-97-0172-8_10

The research emphasizes anthropological perspective, global, and geopolitical concerns. It contains more policy-oriented approaches and explores diverse aspects of how the Chinese population can influence domestic socio-political structures, geopolitical arrangements, and global challenges. A strength and originality of this study is the presence of gender aspects and gender studies that incorporate gender/feminist perspectives.

Book chapters explore various dimensions of the Chinese population that have not been covered by existing literature. Many scholars discuss the rise of China and the counter-measurement of the United States (and the West). A significant volume of research has been done on the impact of the notorious China's "one-child policy" or the population growth until the early twenty-first century. Yet, few, or virtually none, discuss how shrinking and unbalanced Chinese population has domestic and global implications.

With a brief thought-experiment in a new direction, we can easily think of the huge influences of changing Chinese demography on multiple dimensions of our political life. As Barry Naughten's recent version of "Chinese Economy" discussed at length, the demographic dividend (i.e., the favorable ratio between working-age population and the aged population) has been one of the greatest factors that drove the miraculous economic development of China since the beginning of the reform (Naughten 2018).

Now, it is over, as China is aging. China is aging at an alarming speed and with dangerous imbalance, especially sex-ratio. It would, any reasonable China watcher would, expect lead to domestic instability. Domestic instability can lead to uprisings against the CCP or to the strengthened grip of the CCP on its own population. To maintain the domestic political legitimacy of the CCP, the CCP can make more aggressive foreign policies. In other words, the American attempt to contain China may not be the only reason to make Chinese foreign policy aggressive. For this sort of reasoning, we need to see Chinese demography from multi-dimensional approaches and CT viewpoint.

Book chapters provide a groundwork for lively, rational, and realistic discussions on Chinese demography in foreign policy and on Chinese political changes in the near future. Each chapter and the volume as a whole tries to go beyond the existing scholarship that has been overwhelmed by statistical indicators and delimits its discussions to limited issues, such as mainstream demography or labor sociology.

One of the biggest contributions of this study is to interrelate and fill up the gaps between demography, population studies, and CT that links anthropological observation with traditional demography, international relations, in particular geopolitics, gender studies, and global development. The diversity of the chapters allows readers to think in the way of CT. Research findings of each chapter lead to a larger picture of the Chinese demography's impact on global politics and normative/legal approaches.

The China scholarship or demography scholarship in general desperately needs a comprehensive and multidisciplinary review on Chinese demography that deals with its political implications, both domestic and international. This volume has done a great job to fill up the vacuum in the existing scholarship.

This book researches the issue of the multi-layer phenomena, namely demography in China using the methodology of complex thinking, thus taking into account input from different perspectives and study areas, which are not usually considered when analyzing the subject. The layers of complexity, by adding to research on demographical changes nexus, the geopolitical, legal, anthropological, political, migration, and international factors help to grasp the ongoing and globally impacting process in a new light and with deepened understanding.

It is important to notice that the demographical changes in China, due to its importance in the global system, trigger spill-over effects on the world, its economy, political stability, and environmental changes. And secondly, for the CCP, the control over demography is considered as a means to remain in power domestically. China handles demography processes within the ethnonationalist paradigm, which impacts its capabilities to effectively limit negative tendencies decreasing its power globally, but it also consolidates its population on a macro scale internally, which on the other hand evokes internal conflicts with some minorities in the PRC.

The former could be analyzed in the context of progress on China's achievement of UNSDGs 2030, in which observability and quantifiability require the use of complex thinking methodology, in particular when evaluating China, which is a huge subject in the international system, or if the research on the impact of the new BRI (announced by China's State Council Information Office on October 10th, 2023) is conducted in this regard.

The research findings and implications of Chapter 1 point out a significant consequence that China's demographic engineering strategy prioritizes the extension of the Han Chinese population within and beyond mainland China and the "Sinicization" of demographic structures, cultural composition, and institutional restructuring in autonomous regions, such as XUAR, TAR, and IMAR. The Chinese "rejuvenation narrative" symbolizes a "global" Sino-cultural mission oriented to ethnonationalism (Minzner 2018). Thus, an anthropological perspective of Chinese demography highlights a significant and direct effect not only on the local and regional levels in mainland China but also on elsewhere. For example, the analysis of the migration flows can be considered as a tool to shape demography in the domestic and international environment. This layer was investigated in depth on the example of research on China's approach to Xinjiang migration, its purpose, rationality, and repercussions.

Chapter 2 emphasized that the central government in China has exercised its control on local governments through the reforms aimed at decentralization and re-centralization. Under the leadership of Xi Jinping, the latter prevailed. The decentralization of social welfare shifted the responsibility of providing and financing to local governments. Although some scholars claim that re-centralization was introduced in the area of health, the opposite trend seems to dominate—i.e., re-centralization. One of the characteristics of Chinese demography is the rapid aging of the population. This leads to an increased demand for eldercare services. Such services cannot longer be accommodated by traditional family-based care, especially in rural areas. In 1996, new laws regarding eldercare services were introduced, and they greatly transformed them. Local governments were recognized as the main party responsible for providing, regulating, and financing social welfare services. Additionally, the role of family and individual accountability was emphasized. Therefore, home-based care was described as "basis", community-based services as "backing", and institutional care as "supplemental". Two case studies were conducted in terms of the actions of local governments, namely Shanghai and Beijing. These cities were chosen as both are "centrally administered" municipalities, which are prone to be more impacted by central government and the initiatives established in these cities, often are the inspiration and source of national-level regulations. Due to decentralization, local governments have some freedom in creating their models for eldercare health, and can fully embrace, negotiate, or counter-steer national policies. When comparing these models, the main differences between them revolve around timing, prioritization, and support for the third sector. These models are based on essentially different tactics and logics. In Beijing, services are dominated by private and third-sector providers. On the other hand, in Shanghai, there is a mix of private and public spending.

Seeing the problem of an aging society, this study also investigated how China adapts to this situation with respect to the sector of eldercare services. Chapter 2 points to the conclusion that although the central government sets objectives, the fulfillment of the policy is forwarded to local authorities that have some authority in prioritizing and structuring eldercare services in their respective area. The general trend, however, is to base the eldercare services on private and third-sector entities, rather than on the public sector. The research findings present differences (within accepted by the central government framework) in the structure, direction, and priorities of the local state of the eldercare services in Shanghai and Beijing (as case studies), pointing to rather putting the priority on the third sector (Shanghai) or the private sector (Beijing). The research shows us that despite central planning we should expect that the issues connected to the aging of the Chinese population will differ regionally and to better understand China in this regard even more complex research should be conducted (in particular, focusing on quality and delivery of services).

Chapter 3 is a complex analysis of how the demographic and its changes impact the geopolitical situation in China. Demographics in China are characterized by a low fertility rate, gender imbalance, low population growth, and rapid population aging. These patterns are expected to deepen over the next few years. Taking a closer look at the changes in population structure, fertility, and quantity, the authors present several possible assumptions. Demographic shifts are a complex social phenomenon and as such can have a notable impact on geopolitics. These changes influence state power, domestic affairs, and international relations. The population of China is a very good example of how these changes can influence a state's regional and international position, especially in terms of economics, world order, and competition between global powers. Taking as an example the negative population growth: The large population is an essential part of global power, and the structure and size of the population are essential features for strategic capabilities and national power. The negative growth may result in the aging of the population and that can lead to slower economic growth, lower consumption, reduction of savings and investment, and lower corporate profits. Considering the importance of China and its economy, such negative events will affect global supply chains and global markets. A related issue is migration in East Asia. The influx and distribution of Chinese immigrants have a considerable impact on this region. Any changes in migration patterns will lead to demographic changes in East Asian countries and will impact bilateral relations, especially with neighboring countries. They can improve due to positive links to labor and economic development or worsen as a result of cultural, religious, and social conflicts.

Chapter 4 focused on the consistencies and misalignments between the BRI created by the PRC and the UNSDGs 2030. The authors attempted to seek an answer if and to what extent the BRI can support achieving UNSDGs 2030, globally. These two are strategies that share specific broad goals, such as reducing poverty, strengthening international security and peace, stimulating balanced economic growth, and fostering social inclusion. Supporters of the positive connection between the BRI and the UNSDGs 2030 point out that the BRI is a global strategy based on trade, cooperation, and geography and is not limited to the already existing land routes and sea lanes, and is in fact a platform open to all countries, regional, and international organizations. According to the Chinese policymakers, that can foster intergovernmental cooperation, especially on multi-level macro policy and further develop communication systems, promote free trade, provide capital for development objectives, and foster political trust, and economic integration. Free trade is considered the main objective of the BRI. Together with the UNSDGs 2030, these promote a trading system based on consistent, universal, and equitable multilateral WTO rules. Free international trade plays an important role in advancing inclusive growth, sustainable development, and reducing poverty. On the other hand, infrastructure is far from the main source of expenses within the BRI and, according to the UN guidelines, well-developed infrastructure is contributing to achieving some of the UNSDGs. The adversaries of the beneficial impact of BRI on achieving the UNSDGs 2030 mention several issues. The first concern is the "type of cooperation". Most of the BRI agreements are bilateral, and follow the Chinese policies, rules, and procedures. Such solutions will not contribute to the achievement of the UNSDGs 2030, especially if they do not take into account international norms and standards. The second concern is the "lack of transparency". Details about the BRI contracts are usually not published, and thus there is no data about accountability and monitoring. The third concern is "debt sustainability and trade governance". Many questions were raised about Chinese financing strategies leading to debt dependency and sovereign debt obligations or whether the arrangements of the agreements protect them from falling into excessive debt obligations. The BRI has great potential to contribute to achieving the UNSDGs 2030, but all the mentioned concerns and questions should be carefully considered.

In Chapter 4, some noteworthy observations were made while analyzing the impact of the new BRI on the UNSDGs 2030. Bilateral agreements and unilateral regulations related to the BRI occasionally fail to meet global norms and standards for social and environmental protection. The sustainability of debt and trade governance continues to be major issues, as over 20 BRI partner nations could face financial difficulties as a result of onerous debt servicing obligations. Project transparency, a persistent theme due to public knowledge of the BRI, is being limited, and there are insufficient financial measures to assess the efficacy of policies. The findings indicate that this initiative does not strengthen multilateral efforts to achieve the UNSDGs 2030, but rather the initiative uses the UNSDGs 2030 to blur particular Chinese interests.

This book also places great emphasis on the issue of better comprehension and understanding of Chinese normative and hard law. Three respective subjects, which are often misunderstood, are being analyzed to resolve common misperceptions about how China can legally approach the demographic changes in the light of their most important sources of law.

Chapter 5 analyzes the Chinese constitutional preamble from the linguistic angle in terms of the connections between linguistic features and the creation of legitimacy and the exercise of power. The preambles play a prominent role in constitutions or other legal documents. This part serves different functions than the provisions and articles of the legal paper, and this distinction is reflected in the language. The Chinese preamble is an essential factor in establishing the integral rules of China's ideology. The style of this preamble is not homogenous and is usually divided into three parts: historical, ideological, and legal. The latter, which addresses the implementation and status of the "Constitution", consists of brief and precise sentences, written in a language similar to the legal one used further in the "Constitution". Although the section is divergent from the rest of the preamble, according to the author there is not much to analyze. The historical part forms the historical narrative. This section is not very complex to form a clear, coherent narration, and implementation of Chinese history. Especially important subjects are time and history, bringing together two twin pillars of creating and demonstrating legitimacy in China, that is "continuity" and "revolution". The ideological section is the longest of the three aforementioned parts, which allows, together with its amendments, to set out ideological and political basic policies, guidelines, and tasks corresponding with them. This section is filled with political jargon and includes the use of *chengyus* and numerous mentions of proper names of individuals and the CCP, which signalizes the exercise of political power and its shifts.

In Chapter 5, there were adapted linguistic methods to analyze the Constitution of China, thus adding another layer of analysis to the nexus methodology of complexity thinking. The chapter signals the importance of political significance in the case of the preamble of the Chinese constitution rather than as a legal importance, thus contributing to a better understanding of the mechanisms that drive the PRC in the context of social changes happening in this country. This chapter also calls for the reminder that the Chinese political system is set differently than the Western liberal democratic world, and political mechanisms are designed with some exceptional rules that need to be taken into consideration when analyzing China.

Chapter 6 aims to demonstrate Chinese exceptionalism as part of a new agenda for foreign relations law. Exceptionalism includes the idea that something is exceptional and thus is distinctive from others, and as such it demands special treatment. As already mentioned in Chapter 6, Chinese exceptionalism is described as minimalist developmentalism with two distinguished characteristics, "strict sovereignty" and "developmentalism". It can be observed that China's "common but differentiated responsibilities" differed over time and were based on particular stages of development and the capacities of states to comply with international law. In this chapter, the author shows optimism about normalization of Chinese exceptionalism in terms of a new foreign relation law. The author points out that China has been engaged in international law only since the nineteenth century and during that period is continuously trying to incorporate public and private international law as well as other fields of law from Western legal systems. It is due to the fact that foreign relations are crucial to sovereignty, independence, and state-building. Additionally, Chinese scholars are actively engaged in open debates about foreign relations in China and with foreign scholars. With current tendencies to include decolonial perspective and reevaluate the Eurocentric one, China has a place for better understanding in international relations and achieving better inclusion, especially considering the long-lasting lack of trust and prejudice toward China. These trends are not intended to create new hegemonic powers and antagonism, but are aimed at a better understanding of the ideology and history of each state.

Critical thinking in Chapter 6 points to a mismatch in the case of China to adhere to the Western understanding of international law mainly in two regards: sovereignty issue and being equal to international law regardless of the development stage. On the other hand, this chapter points to the fact that exceptionalism in the understanding of international law is a common feature (also for Western powers), and Chinese exceptionalism is similar to the regional perception of the researched phenomena.

Chapter 7 argued the dynamics and relation between intra-party regulations and state law that are of complex nature. It reflects that, in fact, China's governance model is complex and is the result of the nation's legal, political, and economic development. The intra-party regulations are aimed at coordinating the behavior, activities, and members of the "Party". They are sometimes described as the "soft law" (as opposed to the "hard law") as they do not require the state's coercive power for enforcement. Both types of regulation are considered an integral part of the "system of socialist rule of law"), but the relation between them is a constant source for academic discussions and interpretation. They should be treated as two distinctive systems, which differ with constraints, normative affairs, formulating entities, and implementation methods. That leads to many ideas of how these norms fall into conflict, complement each other, and whether one is more prominent than another. However, both are crucial for the formation and evolution of the rule with Chinese characteristics. Although there are a significant number of misalignments, conflicts, and doubts, the author points out that simplifying these regulations to separate distinctive scopes, reorganize, or merge one into another would be insufficient and perfunctory. Rather than simply modifying the regulations, one should inspect the logic regularities, and objectives, and only then take up the challenge to introduce changes. Achieving a connection between these two laws is a fundamental need for the development and improvement of the rule of law with Chinese characteristics.

Chapter 7 adds to the complexity nexus a layer focusing on the domestic legal system of China and its difference in comparison to the Western standards. Understanding the role of intra-party regulations, their functionality, and place in the legal system is a nuance that is the characteristic feature of the Chinese law system. Once again, Chinese system differs from Western patterns, but in principle (not in case of particular rules, configuration, or systematization), the difference may be treated similarly to the differences Europeans face when comparing the common law and continental law system.

Chapter 8 deals with the impact of house prices on the fertility plans of the migrant population in China. The data used for this research comes from the China Migrant Dynamic Survey of 2018. Migrants are important for China's labor supply, especially considering the high demand for labor and the negative demographic changes in the domestic Chinese population, which led to an imbalance of human resource supply following a low fertility rate. Improving the fertility of migrants can alleviate this imbalance and contribute to sustainable economic growth. In China, housing ownership is related to household registration, which corresponds to the eligibility of children for schooling, medical insurance, and other social benefits. High prices make it extremely difficult to allow for property purchase and obtain household registration, and impact the plans to have children among migrants, as they will consider educational and medical resources for their future children. That makes economic and institutional integration more difficult for migrants. As the results show the higher house prices are, the less likely female migrant populations to have fertility plans. When the housing pressure of the migrants is low, their fertility intentions are less affected by the house prices. Additionally, the sensitivity of the fertility plans of the migrant population is affected by the development of infrastructure. Among female migrants, the sensitivity is higher with larger family, higher level of education, and younger ages. Based on the results and the suggestions of the authors, the government can take several actions to improve fertility intentions among the population of migrants. Such initiatives could focus on reforming the household registration system and guaranteeing educational, medical, and other resources for migrants, reducing housing costs and improving the housing policies of the migrant populations.

Apart from the analysis of the aging population, Chapter 8 studies one of the most crucial aspects of the low fertility rate in China, which is the housing situation. The research indicates research findings for the migrant population in China: the higher house prices in inflow cities, the less likely female migrant populations have fertility plans; if the housing pressure of the migrant populations is low, their fertility plans are less affected by house prices; the sensitivity of the migrant populations' fertility plans to house prices is also influenced by the moderating effect of infrastructure development; and finally, the fertility plans of female migrant populations with larger family size, higher education level, and younger age are more sensitive to house prices.

Chapter 9 argued the population aging, the dynamics, and economic policy challenges of the demographic change of the BRICS by considering a "getting old before rich" economic demography transition. Chapter 9 also highlighted that women and children have a deep vested interest in the successful navigating of population change and development in BRICS countries concurrently. Furthermore, adapting some models of economic demography-changed weighted cooperation and lessons sharing is ideally part of the BRICS new population structure dynamics agenda. BRICS countries face rapid population aging as middle-income countries and have agreed to deepen collaboration in this area. In this respect, the BRICS countries are expected to deepen their population age structure dynamics and research cooperation in the area of the BRICS Academic Forum, the BRICS Think Tank Forum, and other long-standing platforms.

The shrink in Chinese demography is essentially an issue of "political action" and "responsibility" of the Chinese authorities. Undoubtedly, the local and national government bodies in China have shared competence and are completely responsible for elderly people, family policies, migration policies, population-planning, and social, economic, political, and legal reforms related to population. In this context, social, political, legal, and economic reforms will be input to state interventions through population change and demographic engineering.

2 Reforms in "Cosmopolitan Chinese Society and Coexistence in the Framework of Ethnopluralism"

"The Ming-to-Qing dynastic transition in the first half of the 1600s coincided with the arrival of Europeans in East Asia by sea. Missionaries followed the trade routes". Goods and fashions were cultural elements that the Jesuits instrumentalized to embed cultural elements in societal lifestyles, habits, and behaviors (Lewis 2009a). “The Jesuit missionaries were learned men capable of dealing with Chinese scholar-officials in intellectual terms. By 1601 the Italian Jesuit Matteo Ricci was permitted to reside in Beijing on an imperial stipend as a Western scholar”. The Jesuits published in Chinese (e.g., over 100 treatises on Western science and technology, over 400 Western works on Christianity and science, over 800 items about religious tracts and translations of scripture, etc.) and they became involved in Manchu court politics (Fairbank and Goldman 2006). In history, the Jesuits were the first reformists and cultural demographers who observed various cultural components and cosmopolitan aspects of Chinese societies.[1] Deng Xiaoping transformed traditional China into a more pluralistic society (e.g., pluralistic values, religious beliefs, ideological orientation, and ways of living). During his cultural reforms, China expanded personal and cultural freedoms, and “Chinese society became diverse and its culture pluralistic. A growing number of Chinese turned to religion, whether Evangelical Protestantism, Roman Catholicism, Daoism, or Buddhism. Along with a revival of Buddhism and Daoism, traditional folk religions, and a resurgence of Islam, Christianity rapidly gained new converts” during his cultural reforms (Fairbank and Goldman 2006). Essentially, China is a multi-ethnic country that has a pluralistic unity of the Chinese nation. However, China’s experiences with colonialism and imperialism in the last two centuries created conflicts, complex issues, and ethnic compartmentalization on the China border and in autonomous regions. Therefore, it is in favor of China’s national interests to promote coexistence in the framework of Ethnopluralism and harmonious ethnic relations that promote autonomy in ethnic minority regions and support diversity policies and fundamental freedoms of minorities (Tsang and Men 2016). Tu Weiming asserted that modernization is pluralistic and that it is wrong to interpret tradition and modernity as two parallel yet unrelated phenomena. He highlighted that “tradition and modernity, Eastern culture and Western culture, popular culture and elite culture, and modernization and regionalization exert mutual influences over each other. He prioritized interactive relationships

[1] The mission of Jesuits was to frankly invite Chinese people to adopt Christian beliefs and values in their life. We learned a lot from the Jesuits’ missionary reports in terms of cultural anthropology, observations, fieldworks, ethnographies, race, and culture.

properly rather than devaluing tradition in the interests of modernization" (Zhao 2016). To put it in a different way, coexistence does not only mean harmony between ethnic groups and cultures but also it means the creation of harmonious order between conflicting things, various phenomena, and mindsets.

The changing demographic structures and diversification/hybridization of Chinese societies brought the issue of "decoupling" and juxtaposition of cosmopolitan and traditional Chinese societies to the forefront. The shrink in Chinese demographic trends pushes local and national authorities to attract and invite qualified labor migrants and foreigners to the internal labor market. China's rapidly decreasing population can be prevented to some extent by external immigration flows and by encouraging foreigners to settle in China. However, the fundamental problem is about how resident Chinese and non-resident foreigners will interact with each other and how the understanding of pluralism will be developed and implemented in China. Thus, the rapid decline in Chinese demography can ensure a paradigm shift from "ethnonationalism" which adopts a totalitarian perspective and imposes traditional Chinese values, interests, and national consciousness to "ethnopluralism/ethno-differentialism" focusing on building a common/democratic collective identity and protecting and reciprocally respecting various border ethno-cultural regions.

An alternative measure for China to counter the negative demographic tendencies is to focus on the inflow of international migration of population, which also one more time may lead to conflicts due to the ethnonationalist approach in managing migration by the PRC.

Ethnonationalism remains one of the main obstacles in the adoption of "reformist" and "responsible" family policies, effective migration policies, and the creation of a multicultural, ethnopluralist, and cosmopolitan social order. Instead of prioritizing living infrastructure, urbanization, and tangible aspects of economic development, it is worth noting that the intangible driving forces of demography, cultural anthropology, and population change have significantly synthesized demography studies with other disciplines by arguing complex phenomena.

The embeddedness of "ethnopluralism/ethno-differentialism" can minimize the risk of demographic de-cosmopolitanization, demographic authoritarianism in China, and totalitarianism. Indeed, the demographic engineering policies of the Chinese authorities do cause a "backlash" that is a very powerful and unexpected adverse reaction to the demographic development of the cosmopolitan Chinese people who support openness and pluralism. Therefore, the rejuvenation of the Chinese nation will be in favor of the proliferation of ethnopluralism and the creation of a common/democratic collective identity.

3 Reforms in "Societal, Economic, Political, and Legal Issues"

Confucius asserted that "To govern (zheng, 政) means to correct (zheng, 正). If you lead by correcting yourself, who would dare to remain incorrect?" (Gardner 2014: 33). Deng Xiaoping (the great architect of reforms in China) initiated the "reform and opening-up" process in 1978 and undertook his "Great Southern Tour" (including Fuzhou) to reinvigorate the reform process in 1992. The 1980s can be considered a golden age of reforms embracing marketization (until June 1989, Tiananmen Square protests and massacre). Since 1978, China has continued the "reform and opening-up" process in societal, economic, political, and legal areas. "Many of the reform-era policy changes originated with local governments. China's entry into the WTO in 2001 saw a new energy committed to internationalization and reform in the economy" including a deeper market liberalization and a growth in export and import activity (Brown 2016). In the reform processes, "leading small groups (LSGs—lingdao xiaozu, 领导小组)", "coordinating small groups (CSGs—xietiao xiaozu, 协调小组)", "coordinating working groups (CWGs—xietiao gongzuo zu, 协调工作组)", and "several commissions (SC—weiyuanhui, 委员会)" have played a key role. "Part of their attraction for elite leaders derives from the fact that they are Party entities convened above the level of ministries, working across policy areas. Xi Jinping is the chair of eight of the best-known and most influential leading groups (1) Taiwan—中央对台工作领导小组; (2) Economics and Finance—中央财经工作领导小组; (3) Foreign Affairs/National Security—中央外事工作领导小组/中央国家安全领导小组; (4) National Security Commission—国家安全委员会; (5) Comprehensively Deepening Reform—中央全面深化改革领导小组; (6) National Defense and Troop Reform—中央军委深化国防和军队改革领导小组; (7) Cybersecurity and Informatization—中央网络安全和信息化领导小组; and (8) Central Military and Civilian Integration Commission—中央军民融合发展委员会". This indicates that Xi is the key actor for a wide spectrum of social, political, security, and diplomatic issues. However, Xi's approach to reformism is to create a balance between the parameters of the "Dengist reforms" and the CCP's "Party reforms" that are rooted in the "Maoist reforms" (which are considered as "blind Westernization") (Brown 2016, 2017; Johnson et al. 2017).

According to the Mercator Institute for China Studies (MERICS), internal reform in China is about "fine-tuning control of the economy" to steer it through domestic hard times with an aging population and sluggish productivity growth. Advancing social reforms, structural socio-economic change, and redistribution have never been the priority and mainstay for the CCP since it embarked on economic reforms (e.g., public spending on health, education, social security, and employment largely remained unchanged). "Contemporary Chinese Marxist political economy (不断开拓当 代中国马克思主义政治经济学新境界) focuses on six key goals: (1) adhere to the people-centered development philosophy (第一，坚持以人民为中心的发展思想); (2) adhere to the new development concept (第二，坚持新的发展理念); (3) uphold and improve the basic socialist economic system (第三，坚持和完善社会主义基本经济制度); (4) uphold and improve the basic socialist distribution system (第四，坚持和完善社会主义基本分配制度); (5) adhere to the direction of socialist market economic reform (第五，坚持社会主义市场经济改革方向); and (6) adhere to the basic national policy of opening up (第六，坚持对外开放基本国策). China will tackle long-lasting structural reforms that will become even more pressing as GDP growth slows, and implement reforms in society ages, working population (which shrinks further from its peak in 2015), and social services. The creation of a large middle class, one of China's biggest economic reform successes, now looks like a potential vulnerability for the CCP. Parts of society may see a stagnation, or even a possible deterioration, in economic well-being. China must provide an economic baseline that ensures employment and income to satisfy the minimum needs of the majority of society. Otherwise, social and regional divisions will likely become a major issue going forward. Record levels of youth unemployment and poor wage prospects have resulted in growing disillusion" (Zenglein and Gunter 2023).

After four decades of market reform and global integration, China faced social challenges as a consequence of a lack of ambitious social reforms. In the last two decades, China has prioritized economic development, growth models, foreign direct investments (FDI), productivity, product and service markets, fiscal and monetary policy, tax system, and international finance. However, China has neglected social reforms while implementing economic and financial reforms. The lack of a progressive era of social and societal reforms has been visible recently. The post-COVID-19 recovery era has indicated that China is very much in need of a reformist movement to accelerate social and societal reforms in social areas, such as child labor law, increasing participation of women in labor market and politics, improving social security and eldercare services, strengthening workers' rights and civil rights, etc. The lack of substantial social and societal reforms is also related to China's contemporary political economy approach that has nothing to do with Western-style socialism and Marxist/feminist perspectives. Furthermore, many members of the CCP oppose especially some political and legal reforms and consider reformism a betrayal of "Chinese-style" communism. In fact, challenges and incoherencies for implementing reforms in social, political, and legal areas are consequences of the high-level of official corruption. The effective way to cope with incoherences and prevent corruption is to use reformist language and legitimate pathways to step up reforms to fight against corruption and deal with galloping inequality (between Chinese men and women, and between Chinese farmers, proletariat class, workers, and Chinese capitalist elites, etc.).

According to Jerome A. Cohen, the heavy hand of censorship and self-censorship in China has recently further limited the interpretation and application of many law reforms, administrative and judicial reforms. The media have had to exercise greater caution than ever in reporting on relevant events and developments. "The biggest obstacle to genuine progress toward the rule of law today in China may be ideological—i.e., the absence of agreed ideals, goals, and principles to guide the formulation and implementation of legal norms" (Cohen 2019a). A detailed blueprint for reforms must comprise new levels of great progress in both human rights and in deeper and speedy political reforms, transparency, accountability, and efficient governance in society. If we are talking about political and legal reforms in China, we exactly mean contemporary reforms that adopt Western universalist values and Western political systems, a much larger role for the non-state sector, "a wider reform of government and administrative functions, and a green agenda" (Brown 2014, 2016, 2017).

4 Reforms in the "Chinese Vision of World Order (*Tianxia Governance*) and Consensus-Based BRI"

Confucius said: "Now throughout the land under the heaven, carriages have all wheels, of the same size; all writing is with the same characters; and for conduct there are the same rules". However, for Confucius, who always maintained an earnest focus on the so-called "Land under Heaven (*tianxia*)", presented only an ideal cultural blueprint and a concept of civilization. Confucius recognized that establishing uniformity in various aspects of social life was one of the important premises for social progress and social reforms (Zhang 2015).

Since 2013, the Chinese government has instrumentalized the BRI to create an expanded version of its millennial "*Tianxia governance*" (i.e., all under heaven), govern the state (*zhi guo*) effectively, and create harmony within the country (*ping tianxia*). Under "*Tianxia governance*", China aims to design the global governance system and create interdependency in relations with neighboring governments. The Chinese dream of national rejuvenation will be a propellant power of "*Tianxia governance*" that will ensure "international advocacy of enlightened and generous Chinese leadership toward a community of shared future for mankind" and replace or alter contemporary international law and global governance (Cohen 2019b; Zhang 2015). Xi Jinping's frequently expressed aspirations for "global Chinese leadership" in dealing with universal problems especially contribute to the improvement of the political sovereignty of "*Tianxia governance*". If Chinese leader Xi Jinping is awarded a fourth five-year term (2027–31) as the nation's re-elected President in 2027, he would likely have (or demand) a "*Chairman*" title (such as "Chairman/Chief of State" Mao Zedong in the past) to legitimate and politically strengthen the "*Tianxia governance*" and create a persuasive Beijing's rhetorical advocacy of "community of shared future for mankind" (Cohen 2023).

"*Tianxia governance*" is a new reconstructed Chinese globalization approach that has not only economic and financial motivations but also cultural and social transformative motivations. The reconstructed Chinese globalization approach will reshape Confucian culture that adheres to the principle of communicative rationality. "Through reinterpreting and restoring Confucianism in order to place Chinese culture on the world stage, China will seek to establish a unique place for itself in the pluralistic structure of the global community. It is also the primary cultural resource brought into dialogues between China's intellectual elite and the West" (Zhao 2016). "*Tianxia governance*" will incorporate the rise of the Chinese economy with the rise in the field of civilization, culture, and society. "Confucius Institutes" which are financially endorsed by the Chinese International Education Foundation and the Ministry of Education of the PRC contribute to the spread of Chinese cultural values, the Sinicization principles, and the embeddedness of the attributes and components of "Chineseness" throughout the world.

During the Beijing 2008 Summer Olympic Games, China emphasized the motto "One World One Dream" which can be converted to "One World" symbolizing an "embedded and reconstructed Chinese-style globalization approach and *Tianxia governance*" and "One Dream" implying "Sinicization of the rest of the world and societal/cultural transformation based on Chineseness".

On October 10th, 2023, China's State Council Information Office released a white paper titled "The Belt and Road Initiative: A Key Pillar of the Global Community of Shared Future". China's new developmental approach to BRI (1) paves the way toward shared development and prosperity; (2) promotes all-round connectivity in multiple fields; (3) injects positive energy into world peace and development; and (4) pursues steady and sustained progress in high-quality BRI cooperation (The State Council Information Office of the People's Republic of China 2023). The new BRI (October 10th, 2023) will be a roadmap to achieve "China's Dream" which is a combination of "sustainable economic development (highly motivated by *Tianxia governance*)" and "societal/cultural transformation" by considering Sinicization mission.

In Xi's "*Tianxia governance*", China has almost completed the economic transformation process of the BRI along the Silk Roads. Now, China will create a holistic development model that incorporates economic development and social/societal development of cultures, cities, civilizations, and people/diverse communities living along the Silk Roads.

Associate Director of King's Silk Roads Programme at King's College (University of Cambridge), Peter Frankopan highlighted the cultural components and the evolution process of the Silk Roads in which complex issues of philosophy, science, language, and religion interact with each other. The "*Tianxia governance*" and the new BRI (October

10th, 2023) will not only attempt to revive the economic history of the Silk Roads but also the cultural richness of the entire Silk Roads that embed economic development in societal and cultural coexistence, ethnic and cultural harmony, environmental sustainability, and compromise (Frankopan 2015). Brakman et al. (2019) indicated that from the beginning of the twenty-first century, the economic center of gravity has shifted back toward China (Brakman et al. 2019). However, it is not only the "economic center of gravity" but also the "cultural and technological center of gravity" has shifted to China.

Generally, if we analyze the demographic changes in China, we should observe a large scale, rapid speed, high aging, unbalanced regional development (urban–rural inversion), and the process of society aging before getting rich. Thus, it should be expected that many challenges will arise particularly connected to the burden of old age pension, high pressure on social security and public services (especially medical services), and the shrinking working-age population.

China's "getting old before rich" syndrome will form barriers to the "*Tianxia governance*", the new BRI (October 10th, 2023), and the holistic development of the Chinese population beyond mainland China. Xi did not anticipate the negative effects of the BRI in 2013. For this reason, China has decided to change the BRI by minimizing its negative effects and side-effects on human healthcare, environmental sustainability, and global development. Recently, China's BRI has started to transform itself because it caused huge debts and raised environmental concerns (e.g., biodiversity/habitat loss, pollution, concerns about carbon emissions, etc.) as well as societal issues, such as human diseases as a consequence of pollution, demographic change, overpopulation/underpopulation, inequality between regions, and so on.

5 Recommendations to Improve the Elderly Care System and the Future of Aging Population in Mainland China and Beyond

Older people mostly prefer to independently make a choice for their housing (the preferred term of UN-Habitat) and care situations and aging in the right place (Farias et al. 2023). However, this is an overly complex issue because many older adults are surrounded by healthcare, socio-economic, environmental, legal, and socio-political conditions and dimensions. Furthermore, psychological motivations, family structures, gerontocracy and geriatrics, public policies, architecture, and urban planning have a significant impact on older people's choice between "ageing in place" (Wiles et al. 2011) or "moving in time". It is crucial to better ascertain of the relationship between housing-related conditions and care needs to address the issue of "ageing in place" in terms of functional, symbolic, and emotional attachments (e.g., sense of identity, autonomy, security, familiarity, etc.) and meanings of homes, neighborhoods, and communities. Instead of posing the question "What is the ideal place and what are the criteria in the housing to grow older?', it is more important to ask, in a more realistic and rationalist way, "Why do many older people live in homes that are not suitable for their health, comfort, and care needs?" From a realist–idealist dichotomy perspective, it is important to argue for the conditions and criteria of the WHO highlighting the evidence-based recommendations on the housing conditions and reducing health risks at home by taking into account the UNSDGs 2030, including those that address health (SDG 3) and sustainable cities (SDG 11).

WHO identified the following "economic criteria and conditions (World Health Organization 2018a)" to improve the housing and care market:

- cost-effective/cost–benefit health benefit of several housing interventions,
- training (e.g., evidence-based training and technical assistance programs to help target communities, specialized training to identify housing problems, etc.) of housing and care market stakeholders (i.e., housing agencies, etc.),
- cross-sector collaboration and co-operation of a broad network of international partners (e.g., government agencies, housing providers, developers, public health professionals, and so on),
- housing environment and climatic conditions (e.g., water and air quality, living space/crowding, accessibility of housing for people with functional impairments, etc.),
- healthy housing including complete physical, mental, and social well-being,

- human right to adequate housing and standard of living (i.e., security of tenure, availability of services, materials, facilities and infrastructure, affordability, habitability, accessibility, location, and cultural adequacy),
- national and local adaptation/harmonization of global regulations, norms, standards, recommendations, housing-related policies and regulations, and their implementation, enforcement measures, and prioritization,
- housing risk factors (e.g., lighting, electric security, housing surroundings, etc.),
- co-benefits (e.g., installation of energy-efficient heating, reduction of energy expenditure, reduction of crowding and carbon emissions, implementation of "green" standards for construction practices and green housing elements, etc.) and housing interventions (e.g., policy interventions, etc.),
- social determinants of housing types, quality, size, and location (e.g., durability, building materials, accessibility, transport infrastructure, etc.),
- providing affordable housing/public housing (funding a supply of affordable dwellings, providing subsidies, such as housing vouchers or tax mechanisms, low-income housing tax credits, etc.).

When comparing layers and the shift from top-down to bottom-up approach, the municipality plays a key role in local governance to cope with living and care conditions for the elderly people. The coordination of the different caregivers operating in the local social medical system ought to be strengthened in a systematic manner. Although traditional healthcare remained largely a responsibility of "central authority at national level", long-term residential care became a responsibility of the "regions", and the "regional competences" with respect to mental care and revalidation care were also extended (De Almeida Mello et al. 2022). A State's Social Protection System ought to protect elderly people, provide sufficient means to prevent and combat elder mistreatment, and develop social services to cope with elder mistreatment (Callewaert 2011).

In practical terms of housing and care, it is true to state that people's freedom of choice is vital. Individual-level choices (regarding lifestyles and residence) have a significant impact on the cost of organizing care for all. In this regard, it is crucial to emphasize the subdivision of detached single-family houses and "obduracy". The subdivision of detached single-family houses remains a rather marginal phenomenon (Bervoets and Heynen 2013; Bervoets et al. 2015). Considering the individual-level choices, lifestyle and residence and "obduracy" of the detached single-family house, it is the "result of a complex entanglement of very heterogeneous elements, such as the materiality of the house, the meaning of home, the local home culture, real estate values, spatial policies, zoning plans, and legislative framework". Thus, embeddedness emphasizes the interrelatedness of elements in an urban sociotechnical ensemble (Hommels 2005). In cities, infrastructure, laws and regulations, urban policies, and town-planning structures are closely interconnected. In specific circumstances, this can result in the obduracy of either individual elements or the ensemble as a whole. The freedoms and obligations that citizens have in their choices in housing, building, and care ought to take into consideration the costs imposed on the community by their choices. A conceptual framework can be proposed to balance the freedom of citizens against the costs imposed on the community by their choices. "This conceptual framework is comprised of six subcategories of indicators: (1) built environment of the housing unit and the surrounding neighborhood, (2) offsite and onsite health and social services and resources, (3) social integration, (4) stability and affordability" (Heylen 2020, 2021) of place (objective and subjective affordability indicators), (5) emotional place attachment (Buffel et al. 2014), and (6) broader political and economic contexts.

During the COVID-19 pandemic era, socialization of care tends to increase family responsibility and has a rather small effect on the neighborhood level (D'Herde et al. 2021). Thus, an efficient strategy is to balance financial sustainability with the provision of social protection against the financial risks associated with the costs imposed on the community by their choices (Hashiguchi and Llena-Nozal 2020). Subsidies for care can be allocated to both care providers and directly to people with disabilities as a Personal Care Budget (PCB). The PCB enables stimulating people with disabilities to move and has a positive impact on housing quality outcomes for those who move, and triggers changes in the provision of housing (Winters and van den Broeck 2022, 2023). These reforms can be seen as a shift to a more demand-side-oriented subsidy (Heylen 2013; Heylen and Haffner 2012) and intend to offer people with disabilities more opportunities to choose where to live, how and with whom, thus enabling people to live more independently and more inclusively.

Biomedical technologies have made substantial advances in recent decades, including monitoring systems and tools to facilitate living and aging at home for frail elderly people. Advanced technologies have been developed in the biomedical sector and contributed to monitoring systems and tools to facilitate living and aging at home. Hi-tech advances have led to the development of many new services and applications of digital tools. Among digital technologies, next-generation telecommunications networks (e.g., 5G) were developed and proliferated, and these ensured that people live independently at home for longer. "New technology, including information and communication technologies, is allowing new types of services such as the use of electronic medical records that can be accessed at any point in the health network and can be a tool for reorganizing health services around the needs of frail elderly people" (World Health Organization 2015). E-health platforms and biomedical technologies support remote management of frail elderly people and communities with a range of healthcare needs through the support of self-care and the use of electronic communications between health care professionals and frail elderly people. In this context, "research and development agencies and technology companies should develop and test cost-effective approaches using mobile and wearable devices to promote physical activity within primary and secondary health care and social services (e.g., mHealth programs)" and to allow people to live independently at home for longer and integrate them properly into a model of care (World Health Organization 2018b).

Residential care is an important care service provided to older people, as it targets the frailest among the older adults' population. Undoubtedly, residential care will play a key role in the care of the most vulnerable among the aging population. "There is some controversy about whether the relation between home care and residential care is supplementary or substitutive. However, residential care provides care to the frailest older adults that, when living at home, would be likely to have to rely on a combination of informal and formal care. Therefore, a low level of residential care should increase both the use of informal and formal care at home" (Suanet et al. 2012). In response to the care recipient's need for care and design a more "humane way of care", the intention of providing care must be based on general attitudes, quality of the relationship, normative beliefs, and perceived barriers (Broese Van Groenou and De Boer 2016). Governments are pinning increased reliance on "informal caregivers to compensate for the cutbacks in residential and professional home care. The reform of long-term care entails a reduction in the intensity of professional care provided at home and stricter criteria for admission to residential care" (Verbakel 2018). There is a division between privately funded and publicly funded residential care. "People who live alone and own a house are not eligible for fully publicly funded residential care" (De Almeida Mello et al. 2022).

The main obstacle for publicly or privately funded residential care premises is that "they hardly engage with the surrounding neighborhood and only attract a public of older people needing care. The residential care zone decouples housing, care, and well-being. All three are organized within the neighborhood and no longer within the institution's walls. Therefore, care and well-being could also be offered to people who still live at home. As a result, older people could stay in their own homes longer, even when their need for care increases. A residential care zone establishes a strong relationship between the available services and the neighborhood. When such a zone is established around a large-scale care facility, it may help to counteract the isolation of the facility from the surrounding neighborhood. The care home comes to the neighborhood residents (e.g., for care and meals), and the residents come to the care home (e.g., for activities and information)" (Coomans et al. 2011; De Vos et al. 2016). In this double integration movement, care homes and residents get to know each other, and care homes become part of the neighborhood.

China's new residential care developments have taken broadly the form of privately governed gated communities since the socialist work-unit housing system was terminated at the end of the 1990s. These new residential forms have emerged in post-reform China after housing privatization reforms and profoundly changed the collectivist neighborhood living and neighborhood attachments—i.e., market-led, mixed, and state-led neighborhoods (Lu et al. 2018). New residential forms in China enable social interaction and participate in neighborhood social events hosted by private governance on a regular basis. These offer a great opportunity to expand networks by becoming members of the homeowner association and increasing social participation under private governance.

However, it is quite difficult to benchmark European elderly care models and services in China. In traditional Chinese culture, older adults are expected to engage in family activities, such as taking care of young children. Thus, living with children has a negative impact on the social participation of older Chinese people over time (Feng et al. 2020). On the one hand, providing care for young grandchildren has harmful effects on grandparents' ADL limitations. On the other hand, it ensures beneficial effects for grandparents' life satisfaction (Wu et al. 2023). It creates a basic obstacle to integrating older Chinese people with the neighborhood residents in urban areas. In rural areas, care services and neighborhood environment fit can become a complex issue due to the negative association of rural residence with social participation and low-income level that forces older Chinese people to continue to work in old age.

In contrast to the family structure based on European individualism, Chinese families are still acting more like traditional collectivists and strengthening their relationships with family members and relatives. Thus, Western eldercare models and interpretations of aging, place, and health are not well suited to China. The current generation of older Chinese is profoundly rooted in pre-reform "Collectivism" and is shaped by socialist ideologies of the past (Yu and Rosenberg 2017). However, China's housing reform significantly increased the rate of homeownership and marketization enforced "Individualism/Communitarianism" in urban China. "Providing urban residents with access to private homes, particularly to improve the living conditions of low-income households, is one of the main goals of China's housing system reform" (Ding and Zhou 2023).

"While there are currently 100 working-age people available to support every 20 elderly people, by 2100, 100 working-age Chinese will have to support as many as 120 elderly Chinese. China's pension payments will grow five-fold from 4% of GDP in 2020 to 20% of GDP in 2100" (Aliu 2023; World Economic Forum 2022). Population aging is responsible for the deceleration of economic growth between 2020 and 2040 (Wang and Conesa 2022). Future predictions suggest that China should encourage internal migration from rural areas to urban areas to increase urban labor supply and balance the aging population ratio in both rural and urban areas. In light of these considerations, China ought to pay attention to seek for effective pathways to strengthen elderly care systems and services and improve the quality of life of frail elderly Chinese people. Monitoring and reasoning the death rates of frail elderly Chinese people and supporting publicly or privately funded projects to improve the level of wellbeing and happiness of these people to ensure steady and prolonged lives are vital issues for the Chinese aging population and demographic change.

Since 1958, China has used the "hukou (戶口)" system (i.e., China's household registration system) to assign each citizen a household registration identity based on the birthplace of his or her parents (Miao and Bierman 2023). From 1958 to 1978, the movement of rural residents to cities was strictly restricted. However, the gap between urban and rural public services has been narrowed through reforms in public services, recently (Li et al. 2023). The hukou system was created to control and regulate migration and limit rural to urban population movement and access to scarce resources within China. In this context, an individual can have agricultural or non-agricultural hukou and there is a division of population into marginalized rural and privileged urban classes—i.e., urban–rural dual land system and two class society (Li et al. 2023; Peng et al. 2023; Zhuge and Lang 2023). Therefore, China's hukou system created "invisible walls", apartheid, and caused inequality between people holding "agricultural hukou" in rural areas and "non-agricultural hukou" in urban areas, as well as gender discrimination between rural women and urban men. Urban/non-agricultural hukou—which is based on geography and blood relations—confers more economic benefits than rural hukou (Chen and Fan 2016; Hu 2023).

Housing ownership is the primary condition for hukou conversion and full citizenship. Hukou system shapes the identity and citizenship (location of residence) and social status (entitlements) of the Chinese population. In contrast to rural populations, the distribution of social services and welfare based on hukou has prioritized cities and urban citizens (Li 2023; Peng et al. 2023). Hukou-associated discrimination and class struggles have a significant impact on family structures (e.g., marriages between rural women and urban men, etc.), elderly care services, and housing issues. "Residents with hukou of a locality (termed local-hukou residents) gain the right to access the welfare services of the locality. On the contrary, migrants (non-local hukou) do not gain access to local social welfare" (Zhou et al. 2023). Non-local hukou/agricultural hukou affects health disparities, adulthood conditions, and cognitive functions of Chinese older adults in later life. The conversion of agricultural hukou status to non-agricultural hukou status ought to be facilitated to overcome the life course impacts of agricultural hukou for many older Chinese adults (Peng et al. 2023). In this context, budgetary concerns should not be an obstacle for the Hukou reforms. The Chinese government should promote more fundamental Hukou reforms, revolutionize

Hukou reforms, and make public services equally accessible to all (Song 2021).

It is crucial to implement reforms in China's Hukou system to improve the elderly care system and the future of the aging population in mainland China. There is a necessity for a "unified residency" hukou that combines agricultural/rural and non-agricultural/urban hukou registration types to balance access to housing, jobs, and healthcare at both rural and urban levels and increase equal opportunities for Chinese people living in rural and urban areas. Reforms in China's Hukou system should prioritize the social services (e.g., elderly, childcare, and assistance in finding employment, help people to access their social rights, etc.) and fundamental freedoms (e.g., freedom of movement/mobility rights, equality rights, etc.) of rural residents with agricultural hukou.

Regarding the implications for future studies, it is crucial to highlight the geopolitical analysis of the role of China in the global and regional system. Population is one of the sourcing factors when power distribution is investigated in political and economic studies. If we consider that the described tendencies will remain, they will decrease the expected global economic growth that for the last decades was to a huge extent driven by Chinese rapid growth.

The decreasing labor force in China leads to enhanced measures to support the economic growth of China through high technologies on the one hand, but on the other when we observe this process, it seems clear that Western countries led by the United States have taken advantage of their technological advantages in the name of safeguarding national security and set strict technological and security thresholds to contain China in high-tech fields, thus rising conflicts in the international system.

If the conflict scenario is also analyzed, then the demographic tendencies may also impact Chinese readiness in this regard as based on comparative studies, the aging population factor may lead to the decrease in military capabilities of China due to the lowering of mobilization abilities, and generally if the dependency ratio of the elderly and young is too high, the social burden may be considered too heavy for China to initiate conflict, in particular in the longer run.

From a complexity-geopolitics nexus in multiplex global governance viewpoint, China's changing demographic trends, policies, and strategies, and social, political, and legal developments can be unraveled by considering a glimpse of the "interrelationships" between the captain of the ship (leader and party), the passengers of the ship (people), the ship (country), the routes of the ship (interdependence, IR, national interests, etc.), the compass (constitution, international law, the UN-SDGs, global standards, etc.), and environmental factors, such as weather conditions and water flows and so on (geopolitics, world order, hard power, soft power, etc.). For the captain on the deck of a magnificent floating/navigating ship in the ocean, the effective and healthier method of running the ship safely is to follow the route properly, act according to a "working" compass, and be constantly aware of the situation of the ship and its passengers. More importantly, the captain must take into account all current forecasts and parameters of environmental factors and turbulent order while floating in the ocean. Otherwise, the captain and the ship will face turmoil and chaos, and for sure the consequences will be devastating and catastrophic.

References

Aliu, A. (2023). Demographic indicators and future predictions of China, Hong Kong, Macao, and Taiwan: A comparative perspective. Harvard Dataverse. https://doi.org/10.7910/DVN/CBU8Y2

Bervoets, W., & Heynen, H. (2013). The obduracy of the detached single family house in Flanders. International Journal of Housing Policy, 13(4), 358–380. https://doi.org/10.1080/14616718.2013.840109

Bervoets, W., van de Weijer, M., Vanneste, D., Vanderstraeten, L., Ryckewaert, M. & Heynen, H. (2015). Towards a sustainable transformation of the detached houses in peri-urban Flanders, Belgium. Journal of Urbanism, 8(3), 302–330. https://doi.org/10.1080/17549175.2014.909368

Brakman, S., Frankopan, P., Garretsen, H., & van Marrewijk, C. (2019). The new silk roads: An introduction to China's belt and road initiative. Cambridge Journal of Regions, Economy and Society, 12, 3–16.

Broese Van Groenou, M., & De Boer, A. (2016). Providing informal care in a changing society. European Journal of Ageing, 13, 271–279. https://doi.org/10.1007/s10433-016-0370-7

Brown, K. (2014). Carnival China: China in the Era of Hu Jintao and Xi Jinping. London: Imperial College Press.

Brown, K. (2016). CEO, China: The Rise of Xi Jinping. London: I.B.Tauris.

Brown, K. (2017). China's World: What Does China Want? London: I.B.Tauris.
Buffel, T., De Donde, L., Phillipson, C., De Witte, N., Dury, S., & Verté, D. (2014) Place attachment among older adults living in four communities in Flanders, Belgium. Housing Studies, 29(6), 800–822. https://doi.org/10.1080/02673037.2014.898741
Callewaert, G. A. G. (2011). Preventing and combating elder mistreatment in Flanders (Belgium): General overview. Journal of Elder Abuse & Neglect, 23, 366–374. https://doi.org/10.1080/08946566.2011.608059
Chen, C. & Fan, C. C. (2016). China's Hukou puzzle: Why don't rural migrants want urban Hukou? The China Review, 16(3), 9–39.
Cohen, J. A. (2019a). Law's relation to political power in China: A backward transition. Social Research: An International Quarterly, 86(1), 231–251.
Cohen, J. A. (2019b). Law and power in China's international relations. New York University Journal of International Law and Politics, 52, 123–165.
Cohen, J. A. (2023). Review: The rise of China and international law: Taking Chinese exceptionalism seriously, by Congyan Cai. The China Journal, 90, 232–234.
Coomans, K., De Smet, H., & Heylighen, A. (2011). In search of a future for large-scale care homes in Flanders. Journal of Housing for the Elderly, 25(4), 329–351. https://doi.org/10.1080/02763893.2011.621858
De Almeida Mello, J., Daems, A., Voorde, C. V., Declercq, A., & Schokkaert, E. (2022). Towards a projection model for the Flemish social protection. Leuven: Steunpunt Welzijn, Volksgezondheid en Gezin.
De Vos, J., Van Acker, V., & Witlox, F. (2016). Urban sprawl: Neighbourhood dissatisfaction and urban preferences. Some evidence from Flanders. Urban Geography, 37(6), 839–862. https://doi.org/10.1080/02723638.2015.1118955
D'herde, J., Gruijthuijsen, W., Vanneste, D., Draulans, V., & Heynen, H. (2021). I could not manage this long-term, absolutely not. Aging in place, informal care, COVID-19, and the neighborhood in Flanders (Belgium). International Journal of Environmental Research and Public Health, 18(12), 64–82. https://doi.org/10.3390/ijerph18126482
Ding, M., & Zhou, S. (2023). A study on the welfare equalization effect of China's housing reform. Journal of Government and Economics, 11, 1–11. https://doi.org/10.1016/j.jge.2023.100086
Fairbank, J. K., & Goldman, M. (2006). China: A new history. Cambridge, MA: Harvard University Press.
Farias, J. C., Brimblecombe, N., & Hu, B. (2023). Early onset of care needs in the older population: The protective role of housing conditions. Health & Place, 81, 1–8. https://doi.org/10.1016/j.healthplace.2023.103007
Feng, Z., Cramm, J. M., Jin, C., Twisk, J., & Nieboer, A. P. (2020). The longitudinal relationship between income and social participation among Chinese

older people. SSM—Population Health, 11, 1–8. https://doi.org/10.1016/j.ssmph.2020.100636
Frankopan, P. (2015). The silk roads: A new history of the world. London: Bloomsbury Publishing.
Gardner, D. K. (2014). Confucianism: A very short introduction. Oxford: Oxford University Press.
Hashiguchi, T. O., & Llena-Nozal, A. (2020). The effectiveness of social protection for long-term care in old age: Is social protection reducing the risk of poverty associated with care needs? (Documents de travail de l'OCDE sur la santé 117). Paris: Éditions OCDE. https://doi.org/10.1787/2592f06e-en
Heylen, K. (2013). The distributional impact of housing subsidies in Flanders. International Journal of Housing Policy, 13(1), 45–65. https://doi.org/10.1080/14616718.2013.764660
Heylen, K. (2020). Targeted affordable housing subsidies in Flanders: Evaluating equity using equivalence scales. International Journal of Housing Policy, 20(4), 513–533. https://doi.org/10.1080/19491247.2019.1608114
Heylen, K. (2021). Measuring housing affordability. A case study of Flanders on the link between objective and subjective indicators. Housing Studies, pp. 1–16. https://doi.org/10.1080/02673037.2021.1893280
Heylen, K., & Haffner, M. (2012). The effect of housing expenses and subsidies on the income distribution in Flanders and the Netherlands. Housing Studies, 27(8), 1142–1161. https://doi.org/10.1080/02673037.2012.728572
Hommels, A. (2005). Studying obduracy in the city: Toward a productive fusion between technology studies and urban studies. Science, Technology, & Human Values, 30(3), 323–351. https://doi.org/10.1177/0162243904271759
Hu, Q. (2023). Social status and marriage markets: Evaluating a Hukou policy in China. Review of Economics of the Household. https://doi.org/10.1007/s11150-023-09663-9
Johnson, C. K., Kennedy, S., & Qiu, M. (2017). Xi's signature governance innovation: The rise of leading small groups. Center for Strategic and International Studies. https://www.csis.org/analysis/xis-signature-governance-innovation-rise-leading-small-groups
Lewis, M. E. (2009a). China's Cosmopolitan Empire: The Tang Dynasty. Cambridge, MA: Harvard University Press.

Lewis, M. E. (2009b). China between Empires: The Northern and Southern Dynasties. Cambridge, MA: Harvard University Press.

Li, A. (2023). Stratified financial inclusion in China based on Hukou and its interaction with city and province development. Journal of Ethnic and Migration Studies, 49(17), 4407–4434. https://doi.org/10.1080/1369183X.2023.2191155

Li, H., Chen, K., Yan, L., Yu, L., & Zhu, Y. (2023). Citizenization of rural migrants in China's new urbanization: The roles of hukou system reform and rural land marketization. Cities, 132, 1–15. https://doi.org/10.1016/j.cities.2022.103968

Lu, T., Zhang, F., & Wu, F. (2018). Place attachment in gated neighbourhoods in China: Evidence from Wenzhou. Geoforum, 92: 144–151.

Naughten, B. (2018). The Chinese Economy: Adaptation and growth (2nd Edition). Cambridge, MA: The MIT Press.

Miao, J., & Bierman, A. (2023). Functional limitations and psychological well-being among older adults in China: The critical role of Hukou as a stratifying factor. The International Journal of Aging and Human Development, 97(3), 327–353.

Minzner, K. (2018). End of an era: How China's authoritarian revival is undermining its rise. Oxford: Oxford University Press.

Peng, C., Burr, J. A., Wu, B., & Li, M. (2023). Hukou status and cognitive function among older Chinese adults: Does support from friends matter? Journal of Aging and Health, pp. 1–12. https://doi.org/10.1177/08982643231206819

Song, Y. (2021). Cost-benefit analysis of the Hukou reform: Simulation evidence from a theoretical labor market model. China Economic Quarterly International, 1, 109–119. https://doi.org/10.1016/j.ceqi.2021.03.001

Suanet, B., Broese Van Groenou, M., & Van Tilburg, T. (2012). Informal and formal home-care use among older adults in Europe: Can cross-national differences be explained by societal context and composition? Ageing and Society, 32(3), 491–515. https://doi.org/10.1017/S0144686X11000390

The State Council Information Office of the People's Republic of China. (2023). The Belt and Road Initiative: A Key Pillar of the Global Community of Shared Future. http://www.scio.gov.cn/zfbps/zfbps_2279/202310/t20231010_773734.html

Tsang, S., & Men, H. (Eds.) (2016). China in the Xi Jinping Era. London: Palgrave Macmillan.

Verbakel, E. (2018). How to understand informal caregiving patterns in Europe? The role of formal long-term care provisions and family care norms. Scandinavian Journal of Public Health, 46(4), 436–447. https://doi.org/10.1177/1403494817726197

Wang, Y., & Conesa, J. C. (2022). The role of demographics and migration for the future of economic growth in China. European Economic Review, 144, 1–18.
World Health Organization. (2015). WHO global strategy on people-centered and integrated health services: Interim report. https://apps.who.int/iris/handle/10665/155002
World Health Organization. (2018a). WHO housing and health guidelines. https://apps.who.int/iris/rest/bitstreams/1161792/retrieve
World Health Organization. (2018b). Global action plan on physical activity 2018–2030: More active people for a healthier world. Geneva: WHO. https://apps.who.int/iris/handle/10665/272722
Wiles, J. L. et al. (2011). The meaning of "aging in place" to older people. Gerontologist, 52(3), 357–66.
Winters, S., & van den Broeck, K. (2022). Social housing in Flanders: Best value for society from social housing associations or social rental agencies? Housing Studies, 37(4), 605–623. https://doi.org/10.1080/02673037.2020.1823329
Winters, S., & van den Broeck, K. (2023). Housing of persons with disabilities: What can be learned from the introduction of more demand-driven subsidies in Flanders? International Journal of Housing Policy, pp. 1–22. https://doi.org/10.1080/19491247.2023.2182622
World Economic Forum. (2022). China's population is about to shrink for the first time since the great famine struck 60 years ago: Here's what that means for the world. https://www.weforum.org/agenda/2022/07/china-population-shrink-60-years-world/
Wu, J., Glaser, K., & Avendano, M. (2023). Does the transition to grandparenthood influence the health and well-being of older people? Evidence from the CHARLS study in China. SSM—Population Health, 21, 1–9.
Yu, J., & Rosenberg, M. W. (2017). "No place like home": Aging in post-reform Beijing. Health & Place, 46, 192–200.
Zenglein, M. J., & Gunter, J. (2023). The party knows best: Aligning economic actors with China's strategic goals. Berlin: MERICS.
Zhang, Q. (2015). An introduction to Chinese history and culture. Heidelberg: Springer.
Zhao, L. (2016). 'Forging a harmonious relationship among the ethnic groups', in S. Tsang & H. Men (editors), China in the Xi Jinping Era (pp. 97–121). London: Palgrave Macmillan.
Zhou, J., Lin, L., & Gu, H. (2023). How attitudes from urban residents shape settlement plans of rural-to-urban migrants in China: The role of Hukou. Current Psychology. https://doi.org/10.1007/s12144-023-05243-3

Zhuge, L., & Lang, K. (2023). Hukou and Guanxi: How social discrimination and networks impact intrahousehold allocations in China, Working Paper 31237. Cambridge, MA: National Bureau of Economic Research. http://www.nber.org/papers/w31237

Index

0–9
2023 BRICS Summit Declaration, 219, 237
20th CCP National Congress, 9

A
Abortion, 75, 76
Accountability, 112, 119, 252, 255, 264
Activities of daily living (ADL), 33, 34, 273
Addis Ababa Action Agenda (AAAA), 113
Administrative and judicial reforms, 264
Advanced technologies, 271
Ageing, 18, 69, 72, 73, 89, 94, 96, 218, 228, 236–238, 240
Ageing in the right place, 267
Agent-based actions, 16
Aging, 33, 39, 42, 51, 243, 244, 253, 263, 267, 271, 273, 275
All under Heaven (tianxia), 265
American exceptionalism, 156
Analysis of policy dynamics, 17
Anthropological demography, 1, 2
Anthropology, 2, 11, 260, 261
Anti-corruption, 180, 181, 184
Antithetical processes, 28
Asian Infrastructure Investment Bank (AIIB), 104, 105, 107, 110, 111, 114, 116, 119, 120
Asymmetric strategies, 9
Authoritarian, 32, 33, 143, 147, 176
Authority, 6, 9–11, 27, 120, 141, 146, 166, 174, 177, 181, 184–186, 253, 261, 269
Autonomy, 6, 28, 31, 32, 159, 260, 268

B
Baby boom, 70
Baby boomer generation, 72
Behavioral economics, 16

A. Aliu (ed.), *Complexity Thinking and China's Demography Within and Beyond Mainland China*,
https://doi.org/10.1007/978-981-97-0172-8

Beijing, 5, 7, 9, 30, 31, 33, 45–55, 108, 219, 253, 266
Beijing 2008 Summer Olympic Games, 266
Belt and Road cooperation, 18
Belt and Road Initiative (BRI), 13, 18, 79, 100–102, 104–107, 109, 111, 112, 114, 115, 117, 119–122, 147, 235, 254, 255, 266, 267
Benefit for all, 17
Best practices, 112, 114
Bilateral, 93, 97, 108, 112, 114, 115, 118, 122, 254, 255
Bilateral tensions, 12
Bingtuan, 5
Biomedical technologies, 271
Biopolitical, 8
Birth control policy, 15
Border control, 82
Border security, 81
Border walls, 87
Bottom-up steering, 32
Brain drain, 78, 82
Brazil, Russia, India, China, and South Africa (BRICS), 107, 108, 218–220, 223, 224, 228, 237, 259
BRICS Academic Forum, 238, 259
BRICS countries, 219–225, 237, 259
BRICS populations age, 238
BRICS Think Tank Forum, 238, 259
Buddhism, 260
Build Back Better Plan of the United States of America (BBB), 18

C
Carbon emissions, 121, 267, 269
Carbon pollution, 121
Carbon pricing, 121
Care homes, 38, 40, 43, 46, 48, 272
Caring responsibilities, 35
Central Asia, 4, 100
Central control over local power, 28
Central government, 5, 6, 27–29, 31–33, 35, 37–39, 42, 112, 252, 253
Centralization, 27, 29
Centralized unified leadership, 9
Centralizing, 29
Central-local relations, 28, 29, 31, 32
Central state, 29
Changing demographics, 18, 261, 275
Chengyus, 134, 141, 145–147, 150, 256
Childbearing, 70, 75, 196, 197, 202, 203, 210
Child labor law, 264
child mortality rate, 221
China, 1, 3, 6, 9, 11, 12, 14, 15, 18, 33, 66, 69, 71, 72, 75, 77–79, 88, 90, 93, 94, 96, 103–105, 108–112, 115, 118, 121, 131, 132, 135, 142, 145, 157–161, 163, 164, 169, 176, 193, 194, 196, 197, 215, 219, 223, 227, 230, 232, 234, 236, 237, 239, 242, 250, 251, 253, 254, 256, 257, 260, 261, 263, 264, 266, 267, 274, 275
China Household Finance Survey, 196
China International Development Cooperation Agency (CIDCA), 18
China Migrants Dynamic Survey (CMDS), 195, 197, 200, 209, 212
China's cultural values, 266
China's economic development, 18
China's grand strategy, 13
China's history, 9, 135
China's housing reform, 273

China's migrant populations, 19
China's National Bureau of Statistics (NBS), 12
China's strategic national interests, 13
China's traditional patriarchal family system, 75
China-UN Peace and Development Fund, 17
Chinese authoritarianism, 10
Chinese authorities, 10, 259, 261
Chinese banks and multinational enterprises, 13
Chinese civilization, 91
Chinese Civil War, 4
Chinese Communist Party (CCP), 4, 6, 32, 132, 149–151, 167, 169, 176, 180, 250, 251, 263, 264
Chinese constitutional law, 152
Chinese constitutional theory, 131, 132
Chinese culture, 10, 145, 195, 203, 265, 272
Chinese demographic authoritarianism, 261
Chinese dream, 10, 265
Chinese economic reform, 4
Chinese eldercare, 39, 56
Chinese elderly, 36, 38
Chinese enterprises, 106, 116
Chinese exceptionalism, 19, 156, 157, 159, 161, 163, 164, 256, 257
Chinese family, 3, 93, 273
Chinese foreign policy, 146, 250
Chinese globalization approach, 265
Chinese government, 3, 10, 15, 28, 72, 94, 106, 113, 116, 118, 120, 265, 274
Chinese interests, 255
Chinese law, 8, 112, 114, 258
Chinese leadership, 265
Chinese legal system, 129, 166
Chinese migrants, 12, 78, 97
Chinese nation, 9, 10, 260, 262
Chineseness, 266
Chinese party-state, 32, 35, 52
Chinese people, 10, 13, 34, 35, 145, 260, 262, 273, 275
Chinese philosophy, 11
Chinese policymakers, 102, 107, 109, 232, 254
Chinese policy process, 32
Chinese political language, 140
Chinese political processes, 29, 32
Chinese political theory, 143
Chinese readiness, 275
Chinese rusticated youth, 5
Chinese society, 15, 70, 76, 260, 261
Chinese State-owned Enterprises, 119
Chinese-style communism, 264
Chinese Turkestan, 4
Chinese women and girls, 10
Chinese youth and workers, 13
Christianity, 260
Civilization, 85, 88, 91, 102, 136, 143, 265, 266
Class struggles, 10, 274
Climate change, 10, 14, 106, 110, 111, 123
Climate/green politics, 10
Coexistence, 29, 55, 102, 111, 113, 157, 176, 184, 185, 260, 267
Cognitive science, 2
Collectivist neighborhood living, 272
Colonialism, 6, 260
Commercialization strategy, 36
Commercial relations, 11
Commercial residential homes, 45
Common/democratic collective identity, 10, 261, 262
Communist China, 10, 148
Community-based care, 36, 40, 41, 43, 44, 46–48, 51, 52, 54, 240
Community-based elder support stations, 43

Community-based services, 36, 40, 44, 48, 252
Community of shared future for mankind, 265
Competitive advantages, 89
Complex challenges, 18
Complexification, 16
Complexity, 2, 17, 19, 28, 139, 140, 150, 168, 258, 275
Complexity thinking (CT), 9, 16, 250, 251, 256
complex macro level analyses, 19
Complex multisectoral agenda, 18
Complex structure, 2, 16
Conflict zones, 10
Confucian culture, 265
Confucianism, 265
Confucian values, 35
Connectivity, 11, 18, 100, 103, 105, 107, 108, 266
Constitutional amendments, 137, 140, 146, 148, 150, 180
Contemporary international law, 265
Contemporary reforms, 264
Continued emigration, 14
Coordinating small groups (CSGs), 262
Coordinating working groups (CWGs), 262
Corruption, 184, 264
Cosmopolitan, 9–11, 260, 261
Cosmopolitan Chinese, 9, 10
Cosmopolitanism, 10, 11
Counter-steer, 253
COVID-19, 11, 15, 90, 110, 223
COVID-19 pandemic era, 270
Cultural demographers, 260
Cultural Revolution, 142, 144

D

Daoism, 260
Death rates, 215, 220, 223, 273
Debt dependency, 112, 255
Debt financing, 117
Debt sustainability, 117, 118, 122, 255
Decentralization, 27–30, 55, 252
Decentralizing, 29
Decentralizing market reform era, 28
Decision-making, 27, 100, 115, 116, 173, 196
Decolonization movements, 113, 157
Deconcentration, 27
Deeper market liberalization, 262
Delegation, 27
Demographical changes, 251
Demographic balance, 4
Demographic change, 3, 6, 14, 16, 66, 69, 79, 81, 87, 89, 92, 93, 96, 97, 219, 232, 254, 258, 267, 273
Demographic competition, 13
Demographic composition, 9
Demographic conjunctures, 1
Demographic data, 14
Demographic decline, 14
Demographic de-cosmopolitanization, 10, 261
Demographic determinism, 15
Demographic development, 10, 262
Demographic dividend, 18, 88–90, 217, 228, 231, 235, 250
Demographic effects, 15
Demographic engineering, 3, 10, 13, 252, 261
Demographic factors, 67, 87
Demographic giants, 218, 219, 237
Demographic indicators, 2
Demographic milestones, 215
Demographic peak, 215, 227
Demographic power, 66
Demographic reality, 236
Demographic shifts, 69, 70, 253

Demographic structure, 1, 14, 252
Demographic transition, 13, 18, 215, 217, 218, 221, 224, 233
Demographic trends, 10, 69, 219, 261
Demography, 1, 2, 9, 12–14, 17, 19, 232, 234, 250–252, 259, 261
Demography studies, 2, 11, 261
Dengist reforms, 263
Deng Xiaoping, 148, 159, 170, 175, 230, 231, 260, 262
Dependency ratio, 84, 235, 275
Depopulation, 70
Developmentalism, 157, 159, 256
Devolution, 27, 28
Diaspora, 4, 13
Diplomatic communication, 14
Direct governmental intervention, 32
Disciplinary actions, 178, 179
Discrimination, 15, 82, 87, 93, 196, 274
Disproportionate effects, 16
Diversity, 15, 82, 251, 260
Domestic instability, 250
Dynamical systems analysis, 16

E
East Turkestan, 4
Economic and fiscal responsibilities, 29
Economic conflict, 17, 92
Economic demography, 11, 219, 220, 232, 236
Economic demography transition (EDT), 13, 218, 228, 237, 259
Economic demography transition strategy, 232–234
Economic empowerment of women, 15
Economic migrants, 69
Economic reforms, 259, 263
Education, 7, 28, 50, 69, 80, 81, 93, 95, 104, 109, 110, 123, 136, 169, 195, 197, 198, 210, 212, 217, 233, 235, 240, 243, 258, 259
Effectiveness, 17, 32, 38, 122, 178, 183
Efficiency, 17, 32, 104, 121, 159, 243
Efficient governance, 264
E-health platforms, 271
Eldercare beds, 38, 42, 48, 50
Eldercare development, 36
Eldercare homes, 39, 44, 46, 49, 54
Eldercare industry, 38, 94
Eldercare infrastructure investment, 42, 48
Eldercare institutions, 39, 43, 46
Eldercare insurance, 43, 47
Eldercare policies, 52, 94
Eldercare providers, 34, 45, 48
Eldercare provision, 34–36, 48, 50, 54, 55
Eldercare service development, 29, 30, 34, 38–40, 42, 46–48, 53, 55, 56
Eldercare service provision, 29, 33, 35, 37, 38, 40, 41, 43, 44, 52, 54
Eldercare services, 19, 29, 35, 39, 41, 42, 48, 52, 53, 56, 253, 264
Eldercare service sector, 31, 33
Elder day-care centers, 43
Elderly care systems and services, 273
Elderly industry, 36
Elderly people, 19, 34, 67, 72, 73, 94, 259, 269, 271, 273
Elderly residents, 34, 43
Elder mistreatment, 269
Elite, 6, 234, 260, 262, 264, 266
Embeddedness, 10, 261, 266, 270
Environmental & social impacts, 17

Environmental impact assessments, 116
Environmental sustainability, 267
Epidemics, 14
Epochal demographic shadow, 219
Epochal population transition, 219
Equator Principles (EP), 115
Equilibrium, 14
Ethnic compartmentalization, 260
Ethnic consciousness, 6
Ethnic groups, 3, 9, 68, 85, 86, 261
Ethnicity, 3, 68, 85
Ethnic minority, 3, 6, 7, 90, 260
Ethnic relations, 9, 260
Ethnic tension, 7, 8, 66
Ethnocentric, 14
Ethno-cultural regions, 261
Ethno-national, 3
Ethnonationalism, 9, 10, 252, 261
Ethnonationalist, 11, 251, 261
Ethnopluralism/ethno-differentialism, 10, 11, 260–262
Ethnopluralist, 261
European elderly care models, 272
European Union Global Gateway (EUGG), 18
Evangelical Protestantism, 260
Excessive debt obligations, 117, 255
Extreme right-wing, 13
Extremism, 8, 96

F
Family care, 47
Family caregiving, 36, 40
Family planning policies, 71, 75, 194, 198
Family reunification, 2
Family structure, 15, 268, 273, 274
Famine, 14, 230
Fear politics, 14
Feminist perspectives, 250, 264
Fertility/natality, 2, 3, 11, 14, 15, 19, 70, 71, 76, 88, 96, 194–203, 206, 207, 209, 210, 212, 253, 258, 259
Fertility rates decline, 215
Financial reforms, 263
Five Principles of Peaceful Coexistence, 101, 102, 157
Five-Year Plans (FYPs), 109, 171, 172, 177, 185, 240–242
Forecasting models, 16
Foreign affairs, 18, 19, 120, 219, 262
Foreign relations law, 156, 163, 164, 256
For-profit providers, 42, 44, 49, 50, 52
Freedom, 3, 9, 10, 15, 111, 252, 260, 270, 275
Fundamental freedoms, 114, 260, 275

G
Gender, 1, 15, 18, 19, 69, 74, 76, 77, 83, 84, 238, 250, 274
Gender equality, 76, 106, 123
General Agreement on Tariffs and Trade, 159
Geographical spatial relationships, 82
Geopolitical, 9, 67–69, 72, 79, 82–88, 91–93, 96, 97, 250, 275
Geopolitics, 9, 19, 65–67, 69, 79, 80, 83, 85, 86, 92, 97, 275
Geriatrics, 268
Gerontocracy, 1, 268
Gerontology, 2
Getting Old Before Getting Rich, 230
Getting old before rich, 13, 236, 237, 259, 267
Global, 15
Global challenges, 13, 250
Global Chinese leadership, 265
Global conflicts, 12
Global constitutionalism, 163

Global economic governance, 100
Global geographic space, 87
Global governance, 13, 15, 110, 113, 265, 275
Global governance level, 12
Global hegemons, 12
Globalization, 11, 65, 77, 89, 90, 114, 161, 266
Global norms and standards, 255
Global post-COVID recovery, 18
Government contracts, 42
Government funding, 42
Great famines (1958–61), 14, 70
Great Leap Forward famine, 5
Great revival, 9
Green agenda, 264
Grey population, 228
Group privilege, 17
Guangxi Zhuang Autonomous Region (GZAR), 3
Guiding Principles on Business and Human Rights, 115
Guomindang (GMD), 5

H
Han, 4–6, 38, 41, 146, 252
Han Chinese, 3, 6, 9
Han officials, 6
Han refugees, 5
Han settlers, 4, 5
Hard steering, 31, 32, 38, 39
Harmonious order, 261
Health care, 28, 36, 67, 93, 95, 242, 243, 271
Heterogeneity analysis, 195, 210, 211
Highly skilled migrants, 78
High-tech, 89, 234, 275
Historical continuity, 142, 147, 148
Hi-tech advancements, 271
HIV/AIDS, 223
Home-based care, 36, 41, 46–48, 51–53, 252
Home care, 241, 271, 272
Homeownership, 273
Household, 2, 43, 45, 194–200, 209, 210, 234, 241, 258, 273, 274
House price, 76, 194–203, 206, 207, 209, 210, 212, 258, 259
Housing costs, 195, 212, 258
Housing privatization reforms, 272
Hukou, 45, 51, 52, 54, 198, 199, 204, 274, 275
Hukou reforms, 274, 275
Human rights, 7, 101, 111, 112, 114, 122, 161, 264, 269
Human rights activism, 15
Hybridization, 9, 33, 44, 50, 261
Hybrid warfare, 9

I
Ideological, 8, 85, 111, 134, 136, 137, 140, 143, 144, 149, 150, 256, 260
ILO Convention on the Rights of the Child, 116
Immigration, 13
Immigration control, 87
Imperialism, 260
Indian Ocean, 13, 100, 103
Infectious disease, 14, 82, 110
Informal care arrangements, 35
In-home care workers, 46
Inner Mongolian Autonomous Region (IMAR), 3, 252
Institutional care, 36, 38, 252
Insufficient welfare provision, 28
Integrated analytical tools, 18
Integration, 85, 88, 92, 97, 103, 108, 180, 181, 186, 194, 196, 199, 241, 258, 270, 272
Interconnectedness, 16, 133
Interdependence, 166, 276
Interdependency, 11, 265
Internal rebellion, 10

International environmental and social standards, 115
International relations (IR), 67, 82, 89, 92, 113, 157, 251, 253, 257
International security, 66, 254
Internment camps, 7
Interventionist, 13
Interventionist population policy, 230
Intra-party regulations, 165–170, 173–175, 177, 178, 181, 183, 184, 187, 257, 258
Invisible China, 234
Islam, 260

J
Jesuit missionaries, 260
Jesuits, 260
Justice, 15, 110, 111, 123

K
Kunming, 7
Kuomintang, 4

L
Labor force, 212, 275
Land under Heaven (*tianxia*), 265
Later, longer, fewer campaign, 12
Law reforms, 264
Laws of historical development, 136
Leadership of the CCP, 132, 136, 143, 149, 150
Leading small groups (LSGs), 120, 262
Legal norms, 166, 264
Legitimacy, 19, 131, 136, 142, 146–148, 150, 151, 174, 250, 255, 256
Life expectancy, 2, 67, 73, 215, 222, 223
Limited territorial autonomy, 3
Linear models of causality, 16
Linguistic anomalies, 130
Local China, 29
Local eldercare development, 35, 55
Local governance, 169, 269
Local government, 27–29, 31, 32, 34–38, 52, 55, 86, 252, 262
Local predictability, 19
Local public service development, 32
Long-term care (LTC), 34, 37, 43, 49, 243, 272
Looming care crisis, 34
Low birth rates, 14, 72
Low SDG commitment countries, 17

M
Macroeconomic, 18, 103, 118
Mainland China, 2, 9, 13, 77, 197, 252, 267, 275
Male chauvinism, 15
Manchu court politics, 260
Mandarin, 8
Mandatory birth control, 15
Maoist reforms, 263
Maritime Silk Road, 13, 100
Marketization, 30, 36, 45, 262, 273
Market reform, 263
Marriage, 2, 14, 15, 76, 77, 82, 84, 93, 274
Meanings of homes, 268
Median age, 73, 223
Mental care, 269
Mergers and acquisitions, 50
Middle class, 263
Migration, 2, 6, 10, 11, 13, 14, 19, 66–69, 77–80, 82, 85–87, 92, 93, 196, 237, 251, 254, 261, 273
Ming Dynasty, 9
Minority culture, 6
Minzu, 3, 6, 9

Modernity, 147, 260
Modes of coordination, 29
Modes of interaction, 29
Modes of state intervention, 31
Mongolia, 4, 117
Mortality, 2, 14, 15, 72, 88, 221
Multi-agent behavior, 17
Multiculturalism, 11
Multicultural societal order, 261
Multi-ethnic, 260
Multilateral environmental agreements, 116
Multilateral governance, 114
Multilateralism, 110, 114
Multi-level steering processes, 31
Municipalities, 28, 33, 39–42, 44–46, 48–50, 197, 252, 269

N
National consciousness, 10, 261
National governance, 166, 173, 175
Nationalist-populist movements, 13
National laws, 35, 161, 166, 167, 170, 173–175, 177, 178, 180–184, 187
National Population and Family Planning Commission (NPFPC), 12
National Security Strategy, 89
National Supervisory Commission, 180
Naturalization, 87
Negative demographic tendencies, 261
Negative effects of the BRI, 267
Negotiation, 32, 110, 158
Neighborhoods, 42, 43, 270, 272, 273
New World Order, 146, 162
Ningxia Hui Autonomous Region (NHAR), 3
Non-linearity, 16
Non-linear system, 16
Non-resident foreigners, 261
Non-state actors, 29, 31, 32
Normative constitutionalism, 131

O
One Child Policy, 15, 67, 230, 231, 250
One World One Dream motto, 266
Ontological, 16
Opening up period, 27
Openness, 109, 110, 119, 262
Openness of the Chinese society, 10
Optimistic, 14, 76, 163
Overall SDG rank score, 17
Overpopulation, 14, 267
Overseas Chinese, 12, 78
Ownership, 43, 44, 56, 199, 203, 274

P
Partnerships (Priority 3), 18
Party Constitution, 169, 170, 175, 177
Party governance, 166, 171–173
Party laws, 169, 182
Party reforms, 263
Party rules, 169, 181, 184
Party's Discipline Inspection Commission, 180
Patriotism, 6
Peace, 12, 101, 102, 105, 111, 113, 254, 266
Pensions, 28, 73, 218, 238, 267, 273
People's Liberation Army (PLA), 5
People's Republic of China (PRC), 8, 70, 102, 109, 113, 130, 158, 160, 161, 171, 256, 266
People and Prosperity (Priority 1), 18
People with disabilities, 270
Pessimistic, 14

Philosophical, 11, 19
Philosophy, 11, 175, 263, 266
Planet (Priority 2), 18
Pluralist, 11
Pluralistic society, 260
Pluralistic unity, 260
Policy coherence, 109, 113, 115, 120
Policy implementation, 31, 120
Political action, 10, 11, 14, 259
Political alienation, 14
Political and institutional power, 17
Political and legal reforms, 264
Political change, 141, 250
Political connotations, 143
Political constitutionalism, 131, 132
Political demography, 2, 3, 15
Political economy, 1, 17, 69, 263, 264
Political ideology, 10
Political philosophy, 10, 11, 146
Political power, 19, 28, 29, 87, 142, 148, 149, 151, 256
Political reforms, 264
Political rhetoric, 14
Political science, 11, 15, 91
Political sovereignty, 265
Political status of women, 15
Political steering theory, 29, 31–33
Political transformations, 140
Population, 1, 3, 5, 6, 9–14, 17–19, 33, 39, 50, 66, 67, 69, 71–74, 78, 80, 81, 83–85, 87, 88, 90, 91, 93–95, 162, 194, 196, 197, 215–217, 219, 224, 226, 228, 232, 233, 235, 237–239, 250, 253, 258, 259, 261, 273, 275
Population ageing, 66
Population age structure change, 219, 237
Population boom, 215
Population change, 2, 3, 11, 80, 86, 259, 261
Population control, 3
Population decline, 12, 14, 222, 226, 235
Population peak, 94, 215, 229
Population replacement rate, 222
Population share of seniors, 217, 223, 224, 228
Population size, 2, 14, 66, 70, 78, 80, 82, 89–91
Population structure, 73, 83–85, 90, 220, 227, 229, 233, 259
Population studies, 13, 17, 19, 251
Population threshold, 217
Power dynamics, 67, 68, 137
Power relations, 15, 80, 96
Power transition theory, 12
Preamble of the Chinese Constitution, 256
Preamble of the Party Constitution, 144, 177
Prevent war, 12
Principle of communicative rationality, 265
Principle of party leadership, 132
Principle of utilitarianism, 17
Private capital mobilization, 107
Private care industry, 37
Private-for profit commercialization, 41, 49
Private governance, 272
Private-Public-Partnerships (PPPs), 36, 43, 120
Privatization, 30, 36, 44
Progressive era of social and societal reforms, 264
Pro-natalist, 14
Public and private care provision, 34
Public care providers, 37
Public debt, 118
Publicly funded eldercare, 35
Public policy, 16, 17, 19, 44, 100
Public welfare, 28, 237

Pure ethnic, 14

Q
Qing, 4, 5

R
Radical revisionist movements, 12
Real politics, 17
Recentralization, 28–30, 55, 56
Recentralizing, 29
Recursive relations, 16
Recursive systems, 16
Reform, 27, 35, 41, 110, 118, 177, 180, 194, 230, 235, 252, 262–264, 270, 275
Reform and opening-up process, 173, 262
Reformism, 264
Reformist language, 264
Reformist movement, 264
Reformists, 260, 261
Reform of government and administrative functions, 264
Regional inequality, 28
Regulatory system, 166, 168, 171, 172, 177
Rejuvenation, 9, 10, 91, 252, 262, 265
Religious extremism, 7
Resettlement, 92, 97
Resettlement programs, 13
Resident Chinese, 261
Residential care, 45, 52, 54, 269, 271, 272
Residential eldercare, 44
Responsibility, 10, 33–35, 52, 110, 114, 159, 178, 252, 259, 270
Restricted code, 140, 142, 150
Revalidation care, 269
Reverse power relations, 12
Reverse power transition, 12
Revolution, 92, 142, 148, 150
Revolutionary history, 142
Ricci, D.M., 14, 260
Role of ideology, 137
Roman Catholicism, 260
Rule of law, 132, 161, 163, 164, 167, 171–173, 175, 176, 187, 257, 264
Rule-of-law governance paradigm, 173
Rural, 15, 28, 34, 46, 51, 76, 194, 196, 217, 221, 234, 240, 252, 273–275

S
Safeguarding national security, 89, 275
SDG index score, 17
SDG transformations, 17
Securitization of the demographic transition, 13
Self-determination, 6, 10, 14
Semantic analysis, 129
Separatism, 8, 93, 96
Several commissions (SC), 262
Sex-ratio, 250
Shadow of hierarchy, 29, 31, 32, 37
Shanghai, 37, 39, 40, 42–44, 46, 48–50, 52, 54, 56, 253
Shanghai Academy of Social Sciences (SASS), 11, 12
Shanghai Civil Affairs Bureau, 42, 43
Shanghai municipality, 40–42
Shared competence, 259
Shrinking workforce, 67
Silk Road Economic Belt, 100
Silk Road Fund, 104, 107, 108, 121
Silk Roads, 104, 147, 266, 267
Silk route, 13
Sinicization, 8, 9, 252, 266
Sino-cultural mission, 9, 252

Sino-US strategic game, 89
Social and environmental protection, 255
Social assistance, 28, 35, 45
Social burden, 84, 275
Social conflicts, 10, 83, 254
Social engineering, 15
Social impact assessments, 116
Social inclusion, 100, 254
Socialist era, 35
Socialist legal system, 167, 168
Socialist rule of law system with Chinese characteristics, 182, 184
Social organizations, 29, 37–42, 44, 50–53
Social progress, 265
Social protection, 28, 270
Social reforms, 263, 265
Social security system, 73, 196, 240, 241, 243
Social services, 35, 263, 269, 271, 275
Social transition, 15
Social welfare, 28, 29, 39, 55, 93, 236, 252, 274
Socio-demographic inventory, 15
Sociological, 19, 66, 84
Soft steering, 32, 35, 37, 38
South-South cooperation, 17
South-South Cooperation Assistance Fund, 18
Sovereign debt obligations, 112, 255
Speech act, 129
Spillover effect, 16, 251
Spillover index, 17
Spillover rank, 17
Spillover score, 17
Stability, 12, 13, 76, 83, 85, 89, 92, 166, 194, 251, 270
Stakeholders, 101, 119, 122, 268
State-building, 15, 158, 163, 257
State-owned enterprises (SOEs), 100, 121
State power, 80, 82, 91, 253
State traditions, 162
Steering capacity, 32
Steering efforts, 31, 33, 34, 38, 41, 52, 53, 56
Steering governability, 32
Steering industry development, 37
Steering local development, 37
Steering modes, 31
Steering outcomes, 31, 32
Strict sovereignty, 157, 158, 256
Structurally complex system, 16
Structural reforms, 263
Sun Yat-sen, 147, 148
Superordinate government levels, 31
Supervision system, 19
Supervision system reform, 167
Supervisory reform, 184
Survey of demographic data, 219
Sustainable development, 15, 74, 91, 99, 104, 106, 111, 121, 123, 254
Sustainable pension schemes, 217
Symmetric relationships, 12
Syntax, 134, 138–141, 143
System of social norms, 166

T

Taklamakan desert, 4, 5
Talent dividends, 89
Tang Dynasty, 9, 146
Territorial integrity, 102, 113, 157, 158
Territorial nation-state, 157
Terrorism, 7, 96, 161
Terrorist, 8, 96
The China Aging Longitudinal Social Survey, 34
Third sector, 29, 37, 38, 42, 44, 45, 51, 54, 55, 253

Third sector actors, 31, 32
Three-tier care system, 46
Tiananmen Square, 7, 262
Tianxiagovernance, 265–267
Tibet, 7
Tibetan cultures, 9
Tibet Autonomous Region (TAR), 3, 7, 9, 252
Top-down steering, 32
Total fertility rate (TFR), 70, 71, 73, 221–223, 231
Totalitarian, 10, 261
Totalitarianism, 10, 261
Tradition, 10, 11, 17, 147, 260, 261
Traditional Chinese, 9, 261
Traditional cultures, 8–11
Transborder ethnicities, 68
Transfer of responsibilities/tasks, 27
Transformation of demographic dividends, 89
Transnational marriages, 66, 77
Transparency, 101, 112, 119, 121, 122, 255, 264
Treaty of Versailles, 159
Turbulent order, 16, 276
Turkestan, 4

U
Unbalanced geographic, 236
Underpopulation, 14, 267
Understanding of pluralism, 261
Unified residency, 275
Union of Soviet Socialist Republics (USSR), 5
United Nations International Organization for Migration (UNIOM), 12
United Nations Sustainable Development Goals 2030 (UNSDGs), 15, 17, 19, 121, 251, 254, 255, 268
United Nations (UN), 72, 73, 107, 110, 114, 160, 219, 225, 228, 239
United States (US), 67, 71, 73, 78, 88, 90, 96, 156, 162, 250, 275
Universal Declaration of Human Rights, 113
Universal exceptionalism, 156
Universalism, 162, 164
UN Population Division (UNPD), 12
Unpredictability, 16, 19
UN Sustainable Development Cooperation Framework (UNSDCF), 18
Urban, 15, 28, 34, 36, 45, 51, 82, 194–197, 199, 203, 221, 234, 270, 273–275
Urbanization, 11, 100, 194, 261
Urumchi, 7, 9
US constitution, 159
Uyghurs, 3, 4, 6–9
Uyghur terrorists, 7

V
Violent conflicts, 13, 86, 91

W
War on Terror, 8
Welfare expenditure, 33
Welfare mix, 29–31, 33, 34, 38, 41, 43, 45, 54, 56
Welfare planning, 33
Welfare provision, 28, 30, 33, 50, 56
Welfare service provision, 39
Western political systems, 264
Western-style socialism, 264
Western universalist values, 264
Woman-related demographics, 15
Working-age population, 73, 217, 224, 226–228, 232, 233, 250, 267

World Trade Organization (WTO), 104, 110, 159, 161, 254, 262
WTO Trade Facilitation Agreement, 106

X
Xi Jinping, 9, 28, 115, 121, 140, 147, 148, 179, 252, 262, 265
Xinjiang, 3–6, 8, 252
Xinjiang Production and Construction Corps (XPCC), 5
Xinjiang Shengchan Jianshe Bingtuan, 5
Xinjiang Uyghur Autonomous Region (XUAR), 3, 5–9, 252
Xi's approach to reformism, 262

Y
Youth bulges, 13
Yunnan, 7, 66, 68, 84, 93

Z
Zedong, Mao, 130, 140, 146–148, 169, 231, 265
Zemin, Jiang, 148
Zero-COVID protests, 15
Zhonghua Minzu, 3, 9

www.ingramcontent.com/pod-product-compliance
Ingram Content Group UK Ltd.
Pitfield, Milton Keynes, MK11 3LW, UK
UKHW020834290926
15470UKWH00004B/1341
* 9 7 8 9 8 1 9 7 0 1 7 1 1 *